Conduct Disorders:
A Practitioner's Guide to
Comparative Treatments

W. Michael Nelson III, PhD, ABPP, is professor and former Chair of the Department of Psychology at Xavier University in Cincinnati, Ohio. He is a Diplomate in Clinical Psychology and in Clinical-Child and Adolescent Psychology from the American Board of Professional Psychology, a Fellow in the Academy of Clinical Psychology, and a Fellow in the American Psychological Association Divisions of Clinical-Child Psychology and Clinical Psychology. After earning his degree in clinical psychology from the Virginia Commonwealth University, Dr Nelson began his work with children and adolescents in low-income families at the University of Texas Health Science Center in Dallas. He also worked with inpatient children at the Millcreek Psychiatric Center for Children for 5 years where he was also the Director of Psychology. He has always attempted to integrate research with practice, as evidenced in a book coauthored with Dr Finch entitled "*Cognitive-Behavioral Procedures with Children and Adolescents: A Practical Guide*" and in their psychoeducational workbook series entitled "*Keeping Your Cool: The Anger Management Workbook.*" His efforts to make empirically supported therapies more "user friendly" are also reflected in the several videos he produced, including the "*Keeping Your Cool:*" *The Anger Management Video*, which serves as an accompaniment to the workbook. Dr Nelson has taught for 27 years at Xavier University, including courses in the areas of childhood psychopathology, cognitive-behavior therapy, and family. Widely published, Nr. Nelson's research interests are primarily on assessment and cognitive-behavioral interventions with children and adolescents.

Alfred J. Finch, Jr., PhD, ABPP, is professor and Dean of Humanities and Social Science at The Citadel in Charleston, SC. He is board-certified in both Clinical Psychology and Clinical-Child and Adolescent Psychology through the American Board of Professional Psychology. Following the completion of his doctorate in clinical psychology from the University of Alabama and his internship in the Department of Psychiatry at the University of Alabama in Birmingham, Dr Finch completed a postdoctoral fellowship in Clinical-Child Psychology at The Devereux Foundation. Dr Finch has been involved in teaching psychology from the undergraduate level to the supervision of postdoctoral fellows. His specialty is in the area of clinical-child psychology and he has published extensively in the area.

Kathleen J. Hart, PhD, ABPP, is a professor in the Department of Psychology at Xavier University and is board-certified in Clinical-Child and Adolescent Psychology through the American Board of Professional Psychology. She received her PhD in clinical psychology from Virginia Polytechnic Institute and State University, and completed an internship through the Brown University Internship Consortium in Providence, Rhode Island. Dr Hart also completed a 2-year postdoctoral fellowship in Clinical-Child Neuropsychology at the Rhode Island Hospital, where she was also a research fellow in the Department of Psychiatry and Human Behavior in the Brown University Program in Medicine. In addition to her teaching, research, and clinical-supervision duties, Dr Hart serves as a consulting psychologist to the Hamilton County Juvenile Court providing psychological, neuropsychological, and forensic evaluations of youths whose behavior brings them in contact with the Juvenile Court. She has published in the areas of child and adolescent psychology, neuropsychology, and forensic psychology.

Conduct Disorders: A Practitioner's Guide to Comparative Treatments

W. M. Nelson III, PhD, ABPP

A. J. Finch, Jr., PhD, ABPP

K. J. Hart, PhD, ABPP

Editors

SPRINGER PUBLISHING COMPANY

New York

Springer Publishing Company, Inc.
11 West 42nd Street
New York, NY 10036-8002

Acquisitions Editor: Sheri W. Sussman
Production Editor: Print Matters, Inc.
Compositor: CompSet
Cover design by Joanne E. Honigman

06 07 08 09 10/ 54321

Library of Congress Cataloging-in-Publication Data

Conduct disorders: a practitioner's guide to comparative treatments/[edited by]
    W. Michael Nelson III,   Alfred J. Finch Jr.,   Kathleen J. Hart.
        p.; cm. — (Springer series on comparative treatments for psychological disorders)
    Includes bibliographical references and index.
    ISBN 0-8261-5615-0 (sc)
    1. Conduct disorders in children—Treatment.   2. Behavior therapy for children.
    I. Nelson, W. Michael. II. Finch, A. J., 1944– III. Hart, Kathleen J. IV. Series.
    [DNLM: 1. Conduct Disorder—therapy.   2. Psychotherapy—methods.
    WS 350.6 C7459 2006]
    RJ506.C65C665 2006
    618.92′8906—dc22

                                                                2005049531

Printed in the United States of America by Bang Printing.

To my family at home (Sarah, Will, and Mer)—"Be nice"
and
my family at work (the Jesuits)—"Service in the context of
scholarship."

—WMN

To my family, teachers, and my students from whom I have learned
all I know.

—AJF

To Doug, Sarah, and Leah

—KJH

Contents

Contributors

Christopher T. Barry, PhD
Department of Psychology
University of Southern Mississippi
Hattiesburg, Mississippi

Wendy Czopp, PhD
Division of Child and
    Adolescent Psychiatry
Department of Psychiatry
Medical College of Ohio
Toledo, Ohio

Virginia DeRoma, PhD, ABPP
Department of Psychology
The Citadel
Charleston, South Carolina

Scott W. Henggeler, PhD
Family Services Research Center
Department of Psychiatry and
    Behavioral Sciences
Medical University of South Carolina
Charleston, South Carolina

Melissa F. Jackson, PhD
Department of Psychology
The University of Alabama
Tuscaloosa, Alabama

M. David Liberman, PhD, ABPP
Private Practice
Highland Park, Illinois

John E. Lochman, PhD, ABPP
Department of Psychology
The University of Alabama
Tuscaloosa, Alabama

Robert D. Lyman, PhD, ABPP
Department of Psychology
    College of Arts & Sciences
Appalachian State University
Boone, North Carolina

Douglas Mossman, MD
Division of Forensic
    Psychiatric Psychiatry
Wright State University
    School of Medicine
Dayton, Ohio

Nicole R. Powell, PhD
Department of Psychology
The University of Alabama
Tuscaloosa, Alabama

Mark A. Reinecke, PhD, ABPP, ACT
Division of Psychology
Northwestern University
Chicago, Illinois

Lisa Saldana, PhD
Family Services Research Center
Department of Psychiatry and
    Behavioral Sciences
Medical University of South
    Carolina
Charleston, South
    Carolina

Janet R. Schultz, PhD, ABPP
Department of Psychology
Xavier University
Cincinnati, Ohio

Christina G. Weston, MD
Division of Child and
    Adolescent Psychiatry
Wright State University
    School of Medicine
Dayton, Ohio

Preface

Psychotherapy has progressed considerably since its humble beginnings at the turn of the 20th century. New developments continue, as do the many controversies, especially among clinicians of differing theoretical persuasions. In the meantime, psychotherapy research has become a vital and evolving enterprise, which at times supplements and at other times confronts the theory-based activities of therapists. Treatment research strives to provide a foundation for the practice of psychotherapy, as practitioners of psychotherapy become more numerous and diverse. In 1982, Garfield identified 60 forms of psychotherapy used in the 1960s, whereas Kazdin noted 400 variants of psychotherapy by the mid-1980s, and over 550 by the end of the 1990s. The emergence of different forms of psychotherapy has occurred independently of empirical evidence. Most practicing clinicians are influenced by the agencies in which they deliver services, by the persons they treat, and by their desire to refine their theoretical understanding of others and improve their methods of helping, rather than by empirical research. Simultaneously, major changes in medical and mental health care reimbursement systems within the United States and structure imposed by managed care organizations also have a pervasive impact on both the delivery of psychotherapy and psychotherapy research. These two enterprises—delivery of psychotherapeutic services and the evaluation of such approaches—have both collided with and complemented each other.

Within this context, the common thread that drives clinicians and re-searchers alike is the quest to find "which treatments are most helpful for patients." Basically, it is the clinician's theoretical orientation that guides his or her clinical interventions with clients. The focus of this book is to have practicing clinicians from different theoretical orientations discuss what they feel works best with children and adolescents who present with conduct-disordered problems.

The first chapter provides an overview of conduct disorder, including the characteristics, incidence and prevalence rates, and etiologic factors. Chapter 2 introduces the case of Michael, a composite portrait of a 13-year-old boy whose character development and life story were developed by drawing on the hundreds of young boys and girls seen by the authors over their combined 81 years of clinical experience. In reading this case of a "typical" conduct-disordered young boy, readers are encouraged to think about their own clients, and how these clients have helped shape the therapists' clinical orientation, therapeutic interactions, and clinical interventions. The questions asked of each contributor are also listed in this chapter. This was done to make it easier for readers to compare alternative approaches for understanding the treatment of conduct-disordered youth. The paramount assumption is that a well-articulated theoretical orientation should be used to guide clinical interventions. As such, we asked each of the contributors to provide an overview of their model, discussion of assessment procedures and the establishment of treatment goals, as well as specific clinical interventions. The discussion of the case concludes with an examination of termination issues, relapse prevention, and recommendations for follow-up.

Chapters 3–10 constitute the heart of the book. Expert therapists representing eight different theoretical perspectives were asked how they would treat Michael had he presented himself to them for therapy. Each chapter describes the theoretical process and offers insights into the practices of therapists of different orientations who have devoted much of their professional lives to dealing with conduct-disordered youngsters. The contributors fall along the continuum of practitioners–scholars, with some in private practice and others in academic institutions. There is wide variation in the settings in which they work and whether they align themselves more on the "practitioner" or "scholar" end of the continuum. Although authors were presented with guidelines with which to organize their chapters, they were given the freedom to modify this format with plans and suggestions most relevant from their clinical/research expertise. They have been asked "to tell of their own experiences" in conducting therapy with such youngsters. Therefore, the authors have developed their individual chapters somewhat independently to reflect their own clinical experience and the methods that have been most helpful in their work, not only with such clients in the therapy office, but also in their teaching and research. The final chapter summarizes and compares the eight treatment models and develops a comparison grid to further elucidate the similarities and differences among the different theoretical orientations.

In the end, we hope that the readers' clinical knowledge and skill are further enhanced by such a comparative presentation of treatment approaches, so that they will have a better developed answer to the question originally posed—"What specific therapeutic interventions produce what specific changes, in what specific patients under what specific conditions, and with what specific therapists?" We realize that the answer to this question depends very much on our assumptions about the nature of human behavior, our own theoretical orientations and clinical skills, as well as the outcome literature and research base. It is our hope that *Conduct Disorders: A Practitioner's Guide to Comparative Treatments* will be helpful for novice and "seasoned" clinicians alike.

WMN
AJF
KJH

Acknowledgments

Until the 20th century, little account was taken of the special characteristics of psychopathology in children. Only since the advent of the mental health movement and the establishment of child guidance facilities at the beginning of the 20th century have strides been made in not only understanding psychopathology in children and adolescents but also assessing and treating it. The recent identification of evidence-based psychotherapies for a number of childhood disorders underscores the strides made in this area. Those working with children, adolescents, and their families realize that we have come a long way, but still have a long way to go. Children are no longer seen as "miniature adults" who are treated with downward extensions of adult-oriented interventions. Within a developmental perspective, clinicians are better able to distinguish among the different disorders of children and adolescents and have a better understanding of the etiology and interventions for our youth. Interventions have moved well beyond simply treating the individual child, as the importance of the family, roles in the community, social, and cultural factors have come to be more appreciated. The struggles faced by severely acting-out children and their families are clearly apparent in examining the demands and costs within the mental health, educational, and juvenile justice systems. Over the course of our careers, we have had the privilege of working with many practitioners and scientists alike who have dedicated themselves to understanding and treating severely acting-out youngsters. We in the field of child and adolescent psychology recognize the influence of those practitioners and scientists who have preceded us, spoken to us, and written books and articles from which we have learned. We owe them a debt of gratitude. In a very direct way, they have made this book possible.

A number of individuals need to be specifically recognized, as their contributions have made this book possible. Our series editor, Art Freeman, provided the initial spark for us to take on this project. Our editor, Sheri Sussman, and the staff at Springer Publishing Company have provided support and encouragement along the way. Their patience and guidance have been truly appreciated. As with any edited book, the "heart" of such a project lies with the contributors whose formidable experience and insights have made this the thought-provoking, practical work that it is.

Finally, we owe a debt of gratitude to the children, adolescents, and families whose struggles and willingness to open themselves up to the therapeutic endeavor have made us all more sensitive clinicians and scientists.

WMN
AJF
KJH

Series Editor's Note

Comparisons are odious...

—Cervantes, *Don Quixote*

The general view of comparisons is that they represent measurements against some standard or that they entail evaluating one experience or object against another. If one has had a sibling, one is likely to come up against the parental statement, "Why can't you be like...?" Teachers also invariably compare students one with the other when they post grades or grade papers for all to see.

This view of comparisons is that they are somehow adversarial—one person, group, or effort "wins" and one "loses." In psychology we often use the construct of comparison as synonymous with the term "versus" (e.g., "The treatment of depression: Psychotherapy versus pharmacology" or "A comparison of treatments for conduct disorder"). This implies that whenever there are two or more systems or objects available, one will be better than another. Yet not all comparisons are clear-cut. One choice may be appropriate for a certain subgroup, whereas another choice may work better in a different setting or with a different population (this adversarial view seems to be very popular among mental health professionals). After all, we are a group that over the years, when under attack, has been known to circle our wagons and shoot at each other!

Our goal in this series is not to examine who is better than whom, or what model works better than other models, but rather to examine and to compare, as clearly as we can, the similarities and differences between different psychotherapeutic approaches. To do this most efficiently, we have used a standard patient. All contributors were asked to respond to the sample case prepared by the volume editors. In this way the reader can compare the thinking, conceptualization, interventions, and questions that would be asked by the contributing authors. We have invited authors who are exemplars of a particular school, understanding that other therapists of the same school might see or do things differently. By aligning apparently diverse therapies side by side, we can look at what models are specific conceptual frameworks, philosophical biases, strategic foci, or technical interventions, as well as help us to make clearer distinctions among therapeutic models.

We have set as our goal the examination of those problems most frequently seen in clinical practice. We have not seen this need for cross-model comparison as an issue of professional discipline inasmuch as these clinical syndromes are seen by psychologists, psychiatrists, nurse practitioners, social workers, pastoral counselors, and counselors.

This series sprang from four roots. First, the powerful influence of the classic "Gloria" series produced by Dr Everett Shorstrum, when he arranged for Carl Rogers (Client-Centered Therapy), Albert Ellis (Rational Emotive Therapy), and Fritz Perls (Gestalt Therapy) to demonstrate their representative model of therapy with a standard patient, Gloria. He gave viewers the opportunity to compare and contrast the three models as practiced by the founders of the particular school of therapy.

The second influence on this series was the present state of affairs in psychotherapy. Between the models that are promoted for their purported science and efficacy and those models that are promoted for their purported humanism and eschewal of science, there are many treatment models. Without attempting to judge the value, efficacy, and importance of a model, we believe that it is important to offer mental health professionals the opportunity to make their own decisions about diverse treatment models.

The third impetus for this series was the availability of so many experts in the treatment of the broad range of psychological disorders, both as editors and as contributing authors. It is their work that is being highlighted in this series.

Finally, the series was the result of encouragement and support from Bill Tucker, former Acquisitions Editor at Springer Publishing Company. When I first approached Springer with the idea for the series, they were enthusiastic and eagerly agreed not to just produce one volume, but committed their resources to a series of several volumes. Given the publishing history of Springer, the breadth and quality of their book list, and the many professional groups that they reach, I can think of no better place to publish this series on comparative psychotherapy.

Arthur Freeman, EdD, ABPP
Department of Psychology
University of St. Francis

CHAPTER 1

Conduct Disorder

Description, Prevalence, and Etiology

A. J. Finch, Jr., W. Michael Nelson III, and K. J. Hart

> Our youth now love luxury. They have bad manners, contempt for authority, and disrespect for their elders. Children nowadays are tyrants.
>
> —Socrates, 470–399 BC

Children who have severe acting-out problems have long been a concern to parents, teachers, and society. Such behaviors have been considered to be the path by which certain youngsters develop a life of juvenile delinquency and adult criminality. Although the most severe forms of youth violence (e.g., homicide) in the United States have been decreasing since the mid-1990s, other forms of severe acting-out have not declined (Brener, Simon, Krug, & Lowry, 1999; Snyder & Sickmund, 1999). During adolescence, there is clearly an increase in behavior that can be considered "problematic" or "at risk," such as the use of drugs, truancy, school suspensions, vandalism, stealing, and precocious and unprotected sex (DiClemente, Hansen, & Ponton, 1996; Ketterlinus & Lamb, 1994; U.S. Congress, Office of Technology Assessment, 1991). In fact, approximately 70% of adolescents engage in some form of delinquent behavior. Again, fewer are involved in more serious offenses (such as robbery, aggravated assault), but many more are involved in problematic but less serious behaviors (such as underage drinking, running away from home, truancy from school, traffic violations) (Elliott, Huizinga, & Ageton, 1985; Farrington, 1995).

Conduct disorder (CD) is one of the most common reasons for referral of a child or adolescent for psychological or psychiatric treatment (Robins, 1991; Selzer & Hluchy, 1991). About one out of every two to three children seen in child guidance clinics have been diagnosed with CD (Comer, 1995; Webster-Stratton & Dahl, 1995). Reasons for this high rate of referral are that the symptoms of CD are external, frequently observed by others, and may bring the youngster into contact with the law or other authorities. In addition, these behaviors are frequently more distressing to those around the youngster than to the youngster who exhibits them. Estimates on the prevalence of conduct problems vary greatly and depend upon the sample being studied. In the general population of approximately 70 million children and adolescents in the United States, it is estimated that from 6 to 16% of boys and 2 to 9% of girls have acting-out behavioral problems (Mash & Wolfe, 2005)—about 5.6–17.5 million youths. There are also longer term consequences for such children as they grow into adulthood, as about 80% of youths who demonstrate severe acting-out are likely to meet criteria for some type of psychiatric disorder in the future (Kazdin, 2004). There are also numerous long-term consequences for others who have to deal with such youths—parents, siblings, teachers, peers, as well as strangers who are the target of aggressive or antisocial acts. CD is one of the most costly psychiatric disorders to society, at least in part because of the large percentage of diagnosed children who remain involved with mental health agencies and criminal justice systems over the course of their lives. Even before they reach adulthood, the economic impact borne by our society is great, with the average cost of incarceration for a juvenile exceeding $60,000/year (Webster-Stratton & Dahl, 1995).

In general, childhood behavior problems can be viewed along the broad dimension of externalized versus internalized conflict. Disruptive acting-out behaviors are "externalized" in the sense that the conflict that occurs is typically in the youngster's relationship with societal norms and other rules of conduct. This stands in contrast to "internalized" disorders, such as anxiety and depression, in which the symptoms lie primarily within the youngster.

Although externalized behavior problems have long been identified in children and adolescents, it was not until 1980 that a formal distinction was made between CD and oppositional defiant disorder (ODD), which are closely linked and can involve defiance of rules, problems managing anger, and failure to assume responsibility for one's behavior. The current *Diagnostic and Statistical Manual of Mental Disorders-IV-TR* (American Psychiatric Association, 2000) describes ODD as "a recurrent pattern of negativistic, defiant, disobedient, and hostile behavior towards authority figures" (p. 100). Such oppositional defiant behaviors are usually apparent by the preschool years and have been linked to problematic temperaments in infancy and childhood (e.g., high reactivity, difficulty being soothed, and/or high motor activity). On the other hand, CD reflects a "persistent pattern of behavior in which the basic rights of others or major age-appropriate societal norms or rules are violated" (p. 93). The problem behaviors associated with CD include aggressive behavior that causes or threatens physical harm to another or an animal, property damage or loss, theft or deceitfulness, and/or serious violations of rules. Three or more of these behaviors must have been present during the last year and one of them must have been present in the last 6 months. Furthermore, the behaviors must have reached a level as to have significantly impacted the individual's social, academic, or occupational functioning. Such acting-out behaviors occur under various conditions and vary in terms of chronicity, severity, and frequency.

The *DSM-IV-TR* (2000) specifies two subtypes of the disorder and three levels of severity. The two subtypes of the disorder are based on the age of onset—childhood versus adolescence. Childhood-onset CD is characterized by the appearance of at least one of the criteria for CD prior to the age of 10, whereas in adolescence onset there are no CD characteristics prior to age 10. Levels of severity vary from mild (when only a few conduct problems are present above the minimum to meet diagnosis, with problems generally involving minor harm to others) to severe (with many problems involved or behavior posing considerable harm to others).

With both ODD and CD, it is important to distinguish between persistent aggressive antisocial acts such as setting fires, cruelty to people and animals, and destruction of property and theft; and the less serious pranks often carried out by "normal" children and adolescents. It should also be noted that both ODD and CD involve behavior that may or may not be considered illegal. Juvenile delinquency is a legal term that refers to violations of the law committed by minors, but a juvenile who has been found to have violated a law may not meet diagnostic criteria for CD. That is, a youth may be adjudicated for vandalism or theft, but if these behaviors do not reflect a persistent pattern of rule/law violations, he is not correctly identified as having CD.

It should also be noted that the behaviors seen in ODD, and especially in CD, can reflect the early stages in the development of an antisocial personality disorder. An antisocial personality disorder involves "a pervasive pattern of disregard for, and violation of the rights of others that begins in childhood or early adolescence and continues into adulthood" (American Psychiatric

Association, 2000, p. 701). In nondiagnostic terms, this type of behavior has been termed psychopathy, sociopathy, or dyssocial personality disorder.

It is often difficult to distinguish between ODD and CD. It is even more difficult to distinguish between CD, a predelinquent pattern of behavior, and the early stages and development of an antisocial personality disorder. Behaviorally, the patterns are similar. Indeed, there is considerable evidence that some children's disruptive behavior problems (especially the early-onset type) develop gradually from childhood onward (Loeber, Green, Keenan, & Lahey, 1995). Thus, it appears that, for some children, there is a developmental sequence from ODD to CD to antisocial personality disorder, and there are common risk factors for these disorders (Hinshaw, 1994). More specifically, virtually all cases of CD (especially in the early-onset subtype) were preceded developmentally by ODD, although only about 25% of children with ODD go on to develop CD within a 3-year period (Lahey, Loeber, Quay, Frick, & Grimm, 1992). Children who develop CD at an earlier age are more likely to develop an antisocial personality disorder as adults than youths who develop adolescent-onset CD (Hinshaw, 1994; Moffitt, 1993). Approximately 25 to 40% of youths diagnosed with early-onset CD go on to develop adult antisocial personality disorder. Over 80% of boys who develop early-onset CD, however, continue to have multiple problems of social dysfunction characterized by disrupted friendships, problems in intimate relationships, and vocational problems, even though they do not meet full criteria for an antisocial personality disorder (Hinshaw, 1994; Zoccolillo et al., 1992). By contrast, youths who develop adolescent-onset CD typically do not go on to develop adult antisocial personality disorders. Instead, their behavior problems are limited to their adolescent years. These "late-onset" youngsters do not share the same cluster of risk factors that "early-/child-onset" cases have, such as low verbal intelligence, neuropsychological deficits, impulsivity, and attentional problems (Hinshaw, 1994; Moffit & Lynan, 1994).

Age of onset of CD has been found to be an important factor not only in the outcome, but also in terms of the severity of the problem presented (Sanford et al., 1999). Individuals who are found to have the child-onset form of disorder tend to be more aggressive, are more likely to drop out of school, tend to have a higher probability of persisting in their antisocial behaviors as adults, and have a higher probability of developing substance abuse problems. In short, they are likely to have more chronic, intense acting-out problems. Thus, it appears that the primary developmental pathway to continued serious conduct problems into adulthood is established during the preschool period (Campbell & Ewing, 1990). This suggests that, perhaps, a strategic point for primary interventions in a CD individual's development may be in the preschool and early elementary school years (i.e., ages 4–7). Unfortunately, not all CD children can be identified early on and practitioners are asked to intervene with such youths over the course of their lives.

Another factor that seems to be important in long-term outcome for those diagnosed with CD is gender. Males with CD who continue to have problems into adulthood are more likely to have substance abuse problems and/or develop antisocial personality disorder. On the other hand, females with CD who continue to have problems as adults are more likely to develop internalizing disorders such as anxiety, depression, and somatization (Robins, 1986).

In sum, it is clear that (a) several million children and adolescents engage in problematic acting-out and are in need of some type of treatment, (b) these children and adolescents experience many and varied types of problems, (c) they frequently experience several problems concurrently (e.g., have comorbid disorders, experience learning problems in school), and (d) these problems can appear at different points in a youngster's life (Kazdin, 2004).

ETIOLOGY OF CONDUCT DISORDER

A variety of etiologies have been suggested for the development of CD, but in truth there are likely a number of different pathways that lead to the various problem behaviors associated with this diagnosis. Because most treatment approaches are based on or are influenced by some conceptual model about the etiology of the disorder, it is important to review briefly the various models.

FAMILIAL AND PSYCHOLOGICAL ETIOLOGICAL FACTORS

Family problems are the most consistent factors found in CD and can be characterized as general family disturbances or specific disturbances in parenting practices. General family disturbances include such issues as psychopathology in the parents, a family history of antisocial behavior, marital conflict, limited financial and emotional resources, family instability, and disturbances in family values (Mash & Wolfe, 2005). For example, Olds et al. (1998) found that families of children with CD are more likely to be dependent on welfare, have greater substance abuse, have more children who are closely spaced, and are more likely to be single-parent families.

Specific disturbances in parenting practices refer to such issues as harsh and excessive punishment, lack of parental supervision and/or support, and inconsistent parental discipline (e.g., Frick, 1998; Patterson, 1996). For example, Reid (1993) has found that some of the most empirically supported risk factors for CD include harsh, inconsistent parenting practices, physical and emotional abuse, reinforcement of aggressive behavior, and lack of supervision, which pave the way for the learning of aggressive behavior, the failure to develop empathy, and the lack of abiding by societal rules.

Related to specific disturbances in parenting, Maccoby (1993) found that punitive, authoritarian parenting styles and inconsistent discipline were related to a lack of social competence, poor communication, and aggression. Authoritative parents are demanding and controlling, while not being responsive to their children's needs. Their lack of communication with their children may produce social incompetence and difficulty in relating to others.

Neglect is another parenting practice frequently reported to be related to CD. Neglectful parents are characterized as rejecting and unresponsive, and lacking control and rule enforcement. Consequently, children who are neglected are likely to show social incompetence as well as a failure to develop socially acceptable behaviors and poor self-control. Related to neglect may be a lack of supervision, which appears to be a factor in the development of the disorder in some studies. For example, Reid (1993) found that by the fifth grade, children who were poorly supervised had a greater probability of exhibiting CD.

Physical abuse has been found to contribute to the development of aggressive behavior and therefore may be a contributing factor to a diagnosis of CD (Mash & Wolfe, 2005). Certainly the learning of aggression by modeling is one of the most documented social learning events.

At times, children may learn inappropriate behavior because of what is encouraged or reinforced within the home. Gardner (1992) found that parents and children who argue and interact in an aggressive manner do not focus on solving the problem. Parents of children who develop CD tend to end arguments quickly. Ending the aggressive confrontation before the problem is solved negatively reinforces the parents because they no longer have to deal with the child's aversive behavior. At the same time, the interaction is reinforcing to the child in that he escapes his parents' demands. This pattern of behavior creates a cycle of the parent and child continuing the negative and aversive confrontations. Consequently, children who develop CD may not learn to develop effective interactions with other children and adults because of the reinforcement of negative behaviors at home.

BIOLOGICAL AND GENETIC FACTORS

Although it is unlikely that there are genetic or biological factors related to specific behaviors, there have been a number of findings that led some investigators to suggest that there are likely biological or genetic factors related to the development of CD (Pliszka, 1999; Simonoff, 2001). A perpetuating cycle seems to occur with low verbal intelligence, mild neuropsychological problems, and other nervous system-based features that set for early onset of CD (Moffit & Lynan, 1994; Slutsky et al., 1997). For example, it may be that a child with a difficult temperament established insecure attachments because parents find it difficult to engage in the type of parenting that would promote a secure attachment. Low verbal intelligence and/or mild neuropsychological deficits may be factors in self-control deficiencies such as sustaining attention, planning, self-monitoring, and inhibiting impulsive behavior. Insecure attachment and mild neuropsychological difficulties, alone or together, appear to be features that contribute to poor behavioral control and, ultimately, to the rule violations and poor socialization that make up CD. Either of these difficulties, or the combination of these problems, appears to "set the stage" for life-long problems in the child's relationships with others, and with society at large.

Other findings that have been used to support a genetic or biological factor in the development of CD have been an extrapolation from research with adults having antisocial personality disorder or substance abuse. For example, in adoption studies, it has been found that there is a stronger relationship with biological parents than adopted ones in the development of antisocial personality disorder and substance abuse problems (Cadoret, Yates, Troughton, Woodworth, & Stewart, 1995a, b).

With children and adolescents, Mash and Wolfe (2005) have pointed out that genetic factors are less clear. Although there is evidence that certain characteristics of children with CD (e.g., impulsivity, mood variations, limited persistence at tasks) are genetically influenced, specific conduct problems are less evident. On the other hand, some research suggests that a family history of mental illness is predictive of the development of CD. For example, Dierker, Merikangas, and Szatmari (1999) have found that parental psychopathology may contribute to the development of CD. Higher than expected rates of CD were found in children whose mothers abused substances, or had anxiety or affective disorders. Similar results were found for children whose fathers had substance abuse problems or antisocial personality disorder. In a similar finding Loeber, Green, Keenan, and Lahey (1995) found that about twice as many mothers and fathers of children diagnosed with CD had substance abuse problems as did parents of children without CD. To the extent that one views substance abuse as having a genetic component, it may be extended to the problems presented by the children of parents with such problems. Also, it could be argued that it is the parenting practices of parents with these problems that contribute to the development of CD.

Several neurobiological factors have been suggested as contributing to the development of CD. For example, Quay (1993) has suggested that an imbalance between the behavioral activation system and the behavioral inhibition system may be a contributing factor. The behavioral activation system serves to stimulate behavioral responses to reinforcing stimuli while the behavioral inhibition system is responsible for the development of anxiety and inhibition. According to this model, individuals who are likely to develop CD are likely to have an overly active behavioral activation system and an underactive behavioral inhibition system.

A host of other biological influences have been proposed to be factors in the development of CD, including birth defects, head injuries, and low birth weight. However, it is impossible to separate these factors out from the numerous other social and environmental factors found to be associated with the disorder.

SCHOOL AND PEER FACTORS

Children with CD frequently have been found to have lower than average intelligence and academic achievement (Martin & Hoffman, 1990). Related to this finding is a frequent report of lower verbal IQ and verbal reasoning problems (Moffit & Lynan, 1994). Children with CD have been found to demonstrate deficits in reading and have a low rate of participation in school (McGee, Williams, Share, Anderson, & Silva, 1986). They tend to be rejected more by teachers, fall behind their peers in school, and have a higher dropout rate, all of which places them at higher risk for the disorder and later difficulties in life.

Children with CD also tend to be rejected more by their peers. This rejection is frequently in response to their negative behaviors and/or ineffective interpersonal and problem-solving skills (Martin & Hoffman, 1990; Short & Shapiro, 1993). Pamella and Henggeler (1985) found children with CD display less social competence and lower levels of positive affect than children without CD. These children tended to have fewer sensitive and responsive exchanges with their peers, and aggressive behaviors become a way of communication. As a result, they are rejected by their peers, tend to associate with other children with conduct problems, and develop increasingly serious delinquent and antisocial behaviors (Dishion & Loeber, 1985).

SOCIAL/CULTURAL FACTORS

A number of studies have found an association between poverty and the development of CD, indicating that this is a clear risk factor. For example, Loeber et al. (1995) found a family background characterized by low socio-economic status to be associated with the disorder. Closely related to the association of socioeconomic status was age of the mother at the time of the birth of her first child. It seems reasonable to speculate that many of the parental and family factors that are associated with CD are related to poverty. Such factors as low parental supervision, lack of involvement in the child's activities, family stress, and family instability can clearly be related to struggles to make enough money to make ends meet. In the United States, minority status has been found to be related to the development of CD with higher rates reported for African American, Hispanic, and Native American groups (Elliott et al., 1985). However, when the effects of socioeconomic status are controlled, these differences tend to dissipate. Overall, however, the specific mechanisms by which these social and cultural factors lead to the development of conduct problems are not known (Mash & Wolfe, 2005).

CONCLUSIONS

This book focuses on youngsters who primarily exhibit CD problems. Nevertheless, the reader is reminded that it is very difficult, if not impossible, to distinguish among the ODD, CD, predelinquent behavior, and early stages in the development of an antisocial personality disorder. Behaviorally, the patterns are alike and may simply represent four ways of describing or accounting for the same problematic acting-out behavior. Although a number of factors have been found to be related to CD, no single one can be identified as producing the disorder. Instead, it likely arises from genetic/constitutional factors, shaped by problematic interactions with parents, teachers, and peers, and influenced by sociocultural factors. It seems most likely that the disorder develops as a result of an interaction of a complex set of factors that result in a spiraling sequence that exacerbates the tendency toward conduct problems and even later antisocial behavior.

The earlier the acting-out behavior becomes problematic and the more severe the behavior, the more likely such patterns of behavior will persist. In general, the earlier the intervention, the more likely it will be effective. Nevertheless, the clinician is called upon to intervene at different stages. In the discussion of the various treatments for CD in the chapters of this volume, the authors' different approaches are influenced by the importance that is assigned to the different etiologic factors. It is possible that a sufficient disruption in any of the factors may serve to produce a chain reaction of improvements. It may be the case that a particular set of factors are more important in the development of the disorder with an individual case and that the particular treatment is more likely to be effective when the individual factors in that case are carefully considered. With such multiple, interacting factors, the task of treating such children and adolescents is clearly more than simply targeting specific presenting symptoms. The challenge for the practicing clinician is not only to address the child him/herself but also to consider and treat the parents, family, caregivers, and other contacts that can support prosocial and adaptive functioning. Thus, the practitioner must consider a variety of factors in developing and implementing a course of treatment for CD youths. Among others, the challenges clinicians must navigate in treatment involve: (a) identifying the problems and framing them in a way to facilitate change (e.g., employing multiple informants and methods of assessment); (b) clarifying the motivation for seeking treatment (e.g., children do not typically refer themselves for treatment and parents/caregivers may or may not recognize problems or want to be involved in treatment); (c) determining who should be treated (e.g., child him/herself, the parents, the siblings, the school); (d) keeping the treatment going until goals are accomplished; and (e) arranging generalization and maintenance of therapeutic improvements before termination.

REFERENCES

American Psychiatric Association. (2000). *Diagnostic and statistical manual of mental disorders-IV-TR* (4th ed.). Washington, DC: American Psychiatric Press.

Brener, N. D., Simon, T. R., Krug, E. G., & Lowry, R. (1999). Recent trends in violence-related behaviors among high school students in the United States. *Journal of the American Medical Association, 282,* 440–446.

Cadoret, R., Yates, W., Troughton, E., Woodworth, G., & Stewart, M. (1995a). Adoption study demonstrating two genetic pathways to drug abuse. *Archives of General Psychiatry, 52,* 42–52.

Cadoret, R., Yates, W., Troughton, E., Woodworth, G., & Stewart, M. (1995b). Gene environment interaction in genesis of aggressiveity and Conduct Disorders. *Archives of General Psychiatry, 52,* 916–924.

Campbell, S.B., & Ewing, L.J. (1990). Follow-up of hard-to-manage preschoolers: Adjustment at age 9 and predictors of continuing symptoms. *Journal of Child Psychology and Psychiatry, 31,* 871–889.

Comer, R. J. (1995). *Abnormal psychology* (2nd ed.). New York: W. H. Freman. Deshion, T., & Loeber, R. (1985). Adolescent marijuana and alcohol use: The role of parents revisited. *American Journal of Alcohol and Drug Abuse, 11,* 11–15. DiClemente,

R. J., Hansen, W. B., & Ponton, L. E. (Eds.). (1996). *Handbook of adolescent health risk behavior.* New York: Plenum Press.

Dierker, L., Merikangas, K., & Szatmari, P. (1999). Influence of parental concordance for psychiatric disorders on psychopathology in offspring. *Journal of the American Academy of Child and Adolescent Psychiatry, 38,* 280–289.

Dishion, T. J., & Loeber, R. (1985). Adolescent marijuana and alcohol use: The role of parents and peers revisited. *American Journal of Drug and Alcohol Abuse, 11,* 11–25.

Elliott, D. S., Huizinga, D., & Ageton, S. S. (1985). Explaining delinquency and drug use. Beverly Hills, CA: Sage.

Farrington, D.P. (1995). The development of offending and anti-social behaviour from childhood: Key findings from the Cambridge study in the delinquent development. *Journal of Child Psychology and Psychiatry, 36,* 929–964.

Frick, P. J. (1998). *Conduct Disorders and severe antisocial behavior.* New York: Plenum Press.

Gardner, F. (1992). Parent–child interaction and conduct disorder. *Educational Psychological Review, 4,* 135–163.

Hinshaw, S. P. (1994). Conduct Disorder in childhood: Conceptualization, diagnosis, comorbidity, and risk status for antisocial functioning in adulthood. In D. C. Fowles, P. Sutker, & S. H. Goodman (Eds.), *Progress in experimental personality and psychopathology research.* New York: Springer Publishing Co.

Kazdin, W. E. (2004). Psychotherapy with children. In M. J. Lambert (Ed.), *Bergin and Garfield's handbook of psychotherapy and behavior change* (5th ed.). New York: Wiley.

Ketterlinus, R., & Lamb, M. E. (Eds.). (1994). *Adolescent problem behaviors: Issues and research.* Hillsdale, NJ: Erlbaum.

Lahey, B. B., Loeber, R. Quay, H. C., Frick, P. J., & Grimm, S. (1992). Oppositional defiant and Conduct Disorders: Issues to be resolved for DSM-IV. *Journal of the American Academy of Child and Adolescent Psychiatry, 29,* 620–626.

Loeber, R., Green, S., Keenan, K., & Lahey, B. (1995). Which boys will fare worse? Early predictions off the onset of Conduct Disorder in six year longitudinal study. *Journal of the American Academy of Child and Adolescent Psychiatry, 34,* 499–600.

Maccoby, E. (1993, April). *Trends and issues in the study of gender role development.* Paper presented at the meeting of the Society for Research in Child Development, New Orleans.

Martin, B., & Hoffman, J. (1990). Conduct Disorders. In M. Lewis & S. Miller (Eds.), *Handbook of developmental psychopathology.* New York: Plenum Press.

Mash, E. J., & Wolfe, D. A. (2005). *Abnormal child psychology* (3rd ed.). Belmont, CA: Wadsworth. McGee, R., Williams, S., Share, D., Anderson, J., & Sliva, P. (1986). The relationship between specific reading retardation, general reading backwardness and behavioral problems in a large sample of Duedin Boys: A longitudinal study from five to eleven years. *Journal of Child Psychology and Psychiatry, 47,* 597–610.

Moffitt, T.E. (1993). "Adolescence-limited" and "life-course persistent" anti-social behavior: A developmental taxonomy. *Psychological Review, 100,* 674–701.

Moffit, T., & Lynan, D. (1994). The neuropsychology of Conduct Disorder and delinquency: Implications for understanding antisocial behavior. In D. Fowlers, P. Sutker, & S. Goodman (Eds.), *Progress in experimental personality and psychopathology research* (pp. 233–262). New York: Springer Publishing Co.

Olds, D., Pettitt, L., Robinson, J., Henderson, C., Kitman, H., Cole, B., & Powers, J. (1998). Reducing risks for antisocial behavior with a program of prenatal and early childhood home visitation. *Journal of Community Psychology, 26,* 65–83.

Pamella, D., & Henggeler, S. (1985). Peer interactions of Conduct Disorder, anxious-withdrawn and well adjusted black adolescents. *Journal of Abnormal Psychology, 14,* 1–11.

Patterson, G. R. (1996). Characteristics of developmental theory for early onset delinquency. In M. F. Lenzenweger, & J. L. Haugaard (Eds.), *Frontiers of developmental psychopathology* (pp. 81–124). New York: Oxford University Press.

Pliszka, S. R. (1999). The psychobiology of Oppositional Defiant Disorder and conduct disorder. In H. C. Quay, & A. E. Hogan (Eds.), *Handbook of disruptive behavior disorders* (pp. 507–524). New York: Kluwer.

Quay, H. C. (1993). The psychobiology of under socialized aggressive Conduct Disorder: A theoretical perspective. *Development and Psychopathology, 5,* 165–180.

Reid, B. (1993). Prevention of Conduct Disorder before and after school entry: Relating intervention to developmental findings. *Development and Psychopathology, 5,* 243–262.

Robins, L. (1991). Conduct Disorder. *Journal of Child Psychology and Psychiatry, 32,* 193–212.

Robins, L. N. (1986). The consequences of Conduct Disorder in girls. In D. Oleos, J. Block, & M. Radke-Yarrow (Eds.), *The development of antisocial and prosocial behavior: Research, theories, and issues* (pp. 385–414). Orlando, FL: Academic Press.

Sanford, M., Boyles, M. H., Szatmari, P., Offord, D. R., Jamieson, E., & Spinner, M. (1999). Age-of-onset classification of Conduct Disorder: Reliability and validity in a prospective cohort study. *Journal of the American Academy of Child and Adolescent Psychiatry, 38,* 992–999.

Selzer, J. D., & Hluchy, C. (1991). Youth with Conduct Disorder: A challenge to be met. *Canadian Journal of Psychiatry, 36,* 405–414.

Short, R., & Shapiro, S. (1993). Conduct Disorders: A framework for understanding and intervention in schools and communities. *School Psychology Review, 22,* 362–375.

Simonoff, E. (2001). Gene-environment interplay in oppositional defiant and conduct disorder. *Child Adolescent Psychiatric Clinical North American, 10*(2), 351–374.

Slutsky, W., Heath, A. C., Dunne, M. P., Statham, D. J., Dinwiddie, S. H., Madden, P. A. F., Martin, N. G., & Bucholz, K. K. (1997). Modeling genetic and environmental influences in he etiology of Conduct Disorder: A study of 2,682 adult win pairs. *Journal of Abnormal Psychology, 100*(2), 266–279.

Snyder, H. N., & Sickmund, M. (1999). *Juvenile offenders and victims: 1999 national report*. Pittsburg, PA: National Center for Juvenile Justice, US Department of Justice.

U.S. Congress, Office of Technology Assessment. (1991). *Adolescent health*. (OTA-H-468). Washington, DC: U.S. Government Printing Office.

Webster-Stratton, C. & Dahl, R.W. (1995). Conduct Disorder. *Advanced abnormal child psychology*. Hillsdale, NJ: Erlbaum Associates.

Zoccolillo, M., Pickles, A., Quinton, D., & Rutter, M. (1992). The outcome of conduct disorder: Implications for defining adult personality disorder and conduct disorder. *Psychological Medicine, 22,* 971–986.

CHAPTER 2

The Case of "Michael"

W. Michael Nelson III, K. J. Hart, and A. J. Finch, Jr.

CLINICAL CASE PRESENTATION:
THE CASE OF "MICHAEL"

Mike was brought to my private practice office by his mother in a large midwest city after school on Thursday afternoon. He immediately struck me as a handsome, capable 13-year-old who obviously did not want to be here. His 38-year-old mother was a tall, slender, attractive woman who worked as a medical secretary in a professional building. She was frustrated and upset, although beneath this "put out" demeanor was a caring concern for her son. They entered my office and sat in the chairs, with Mike plopping down in the most comfortable chair. While his mother took the chair directly across from her son, I took the chair in the middle. Mike avoided eye contact with me as he laid claim to his chair, making sure that both his mother and I understood that he was not pleased to be here. His mother, clearly irritated with the "impoliteness" of her son at this first encounter, seemed hesitant to confront him. Such hesitancy appeared to stem from a fundamental insecurity on her part but seemed coupled with a resignation that I often see in patients who have had a long, unsuccessful history of helplessly raging against the tyranny of their child. She did not seem to be passive by nature but there was an air of helplessness and ineptness when it came to dealing with her son who had obviously been very frustrating to her, particularly over the last 2 years when she and her husband of 19 years decided to separate and divorce. She did not seem to have that completely defeated look that oftentimes characterizes parents with severely acting-out children: such parents are hopeless, emotionless, and have given up in the frustrating interactive cycle with their child.

After a brief social stage where I tried to make contact with each of them, albeit not very successfully with Mike, I shifted into the "getting down to business" stage and asked, "How can I help you out?" Mike's mother callously looked at him and said, "Why don't you tell the doctor?" to which he simply stared at the floor and remained defiantly silent. It was obvious to me that Mike was not going to volunteer any information, so I matter-of-factly pointed this out and asked his mother to let me know what brought them to my office.

Mike's mother, in a somewhat cautious fashion so as to not further agitate her son, stated that the immediate crisis was her son's arrest for shoplifting. Mike was caught with one other youth when he and four friends "swarmed" a convenience store and took items before running down the street. According to his mother, Mike blamed his friends for getting caught because they apparently left him behind while making their escape. He was charged only with shoplifting, however, after the police apprehended him. Mike rather defiantly expressed no remorse, although his mother said that she knew he was fearful of what might happen to him when he goes to court. As part of the probation investigation, a magistrate ordered a psychological evaluation (see the evaluation at the end of this chapter), which had been conducted and had recommended therapy. She stated that this was the primary reason why they had made an appointment with me, although she admittedly had considered getting Mike into therapy before the incident because of her growing concerns about him and her difficulties in effectively managing his behavior at home. Mike's mother went on to report that he had some other "brushes" with legal authorities due to his occasional truancy and cutting class. He had missed 13 days of school in the first two quarters (his mother had recently learned that he cuts classes with friends) and the school threatened to file truancy charges against him. Besides the shoplifting charge, she thought that Mike had been stealing small items at home and they had struggled around curfew violations and his current group of friends whom she really did not know much about but wondered if they were a "bad influence" on her son. She was particularly concerned about his "short fuse and hot temper," stating that he sporadically becomes so angry that he has threatened to "really hurt" and even kill his 15-year-old older sister (who was not having any emotional/behavioral difficulties and was excelling in school). Although Mike has threatened to hit his mother on occasion, he has always kept a large distance and backed off when approached by her. He and his sister, however, have gotten into shoving matches where she runs and handles it by complaining to the mother, so that "I have to get involved." Mike becomes very angry at times, but he has only done minimal damage usually to invaluable things. For example, he threw a ball that accidentally broke a vase in the family room about 4 weeks ago. Mike has gotten into several fights in the neighborhood where he tries to present an image of being a "tough guy." Mike's mother noted, however, that he has not "really" gotten into fights at school, "yet."

Somewhere in her description of "Mike's problems," Ms. D. noted that "his temper is just like his father's." Though she reported that Mr. D. was never physically abusive with her, their relationship was conflictual much of the time. Mike's mother also made it clear that her ex-husband had verbally threatened her during their 19-year marriage and even had shoved her on two or three occasions during the last year of their marriage. She complained that her ex-husband has threatened to withhold child support, which she sees as "unfair to the children." She also made it abundantly clear that she was forced to find a secretarial job after the divorce, which has interfered with her ability to "be there for the kids."

Mike sat in a rather defiant, slouched position in his chair while his mother talked. He punctuated her story by occasional interjections that "you don't know what you are talking about." He obviously had a different view of the situation than his mother. Finally, he blurted out that he was "sick and tired of being called the black sheep of the family" while everyone thought his "goody two shoes" sister was "perfect." He said that he was also "sick and tired" of being told what to do and when to do it. He threatened that he had even considered running away, at which his mother seemed surprised, stating that "this was the first time you've said that." His mother stated that "Mike's been like this" ever since she and his father decided to separate 2 years ago. She remained with the two children in their middle-class house while Mr. D. rented a two-bedroom apartment not far from where they live. She was purposefully vague in discussing their marital difficulties, but was clearly irritated with her ex-husband and the events that led to their separation. She said that after 2 years, she finally realized "it's probably over for good." The visitation arrangement hastily worked out was inconsistently followed by Mike's father, which his mother said used to upset her son a great deal. Mike vehemently denied this, stating that "sometimes I don't want anything to do with him!" Mike's mother noted that her daughter, who has never given her much trouble, has made it clear she does not want to visit her father.

At the end of the first session, Mike was asked about his current situation and goals for the future. He confided that he really did not expect to receive serious consequences from the judge on the shoplifting charge and, although his grades were average to somewhat above average prior to his parent's divorce, his problems in school made him question whether he wanted to complete his high school education. He was indifferent to suggestions made by his mother about attending a school vocational program, stating cryptically that he "wasn't going to a school for dummies" and that "all I need is my friends anyway."

A subsequent interview with Mike's father confirmed some of Mike and his mother's initial reports, although it was clear that his father was not well informed about his son's behavior. He caustically noted that he and his wife never were able to get along that well and that he did not think Mike's shoplifting charge would result in any significant jail or community service sentence. His father stated that Mike was usually compliant with him at home but that his son was often with his friends during the day and occasionally at night. He was unsure of what his son did when he was away from home and speculated that he was with friends playing basketball and video games. He was concerned that Mike finish high school and then "get a job if he wants." His dad was not uncooperative during the interview but he seemed careful to justify his actions as a parent and not assume too much blame. He complained that having to work as much as he did in the factory was difficult, claiming that he typically worked 50–60 hours a week. He also claimed that his wife did not tell him much about the difficulties she was having with Mike because "it would always end up where we'd be arguing." Mr. D. said that he wanted to help his son "get on the right track" and was hopeful that I could "get through to Mike" in individual counseling. Overall, I got the message that he did not see the need to expend a lot of personal effort with Mike's treatment.

QUESTIONS FOR CONTRIBUTORS

The case of Mike is actually a composite of several youths who have presented with more severe acting-out, defiant, conduct disorder problems. This case was constructed to represent a patient often seen in clinical practice. The contributors in this text were asked to consider the case of Mike and respond to the following questions based on their theoretical orientation.

    I. Treatment. Please describe your theoretical orientation and treatment model in working with such a patient.

    II. Therapists skills and attributes. Describe the clinical skills or personal attributes of a treating clinician that are essential to a successful therapeutic approach.

III. The case of Mike. The goal of this book is to provide the readers with some insight into what you think are the important elements in therapy needed to deal with such an acting-out, defiant youngster. Consider each of the following topics and questions regarding the case of Mike.

A. Conceptualization, assessment, and treatment planning.

1. What additional information would you want to assist you in conceptualizing and structuring this patient's treatment? Are there any specific assessment tests/tools you would want? What would be the rationale for these?

2. Therapeutic goals, both primary and secondary. What would be your therapeutic short- and long-term goals for this patient? What level of adaptation, coping, or functioning would you see this patient reaching as a result of therapy, both short-term and long-term.

3. Length of therapy. What would be your timeline or duration for therapy? What would be the frequency and duration of sessions and who would be included (e.g., patient, parents, school personnel, legal personnel)?

4. Case conceptualization. What is your conceptualization of this patient's personality, behavior, affective state, cognitions, and functioning. How would you assess the level of danger to self and others. Also include the patients strengths that could be used in therapy.

B. The therapeutic relationship. How would you describe your goals in establishing a therapeutic relationship between the therapist, patient, and, if included, significant others? Examples would include establishing confidentiality, development of trust, boundaries, limit setting, self-disclosure, transference, and countertransference.

1. Roles in a therapeutic relationship. What are the appropriate roles of a therapist/patient as well as significant others (e.g., parents, school, legal authorities) in your model of treatment and what might you do to facilitate these roles? For example, who is included and when in therapy? What is the therapist's degree of directness and activity level? For example, is the therapist more active or passive in working with such a patient? To what extent is the therapeutic relationship collaborative?

C. Treatment implications and outcome.

1. Therapeutic techniques and strategies. Are there specific therapeutic techniques that you would or would not utilize

in therapy? If so, what would they be and why? What other professionals you would want to collaborate with on this case and how would you work together? Would you want to involve significant others in the treatment (e.g., parents, school personnel, legal representatives)? Would you assign out-of-session work (e.g., homework) with this patient, and, if so, what kind?

2. Mechanisms of change. What would you see as the hope for mechanisms of change for this patient, in order of relative importance?

3. Medical and nutritional issues. How would you handle any medical or psychopharmacology issues involved in working with this client? Are there any nutritional issues that you would consider in working with this adolescent?

4. Potential pitfalls. What potential pitfalls would you envision in your therapy? Would you envision as the source(s) of these difficulties and how would you handle them? Are there any special cautions to be observed in working with this patient? Any particular resistances that you would expect, and how would you deal with them?

5. Termination and relapse prevention. When would you consider termination to be appropriate for this patient and how would that be addressed in therapy? How would you envision relapse prevention and how would this be structured?

COUNTY JUVENILE COURT CLINIC SERVICES
PSYCHOLOGICAL EVALUATION

Name: Michael D.
Court ID: 123456
Date Evaluated: September 6, 2003
Age: 13 years, 4 months
Birth Date: May 2, 1990
Education: 7th grade
Referral Source: Probation Officer

Reason for Referral

Michael D. is a 13-year-old Caucasian male referred to the County Juvenile Court Psychology Clinic by his probation officer to aid in dispositional planning. He is before the Court on a charge of Theft (M4) resulting from an incident at a convenience store in which he, along with a group of friends, allegedly distracted a convenience store clerk and took several food items and magazines without paying. This is Michael's first contact with the Juvenile Court.

Assessment Procedures
    Review of File Information
    Interview with youth
    Interview with father, Greg D.
    Interview with mother, Sarah D.
    Wechsler Intelligence Scale for Children-IV (WISC-IV)
    Wide Range Achievement Test - Revision 3 (WRAT-3)
    Incomplete Sentences Blank
    Kovacs' Children Depression Inventory (CDI)
    Minnesota Multiphasic Personality Inventory for Adolescents (MMPI-A)
    Substance Abuse Subtle Screening Inventory (SASSI-A2)
    Child Inventory of Anger (ChIA)
    Achenbach Child Behavioral Checklist (completed by mother)

Background Information
Background information is based on the social history prepared by the probation officer and interviews with Michael and his parents, all of whom were interviewed separately. Michael is the second of two children born to his biological parents who separated and divorced 2 years ago. Also in the home is Michael's 16-year-old sister who is reportedly "doing great" in school, and poses no significant behavior problems at home.

    Ms. D. reported that she and her husband of 19 years divorced about 2 years ago. Although she said, "there was a lot wrong with the marriage," the divorce was precipitated by her "fear" of her ex-husband's temper. Specifically, she reportedly felt her husband was overly strict with the children, often imposing harsh punishments such as very lengthy groundings. He also "raged" at the children when he was angry, and she feared that he would harm them with physical punishment, although he had never done so. She also worried that Michael was "becoming just like his father—he has the same temper."

    In describing Michael's development, Ms. D. reported that he was born following a full-term pregnancy and uncomplicated labor and delivery. From early in his life, she found him to be challenging: he did not seem to sleep much, and he was "several months old" before he slept through the night. He also developed colic and "cried for 4 months straight." As a toddler, he was prone to severe temper tantrums that she found difficult to manage. His early adjustment to school was "ok," although he "got in much more trouble than his sister ever did" at school. She saw some of his behavior as "typical boy—very active, into sports." She stated that his 3rd grade teacher described him as restless in school, and Ms.D. wondered if he might "have ADD." She discussed it with Michael's pediatrician who took a "wait and see" approach in light of Michael's adequate academic performance in school. His academic performance remained good in the 4th grade, and the issue "passed." However, Michael's grades in the 5th grade dropped "from mostly As and Bs" to "a lot of Cs" and he has continued to "struggle" academically. His parents' divorce occurred during that year, and Ms. D. attributed his difficulties to that event. However, he has continued to struggle academically since that time, and his behavior at school has also become more problematic. Ms. D. was most distressed by the recent revelation at a school conference that Michael has missed several days of school (without her awareness) and has been "cutting" classes. Because of the number of days missed (13 days in the first 2 quarters), the school has threatened to file truancy charges if the situation does not improve. In addition, Michael has had a series of suspensions and Friday School assignments for smoking, insubordination, inappropriate behavior, nonparticipation in class, and disruptive/uncooperative behavior. Most recently, he received a suspension last week for smoking in the bathroom and defiantly challenging the teacher who caught him; he will serve 4 days of in-school suspension starting tomorrow. The disruptive/uncooperative behavior refers to verbal arguments between Michael and peers that his mother says "would have resulted in punches if the teachers hadn't broken it up" and the insubordination is related to "shouting matches" with teachers. Ms. D. also expressed concern about the boys with whom Michael has been associating; she sees them as "losers and troublemakers."

Regarding Michael's adjustment in the home, Ms. D. reported that he is surly and uncommunicative and he engages in frequent arguments with his sister, some of which have ended in "shoving and slapping." In addition, Michael regularly violates the curfew she has set for him, and refuses to follow any consequences she places on his behavior. For example, when Michael argues with his sister, she sends him to his room, but he refuses, and this often seems to "fuel the fire," and escalate the argument. Ms. D. is concerned that Michael is regularly smoking marijuana.

Mr. D. has weekly visitation with Michael and he pays child support, although Ms. D. indicated that Mr. D. has not only threatened to withhold payment, but has actually done so at times, which has resulted in her contacting an attorney. Conflict over support payment has arisen because the 16-year-old sister has refused to visit her father regularly. His father expressed distress over continuing conflict with his ex-wife, claiming, "she can't handle him, and she's turned my daughter against me." According to Mr. D., Ms. D.

allows Michael to "get away with murder" and makes excuses for his behavior. In contrast, Mr. D. reported (and Ms. D.'s report corroborated) that he will "threaten to get out the belt" when he feels that Michael is "getting out of hand." Mr. D. admitted that he used physical punishment (e.g., spanking) when Michael was younger, but that he "mostly yells" now and threatens physical contact. He finds "that usually works to get my message across, so I don't really have to hit him." He claimed that his ex-wife "always tried to protect Mike" from the physical discipline and verbal threats, stating, "she believes in the soft approach" of reasoning and time-outs.

Interview with Youth

When asked why he was charged with theft, Michael stated, "We were just having fun—goofing around. It was really no big deal."

Michael described his relationship with his parents as "alright" but would not elaborate initially. Later in the interview, he stated that he "kind of" gets along with his father, but added, "If I don't do something perfect, he yells and grounds me." He added that his father used to drink heavily but has cut back on his drinking. Michael dislikes school because "you have to work, and get no respect from the teachers." Michael claims that he "used to" associate with youths who got into trouble and smoked marijuana but has recently "stopped" seeing them; this is inconsistent with his mother's report. He was not able to describe how he currently spends his free time or with whom he currently associates. He commented that he dislikes being at home and tries to spend as much time away as he can.

Michael said that he does not have problems making or keeping friends. He hopes to finish high school, and enter the armed services, and/or become a professional football player. According to Michael, he first tried marijuana at age 11 at a friend's house, and he currently smokes "on the weekends." When pressed about how he is spending time when he skips school, he admitted that he and friends "smoke pot and play video games" at each other's homes.

Michael admitted that he has "a bad temper" but he does not feel he has an anger management problem and he sees no need for treatment. He reportedly has no sleep or appetite problems and claims to usually have adequate energy. He denied ever having been sexually abused.

Behavioral Observations

Michael arrived promptly for his appointment at the Juvenile Court Psychology Clinic, escorted by his mother. He accompanied this examiner to the testing area and seemed to understand the purpose and nonconfidential nature of the current evaluation. Michael is a 13-year-old Caucasian male of average build who was casually but neatly dressed for his appointment. He had blonde hair, freckles, and wore his jacket throughout the entire evaluation. He related in a grudgingly polite and distant manner during the interview, generally denying or minimizing issues or problems. There was no evidence of the restlessness that his mother had reported. Indeed, he seemed somewhat lethargic and yawned several times throughout the evaluation. He complained that he was tired because he stayed up late the previous night and had to get up early this morning. Michael responded appropriately to questions but maintained poor eye contact. His thinking appeared adequately organized and his thoughts were logical and coherent.

During psychological testing, Michael was more cooperative than he had been in the interview, and he appeared to be adequately motivated. Michael approached tasks systematically, but he gave up fairly easily when challenged on academic testing. Based on his overall cooperation and motivation, the following test results are believed to be valid and reliable estimates of his current functioning.

Test Results

On this administration of the WISC-IV, Michael obtained a Full Scale IQ score of 97, which is in the Average range at the 45th percentile. His scaled scores on individual subtests and the Index scores are listed:

Verbal Comprehension	SS	Perceptual Reasoning	SS
Similarities	9	Block Design	11
Vocabulary	8	Picture Concepts	10
Comprehension	8	Matrix Reasoning	9
Information	(8)	Picture Completion	(10)
Word Reasoning	(9)		

Working Memory	SS	Processing Speed	SS
Digit Span	9	Coding	12
Letter-Number Seq.	10	Symbol Search	10
Arithmetic	(7)	Cancellation	(9)

Verbal Comprehension Index	91
Perceptual Reasoning Index	100
Working Memory Index	97
Processing Speed Index	106

Michael is currently functioning in the average range of intelligence, which is consistent with his clinical presentation. The differences in his scores are not significant, but he demonstrates slightly greater facility when dealing with nonverbal material relative to verbal material.

On this administration of the WRAT-3, Michael achieved scores that are fairly consistent with overall cognitive skills and with his current grade placement. Although this is only a screening, there is no evidence to suggest that he experiences a specific learning disability. The scaled scores (SS, based on age), percentiles, and grade scores in each of the areas measured are listed as follows:

	SS	Percentile	Grade Equivalent
Reading	94	34	6
Spelling	97	42	6
Arithmetic	99	47	7

Michael produced a valid profile on the MMPI-A. Only two of the clinical scales reached the clinically significant range: Ma (T = 78) and Pd (T = 67). With the exception of Hy (T = 45), the remaining clinical scale T scores vary between 54 and 63. Youth who produce similar profiles are described as having limited insight into themselves or the motivation for their behavior. They tend to be immature, insecure, and dependent. In addition, they tend to be easily bored and restless, and to display difficulties with impulse control. These individuals tend to have high energy levels, but they have difficulty using that energy to their advantage, and they have difficulty completing projects. They typically have a low frustration tolerance, which can result in hostile and angry outbursts. Although they can make a good first impression in their interactions with others, they tend to maintain fairly superficial relationships. The content and supplementary scales were significant for cynicism and distrust of others, and a tendency to assume the worst of others. There are indications that Michael is developing anti-social attitudes, in addition to his conduct problems. He also appears to be developing substance use related to his delinquent behaviors.

Themes of Michael's responses on the Incomplete Sentences suggest that he is disinterested in school, experiences conflict with his parents, and is easily angered. With regard to his view of authority figures, he presents a "leave me alone" attitude. Michael did not endorse symptoms of depression on the CDI, and he denied current suicidal ideation. On the ChIA, a self-report measure of anger, Michael's scores suggest that he is easily frustrated and responds to problem situations with ready anger, including verbal and occasional physical aggression. He is most likely to demonstrate indirect aggression. Although he reports conflicts with authority figures, he sees his relationships with his peers as adequate. On the SASSI, he reported that he abuses substances, and he endorsed attitudes and beliefs that make him particularly susceptible to substance abuse.

Michael's mother's responses to a measure of social and emotional functioning indicate that Michael exhibits primarily externalizing aggressive and rule-breaking behavior. Michael's mother also endorsed some symptoms of attention problems such as daydreaming, impulsivity, inattentiveness, and poor school performance, although this score fell just short of the clinically significant range. There was no indication of internalizing problems such as anxiety or depression.

Diagnostic Impressions

Axis I:	312.82	Conduct Disorder, Adolescent Onset Type
		Rule out Cannabis Abuse
Axis II:	71.09	No diagnosis
Axis III:		No known physical or medical difficulties
Axis IV:		Legal difficulties, divorce of parents 2 years ago, academic difficulties
Axis V:	GAF = 55	(current)

Recommendations

In light of the preceding information, it is recommended that Michael be placed on probation with the goal of ensuring that he receives supervision and treatment, which might include psychotherapy and community/school interventions. It is also recommended that he seek psychiatric consultation to determine if medication might assist in his overall adjustment. It is further recommended that all parties who are responsible for disciplining Michael become involved in his treatment to ensure consistency of discipline and expectations. Finally, it is recommended that, as a condition of his probation, Michael receive a substance abuse evaluation, regular urine screens, and treatment as indicated.

Jane Q. Doe, Ph.D.
Court-Appointed Psychologist

CHAPTER 3

The Psychoanalytic Approach to the Treatment of Conduct Disorder

M. David Liberman

TREATMENT MODEL

In this chapter, I will be discussing this case from the perspective of a psychoanalyst with a strong commitment to the self psychological position of Heinz Kohut. The self psychological model focuses on the vitality and the sense of cohesion of the self. Procedurally, the self psychologist functions within the same framework as does the classical psychoanalyst: The analyst listens and interprets the patient's associations while paying particular attention to the kinds of transferences that arise during the course of treatment. Although self psychology retains the emphasis on both interpretation and transference, the goal of the self psychologist is to understand the patient through empathic immersion in the patient's subjective world. As the patient works through the feelings and transferences generated by the analytic setting, the sense of understanding that is communicated by the analyst to the patient is an important component of the curative aspect of the self psychological treatment.

The self psychological position holds that the vitality, cohesiveness, and resilience of the self are dependent on the development and transformations of narcissism. Following classical theory, Kohut (1971) originally envisioned the infant as existing initially in a state of objectless "bliss." Because of the inevitable failures in mothering, this state of bliss is ruptured. In order to re-establish this primary narcissistic state, the infant develops the image of a perfect parent (i.e., the idealized parent imago) and of a perfect self (i.e., the grandiose self). In order for growth to take place, the developing child must experience a series of manageable disappointments in both the idealized parental imago and the grandiose self. As Kohut (1971) originally theorized, this series of manageable disappointments allows the child to internalize or draw back into himself the narcissistic libido or energy that has been attached to the idealized parental imago. If these disappointments are too intense, the developing individual will be traumatized. The development of mature narcissism (i.e., realistic and resilient self-esteem) starts to occur as the child begins to realize that neither the idealized other nor the grandiose self is quite as perfect or as powerful as the child had imagined. These manageable disappointments lead to a more realistic sense of both self and self-esteem.

In addition to their restitutive functions, the development of both the idealized parental imago and the grandiose self leads to the development of significant sources of motivation for the growing self. The development of an idealized parental imago allows the child to develop an image of how he will want to see himself: in other words, it allows for the development of ideals. The development of the grandiose self provides the individual with the direction and underpinnings for what he may hope to achieve or, again in other words, for the development of ambitions. As Kohut said, "The individual is led by ideals and pushed by ambitions" (Siegel, 1996). Kohut (1977) expressed this motivational tension between ambitions and ideals as the "Bipolar self" with an arc of talents existing between the twin poles of ambition and ideals.

It is believed that patients who suffer from disorders of the self have been either traumatized by or simply denied these needed relationships and experiences. As a consequence of this, people will develop distortions and defenses that stifle and impair their developmental processes. In order for self development to resume, the patient needs to work through the defenses and distortions so that he can establish the kinds of relationships that were appropriate to the phase in which his development was stopped. These relationships are recreated clinically in the transferences that power the self psychological treatment. Self psychology recognizes the development of unrealistic perceptions or expectations of the analyst or therapist as important recreations of the patient's interrupted development. The kinds of transferences that are established with the therapist are crucial to the resumption of the patient's development. Diagnostically, the kinds of transferences that arise in the course of therapy indicate not only what initially went wrong in the patient's developmental process but also where and with whom. Kohut (1971) initially described a number of different kinds of transferences, but only the two main categories are described here: the mirroring and the idealizing transferences. If the therapist is seen as merely someone who is there to reflect the "wonderfulness" of the patient, then we have the development of the mirroring transference, which is crucial to the development of the grandiose self. The self psychological position recognizes that the re-establishment of the grandiose self is a crucial step in growth. Although the patient's grandiosity may be interpreted, the self psychologist recognizes it as an important stepping-stone to mature self-esteem. On the other hand, if the analyst is seen as being "perfect," the patient is in the midst of an idealizing transference. Idealizing transferences are critical in the re-establishment of the idealized parental imago.

The forward movement of the therapeutic process is dependent on the therapist's ability to re-establish an empathic atmosphere in which the patient feels deeply understood by the therapist. Operating from a position of an empathic immersion, the therapist is able to both understand and empathically—not traumatically—interpret to the patient what is transpiring between them. The self psychologist undertakes two tasks in this kind of treatment. The first is to understand and to interpret the patient's resistances to the awakening and reawakening of his frustrated narcissistic needs. Once the process is underway, the second task is to empathize with and interpret the vicissitudes of the patient's idealizations and denigrations of the analyst and/or the patient. If this process is successfully negotiated, the self-development of the patient will resume.

Failures in the empathic connection between the therapist and patient are recognized not only as inevitable but also as necessary. These failures can bring about anger and rage in the patient. The self psychological analyst sees the patient's anger and rage as a breakdown product that results from a rupture or failure of the empathic bond between the therapist and patient. Further, the self psychological position holds that it is the successful repair of these empathic failures that moves the individual's development forward. Empathic breaks between the therapist and the patient are not viewed as unfortunate setbacks but rather as new opportunities for growth and progress. The successful understanding and interpretation of the patient's frustration with and disappointment in the therapist are a crucial component to the development of the self. Those things, which were initially admired in the idealized parent, are made part of the self through the manageable disappointments in the idealized parental imago. Kohut (1971) described this as the process of "transmuting internalization." It is through this ongoing process of transmuting internalizations that the individual builds up the psychological structures that help the individual to regulate internal tension and in self-soothing. The developing individual becomes more and more capable of taking over the functions of emotional homeostasis that were originally managed—or mismanaged—for the patient by others.

Kohut (1971) saw that interference at different stages of development would give rise to different impairments in the development of either the idealizing process or the grandiose self. One of the consequences of this interference is the development of what Kohut referred to as the "vertical" split. The vertical split was distinguished from the "horizontal" split of classical analysis because it was a split in or, perhaps more correctly said, within consciousness. Unlike the horizontal split, the individual is aware that he or she is holding two opposing views, but the contradiction does not appear to cause conflict in his or her mind; the synthesizing function of the ego does not appear to be operating. It is through the healing of these vertical splits that the developing individual is able to reclaim a sense of cohesion and wholeness.

THERAPIST'S SKILL AND ATTRIBUTES

The process of the self psychological treatment depends on the ability of the analyst to empathize with his or her patient. A core requirement for the self psychological approach is the ability of the therapist to genuinely feel, understand, and accept the meaning of an experience for the other person. This skill requires that the therapist is both willing and able to recognize his or her own countertransferences and resistances to the therapeutic process. It also requires that the therapist be able to accept a genuine recognition of his or her own limitations in understanding the experience of another person. This process is particularly important in a self psychological treatment, as the self psychologist becomes the self-object onto which the patient's early narcissistic needs and disappointments are transferred. The analyst must continuously strive to be comfortable with the patient's idealizations and denigrations and to maintain his or her empathic stance. Sometimes this can be quite trying. Patients may react with rage when their narcissistic needs are disappointed or frustrated. The therapist must be able to concurrently recognize his or her own discomforts with the process and then work through them. In order to continue the empathic immersion in the patient's world, the analyst has to be able to stay in emotional contact with the patient through the ups and the downs of the therapeutic process. These empathic demands require not only the ability of the therapist to understand the feelings of the patient, but also that the therapist be willing to continuously struggle to stay in touch with the patient, to remain emotionally steady through this process, and to sensitively interpret what is being recreated between the two of them.

It is also crucial that the therapist be able to work through the counter-transferences and the resistances that are the fabric of the self psychological exchange. A successful therapeutic process requires that the therapist continuously work through his or her resistances and countertransferences, even as the patient is dealing with his or her own resistances and transferences. I have found that therapy often stalls as I struggle to catch up in my own self-analysis with the analysis of the patient. Kohut (1977) discussed some of the major countertransference problems that are encountered by the therapist in a self psychological treatment. A therapist who has not sufficiently worked through his or her own deficits in the grandiose self will be made uncomfortable with the patient's idealization, and will be unable to accept the patient's regard in the idealizing transferences. Conversely, a therapist whose grandiose self was not sufficiently nurtured may become caught up in the patient's idealizations and lose sight of the transference nature of the patient's feelings. The demands on the therapist can be equally intense when the patient's grandiose self is the focus of the work. The self object nature of the transference can become quite difficult to tolerate. The patient's treatment by the therapist may range from a mild condescension to intense denigration. The patient might also demand perfect attunement and mirroring from the analyst. In the mirroring transferences, the treatment can evoke feelings in the therapist that range from frustration to rage, or from boredom to a feeling of "deadness" in the presence of the patient. Again, it is critical that the therapist be able to tolerate these feelings, understand them, and work them through to the point where the therapist can again re-establish emotional contact with the patient. If the therapist is able to handle these multiple demands, then he or she can function as an effective self-object. An effective self-object for the patient would be a new self-object that is able to tolerate both the idealizations and the deidealizations of the different idealizing transferences as well as being able to accept and understand the intense demands and deadening impact of the various mirroring transferences.

To this list, I would add another potential source of interference: a variety of resistance that I have started to think of as "Repudiation." True empathic immersion is a particularly demanding aspect of the self psychological treatment process. This not only requires that the therapist be able to understand what the patient is feeling, but also that the therapist be able to relate the patient's feelings and experiences to similar feelings and experiences that the therapist has had. Quite often, we find that we are viewing the patient's experiences or feelings from a distance. Perhaps wondering, "How could *he or she* possibly feel or do such a thing?!" In my experience, this is almost inevitably the result of my resistance to being empathic with the patient. The patient is stirring up feelings and/or memories that I do not want to re-experience. As a result of my resistance, I insist that I cannot relate to the patient's feelings or experiences. This kind of resistance on my part makes a true connection with the patient impossible. Sometimes it takes considerable self-analysis before I can reconnect with the experiences and the feelings that correspond with those that the patient is telling me. In effect, I have "repudiated" the experiences and feelings that would allow me to genuinely understand, empathize, and relate to those experiences that my patient is describing. I have since come to think of this as a kind of resistance on the part of the therapist—or, as it often turns out, on the part of the parent—as "repudiation."

THE CASE OF "MIKE"
Conceptualization, Assessment, and Treatment Planning
Additional Information and Assessment

The question of assessment and structuring of the treatment touches on a central note about this patient having to do with Mike's current diagnosis of conduct disorder. Kohut (1977) actually described two kinds of narcissistic patients: the narcissistic personality disorder and the narcissistic behavior disorder. In terms of self psychological conceptualization, Mike's description might better fit into this latter category. Considering a patient for self psychological treatment, or any form of psychoanalysis, it is necessary to make an intrapsychic evaluation of the patient. The critical factor for the self psychological psychoanalyst or therapist is in the determination of the essential state of the patient's self. The self psychological therapist, who is uncertain about the self-state of the patient, must make that determination through patient and careful observation of the patient. In fact, it is often the patient's response to treatment that allows the therapist to arrive at a definite appraisal of the patient's self-state. If there is sufficient concern about the patient's self-state at the beginning of treatment, then a referral should be made for psychological testing that included a comprehensive work-up that included projective testing. As a result of Mike's propensity for acting-out, I would want to spend some time in evaluation. Intensive psychotherapy and psychoanalysis can put a severe strain on the individual's functioning capacities, and an in-depth evaluation made of this young man's reality testing and ego strength would help to determine if there were any contraindications or particular cautions that could be identified. In particular, it would be important to rule out an unrecognized biological condition, as these disorders can produce outbursts such as Mike's. However, these same behaviors can result from psychologically based deficits reflecting his ability—or inability—to control impulses or self-soothing. It is possible that projective testing could help to distinguish between these two possibilities.

In addition to the projective testing, I would want a formal evaluation to rule out the possibility of attention deficit hyperactivity disorder (ADHD) for this young man. There is sufficient scope to wonder if there might be a biological component to this aspect of his difficulties. Is Michael's tendency to explode a result of ADHD, identification with his explosive father, or an inability on Michael's part to soothe himself? There is a developmental history that might support any or all of these possibilities. Although these questions could ultimately be answered in the therapy, it might also be possible to make some tentative determination early in the treatment.

Therapeutic Goals

The ultimate goal of treatment for the self psychologist is always the same: to help restart the development of the self that has become blocked in the patient. Kohut (1984) believed that the real goal of treatment was to help the individual to feel that he could live a satisfying and fulfilling life and to be able to appreciate and make use of his talents and abilities. Kohut was writing about adult patients; Michael is demonstrating the beginnings of these kinds of failures in the development of the self of an early adolescent.

Short-term goals. The short-term goal for a patient like Mike would be to establish a therapeutic atmosphere in which he could begin to talk about his feelings instead of acting them out.

Long-term goals. The most important goal of long-term therapy with someone like Michael is to help him develop a sense of cohesion and resilience so that he does not "come apart." His current functioning is of a youth who is already showing serious deficits in self-cohesion. Most of Kohut's writing describes the treatment of adults who failed to develop cohesive "selves" as a result of developmental failures that had taken place earlier in life. In the description of Michael, brief as it is, we see an early adolescent youngster who is currently experiencing the kinds of developmental failures described by Kohut. Without correction of these developmental failures, Mike will continue to "fragment" in developing self, resulting in the type of adult pathology that Kohut treated.

Kohut saw the development of the self as being powered by the twin poles of ambition and ideals (Kohut, 1977). Ideals initially develop from our idealization of an early-idealized figure, which often is of the father. When this kind of idealization fails—because either the parent is unavailable, unreceptive, or absent—the child is unable to develop this aspect of the personality. As a result of this failure, the child will often turn to other young-sters to fill this unmet idealization need. Delinquency and gang membership are often the result of a younger person's attempt to compensate for this kind of developmental deficit. Mike's history seems to be the type of situation that could easily provide this outcome: a father who is rejecting, critical, and both emotionally and physically unavailable. Idealization fails and the need for an idealizable parental imago goes unmet. In a self psychological therapy, we would hope that the analyst or therapist could re-engage with Michael's narcissistic development and restart the idealizing process. Children like Michael demonstrate the narcissistic behavior disorders described by Kohut: the individuals who tend to act out rather than quietly suffer from these kinds of failures in self-cohesion.

A major difficulty for the narcissistic disorders is the failure in self-soothing. A younger person—such as Mike—is still very much in need of the calming influence of the parent. Another long-term goal of therapy would be to help Mike in self-soothing. In the case presentation, Ms. D. states that she is "particularly concerned about Mike's short fuse and hot temper, stat-ing that he sporadically becomes so angry that he has threatened to really hurt and even kill his 15-year-old sister," that "he has verbally threatened his mother," has "gotten involved in shoving matches with his sister" and has broken things when he was very angry. Within a self psychological frame-work, these behaviors would be understood as resulting from fragmentation of the self. Although Ms. D. implied that Mike might be identifying with his father's temper, an equally plausible explanation is that Mike's father is not able to calm himself such that he has been of little help to his son in this regard. Furthermore, Ms. D. has not acted as a calming influence on her son so that this young man has internalized no soothing influences. An aim of the analysis or therapy would be for Michael to experience and internalize the safety of the setting and the settling capacities of the therapist so that his "self" would no longer be subject to fragmentation.

The twinship type of mirroring that is so necessary to adolescence ap-pears to be totally absent in Michael's relationship with his parents. One of the striking things about the description of Michael was the apparent joylessness of his existence. His actions were not the result of adolescent exuberance as described by Erikson (1950). There was no sense of pleasure or excitement as this young man's experiences were related either by himself or by his parents. Michael's activities were angry actions, not vitalizing experiences. It appeared that neither Michael nor his parents were enjoying his adolescence. Instead, what we are told is that the mother showed "an air of helplessness and inept-ness when it came to dealing with her son." The examiner characterizes this parent in a somewhat more hopeful manner than other parents, whom he has seen, who are "hopeless, emotionless, and resigned." The examiner goes on to say, "They have given up in the frustrating interactive cycle with their child." The descriptions are profound. This adolescent's mother—as well as the other parents described—has entered into a negative mirroring of her child in which the desperation of the child is met with an equal joylessness and despair by the parents. This macabre dance between parents and child can only lead into further downward spiraling. I would hope that by the end of this therapy, Michael would have some opportunity to connect or, perhaps, reconnect with the joyfulness and exuberance that is an essential part of adolescence.

A collateral long-term goal of therapy would also be to help Ms. D. regain some sense of her own authority. One of the examiner's first comments is his impression that Ms. D. reminded him of other parents "who had a long and unsuccessful history of dealing with the child's tyranny." How does a child become the parent, and a "tyrannical" one at that? It often comes about when the parent makes a transference to the child and it inevitably interferes with the adult's ability to relate to the child *as a child*. In a number of cases like this one, I have found that it was crucial to engage either one or both of the parents into therapy as their self-object use of the child was seriously interfering with the child's emotional development.

Level of adaptation.   It is possible that Michael might gain an immediate sense of relief from his treatment. Self psychologists believe that a crucial part of an individual's ability to function and to grow is his experience of feeling understood. A patient like Michael is in desperate need of a continuing experience of feeling understood. The intensity and regularity of psychoanalytic treatment could meet that need and offer him an immediate sense of relief. If Michael and his therapist were able to develop a therapeutic framework for their relationship such that Michael would have some sense of what he could and could not expect from his treatment, then I think it is possible that Michael might settle down and experience feelings of stability, understanding, and respect that have not been part of his life. The availability of an understanding therapist several times a week could provide Michael with some relief from his chronic disappointment in the figures he needs to respect, as well as the possibility of finding a continuing source of acceptance and soothing. If the therapeutic "fit" were initially successful (i.e., the therapist was able to quickly establish an empathic connection), then rapid improvements in behavior are possible. Within the first several months, I would hope school functioning would improve, the frequency of outbursts would decrease, and

Michael would show greater willingness to bring his feelings into therapy to be discussed.

The ultimate goals of self psychological treatment are the development of an ability to appreciate oneself and maintain both a sense of self and one's self-respect in the face of disappointment and frustration, and the development of the ability to calm oneself in the face of upset. In long-term therapy, such as analysis, I would also hope to see Michael develop a resilient sense of self so that he would not fragment or act out in the face of frustration and disappointment. Self psychological therapists engage in an intense therapeutic process over an extended period of time in order that the patient can build up and maintain a resilient self so that even after he or she has completed treatment, he or she is able to maintain cohesion. Based on the information available, I think that it is possible for Michael to achieve that level of self-development. In terms of the long-term prognosis, if therapy or analysis were ultimately successful, I would think that Mike could eventually "catch up" with himself and function at an age-specific level.

Length of Therapy

This is always a problematic issue in psychodynamic treatment, and psychoanalysts and psychodynamic therapists are sometime viewed as avoiding this question. The reason that it is difficult for us to say how long a therapy will take is a result of the fact that we are looking for psychic growth rather than behavioral change, and psychic growth is not easily predicted. Mike is not only in need of help to psychologically catch up with himself as a 13-year-old, but also in his efforts to finish up growing through adolescence. At present, this is being done in an environment that appears to be sadly lacking the needed ingredients. If Michael's parents are unable—or unwilling—to provide the kind of understanding that this youngster needs, then this task becomes the job of the therapist. If the parents cannot complete the work of helping him grow through adolescence, then the therapist and the therapeutic setting may ultimately need to function as a surrogate parental environment for the patient, even after he is able to function at an age-specific level. If the parents continue to be unable to shepherd this growing adolescent into young adulthood, there is a risk that the therapeutic work will be undone. In terms of frequency of sessions, I would recommend this patient to be seen in psychotherapy at least twice a week. If psychotherapy does not provide sufficient involvement, I would recommend psychoanalysis four to five time per week. I would also recommend that the parents begin therapy. It is evident that they have not been successful in their attempts to raise Mike.

Case Conceptualization

Mike appears to be a young man whose self-development is being seriously compromised by failures in both lines of narcissistic development. It seems that he is reacting to the loss of his father as both a presence in the home, and as a figure that he can look up to and hope to emulate. Ms. D. reports that his school performance began to fall apart around the time of the separation, but it also appears that she is at a loss to understand this relationship. Her inability to understand this alone is telling. It appears that Mike is continuing to suffer from both the physical and psychological loss of his father. Further, Mike may be feeling a disappointment in his father that he has not acknowledged. Mike's father does not appear to be someone to whom Mike could either feel close or could realistically idealize. The lack of an idealizeable male figure can be crippling to a growing adolescent. Chasseguet-Smirgel (1984), quoting Freud, describes the need of the child to be able to project his narcissism onto the parents in order for the child to develop an Ego Ideal. "Projection of infantile narcissism onto the parents, which results in the Ego Ideal, is a step towards the conquest of reality and object love," as "the Ego ideal implies that there is a 'plan,' 'hope,' and 'promise.'" In Mike's case, it appears that he does not have figures onto whom he can cast his hopes for himself in the future. Adolescents who cannot find these kinds of figures will often angrily turn away and, because a real idealizable object is not available, develop a fictional male identity—a "tough guy"—into whom they try to form themselves. This appears to be the case with Mike: He is angrily turning away from his family and school, which reflects his failure to find an appropriate figure whom he can admire. Instead, he has turned to his nascent "gang" for a sense of belonging and a group that he can respect.

Along these same lines, Kohut (1977) described the self-objects of the idealizing transference as being the sources of our ideals and our hopes for the future. Mike does not appear to have such a figure available. In a self psychological treatment, there is another opportunity to remobilize the kind of idealizing transference that he needs to remobilize the idealized parent imago and allow a maturing of the self to continue. It appears that Michael has attempted to develop an idealizing relationship with the other members of his "gang." This attempt is not an uncommon compensation for latency-age youths or adolescents who do not have a suitable object for idealization. In a self psychological treatment, the job of the therapist would be to allow these needs to emerge in the therapeutic relationship and then to help the patient to understand and fulfill them. With many patients, this is a slow process. They have learned to defend themselves against the potential disappointments that they have already suffered by not allowing others to disappoint them again.

The empathic interpretation of this defensive "strategy" is also very much part of the self psychological treatment of this kind of condition.

In addition to Mike's difficulties in his development of the idealizing parent imago, it appears that there have been difficulties in the development of some of the self-soothing functions associated with the grandiose self. Mike's mother reports that he was difficult to calm down since birth. A colicky baby is a challenge for a young mother even in the most secure situation. In this kind of situation, it is difficult for the mother to be able to provide the generally consistent understanding and soothing presence that will allow for this aspect of self-development. It appears that in this earlier area, also, Mike's self-development has stalled and that he is steadily becoming both more frustrated and less able to handle his upsets and disappointments. The use of drugs and alcohol is often a substitute for the inability to soothe oneself. We have examples of Michael's attempts to meet his current needs in the case material. When his tension gets too great, he explodes. Mike presents the picture of a young man who is beginning to endanger himself. His emotional needs are causing him to become desperate and to play closer and closer to the edge. Adolescents who do this sometimes go over the edge without ever having intended to do so.

Strengths.   It appears that Mike has at least average intelligence and enough social sense to be able to be part of a group. Part of the tragedy of this kind of youngster is that he or she often has a number of strengths and talents that he or she cannot show because of difficulties in maintaining a cohesive self.

The Therapeutic Relationship
Goals in Establishing the Therapeutic Relationship
The most immediate task in self psychological therapy is the establishment of an empathic environment in which Mike would be able to settle down. The job of the therapist is to create a situation in which Mike could begin to feel safe and secure enough to expose and acknowledge his needs for admiration, understanding, and an adult figure that he could admire. In order to facilitate this process in the early phases of treatment, the therapist does not interfere in the development of transferences by the patient. It is the task of the therapist to accept the developing transference and to be careful to interpret only the patient's resistances to the unfolding of these needs (Kohut, 1971). It is often the case that an adolescent of this age needs the therapist's understanding and the provision of self-object functions (such as soothing, calming, and the restoration of self-respect) more than the development of insight into his own psychic processes. In fact, adolescents often resent the therapist

trying to "get into their heads," and analytic therapists must be particularly cognizant of this resentment

Confidentiality is a crucial part of our therapeutic agreement. We do not discuss what is going on in the sessions with other people unless the safety of the patient or of another is in question. Psychoanalytic work is founded on developing a sense of reliability and safety between patient and therapist. Generally, the best way to approach this issue is to be forthcoming with someone of Mike's age. At the onset, I explain what I can and cannot say to others and the conditions under which confidentiality might be compromised.

Trust is developed on the basis of experience. I do not expect anyone to "trust" me when our relationship is just starting. In self psychology, we believe that the genesis of the individual's problems began when he found that he could not trust the people on whom he was depending. At the beginning of therapy, what I am really talking about is the question of whether or not a new patient can have enough faith in me to begin talking about himself. Trust will generally follow if, based on the patient's experiences with me, I have treated him with respect and have shown myself to be reliable and sensitive to his feelings. However, if trust does not seem to be developing, this is not a contraindication for therapy but rather an obviously critical issue to be addressed by the therapist and patient.

Limit setting is another of those issues that is better discovered than pronounced. I try to make the most obvious of my needs known at the onset of our relationship. I try to do this with the understanding that even adult and psychologically sophisticated patients will experiment and test those limits to see how I will handle their incursions. At the start of psychoanalytic therapy, it is very important to explain to the patient the process of psychoanalytic treatment and the limits within which the analyst or therapist works. In the past, too often, this was not done. Instead, the patient's ignorance of what could and could not be expected was often interpreted as his or her "resistance" rather than simply being understood as a reasonable ignorance of the process of psychoanalysis. As a rule—and particularly in a case like this—I explain to my younger patients that we sometimes have to forgo the normal social conventions such as my answering personal questions or saying the things that one would normally expect another person to say. I explain that this is not meant as a discourtesy but rather to allow for a relationship in which the patient has the opportunity to develop a deeper understanding of him- or herself. I think that it is also a good policy to acknowledge that these limitations can be frustrating and upsetting but that ultimately they do have a use and a purpose. With younger patients, it has to be understood from the outset that they will find these things out from their experiences with our interactions and not from my explanations.

Given the current circumstances, I would urge Michael to try not to act on his feelings of frustration and anger and his wish to just blow things off. I would encourage him to try to begin to be aware of his feelings, contain himself, and then try to bring these feelings into his sessions. I would ask him to do this in order to allow me to see if I could help him handle these feelings and explain that by working with his feelings, he may begin to feel better and not so upset and frustrated.

Self-disclosure on the part of a therapist is a possibility but the psychoanalytic therapist is generally aware and thoughtful about how much he or she brings his or her own personality into the sessions. Each instance of self-disclosure is generally a carefully considered matter.

The idea of *boundaries* has always been problematic in therapy. We talk about the patient "testing the limits" and "the boundaries of the therapeutic relationship." It is easy to confuse and antagonize a patient by telling him what the boundaries and limits are as if we are setting these on him. Individuals, who are already having difficulties maintaining their level of self-esteem, do not need a therapist to set up new standards that they do not want or simply cannot meet. I try to clarify that the boundaries are my limitations and not theirs. I try to make it clear to my patients, particularly patients like Michael, that there are certain limitations that *I* have, and that these are the kinds of agreements that *I* need in order for *me* to be able to function. Further, I explain that if they violate the limitations that I have, then I will not be as good for them as a therapist because I do not function well outside of these limits.

Transference and counter transference are the driving forces of psychoanalytic therapy. We generally attempt to interpret transference to the patient. Countertransference—as mentioned in the beginning section of this chapter—is a crucial aspect of the self psychological approach. We are always trying to understand a patient's emotional state, and our ability to empathize and convey that understanding to the patient is crucial. Our emotional reactions can be clear indicators of the patient's reality *or* of our attempts to avoid understanding that reality. When it is correctly used, it can deepen the therapist's ability to empathize with the patient's reality, particularly with the younger patient.

Roles.   The ultimate therapeutic role of the self psychologist is to understand the nature of the patient's deficiencies in self-development and to convey this understanding to the patient within a stable and empathic relationship. The activity level of the therapist is determined by the needs and the kinds of self-object transferences made by the patient. Concretely, this may mean that the idealizing transference of one patient may require the therapist to be direct and active although the idealizing transference of another patient may require the therapist to remain generally quiet. I do not know that I would generally describe the self psychological position as "collaborative" except, perhaps, in the twinship transference where equality is a central issue. However, regardless of the nature of the transference, the self psychologist, by definition, needs to be respectful of the patient and the patient's view of his world.

Treatment Implications and Outcome
Therapeutic Techniques and Strategies
The specific "technique" of self psychology is the same as that for all schools of psychoanalysis: namely, interpretation. The role of the psychoanalyst is to interpret the patient's actions and associations in a way that the patient can use. There are no other techniques or strategies; effective use of this technique requires high levels of training, years of practice, and ongoing self-reflection and analysis.

Collaboration and homework. When it is in the best interests of the patient, the modern analytic therapist collaborates with other professionals, as long as the information that is shared does not undermine the therapeutic relationship. This collaboration might include school personnel, probation officers, other juvenile court authorities, or the parents. Bringing others into any psychoanalytic therapy is not ideal, as it can impinge on the therapeutic relationship, and, by extension, on the therapy itself. However, with a younger patient and particularly with a patient with these kinds of issues, it would be necessary to have ongoing contact with the court, the school, and the parents.

Homework, as such, is generally not a part of any school of psychoanalytic thought. Homework might be in the nature of encouraging the young patient to try to be aware of his feelings and to bring them into the session rather than acting them out.

Mechanisms of Change
The mechanism of change in self psychological treatment is through the remobilization of the self-object needs in the therapeutic transferences, most commonly expressed in the idealizing, mirroring, or twinship transferences. It is through the re-emergence and expression of these needs either to be idealized or to have someone to idealize in the transferences that the patient is able to revitalize the thwarted self. As these needs are expressed and worked through in the self-object transferences, there is a restructuring of the defective or stunted aspects of the self. Kohut described this remobilization and working through

of the self-object needs and the complementary self-object configuration as the process of transmuting internalization. In the process of transmuting internalization, the old, thwarted, and defective self-object structures are reworked again in the transference. In a successful working through, the patient is able to recognize his needs, experience these needs differently, and find new resolutions to these failed relationships or develop new structures to compensate for them. Compensatory structures work to satisfy the individual's needs in a healthy way. Kohut viewed the development of compensatory structures as a replacement for the needed but unsatisfying defensive structures; he saw the development of these new and healthier compensatory structures as a successful outcome to treatment. However, younger patients still have time to have the primary experiences needed to develop the primary psychic structures before compensatory structures are deployed.

Medical and Nutritional Issues

As mentioned before, I would want to have Michael evaluated to rule out medical conditions that might help explain his outbursts and his poor school performance. Specifically, I would encourage the parents to consult with a child psychiatrist, as that individual is likely in the best position to determine if a condition exists, and whether that condition might respond to medication.

Potential Pitfalls

As is common with younger patients, Michael's acting-out poses a potential problem. Michael is already acting-out his feelings. As therapy proceeds and Michael begins to drop his old defenses against the recognition of his feelings and needs, he will begin to experience his feelings and needs more intensely. This, in turn, can result in more overt attempts to assuage hurts or to satisfy the needs that he is now experiencing more intensely. In light of Michael's history of acting-out, his therapist would have to be very alert to the possibility of increased acting-out in response to both situational elements and the ups and downs of his therapy. I would try to enlist Michael's co-operation, as much as possible, in understanding this as a potential impediment to our work and to urge him to try to bring his feelings into therapy instead of acting on them. However, with someone of this age, it is always problematic to try to enlist his or her support in the therapy. I try to make myself as available as possible to patients who act out, particularly when they are young. I encourage them to contact me whenever they felt that they are going to act out on their feelings. I also try to be available to the parent as a consultant as long as our contact does not compromise my work with the child.

Younger patients who have missed out on intense mirroring and have demonstrated poor impulse control are more prone to try to convert the therapist from a transference object to an object of reality. This attempted conversion is true particularly with younger patients diagnosed with narcissistic conduct disorders. The younger patient is more prone to act out in order to test if the analyst will disappoint him as previous idealized parent imagoes have. This would only be the opening phase of treatment. As therapy proceeds and patients feel more and more vulnerable to their needs and hurts, acting-out can become a regular, and very tiring, part of the therapy. Often, at the beginning of therapy, I warn the parents and the schools—as well as myself—to be prepared for things to look worse before they get better.

There is also another very painful potential pitfall in the treatment of a younger patient such as Michael. In a number of my cases involving younger patients, I concluded that the families needed the young person to be the "sick" member of the family in order to maintain a status quo of family functioning. In these family situations, when the "sick" member's behavior improves, the family either begins to undercut the therapy or pulls the patient totally out of treatment. It is particularly important to assess the role that the young patient's illness may be playing in maintaining the family dynamics. I have found too often that young patients were playing a very important self-object role for the parents. The parents needed the young person to be "ill" in order to bolster the parents' shaky sense of self. As the young patient got better, it threatened the parents' self-object needs and they began to compromise or even end the therapy. I have learned that when I have a younger patient, I must make as strong an alliance as possible with the parents. Many times, it has turned out that it was crucial to get the parents into therapy so that they can "survive" their child's growing sense of self-respect.

Finally, there are some other cautions that the psychoanalytic clinician might want to take with this patient. It is possible that Michael's level of reality testing is slightly impaired. Although Michael appears to be desperately hungry for an intense relationship, he may be unable to maintain the therapeutic alliance as he encounters frustration and disappointment. As the therapist allows the unfolding of an idealizing or mirroring transference, Michael could begin to misinterpret the understanding stance of the therapist and begin to believe that the therapist was there to gratify his unmet need for a "real" relationship. Michael would become unable or unwilling to accept the limitations of the therapeutic relationship and might begin to demand that the therapist meet his needs. Patients with an intense need for mirroring, poor impulse control, and an unclear sense of social boundaries are more prone to try to convert the therapist from a transference object to an object of reality. As the patient's wishes are interpreted rather than acted upon, the patient may experience this process as another injury to his self-esteem and either leave treatment or resume acting-out.

This same kind of reaction can be used as a resistance. The patient who is unwilling to accept either the pain of his past or the emptiness of his current living situation may also attempt to change the parameters of the therapeutic relationship. His efforts are not always caused by an inability to tolerate his psychic distress, but rather as an effort to escape facing his inner pain and its consequences. The "acting-in" becomes a manifestation of resistance, although it can also become a path of realization if the analyst is able to understand what the patient is re-enacting in the therapy session. Although understanding the patient's actions is difficult enough, in order to be truly effective, the analyst needs to be able to achieve this understanding while maintaining his or her empathic stance and emotional connection with the patient.

Work with the narcissistic patient requires the therapist to constantly engage in a process of self-analysis. The therapist continuously needs to work at resolving his or her own resistances that he or she will set up against empathizing with the patient's actions. The therapist's resistances prevent the therapist from being able to maintain a genuinely empathic connection with the patient as the patient works his or her way through these feelings. As can be imagined, this is an ongoing and emotionally taxing process. It can be particularly difficult to maintain this stance with a younger patient like Michael, because it is tempting for the therapist to write off the breakdowns in therapist–patient empathy as more of the patient's "foolishness" or "merely acting out." Sometimes it is much easier for the therapist to avoid looking into him- or herself. Patients like this can remind us of things about our current or past selves, of which we would rather remain unaware. The result of this pain is that we deny any understanding of the actions of the patient, and our empathic understanding becomes hollow. In this way, we can engage in a re-enactment of what Michael is going through with his parents as they seem to deny any real empathy with this young man or with his struggles.

Termination and Relapse Prevention

The termination process is likely to be a critical part of Michael's therapy. Termination always reflects the individual's history in handling loss, and the loss of Michael's father was certainly one of the most significant events of this young man's developmental history. I wonder how much of Michael's difficulties from the onset are actually re-enacting the loss and devaluation of his father. Through the termination process, Michael would again be "losing" an important figure in his life and this would need to be understood and sensitively handled. Michael lost the focus of his idealizing parent imago and the motivator for his goals. In termination of the therapy, all of this would be reworked and, I hope, resolved in a much healthier fashion.

Another aspect of the termination process that complicates this period of treatment is the re-emergence of all the old issues that had initially brought the patient into treatment. When a patient is terminating an intense analytic therapy, it is quite common for all the old issues to flare up again. It can be quite discouraging for the therapist and for the patient when it seems that all the issues that had already been worked through appear again in the therapy. I have seen both patients and therapists who did not understand that this recrudescence of old material in the last stages of treatment is very much part of the patient's termination process. It can serve as a last desperate attempt, if you will, on the part of the patient to stave off the healthy separation toward which they are moving. It needs to be understood and interpreted with compassion. It is easy to misunderstand these events and, because of this misunderstanding, not to stay in touch with the patient's simultaneous needs for closeness and separation. (Parenthetically, this aspect of termination is the same dilemma often faced by the parents of a teenager as the child-adult is preparing to leave home and go to college or move out and get a job. This same regressive, angry, and contradictory behavior can drive the parents to distraction as even the previously "best" child's behavior ranges from the difficult to the impossible.) For some patients—and I think that Michael may very likely fall into this group—the understanding manner of the therapist is critical to the patient's ability to separate from the treatment. I have seen therapies that seemed to be completely undone because of the therapist's unempathic handling of this aspect of the termination process. It is therefore critical that the therapist keep the issue of approaching termination clearly in the foreground between himself and the patient at all times.

Technically, in terms of initiating, interpreting, and structuring the termination phase, therapists doing analytic therapy take their lead from the patient. As issues of separation and termination show up more frequently in the patient's associations and dreams, the therapist will begin to point out that leaving seems to be on the patient's mind. At some point, the patient will generally discuss with the therapist how this should be accomplished. Often, this is actually a question that the patient cannot quite bring himself or herself to ask to the therapist. If the questions could be posed, it might be: "Are you going to support my wish to stop seeing you?" or, even more poignantly, "Will you miss me as much as I'm going to miss you?" Again, this is a part of the separation process. If the parents did not sensitively handle the separation issues when the patient was small, this can be a second chance for a previously unhappy experience to be reworked.

Usually, in an analytic therapy, some kind of time frame is established for the ending of the treatment. As the therapy proceeds, the patient becomes more confident of both his ability to take care of himself and the therapist's ability to handle the loss. Usually I follow the patient's lead in setting a definite termination date. In order to avoid retraumatizing the patient and precipitating a regression during the termination process, I would not hold Michael to the termination date. It is important to allow the patient to decide if he can manage to actually stop on the termination date that he has set. It is also important to make it clear that the patient can always return to therapy if he feels it is necessary. Again, the therapist needs to be very empathic to the contradictory needs that the patient is again working through with the analyst.

Relapse prevention.   The question of relapse is also quite complex. Everyone stumbles and falls; that is part of life. To look at a patient's stumbling or falling as a "relapse" is destructive to the patient and to the work that has been done. Some people never need to return to therapy, some people never want to leave therapy, and some simply cannot return to therapy. If a patient has experienced a resurgence of symptoms, I think that it is critical that he feel that he can return to see his therapist without feeling that he has failed. I have found that one of the best ways to help people make the transition out of treatment is to make sure that they understand that they are always welcome to come back and see me. I also try to make it clear that I do not see their feeling that they need some more time with me as a failure in their treatment. There have been times when I failed to understand this, and it was a further blow to the patient's already weakened self-state. This understanding is particularly important for the younger patient, like Michael. It could be important and appropriate for him to return to a trusted and respected adult as he continues with his development. In this case, if it is the therapist who is the trusted adult, it is particularly crucial that he leaves with the feeling that he can return without feeling stigmatized.

Another issue related to termination is that it appeared that there were two areas of difficulty in the development of Michael's self. The more obvious one was the physical loss of his father. His father was the most immediate and appropriate self-object through which he could develop the idealizing relationship that he needed. However, it appears that there may have been an earlier failure in the development of the grandiose self. Michael's mother re-lates that his early months were filled with frustration. She described him as a colicky baby whom she could not comfort. What was particularly noticeable was that in the mother's description of both Michael's loss of his father and her own inability to calm Michael as an infant, there did not seem to be any hint of understanding, insight, or compassion. In other words, Ms. D. did not appear to have any empathy for either her son's struggles or his losses. One hopes that this reflects only her current frustration with her son's actions but one must also wonder if this seeming lack of empathy is also a cause of some of Michael's current difficulties. As therapy proceeded, if this did turn out to be the case (i.e., that there was a definite lack of maternal empathy), it becomes particularly crucial to the termination phase that the same lack of understanding not be shown to Michael by the therapist, particularly as Michael separates himself for the last time from the one source of empathy that he may have experienced in his young life. An empathic failure of this sort at this point in Michael's termination could have crushing consequences. The therapist would have to be particularly alert to his young patient's feelings as Michael was saying goodbye.

REFERENCES

Chasseguet-Smirgel, J. (1984). *Creativity and perversion.* New York: W.W. Norton.

Erikson, E. (1950). *Childhood and society.* New York: W.W. Norton.

Kohut, H. (1971). *The analysis of the self.* New York: International Universities Press.

Kohut, H. (1977). *The restoration of the self.* New York: International Universities Press.

Kohut, H. (1984). In A. Goldberg (Ed.), *How does analysis cure?* Chicago: University of Chicago Press.

Siegel, A. M. (1996). *Heinz Kohut and the psychology of the self.* London: Routledge.

CHAPTER 4

Family Therapy

Structural and Bowenian Perspectives

Virginia DeRoma

Family—that dear octopus from whose tentacles we never quite escape, nor, in our innermost hearts, ever quite wish to.

— Dodie Smith

TREATMENT MODEL

Our attempts to understand individuals in context of the family date back to Freud's proposal that childhood relationships with parents were the root of most neurotic conflicts in adulthood (Guerin & Chabot, 1992). In the 1920s, the Child Guidance movement emphasized the need for parental involvement in the treatment of a child, although interventions initially leaned only toward involvement of a parent through separate counseling (Wells, 1988). The interaction of families eventually became a point of interest in therapy, but the focus was initially narrowed to understanding how parents' pathological behavior might contribute to their child's psychopathology (Nichols & Schwartz, 2001). Eventually, an emphasis on how the entire family contributed to problems presented by the family evolved into the family therapy movement. In the field of family therapy, examination of family interactions is considered the most powerful avenue for understanding individual behavior

(Santisteban et al., 1997). Unlike other treatment conceptualization models, family therapy incorporates a number of traditional theoretical (e.g., cognitive-behavioral, behavioral) orientations (Springer, McNeece, & Arnold, 2002). Using a family therapy framework, the therapist's focus eschews a linear view of how any *one* family member *causes* a reaction to another. Instead, the therapist examines the complex patterns of reactions among family members (Fishman & Fishman, 2003). Using this model, diagnoses of disorders of individuals, per se, are considered too narrow; the diagnosis of family system functioning is more suitable.

Numerous schools of family therapy have developed over the years, with different approaches to conceptualizing and treating family relationships within the family system. The prominent schools in family therapy include intergenerational, symbolic-experiential, structural, strategic, brief, narrative, and systemic family therapy (Gurman & Kniskern, 1981; Haley, 1976; Liddle, 1983; Nichols & Schwartz, 2001). Two of these seven family systems approaches are used in the case formulation in this chapter—structural family therapy, developed by Minuchin (1974), and intergenerational (Bowenian) family therapy, founded by Murray Bowen (Bowen, 1978). These two approaches, which can be used in isolation or combination with one another, are compatible in that they ascribe importance to the family as a system, where individual behavior is viewed as a product of reciprocal influences in family interaction.

Although empirical evidence on the efficacy of many models of family therapy has been slow to emerge, the research base has accelerated in recent decades. Specifically, success has been noted with family therapy for substance-abuse (Edwards & Steinglass, 1995; Sand-Pringle, West, & Bubenzer 1991; Waldron, 1997) and delinquency issues with adolescents (Diamond & Siqueland, 1995; Horne, 1993), both of which are presenting concerns in the current chapter's case. Both structural and Bowenian models of family therapy have been utilized with success to treat families with such problems (Todd & Selekman, 1974).

Many of the concepts and terminologies used to describe family processes for each model are similar. For example, both schools emphasize *current* family relationships, define the presenting problem based on how family members *behave*, and place importance on patterns of interactions (such as triangulation) within the family (Springer et al., 2002). Distinct differences between the two approaches can also be noted. Among the most important are the Bowenian emphasis on the role of anxiety in emotional processes, the Bowenian exploration of past versus present, and the structural therapist's value of an active affiliation with the family and with a wider scope of family members involved in the session. Although structural therapists value the examination of patterns of past generations, they would prefer to limit the family present in the session to those members who are part of the current household. Bowenian therapists, on the other hand, view the family of origin and individual family members as the family unit interest; they do not require all family members of a current household to be present (Oehrle, 1997). In fact, Bowenian therapists work comfortably with parents only, with a focus on patterns of prior generations of those family members (Guerin & Chabot, 1992; Sayger, 1992).

Structural Family Therapy Model

The structural family therapy model asserts that members of a family form certain interlocking arrangements, much like those of a jigsaw puzzle, and that particular family interaction patterns are associated with these arrangements (Callapinto, 1988). Although not explicitly communicated, these arrangements can be discerned through examination of interactions, or transactional patterns, in the family. One important arrangement in the structural family system is that of subsystems. Subsystems (e.g., marital, parental, sibling) are comprised of family members who share certain duties, functions, or power.

Functioning between subsystems is optimal when boundaries that define these subsystems are present and permeable to an appropriate degree (Horne, 1993). Subsystem functioning may become problematic when boundaries are too inflexible and rigid or, alternatively, too loose and chaotic (Larson & Wilsoon, 1998). According to this model, problems in boundary functioning make it difficult for the family to accommodate stressors introduced into the family. Therefore, changing the family structure is the key to altering family interaction patterns so that families can deal effectively with problems (Chamberlain & Rosicky, 1995; Clarkin & Carpenter, 1995). Structural family therapy has been identified as most appropriate for families presenting with a symptomatic child and disturbances in generational boundaries (Sayger, 1992). The case in this chapter involves a family whose presenting problems revolve around their symptomatic son, Mike, and whose generational boundaries between both parents and their children are clearly problematic.

Bowen's Intergenerational Family Therapy Model

Bowen's intergenerational family systems theory views the family interactions from past generations as the strongest influences of current family functioning (Framo, 1990). Using this model, family members' sensitivity and reactivity to anxiety in the family environment is examined, particularly with respect to a person's ability to separate him/herself from anxious others in the family (Brown, 1991). A person's ability to make choices based on rational, deliberate thought processes versus automatic, reactive, emotional processes is viewed as an important element of this separation (Edmonson, 2001). Healthy family processes are defined by this ability to individuate or differentiate oneself from others. The ability to adopt a calm and reflective position in the context of high levels of family emotionality would be assumed to help the D. family members to function more effectively as a family.

Differentiation does not denote mere autonomy, however. Differentiation represents a balanced response to the opposing forces of group affiliation and autonomy (Kerr & Bowen, 1988). According to Bowenian theory, a person's anxiety often drives the degree to which she or he gravitates toward togetherness. Excessive pressures for togetherness lead to excessive closeness, sensitivity toward the environment, and emotional reactivity to persons in it. A person's level of differentiation is central to understanding other concepts, such as: (a) the involvement of outsiders to resolve problems (triangulation); (b) unresolved emotional sensitivity to one's parents (often managed through emotional cutoff), and (c) a parent's inability to see the child as a being that is separate from self (family projection process).

Unlike structural family therapy, the goal is not to modify family interactions directly, but to promote insight into early family experiences and their influence on current family processes so that the family member might make different choices. Bowenian therapy has been considered most appropriate for families with high levels of motivation and compliance (Sayger, 1992). The therapist's remark that Ms. D. appeared to have a caring concern for her child, coupled with the observation that she did not have the completely defeated look so often present for a parent struggling with an acting-out child, supports the presence of high maternal motivation.

THERAPIST SKILLS AND ATTRIBUTES

Implementation of family therapy under each of these models involves a number of specialized skills, often shaped through rigorous training programs, such as the Bowenian family therapy training sponsored by the Family Center, a division of Georgetown University Medical School's Department of Psychiatry (Kaslow, Dausch, & Celano, 2003) and structural family therapy training obtained through the Philadelphia Child Clinic's Family Therapy Training Center (Guerin & Chabot, 1992). These training programs often accept trainees whose interest in a particular school has been fostered by prior exposure (e.g., coursework, readings) in family therapy theory (Minuchin &

Fishman, 1981). Expertise is shaped through lecture and supervision, which uniformly focuses on broadening trainees' perspectives so that they are better able to "think systems" (Papero, 1988, p. 74). Systems-thinking involves conceptualization of family problems and their reciprocal, rather than linear, processes (Fishman & Fishman, 2003). However, it is not enough to think nonlinearly. The therapist must possess skills in raising alternative explanations to a family's linear view of events in a way that families will accept. To accomplish this, the therapist must be attuned to the importance of timing in the delivery of any interventions.

Structural family therapists place a high priority on engagement skills with a family. Although skills in engaging *individuals* in therapy provide a good foundation for rapport building in family therapy, they should be viewed as skills that are necessary, but not sufficient for family engagement. To build rapport with a family, the therapist must be skilled in setting aside bias, conveying an objective and nonjudgmental stance toward all family members, and showing interest in and encouraging participation of all family members. For example, when attempting to understand the nature of the problem, the therapist must involve all family members and phrase questions in a way that suggests that no single family member alone is to blame for the presenting problem. Ironically, objective, fair, and balanced treatment of all family members must sometimes be offset with strategic alliances at certain points in treatment. Use of empathy, humor, and playfulness has been noted to help therapists maintain connections with all family members during a therapist's purposeful introduction of strategic power-unbalancing (Fishman & Fishman, 2003; Weiner, 2003).

The structural therapist should be spontaneous, assertive, tolerant, and flexible—all skills required for navigation through the many complexities of family work. First, the therapist should be flexible in his/her conceptualization of assessment, which is best viewed as an ongoing process, rather than a distinct phase of therapy (Cox, Farr, & Parish, 2003). In essence, the therapist should be comfortable outside of the role of expert, adopting the role of teacher and learner with equal enthusiasm. Second, the therapist must be able to experientially join the family, while simultaneously maintaining enough distance to monitor his/her own subjectivity. This moving in and out of participant and observer roles requires a therapist style that is dynamic, active, and often provocative. Third, using this model, the therapist must feel comfortable being spontaneously assertive, pushing families to take risks to behave differently (Minuchin & Fishman, 1981). The therapist's recognition that the family is reluctant to change is an effort to maintain homeostasis in the family typically reduces any premature attempts to address resistance in therapy. Fourth, the therapist should also be flexible enough to appreciate the need to develop an agenda for a session that takes form as the session progresses, rather than one that is carefully planned in advance and then rigidly applied throughout the session. Finally, it is important for therapists to be skilled at dealing spontaneously with unexpected outcomes that arise from unstructured role-plays or enactments that so often make up structural family therapy sessions (Weiner, 2003).

From a Bowenian therapist's standpoint, skillful management of self is viewed as critical for successful work with a family (Minuchin & Fishman, 1981). The therapist should always be aware of the role that s/he is playing in the therapy process and how that role is affecting family anxiety. Under this model, therapists function optimally when they successfully avoid getting caught up in the family's emotional reactivity and, instead, develop skills in monitoring and managing their own anxiety (Freeman, 1992). To accomplish this, therapists need to master the art of becoming close to a family, while maintaining a sense of separateness. This separateness will allow family therapists to form their own, objective appraisal of family influences and patterns, rather than accepting the initial interpretations of problems introduced by family members. Without this separateness, the therapist has the potential to inadvertently fuel the family's anxiety, and, subsequently, miss opportunities to model objective, thoughtful reflection in the context of family dilemmas.

Kerr (2003) has asserted that the best family therapists have also engaged in some level of self-examination in relation to their own family of origin. A curiosity about and willingness to understand family differentiation patterns at work in therapists' own families may help the therapist to develop respect for the benefits of an individual's increased emotional autonomy in the context of family. Ideally, this exploration will place the therapist in a position to better model genuine enthusiasm about discovering family patterns at play in past generations. This, in turn, will encourage family enthusiasm in uncovering patterns in their own intergenerational transmission processes.

THE CASE OF "MIKE"
Conceptualization, Assessment, and Treatment Planning
Additional Information and Assessments

Options for assessment tools are presented separately for structural and Bowenian therapy. Although several assessments presented can be considered appropriate for either model, they are categorized under the school in which they most likely would be used.

Structural family therapy assessment tools.   During the interview, the therapist asks questions about and observes family behaviorthat might reveal system structures that can later be mapped (Nelson & Utesch, 1990). In conducting such probes, the therapist involved with the D. family could explore: (a) members' proximity to one another as reflected in seating arrangements that may be indicative of family alignments (Watzlawick, 1990); (b) processes of enmeshment, often observed through pressures for agreement in perception; (c) affiliations (groupings that serve support functions) that might be detected through exchanges of support (e.g., touching or eye contact) between certain family members; (d) collusions that align two members of a family and exclude a third (i.e., coalitions), possibly noted through two members of a family talking about a third; and/or (e) triangulation detected through involvement of a third party in conflict that would more appropriately be kept between a dyad.

FAMILY MAPPING.   Subsystem arrangements and boundaries that exist between family members can be mapped through a diagramming process that reveals relational patterns in the family (Horne, 1993; Nichols & Schwartz, 2001). For example, using this system: (a) clear boundaries can be represented by dashed lines (------------), (b) diffuse boundaries are represented by dotted lines (..............), and (c) rigid boundaries are denoted by solid lines (_____). Diffuse boundaries between Ms. D. (M = Mother) and her children (C) and rigid boundaries between Mr. D. (F = Father) and his ex-wife and children could be mapped (see Figure 4.1) to illustrate boundary dysfunction. Scapegoating patterns that function to detour conflict between Mr. D. and Ms. D. could also be mapped (see Figure 4.2).

FAMILY ADAPTABILITY AND COHESION EVALUATION SCALES III.   The Family Adaptability and Cohesion Evaluation Scales III (FACES-III; Olson, Bell, & Postner, 1978) is based on the Family System Circumplex Model developed

FIGURE 4.1   Mapping of family boundaries.

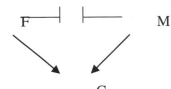

FIGURE 4.2 Detouring of conflict from parents to child.

by Olson, Russell, and Sprenkle (1983). FACES III is a 20-item self-report instrument developed to assess two primary dimensions: cohesion and adaptability. Both of these constructs are relevant for conceptualizing dysfunction in this family. Although the measure was designed for intact families, it has been adapted for families with a single, custodial caretaker. Both parents and adolescents in this family can complete this measure.

Cohesion and adaptability scale scores on the FACES III can be plotted and illustrated graphically, with four levels of cohesion (disengaged, separated, connected, and enmeshed) and four levels of adaptability (rigid, structured, flexible, and chaotic) that combine to form 16 family types. Based on the Circumplex model, a curvilinear relationship can be noted between healthy functioning and both cohesion and adaptability, with moderate levels of each viewed as optimal. Mr. D.'s plotted scores of family interactions might place him in the rigidly disengaged category, whereas Ms. D.'s plotted scores would be expected to place her in the chaotically enmeshed category.

THE FAMILY UNPREDICTABILITY SCALE.   The Family Unpredictability Scale (Ross & Hill, 2000) is a 22-item measure designed to assess inconsistent family behavior patterns. Parent report provided by this measure provides information on the consistency with which family's responsibilities are performed. Higher scores on this measure are indicative of greater family unpredictability and suggestive of problems with leadership in the parental subsystem and chaotic family organization. In addition to a total score, scores can be calculated for the following scales: (a) discipline (7 items), (b) nurturance (7 items), (c) meals (5 items), and (d) money (3 items). Discipline, nurturance, and monetary issues have all been noted as targets of interest for this family. This measure could help the therapist working with this family to identify areas in which Ms. D. might develop structured routines to replace chaotic organization patterns in the family.

INTERVIEW.   In interview, the therapist can collect information about the father's drinking patterns and how these patterns might set the stage for certain roles to be adopted in the family (e.g., enabler). The therapist could also assess the structural arrangement and grouping patterns of living family members in other generations (e.g., a coalition between Mike and his grandfather). Reports of nuclear family relationships prior to Mr. D.'s departure from the home would provide valuable information about the kinds of adaptation required of the family following the dissolution of the marital relationship. If, for example, a subsystem grouping (perhaps based on gender) existed between Mike and his father prior to the separation, Mike's acting-out behavior might be viewed as an inability to form appropriate, new structures following an abrupt disruption in this relationship structure.

Information on family relational rules (e.g., how is affection expressed? How does one get attention? How is anxiety reduced? How are rule violations handled?), routines (e.g., Do they eat together as a family?), and rituals (e.g., How does the D. family celebrate holidays?) should be collected in order to better understand family structure (Cox, 2003b; Frankel, 1990; Sayger, 1992). However dysfunctional, these rules help create and maintain family structures. For example, the indirect conflict expressed between Mike and his mother (e.g., callous looks by Mike's mother, Mike's defiant, slouched position in the chair) may relate to an unspoken family rule about the inappropriateness of open and direct conflict in public.

In addition to rules, more information should be collected on family structural strengths: When have appropriate boundaries between child and parent subsystems been established and maintained? When has cohesion been optimal? What are examples of the family's successful accommodation to new demands introduced to the family? In light of the fact that Mike has not engaged in physical aggression toward adults, how have family rules and expectations related to physical aggression toward authority figures been communicated?

Bowenian family therapy assessment tools. Therapist observation of family patterns (e.g., emotional sensitivity and reactivity, patterns of disengagement or fusion) is also an important part of introductory Bowenian assessments. The tools outlined in this section are standard assessment devices utilized by therapists who operate from a Bowenian perspective.

The genogram. The genogram is a tool used to collect data on family history that can be mapped out for purposes of generational pattern identification (DeMaria & Hannah, 2003). Although most uniquely suited for Bowenian therapy's intergenerational focus, the structural model also employs the use of the genogram to examine family patterns. Mike's parents could use the genogram to map out gender, birth order, addiction patterns, domestic violence, divorces, power plays against authority, and boundaries between family members. Family members can also identify adjectives that would best describe each person on the genogram. Geographical cutoffs involving a family member moving away to create needed distance from intense family anxiety can also be mapped. This work can help family members to understand how current patterns relate to past family scripts and invisible loyalties to implicit family culture (Gordon-Rabinowitz & Rabinowitz, 2003).

DIFFERENTIATION OF SELF-INVENTORY.   The Differentiation of Self Inventory (DOS; Skowron & Friedlander, 1998) is a 43-item measure developed to assess an individual's ability to sustain an autonomous sense of self in the context of family relations. It results in scores on four scales: (a) emotional reactivity (11 items), (b) I position (11 items), (c) emotional cutoff (12 items), and (d) fusion with others (9 items). Given problems with differentiation hypothesized for members of Mike's family, this measure seems particularly appropriate.

PERSONAL AUTHORITY IN THE FAMILY QUESTIONNAIRE.   This is a self-report measure that assesses levels of differentiation across three generations (Bray, Williamson, & Malone, 1984). The concept of personal authority is defined as the ability to balance relational closeness and individuation. Different forms of the measure are available for adolescents or young adults without children, adults with children, and adults without children. Five of the measure's eight scales would be of particular interest in this case: (a) intergenerational fusion/individuation, (b) intergenerational intimacy, (c) intergenerational triangulation, (d) intergenerational intimidation, and (e) personal authority.

THE FAMILY-OF-ORIGIN SCALE.   The Family-of-Origin Scale (FOS; Hovestadt, Anderson, Piercy, Cochran, & Fine, 1985) is a 60-item self-report scale developed to assess a family member's perceptions of intimacy and autonomy in his or her family of origin. The total score is based on scores on 10 constructs (with four items represented by each construct): (a) clarity of expression, (b) responsibility, (c) respect for others, (d) openness to others, (e) acceptance of separation and loss, (f) range of feelings, (g) mood and tone, (h) conflict resolution, (i) empathy, and (j) trust. Higher scores represent healthier perceptions of one's prior home environment. The FOS could be administered to Mike's parents in order to identify unresolved issues between Mr. D. and Ms. D. and their parents. Results from this measure might help Mr. D. and Ms. D. to gain insight into how events in their own families might be affecting current family experiences. Scores on this measure could be used as pre-post change measures because responses to probes of early childhood experiences with one's family of origin would not be expected to change after therapy.

INTERVIEW.   The therapist would use the interview to inquire about events in the nuclear family history that reflect family projection—a pattern whereby adults project their unresolved differentiation issues onto a child (Nelson, 2003): At what stage of differentiation were Mike's parents when he and his sister were born? How could the differentiation level of each parent be related to the degree to which each child received positive or negative parental attention differently at various stages of family development?

Given Springer et al.'s (2002) recommendation that therapists examine a family member's substance-abuse behavior in context of the entire alcoholic family, generational patterns of alcohol abuse, as well as recovery, in the D. family should be probed. The therapist should inquire about who in the nuclear family has been most affected by Mr. D.'s patterns of substance abuse. Emotional and geographical cutoff from extended family should also be identified, as such patterns represent extreme forms of distancing that often arise from an inability to manage self autonomously. Attention should also be devoted to identifying family strengths with respect to management of anxiety: When have family members resolved conflicts in the past with objectivity versus reactivity? What are the instances in which dyads successfully managed anxiety without involving a third party? When have family members been most successful in not over-reacting to another family member?

Family system issues, such as those related to cohesion, are more often associated with suicide behaviors that are nonfatal (Wagner, Silverman, & Martin, 2003). A number of additional family risk factors associated with youth's suicide are noted in Mike's family, including high conflict, low closeness, parental divorce, and alcohol-/substance-abuse patterns (Wagner et al., 2003). However, the therapist should consider the possibility that a suicide gesture by Mike might function to perpetuate a dysfunctional family structure. For example, a suicide gesture by Mike following his father's aggressive behavior toward him might serve as an attempt to triangulate his mother into conflict between him and his father. From the Bowenian perspective, poor differentiation and high emotional reactivity in the family may also place Mike at risk for impulsivity manifested through self-harm. Overall, danger to self does not appear to be a significant threat for Mike's given test results indicating low levels of depression and the absence of suicidal ideation.

Therapeutic Goals

The family therapist focuses on the network of family relationships in goal setting, asserting that there is a reciprocal influence among family members that can explain presenting problems. Therapists in both schools assume that family members are unable to accurately identify the important elements of dysfunctional family patterns that need to be addressed in therapy. The first goal of therapy with this family would be to reframe the family's presenting problem so that the family's focus is shifted to the family and away from Mike as the problem individual. In essence, the goal is for family members to assume responsibility for their role in family's problems.

Once this goal is reached, family members will be more likely to take responsibility for change to self, instead of attempting to blame or control one another. As progress is made toward this goal, defensiveness of family members typically declines enough for family change goals to be addressed. Initial, short-term goals that might follow this successful family reframing of the problem are highlighted for both structural and Bowenian family therapy. The goals for each school are, for the most part, compatible, although the terminology or framework used in goal setting differs for each.

Structural therapy goals.   Short-term goals for structural family therapy would involve rearrangement of the family structure through boundary modification (Sand-Pringle et al., 1991). Specific goals for this family could include: (a) strengthened boundaries in parental subsystem through agreement on clear boundaries for children; (b) increased proximity and contact between members of the sibling subsystem and between Mr. D. and his children; and (c) decreased emotional involvement between Ms. D. and her children.

Long-term structural therapy goals for this family would include: (a) rearrangement of dysfunctional subgroupings (coalitions) characterized by new family structures without the intervention of a therapist, (b) increased adaptability (vs. rigid or chaotic organization that prevents adoption of new family structures) when faced with developmental transitions for family members, and (c) restored successful hierarchical functioning in the family. Minuchin and Nichols (1998) identified a family's greater involvement and interest in family processes as an important process goal to work toward in the therapy process.

Bowenian therapy goals.   Short-term goals for Bowenian therapy for the D. family could include: (a) decreased emotional fusion between Ms. D. and her children, (b) increased adoption of "I position" and differentiation of all family members, (b) decreased emotional reactivity by all family members, and (c) decreased emotional cutoff of family-of-origin members by Mr. D. and Ms. D. If even one family member meets these goals, the decreases in reactivity among family members is typically enough for the family, as a whole, to experience increased autonomy among its members (Kerr, 2003; Minuchin & Fishman, 1981).

Eventually, as progress in reaching short-term goals aimed at fostering differentiation is made and family-of-origin issues are explored, we can expect altered family patterns: (a) employment of conscious, alternative choices in their family of procreation; (b) increased acceptance of other family members' differences; and (c) increased appreciation of how current patterns in family are influenced by the multigenerational influence. Goals of reconnecting Mr. D. and Ms. D. to family-of-origin members would be encouraged where appropriate, although no information on the feasibility or appropriateness of accomplishing this is presented in this case.

With both schools of therapy, as boundary patterns that accompany fusion and disengagement are addressed, the degree of intimacy and cohesion between family members would be expected to increase. Family therapy may differ most from other therapeutic approaches in its failure to identify explicit goals to reduce Mike's substance-abuse and acting-out behavior. Instead, Mike's substance-abuse and acting-out behaviors would be expected to decrease more as a *by-product* of improved family functioning, rather than as a result of direct attempts to change these behaviors.

It is unrealistic to expect family members to have the skills to consistently reorganize into more effective structures when needed (with structural therapy) or completely guard oneself against the infectious spread of family anxiety (with Bowenian therapy) immediately following participation in therapy. Rather, the therapist might expect Mike's family to leave therapy with a heightened understanding of family role dynamics and some instances of success in changing their role in these dynamics. Leaving therapy as a more objective observer of family transactions, Mike's family members should be in a better position to recognize problematic structures and processes and then use the repertoire of alternative responses learned in therapy to guide effective coping.

Length of Therapy

Length of treatment for this family under both schools would be relatively brief, with a typical course of therapy lasting approximately 12 sessions (Frankel, 1990; Sayger, 1992). The first four to six sessions with Mike and his family should be scheduled weekly so that a solid relationship with the family can be secured through joining. These sessions are viewed as important for helping family members shift their attention to family processes, versus family content, as the focal point of therapy. Initially, when family members are more seriously considering their own roles in family problems, reflections of how s/he plays a part in family relationship problems may raise anxiety. However, as family members become more curious about family structures (and their connections to the past), anxiety gradually decreases and enthusiasm for family changes increases. At this point, the family's move from a reactive to a more proactive stance allows the therapist to adopt a more flexible approach in the frequency of scheduled sessions.

Case Conceptualization

Many, but not all, of the key concepts of structural and Bowenian therapy will be used to understand the dynamics behind family member dysfunction. Concepts used in the conceptualization of each approach often involve a shared view of constructs, although the language used to describe processes (e.g., enmeshment, fusion) and conceptualizations of causal influences may differ. Several concepts introduced for each model also represent unique aspects of each of these approaches to understanding the family. For both models, the adoption of the family systems perspectives precludes an exclusive focus on Mike's individual behavioral, affective, and cognitive functioning. For both approaches, information on Mike's functioning, which is most valuable, is considered in the context of the family.

Case conceptualization from a structural perspective.   Three key concepts of the structural model have been selected to conceptualize this case: Subsystem dysfunction, family structure, and cohesion.

SUBSYSTEM DYSFUNCTION.   In families presenting with parental control issues, some degree of disturbances in functioning of the executive, parental subsystems is often present (Minuchin & Fishman, 1981). The central question to ask in constructing a conceptualization of the hierarchical organization of the family is, "How is authority shared between parent and child subsystems?" To answer this, the structural therapist typically employs the concept of boundaries—the rules that define the degree of contact between groupings of individuals. Boundaries between subsystems can be conceptualized on a permeability continuum, with diffuse, overpermeable structures at one extreme and rigid, impermeable boundaries on the other (Horne, 1993). Optimally, boundaries are permeable enough to allow for appropriate contact between groupings of family members, but rigid enough to prevent interference from other subsystems (Liddle, 1983).

When power is regulated appropriately within a system, boundaries are assumed to be clear and permeable. Problems with parental authority, on the other hand, imply that diffuse boundaries are present, failing to protect the parental subsystem from outside interferences of child subsystems. Transactions observed between Mike and his mother, such as his asserting that he was tired of being told what to do and when to do it, represent child subsystem challenges to the parental subsystem authority. Such challenges are often present when diffuse boundaries in the parent subsystem exist. Mike's history of breaking rules and his stated intentions of running away also suggest dysfunction in the authority of the executive system.

Approximately half of adolescents engaged in substance-abuse treatment have reported a history of family problems (Daroff, Marks, & Friedman, 1990). Generational boundaries in families with substance-abusing adolescents have been characterized by therapists as diffuse (Friedman, Utada, & Morissey, 1990). Mike's history of coming close to hitting his mother and his display of dominance in securing the privileged chair in the therapist's office suggest that Mike views himself as entitled to power in the executive role of family functioning. His father's assertion that his mother allows Mike to "get away with murder" and that she takes a "soft approach" to disciplining him is consistent with this notion of executive, parental functioning failings. Ms. D.'s hesitancy in confronting Mike's rudeness and cautiousness in broaching the discussion of Mike's regular violation of curfew suggest that Ms. D. is uncomfortable erecting boundaries around authority in the parental subsystem. The therapist's perception of ineptness on the mother's part and reports of Mike's refusal to follow consequences further validate the presence of an overly yielding parent, which so often characterizes weak parental subsystem boundaries. This parenting characterization is consistent with patterns of inconsistent limit setting or structuring noted for parents in drug-abusing families (Friedman, 1990).

Peck and Brown (1991) have recommended that the family processes surrounding divorce in a family serve as a focal point of therapy. Changes in family composition, and resulting shifts in family member roles following parental separation, have likely impacted the D. family in numerous ways. Although the divorce circumvents the need to conceptualize the functioning of Mr. D. and Ms. D. as a couple subsystem, these parents still share roles in the parental subsystem, which have been changed significantly. For example, if the authority of the parental subsystem was primarily vested with the father, as is often the case in families, restructuring would be essential so that Ms. D. could strengthen boundaries and exert more authority in the parental subsystem following divorce. Mr. D.'s reports that Mike was generally compliant with his father at home support this notion that the father was the primary authority in the parental subsystem prior to the family's separation. Ms. D.'s failure to adjust to parental separation may have rendered parental subsystem boundaries in the custodial home weak and subject to interference by the child subsystem.

Members of the sibling subsystem are also an important focal point of interest in structural therapy (Minuchin & Fishman, 1981). In its optimal state, members of the sibling subsystem are cooperative and supportive toward one another, sharing important joint functions (e.g., chores, alliances, challenges of the parental subsystem authority). However, the sibling subsystem in this family appears to have excessive distance between its two members. This distance is evidenced by Mike's characterization of his sister as the perfect child, his serious threats toward her, and the reports of periodic physical altercations occurring between them. Mike's sister's refusal to visit her father suggests that a coalition has been formed between his mother and sister, with Mike and Mr. D. as outsiders. This affiliation between his mother and sister can exacerbate existing distance in the sibling subsystem grouping.

STRUCTURE.   Structure refers to how the family is organized around predictable patterns of interaction (Vetere, 2001; Wells, 1988). When delinquency-related presenting problems are present, communication patterns in a family are often characterized as chaotic, emotionally laden, and disconnected (Minuchin & Fishman, 1981). Communication patterns between Ms. D. and Mike involving multiple topic shifts with high emotion, but no resolution, are consistent with this characterization. Although interactions are only available from one session for this family, the therapist can formulate hypotheses about family structures that can be revised as more opportunities to observe the family unfold. These formulations are based on how a family interacts, rather than what the family talks about, in a session (Kaslow et al., 2003).

One spontaneous pattern of interaction observed in this family was Mike's defiance in response to his mother's displays of contempt, as noted by his refusal to speak when she asked *him* to explain to the therapist why they needed help. Another structure is formed by Mike's altercations with authority being followed by Ms. D.'s reaction of assigning responsibility for Mike's problem behavior to others (e.g., his peers, his father). A patterned transaction can also be noted related to verbal aggression. It appears that Mike backs away from a threat that he has made to his mother when she approaches him (i.e., calls his bluff). Mike's interruptions of his mother's conversation and his mother's responsiveness to these interruptions reveal family structure related to poor boundaries. Finally, Mike's mother's nonverbal expression of disapproval following his displays of defiance is hypothesized as an established structure.

COHESION. Patterns of closeness are often described with respect to boundaries—more specifically, the permeability of those boundaries (Horne, 1993). In this case, permeability describes the degree to which closeness is allowed between parties (e.g., individuals, subsystems). Cohesion at either extreme of the boundary continuum is characterized as problematic, with enmeshed (overly close because boundaries are too diffuse) at one extreme and disengaged (overly distant because boundaries are too rigid) at the other (Fishman & Fishman, 2003). Families with high levels of marital dissatisfaction have been noted to have family cohesion disturbances, often manifested through disengagement (Henderson, Sayger, & Horne, 2003). Conflict in the D. parental subsystem appears to have been high during the marriage, as evidenced by frequent arguing and instances of physical altercations reported for the couple.

Families with substance-abuse problems have also been noted to have difficulties with both bonding and autonomy, with families of users reporting less family cohesiveness and more family disengagement than families of nonusers (Protinksy & Shilts, 1990; Utada & Friedman, 1990). Disengagement in families has, in fact, been associated with behavior problems in the child subsystem (Lindah & Malik, 1999). Many fathers are less engaged in contact with their children than the mother, especially following separation and divorce (Sholevar, 1995). Cohesion between Mr. D. and his children reflects one of disengagements. Mr. D. has not formed a close relationship with Mike, as evidenced by his failure to remain informed about his son's behavior, his uncertainty about his son's activities when he is away from the home, and his lack of emotional investment in his son's future or career. Further, Mr. D.'s yelling and grounding Mike for less than "perfect" behavior, coupled with his statement that he wanted to "get through to Mike," suggests that boundaries in the father's executive subsystem are too rigid to allow for input or feedback from the child subsystem. Utada and Friedman (1990), in fact, have proposed that many adolescents engage in drug abuse in order to gain attention from family members who are not involved with them.

Substance-abuse may also function to maintain the homeostasis of disturbance in the family (Kaufman, 1990). Friedman (1990) recognized the whole family as disturbed in such cases, although the substance-abusing family member alone functions as the transporter of family symptom dysfunction. Mike's substance-abuse, truancy, and shoplifting may serve to maintain involvement and contact between his divorced parents. Issues of concern over Mike may also serve as the focal point of all familial problems that enable his family members to bypass or detour conflict from other family interactions (Diamond & Siqueland, 1995; Kaufman, 1990).

Unfortunately, children report more self-blame for conflict in families where detoured couple conflict is identified (Kerig, 1995). Mike self-identified his role of scapegoat in the family, a part that his parents may need him to play in order to maintain the homeostasis of targeted dysfunction in the family system.

Interestingly, although ratings by parents of drug-abusing youths indicate that they consider their family relationship to be disengaged, therapist ratings suggest that they would characterize the relationship as just the opposite—enmeshed (Friedman et al., 1990). Parents with unsatisfactory couple relationships, such as Mr. D. and Ms. D., often attempt to establish an enmeshed relationship with a child to maintain cohesion patterns in the family (Friedman, 1990). Separation of parents may be especially likely to provoke enmeshments and coalitions between a "needy, custodial parent" who has lost the physical presence of a spouse and a child (Abelsohn & Saayman, 1991, p. 179). Mike's relationship with his mother appears to be defined by boundaries that are excessively diffuse.

Mr. D.'s assertion that Ms. D. makes excuses for Mike's behavior attests to Ms. D.'s overinvolvement, with enmeshed boundary dysfunction. Ms. D.'s minimization of his law-breaking behavior as "brushes" with legal authorities also suggests that she is unable to acknowledge the inappropriateness of his antisocial behaviors because of emotional overprotectiveness. Her cautious approach in discussing reports of his inappropriate behavior, and the degree to which she was emotionally affected by his belligerence in the session, are also suggestive of patterns of overinvolvement, which is also characteristic of enmeshment patterns.

Children from enmeshed families have been characterized as insecure and dependent, while those from disengaged families have reported difficulties forming close relationships with others (Wells, 1988). It is noteworthy that there was evidence for both patterns of interactions for Mike during testing. Behavioral observations indicated that Mike was related to the examiner in a distant fashion. Yet, test results from the Minnesota Multiphasic Personality Inventory for Adolescents indicated that his profile was similar to individuals who tend to be immature, insecure, and dependent.

Delinquent behaviors in youths have been associated with both forms of cohesive dysfunction in families—enmeshed and disengaged (Horne, 1993; Sholevar, 1995; Wells, 1988). Thus, Mike's oppositional behavior may be viewed as associated with both patterns of dysfunctional cohesion transactions—enmeshment with his mother and disengagement with his father. In families in which a parent's high degree of involvement infringes on the adolescent's emerging need for autonomy, the adolescent affinity to the delinquent peer group can be viewed as an attempt to gain respite from the intensity of this family overinvolvement (Horne, 1993). In this case, Mike's strong connection with a peer group outside of the family system may represent an attempt to escape demands for connectedness from his mother. Such demands from Ms. D. have probably increased as distance in the couple subsystem has increased. Mike's substance abuse may also function as an attempt to re-engage with a disengaged father. To that extent, Mike's attempts to cry for help may represent a fight for cohesion needed to establish new, more functional family structures around his absent father. Lacking this, Mike may continue to look outside of the family system toward peers to fill the needs of support and involvement.

ADAPTABILITY.   Normal developmental change processes in families require the structure of a family to change (Partridge, 2000). Recently, the D family has experienced numerous developmental and situational transitions that have created adjustment demands for the family. Divorce represents a significant disruption to this family system that has also impacted the family structure. Abelsohn and Saayman (1991) have noted that families adjusting to divorce are often faced with disruptions in the hierarchical structure and dysfunctional groupings, sometimes spurred by parental pressures for loyalty. In this case, such disruptions and pressures for divided loyalty are apparent. Two members of the child subsystem have also entered adolescence, a transition that requires adjustments in boundary permeability to accommodate for adolescent needs of increased input and responsibility (Minuchin & Fishman, 1981; Young, 1991). Parents of adolescents must learn to restructure roles so that authority can be negotiated differently (Minuchin & Fishman, 1981).

The degree of flexibility in a family has been noted to play an important role in the development of pathology during times of transition. In fact, pathology has been identified as the consequence of a family system's inability to change when new structures are demanded. Level of family adaptability is determined by the level of flexibility demonstrated by individual family members (Abelsohn & Saayman, 1991). A family that lacks flexibility in its response to adjustment demand is characterized as rigid, while a family that lacks structure in its response to stress is characterized as chaotic in its organization.

Flexibility of families with adolescents who engage in substance abuse has been characterized as disturbed at both extremes—rigid and chaotic (Friedman et al., 1990). In both Mr. D. and Ms. D.'s postseparation homes, patterns of poor flexibility can be noted to accompany normal developmental transitions and unexpected disruptions to this family system. Ms. D.'s family environment might be characterized as more chaotically organized, with an approach that is so flexible and over-responsive that family organization is compromised. Ms. D.'s statement that she thought the relationship was "probably" over after *two years* of separation signifies her difficulty in adjusting to the termination of the relationship. Without such adjustment, important, new, structural arrangements cannot be formed. In the noncustodial parent system, Mr. D.'s functioning would be polarized at the other end of the adaptability dimension—rigidity. He lacks flexibility in responding to the parenting changes demanded by transitions of adolescence, namely increased permeability in boundaries.

The family's responses to the therapist's suggestions and interventions during enactments provide information about a family's adaptability and have the potential to increase the likelihood for greater "complexity, flexibility, and variety" of future responses (Powell & Dosser, 1992, p. 255). Powell and Dosser (1992) have described the new patterns that are established with enactments as grooves that are worn into the template of family experiences.

Case conceptualization from a Bowenian perspective.   Three key concepts are utilized to understand this case from the Bowenian perspective: Differentiation, triangulation, and multi-generational family process.

DIFFERENTIATION.   Bowen (1978) has described two opposing forces in systems—one that drives people toward togetherness and approval and the other that drives people toward separateness and individuality. Without some drive for togetherness, the D. family would become completely autonomous; without some drive toward separateness, D. family members would not move toward healthy individuality (Papero, 1988). An established, healthy balance between emotional autonomy and closeness is identified as differentiation, the concept that serves as the "cornerstone of Bowen's theory" (Nichols & Schwartz, 2001, p. 140). However, extremes of either of these forces can impair family member's functioning. Too much togetherness can make individuals overly sensitive to the reactions of another and unable to function outside of the presence of the other family members. Too much separateness, on the other hand, may place family members at risk for having little emotional connection to a family.

Parents who can contain or bind their anxiety successfully allow their children the space to separate from them appropriately (Kerr, 2003). Family members lacking the self-control to bind their anxiety, however, often attempt to anxiously attach to others (Kerr, 2003; Nichols & Schwartz, 2001). The anxious family member will often engage other family members in excessive closeness by expecting them to think and feel the same way that they do. When boundaries between subsystems are too weak, family members succumb to this pressure for excessive closeness and fusion occurs. Togetherness develops at the cost of impaired autonomous functioning, as patterns involving excessive sensitivity and emotionality develop. Emotional fusion (likened to enmeshment in the structural model) between a parent and child can be manifested in one of two ways—a conflictual relationship, characterized primarily by anger, or a dependent relationship, characterized by warmth (Oehrle, 1997). Fusion between Ms. D. and her children is manifested in this family through both conflict and dependency—as evidenced by a highly emotional and conflictual relationship with her son and a seemingly more dependent involvement with her daughter.

Families who have low levels of differentiation are emotionally reactive and have difficulty allowing rational, intellectual processes to override their more reactive feeling processes (Friesen, 1995). Reports of Mike's "short fuse" and "hot temper" indicate that Mike is operating at a low level of differentiation, failing to achieve the more appropriate governance of the intellectual system. Parents' aggression against their children has also been explained by control issues associated with low levels of differentiation. Parents' emotionality arises from the inability to behave rationally when faced with differences in thinking and feeling of another family member (Minuchin & Fishman, 1981; Nichols & Schwartz, 2001). Mr. D.'s history of becoming aggressive with Mike implies this possessive, low level of differentiation.

Patterns of avoidance of core issues have been noted for individuals with poor differentiation (Goodrow, 1997). The therapist's perception that Ms. D. was "purposefully vague" about discussing reasons for her marital separation is suggestive of this pattern. Individuals who operate on a more emotional level of functioning would also be expected to engage in avoidance through externalizing, blaming behaviors during conflict. Ms. D.'s irritation with her ex-husband and assignment of blame to him for the divorce and Mike's behavioral problem, and her victimization portrayal of being "forced" to work are consistent with this profile of blaming others. Mr. D.'s blaming of his ex-wife for his son's behavior and his own strained relationship with his daughter also support the presence of poor differentiation. Mike's angry and rebellious stance toward his mother and other authority figures suggests decreased responsibility for his anger. Only with an ability to individuate can Mike learn to view his actions as conscious choices for which he can safely assume responsibility.

Level of differentiation has also been related to the ability to deal effectively with conflict in the family (Kerr, 2003). Reports that Mr. D. and Ms. D. were "never able to get along" well, coupled with patterns of high-intensity disagreements noted between Mike and other family members, corroborate these emotionally reactive, conflict patterns throughout the family. During the session, numerous instances of emotional reactivity between Ms. D. and Mike were also noted. For example, Mike's attempts to make his displeasure in the session obvious to his mother, and Ms. D.'s adoption of a cautious demeanor "so as not to further agitate" Mike, suggest patterns of hypersensitivity to one another. Mike's emotional outbursts and Ms. D.'s emotional responsivity (e.g., exhibiting surprise) to his threats in the session are further evidence of emotionally reactivity in the system.

Although family symptoms may not have been present under conditions of lower stress (and thus anxiety), problems related to low differentiation emerged in the D. family under conditions of heightened anxiety, a pattern noted in many families (Bartle-Haring, Rosen, & Stith, 2002). Indeed, Daroff et al. (1990) have identified divorce as an event that leaves the family in a state of chronic, heightened anxiety. Ms. D. has experienced significant anxiety (which has not subsided) following her separation from her husband. This was evidenced by her obvious discomfort with working and her failure to accept the relationship ending. Ms. D.'s remark that she was "forced" to work after her divorce reflects that this event raised anxiety for her. If Ms. D. was unable to bind this chronic anxiety independently, she may have transferred this anxiety to Mike, possibly through pressures for excessive involvement or connectedness.

When parental anxiety is bound through projection onto children, the anxiety level of the children is typically heightened (Sayger, 1992). Mike's restlessness noted in the presence of the mother, but not in the presence of the test examiner, suggests that his anxiety relates to family dynamics. Mike's difficulties in school began directly after his family's separation and can be viewed as possible manifestations of the heightened anxiety that he experienced through the family. As the younger child at the time of the separation, he may have experienced a stronger pressure for his mother's pull toward intimacy than his sister, thereby absorbing a disproportionate amount of anxiety relative to her.

Family members who resist pressures for fusion may appear to have achieved balance between separateness and connectedness. Upon closer examination, however, it becomes clear that they have simply adopted behaviors that help them escape family anxiety. Although Mike's acting-out behaviors (i.e., drug abuse, delinquency) may serve to distance him from his mother's over-involvement and achieve some level of autonomy, playing the role of the problem child actually perpetuates his absorption of his mother's anxiety. When his mother reacts to his attempts to distance by worrying about him more, Mike's anxiety (and the likelihood of future rebellion) is also raised. Mike's shoplifting behavior represents the most recent climax of his rebellion toward authority. Ms. D. responds to Mike's rebellion by increasing her concern over and involvement with him. Bowenian family systems' theorists have also noted that family fusion anxiety has been associated with later problems in career decision-making (Larson & Wilsoon, 1998). Mike's reported uncertainties about his post-high school future suggest the beginning of his career commitment and decision problems.

It is typical for the father in a family to react to family's anxiety by giving more attention to work (Kerr, 2003). Mr. D.'s reports of his 50–60-hour weekly work schedule suggest that he escaped family anxiety through work. Mike's father may be much less anxious about his son's substance-abuse and delinquent behavior than Ms. D. because of his own, similar choices in his youth. Without intervention, patterns of emotional distancing (through conflict and substance abuse) and poor differentiation are likely to emerge in future generations of Mike's family.

According to principles of complimentarity, family members develop transactions that offset or compliment the role of other family members (Friesen, 1995). Complimentary behavior patterns adopted in families often include pursuing/distancing and overfunctioning/underfunctioning family member (Nichols & Schwartz, 2001). In this family, Ms. D. is overfunctioning by adopting the role of a motivated problem-solver, and this is associated with Mike's adoption of the complimentary role of unmotivated engager. Observations during testing suggest that Mike was indeed unmotivated, giving up on tasks easily and interacting begrudgingly during the interview. At present, Ms. D.'s protestation of her son' delinquency is complimented by Mr. D.'s passive acceptance. Her concentrated interest in developing Mike into a healthy adolescent is complimented by his indifference regarding the types of choices that his son Mike is making in his life.

TRIANGULATION.   Families characterized by negative affect and marital conflict are associated more with patterns of triangulation than families characterized by cohesion (Kerig, 1995). Family members involve a third party in order to reduce the anxiety associated with the distance brought about by conflict in the marital dyad (Bowen, 1978; Nichols & Schwartz, 2001). Nichols and Schwartz (2001) have described triangulation as resulting from an overwhelming "urge to confide in someone else" (p. 141). Although this triangulation of a third party might function to reduce anxiety, it occurs at the expense of the dyad failing to reach some resolution to the problem that originally created the anxiety.

A common pattern in families is the triangulation of a child by parents who are experiencing distance in their relationship with one another (Sayger, 1992). In this case, Ms. D.'s references of Mr. D.'s withholding of child support as problematic for and "unfair" to the children is suggestive of her attempt to triangulate her children in the conflict with her husband over monetary support. Additionally, her references to how Mr. D.'s failure to follow the visitation schedule upset her son, in context of his objection that this was not true, suggests that Ms. D. has attempted to pull Mike into conflict between her and his father.

Parents' triangulation of an adolescent into parental conflict during the adolescent's attempt to separate from parents can be particularly problematic to healthy individuation (Coco & Courtney, 2003). In this case, both Mike and his sister are attempting to increase autonomy from parents. Children triangulated into their parent's problems, especially at this developmental stage, are often caught in the bind of complying and feeling angry or feeling guilty because they refuse to be triangulated (Oehrle, 1997). On a positive note, Mike's objections to his mother's assertion that he is upset by his father's behavior suggest a significant family strength—thwarting of parental efforts to triangulate.

Mike's sister has successfully triangulated her mother into conflict with Mike, as noted by Ms. D.'s reference that her daughter complains to her about her brother. Ms. D.'s statement that her daughter "has to get involved," suggests that she participates in this triangulation, an event that likely precludes problem resolution between Mike and his sister. Bowen (1978) described the widespread pattern of involvement of third parties in families as a system of overlapping triangles. Ms. D.'s descriptions of her daughter as the "perfect child," and patterns of her daughter siding with her against her ex-husband suggest an alliance between mother and daughter. The daughter's close alliance with her mother may also be interfering with her desire to visit and build a closer relationship with Mike and her father, who are both outsiders. If these patterns of triangulation continue without interruption, they will likely be extended into strained sibling relationships in adulthood.

Family secrets, which often raise anxiety, may be a stabilizing pattern playing out in this family (Cox, 2003b; Knauth, 2003). Ms. D. appears to be withholding information related to the reasons for the divorce. Secrets, if shared strategically with certain family members (e.g., only Mike's sister is made privy to knowledge about an affair) can place the family at risk for dysfunctional triangular subgroupings in the family.

MULTIGENERATIONAL FAMILY PROCESS. Bowen's theory asserts that differentiation levels are transferred down through generations of a family

(Goodrow, 1997). The Bowenian family therapist views knowledge of the emotional processes of past generations as the key that unlocks insight into the development of current family system patterns (Friesen, 1995). Using this approach, family functioning for Mike's parents would be examined across a number of generations. This exploration might reveal that the origins of Mr. D. and Ms. D.'s low levels of self-differentiation lie in their own family-of-origin patterns.

Without case information on Mike's parents' family history, hypotheses about other transgenerational patterns are limited. However, the therapist can speculate that patterns of scapegoating, triangulation, and family secrets revealed for this nuclear family may all be a product of multigenerational influences. Inquiries can be made into how patterns of distancing might be played out in Mr. D.'s own family of origin. Like his father, Mike seems to be experiencing transgenerational patterns of distancing in response to family anxiety, as evidenced by belligerent behavior and substance abuse.

PARTICIPANTS AND FREQUENCY OF THERAPY. In structural therapy, all members of Mike's nuclear family are included, often in different groupings of individuals and subsystems, in order to reinforce the notion that the current household is the priority unit of interest. Although Mr. D. and Ms. D. are divorced, both would be invited to participate in therapy. If Mike's parents were remarried, step-parents, as new members of the family households, would be included in family therapy sessions as well.

Bowenian therapy would be more likely to hold sessions less frequently, often twice per month (Kolevzon & Green, 1983). Therapists using the Bowenian model are more likely to involve the parents of a family. In fact, in a survey of practices, Bowenian family therapists indicated that they involved the entire family in 7% of their cases (Kolevzon & Green, 1983). In Bowenian therapy, members of Mike's nuclear family would be seen during the period that the therapist addresses issues related to family anxiety and differentiation. During the portion of treatment addressing intergenerational processes, the parents alone could be seen. Mr. D. and Ms. D.'s extended family members might be invited into sessions (or contacted through letters or phone) and interviewed about past family processes or patterns. Ultimately, one goal of extending contact to family-of-origin members, in any form, is to gain a better understanding of how patterns in the current family relate to patterns of prior generations.

Although interactions with other systems are acknowledged as a source of family influence, individuals from outside systems typically would not be consistently involved in the therapy sessions in either school of family therapy. Given that a family's contact with other social support systems has been noted to diffuse family anxiety (Kerr, 2003), the permeability of boundaries between the family system and other social systems should be explored. Specifically, attention should be devoted to how family rules and family system openness permits contact from outside systems. Boundaries between this family and school personnel, law enforcement agencies, the court system, and even members of their neighborhood and church communities should be examined. Dysfunctional subgroupings between members of the family and other social systems (e.g., collusion between Ms. D. and law enforcement to blame Mr. D.) should also be addressed in the D. family in order to increase the likelihood of healthier boundaries.

The Therapeutic Relationship

Building a therapeutic alliance with a family system is one of the most important tasks in family therapy. In structural therapy, this alliance building is referred to as joining (Minuchin & Fishman, 1981). Joining is often accomplished through therapist mirroring of family actions and accommodating to family patterns, while still maintaining his/her position of leadership (Goldberg, 1994). Accommodation involves embracing, and even adopting, a family's style of relating to one another in order to increase acceptance by the family. This can increase family members' ability to relate more comfortably in the therapist's presence (Freeman, 1992). With the D. family, the therapist accommodated by allowing Mike to use silence to communicate and by agreeing to direct attention to Mike when he interrupted the family.

Adopting a nonjudgmental stance with all family members is important for establishing trust in the therapeutic relationship. In a family system with many members, this task is like a juggling act, with the therapist dividing attention among all family members. In joining with family members, the therapist builds an alliance with all members of the family by listening to the perspective of every family member and connecting with them through their story. Joining is critical for setting the stage for future, inevitable relationship strains in therapy. Family members would prefer assigning blame to someone else for family problems and the therapist risks damaging this relationship when they intimate that this notion is not shared.

The therapeutic alliance may also experience strain when the therapist attempts to expand each family member's notion of responsibility for change. To preserve the relationship with the family, the therapist approaches with caution, validating a need for change in the family, but also pointing out the benefits of involving the entire family in changing dysfunctional patterns. The therapist must be cautious not to insinuate judgment toward any one family member as s/he addresses dysfunctional hierarchies or emotional pro-cesses. The therapist's use of nonblaming statements when reflecting upon sequences of family transactional processes helps families see how their roles are connected in a neutral way (Alexander, Waldon, Newberry, & Liddle, 1990). There is a risk that Mike's parents would misperceive the therapist as being judgmental about their relinquished power in the executive sub-system. The therapist's ability to frame Mike's behaviors as patterns that all family members contribute to (or as part of a transgenerational process) can decrease this family defensiveness.

Particular threats to relationship building with the family can be spe-cific to different schools of family therapy. For example, a relational strain in structural family therapy may arise when the therapist unbalances by aligning with certain (i.e., less powerful) family members. If the therapist's relation-ship with all family members is strong, family members can typically trust that this alliance is temporary (Wetchler, 2003). Using the Bowenian model, strain might be introduced when family member's perceptions of past gen-erational patterns are challenged. To the extent that the Bowenian therapist can also normalize processes involving pressures for fusion under conditions of high anxiety, family members will develop trust that the therapist will not scapegoat a family member.

Therapist Role

The role of the family therapist demands constant engagement in two differ-ent processes—directing and discovering (Callapinto, 1988). Although both models of therapy involve a collaborative relationship with families, the de-gree of directiveness used in the delivery of each model is different. The role of the therapist in structural therapy is more directive (Panichelli & Kendall, 1995). However, the family is by no means viewed as a passive system that the therapist acts on, but rather as an active entity that the therapist refocuses (Callapinto, 1988). Therapists take an active role in restructuring activities, such as identifying boundaries, education, restructuring boundaries, and assigning tasks. Typically, the goal is to facilitate communication between family members in session, rather than to serve as the focal point through which all family members communicate (Matusi, 1988). Thus, the role of therapist is directive, but decentralized as the therapist focuses on prompting the family to be more involved with one another.

The role of the Bowenian therapist has been noted to involve a less active use of self in therapy than other schools of family therapy (Kolevzon & Green, 1983; Minuchin & Fishman, 1981). Using this model, the therapist is less likely to set the stage for family re-enactments or to be involved in the orchestration of replayed events in therapy. Instead, the therapist is more likely to analyze and theorize with Mike's family. Bowenian therapists help family members to examine their role in family emotional processes and the transgenerational influences of these roles. In contrast to structural therapy, the Bowenian therapist is more likely to take an outsider position in serving as a catalyst for change by asking process questions (Frankel, 1990; Nichols & Schwartz, 2001). The therapist's role of asking process questions to help clients independently uncover family processes is referred to as coaching (Nichols & Schwartz, 2001). Ideally, Mike's family would be involved in therapy to the extent that they will *appear* to be making progress independently, without the aid of the therapist (Kerr, 2003). Unlike structural therapy, the Bowenian therapist may endorse centralized communication directed through the therapist in order to decrease emotional reactivity of family members toward each other (Nelson, 2003).

Therapeutic Boundaries

Boundaries between the structural therapist and the family can be viewed as clearly defined and appropriately permeable when considering the therapist's role of director or leader of family transactions. Rules become more uncertain around boundaries when considering the therapist's formation of alliances with family members to unbalance unhealthy structural arrangements. Also, therapist disclosure in structural family therapy sessions is typically routine, albeit strategic. For example, the therapist's emphasis on circularity versus causality in Mike's family may lead the therapist to routinely comment on emotional reactions that she or he might experience if she or he was a particular family member. Since the approaches used with the Bowenian model are more straightforward, boundaries between therapist and family members are typically clearer, and disclosure is fairly minimal.

Use of limit setting is employed in both schools of family therapy as a form of setting boundaries. The therapist must set limits in therapy that make it safe and comfortable enough for family members to participate in the process of therapy (Freeman, 1992). Eventually, therapists in both schools might play an active role in setting limits to minimize criticism so that the comments or perceptions of all Mike's family members are respected. In structural family therapy, limit setting is also employed frequently to reorganize transactional patterns in therapy. For example, at some point, the therapist might direct Ms. D. to set limits on Mike's interruptions of her in order to reinforce the boundaries between the parental and child subsystem. In Bowenian therapy, the therapist may set limits by encouraging family members to reduce criticism of family members in their family of origin (e.g., parents) by adopting the view that their family did the best that they could with the resources they had at the time.

Unfortunately, family members repeat what is familiar, even though the repeated pattern may be self-limiting. Intervention themes for both schools of family therapy are aimed at helping the family move beyond *self-limiting* behaviors to expanded options. Structural therapists might frame treatment as efforts to help family members to refrain from familiar, but self-limiting behaviors (in the form of transactions) that are repeated over and over in Mike's family, in spite of their failure to resolve problems. Bowenian therapists, on the other hand, might view their efforts as primarily aimed at moving family members beyond the limits defined by repetition of familiar generational patterns.

Treatment Implications and Outcomes
Therapeutic Techniques and Strategies
Goldberg (1994) noted a concordance in treatment techniques across schools of family therapy. Indeed, structural and Bowenian therapies comprised more consistencies in philosophy than discrepancies. One primary difference between the techniques employed by the two schools is that structural techniques tend to be more action oriented and experientially based (Vetere, 2001), whereas Bowenian techniques are more insight oriented (Freeman, 1992). Eight primary interventions that would be suitable for each model of therapy are outlined in the next sections.

Structural family interventions.   Boundary modification is the central theme in structural family therapy. Boundary-making is not identified as an explicit technique in this chapter, however, but as the goal that underlies many of the strategies that will be outlined. The primary task of the therapist is to restructure boundaries by strengthening those that are too weak and by increasing openness in boundaries that are too rigid or distant (Panichelli & Kendall, 1995).

CHALLENGING UNPRODUCTIVE ASSUMPTIONS AND REFRAMING.   Reframing assumptions about ownership of the presenting problem is an important therapeutic task (Alexander et al., 1990; Nichols & Schwartz, 2001; Vetere, 2009). The therapist in this case could begin to refer to altercations between Mike and his mother as "family arguments" to clarify the shared role members have in any disagreement. In reframing the problem as belonging to the family, the therapist could also ask about Mike's family interactions (and their impact) in a circular fashion. For example, the therapist could ask Mike about his reaction when his mother expresses concern and becomes involved with him and then ask his sister and parents how they react when he responds by distancing. This can help family members to appreciate the extent to which their roles influence one another. In turn, this may increase the likelihood that the family will shift its focus from a single problem family member to problematic family interactions.

Family members tend to act out roles that are assigned to them by other family members. These roles are prescribed not only by the labels that are used when talking about an individual family member, but also by the way they relate to him/her (Nichols & Schwartz, 2001). Ms. D.'s derogatory references to Mike's friends as "losers and troublemakers" communicates a lack of confidence in Mike's ability to attract friends who are "winners." The therapist could challenge assumptions about Mike's peer group by asking about what competencies in his friends attracted him to them. Such challenges can unfreeze assumptions about Mike's "certain future" of limiting friendships to individuals with antisocial tendencies.

EDUCATION OF STRUCTURAL FAMILY SYSTEMS CONCEPTS.   The D. family should be introduced to concepts related to how boundaries function, disengagement, enmeshment, the role of subsystems, the parent–child hierarchy, and how triangles, alliances, and coalitions are formed (Wetchler, 2003). The therapist may elect to introduce a concept and use the D. family dynamics to illustrate it or, alternatively, wait until the pattern is noticed in the family and then take this opportunity to label and define it.

RESTRUCTURING TRANSACTIONS THROUGH ENACTMENT.   Enactment is a technique commonly used in structural therapy in which the therapist asks the family to act out the way that they typically relate to one another around a conflict (Horne, 1993; Minuchin & Fishman, 1981; Parr & Zarski, 2002). Minuchin and Fishman (1981, p. 79) refer to this technique as one in which the therapist "asks the family to dance in his presence." Initially, the therapist directs the family to spontaneously act out their roles in a conflict, while the therapist positions him/herself as an objective observer of interaction sequences.

With Mike's family, the therapist might ask the family to participate in enactments of the last argument about Mr. D. being unfair to the children or a recent discussion about Mike's post-high school career plans. Observing the process allows the therapist to make judgments about transactions that need to be changed in the session, often with less bias than if the family relayed this information verbally (Friedman, 1990). In the first family enactment, the therapist could observe the degree to which either parent triangulated a member of the child subsystem. In the second, the therapist could observe the degree to which Mike's parents were supportive of his thoughts about his future (e.g., making a commitment to the military), without directly endorsing or denouncing his options. Such a transaction would reflect the presence and permeability of boundaries between the parental and child subsystems. In essence, the therapist is evaluating permeability by assessing the degree to which the parent was open to dialog involving a future that differed from their values. Through this observation, the therapist may also be better able to identify rules that govern family transactions revolving around conflicts (Minuchin & Fishman, 1981).

The therapist takes a more active role in the intervention phase of this enactment process. S/he has a number of intervention choices available to evoke alternative transactions (Minuchin & Fishman, 1981), including: (a) increasing intensity of elements of the transaction (e.g., replay the part of the enactment in which Mike insists that his mother does not know what she is talking about over and over); (b) prolonging the time of the interaction (e.g., giving instructions to Mike's family to continue the transaction when they attempt to end it); (c) rearrangement of family members involved in the transaction (e.g., include Mike's sister in the transaction); and (d) provoking alternative transactions (e.g., blocking Ms. D.'s overprotective behaviors and directing her to validate Mike's competence).

Cowan (2001) examined the behavior of experienced and inexperienced therapists' enactment techniques and found significant overlap. Overlap between enactment techniques detected in enactments labeled as productive and unproductive was also noted. These results suggest that the way that therapists behave during enactments may not be a determining factor in how successful the enactments turn out. However, there were a number of clear differences in the behavior of *family members* that characterized unproductive enactments, including arguing, attacking, blaming, decreased eye contact, and low response rates. These data suggest that therapists working with Mike's family should consider taking an active role in prompting family members to participate actively, engage nonverbally, and curb hostility during the intervention phase of enactments.

STRUCTURAL MODIFICATIONS THROUGH PROXIMITY AND DISTANCE.   After a structural diagnosis of family functioning is developed, the therapist can experiment with the formation of new subsystems in Mike's family by manipulating space (Freeman, 1992; Horne, 1993; Panichelli & Kendall, 1995). For example, the therapist might address disengaged boundaries between

Mr. D. and his children by seating them closer together. With this rearranged seating, the therapist could ask Mr. D. and his children to plan an activity that they could participate in together during the next scheduled weekend visitation. Ms. D. could be asked to move to a seat across from the children and observe this interaction without interruption. By increasing proximity between Mr. D. and the children, the disengaged boundary may open more; by decreasing proximity between Ms. D. and the children, the boundary between the enmeshed parties might be strengthened. This changing of geographic proximity sets the stage for family members to deal differently with psychological space (Vetere, 2001).

REORGANIZING SUBSYSTEM MEMBERSHIP OF HIERARCHIES.   Appropriate family boundaries (e.g., family structure involving clear parental limits and consequences) have been associated with a lower likelihood for adolescents substance-abuse (Kaufman, 1990). Mr. D. and Ms. D. could be prompted to agree on age-appropriate expectations and consequences appropriate for rule violations for Mike in order to re-establish power in the subsystem. Minuchin and Fishman (1981) have conceptualized this process as one involving demotion of the child from the parent executive subsystem. Relationships could also be strengthened between the sibling pair in this family by directing them to engage in a task that excludes members of the parental subsystem. For example, Mike and his sister could be directed to discuss how they think and behave differently from their parents.

UNBALANCING.   Therapist's alignment with a particular family member in order to disrupt deeply rooted structures in a family can be a powerful tool (Fishman & Fishman, 2003; Panichelli & Kendall, 1995). In this case, strategic alignments or coalitions with a parent can strengthen boundaries between parental and child subsystems and help to restore appropriate hierarchical organization to the family (Minuchin & Fishman, 1981). For example, the therapist could unbalance Mike's position of power in the family by encouraging Ms. D. to actively set limits (e.g., not tolerate interruptions) in therapy sessions. The therapist could also direct Mike to leave the room so that they could discuss how he could make restitutions for expenses incurred in court.

The therapist could also align strategically with Mike to decrease Ms. D.'s overinvolvement by pointing out instances of his mother's over-involvement and asking him which of those he is most uncomfortable with during a particular session. Ms. D. could be asked if she intends to communicate a lack of faith in his emergence as an autonomous adult during those instances.

If Mr. D. agreed to be a participant in family therapy, the therapist could unbalance the homeostasis in the system by siding with Mr. D. in his assertion that he is being placed in the role of outsider in the family. All of these unbalancing interventions have the potential to disrupt the comfortable, but dysfunctional homeostasis of the family.

INCREASING FAMILY/SOCIAL SYSTEM PERMEABILITY.   The role of the therapist in drawing connections between families and community-based activities is an important one. Doherty and Carroll (2002) have recommended that all therapists identify themselves with family-centered community building, a movement that puts families in closer contact with community resources that help families to develop cohesion and perceived support. The D. family is in need of increased involvement with outside social systems that could support healthy family functioning. To accomplish this, the therapist should address how to increase permeability of membranes between societal systems and the D. family system (Partridge, 2000).

In troubled families, rigid boundaries around the family permit limited access to the community and can be especially problematic when legal problems arise (Cox, 2003a). Parental minimization of the possibility of Mike receiving serious consequences for the shoplifting charge suggests that the boundaries between the juvenile justice system and the family may be rigid. Openness in the boundaries between family and the legal system can be encouraged through increased contact (i.e., appointments with a juvenile counselor). Reinforcement of the seriousness of Mike's offenses by both systems can only help to strengthen the authority in the parental hierarchy. Mike's dismissal of the option of vocational school also indicates that family boundaries provide limited access to support from the educational systems and suggests that increased contact is needed. Permeability between adult and child subsystems and community membership systems should also be opened. The therapist might promote adult's social contacts through club (e.g., book club, gym) involvement for the parents and involvement in community youth sports programs of interest (e.g., football) for Mike.

ENHANCING FAMILY STRENGTHS.   Family descriptions of positive attributes of family members can be highlighted by the therapist to increase the likelihood that the family member will relate to others in a way that is consistent with the family labels (Friedman, 1990; Nelson, 2003; Nichols & Schwartz, 2001; Parr & Zarski, 2002). For example, Ms. D.'s description of Mike's adoption of a "tough guy" image reflects a recognition of the more vulnerable, affectionate side of Mike that is strategically hidden. Mike's backing-off from threats may represent behavior patterns that are consistent with this profile of a nice person whose tough exterior is only a bluff that helps him to retreat.

Therapists should highlight family strengths that relate to flexibility in responding to changes in the family system. However inconsistently it was followed, strength can be noted in the rapid development of a visitation arrangement shortly after Mr. D.'s departure. Mr. D.'s maintenance of close proximity to the family through his selection of an apartment close to the family house when he moved can also be highlighted as a noble effort to open boundaries between himself and other family members.

Family resources that allow the D. family to be effective in developing or maintaining family structure should also be identified in descriptions of past transactions. For example, Mike's ability to voice objections to his mother's assertions that he was unhappy with his father's involvement represents a healthy refusal to participate in patterns of triangulation into family conflict. Further, Mike's ability to initiate and maintain friendships in the context of his strained relationships with adults represents a flexible approach to boundary permeability with others. Also, Mike's report that he has stopped associating with individuals who engage in marijuana use is promising in that it reflects an attempt to construct a different reality around peer affiliation patterns than those scripted for him by his family.

The sibling subsystems history of academic achievements can be highlighted to draw attention to its shared capabilities. Intellectual strengths and challenges of Mike's failure to fully utilize academic competencies can be brought out through a "stroke and kick" technique (Nichols & Schwartz, 2001, p. 259). This technique, described by Minuchin (1974), involves restructuring through the delivery of a compliment (often made directly to the individual) and a critique (often made indirectly by raising an objection to an individual's behavior with another family member). In this case, the therapist could comment on Mike's intellectual strengths (stroke), then turn to his sister and comment on how Mike does not seem up to the challenge of competing with someone if there is the chance that he might not outperform academically (kick).

OUT-OF-SESSION TASKS.   The therapist could assign tasks outside of therapy that would support involvement between Mr. D. and his children. It should be noted that these tasks, in part, serve as probes of a family's openness to change (e.g., Kaslow et al., 2003). Mr. D. could be asked to call each of his children and ex-wife and hold a 10-min conversation each time. Often, assigning therapeutic tasks with different roles for enmeshed family members helps to support attempts to move them toward separateness. Ms. D. could be given tasks that encouraged her to decrease her involvement in activities that Mike plans. Mike might be asked to put in applications for jobs in order to help pay for his court costs. Ms. D. would be asked to refrain from assisting with this task (i.e., giving input into the types of jobs that he applied for or suggesting how he should approach the application process).

Bowenian family therapy techniques.   Kerr (2003) outlined the importance of teaching the family about a different framework to use in thinking, rather than teaching them specific thoughts that should be involved in changing behavior. A family must first reduce emotional reactivity so that they can recognize that everyone plays a role in maintaining the problem; then the therapist can develop a family's understanding of important family therapy concepts (Freeman, 1992; Kerr, 2003; Nelson, 2003). Concepts important to address in conveying this new way of thinking include, but are not limited to: (a) fusion anxiety, (b) differentiation, (c) family projection process, (d) multigenerational processes, (e) distancing, (f) emotional cutoff, and (g) triangulation. The relationship between low levels of differentiation and negative adjustment outcomes should also be highlighted in this family education.

DECREASING EMOTIONAL REACTIVITY.   Each member of Mike's family can be taught to identify and monitor the degree of sensitivity that she or he has toward others (Sayger, 1992). Then, he or she could be asked to consider the extent to which she or he uses emotional versus intellectual processes in responding to other family members. In this family, Ms. D. and Mike could be encouraged to balance their excessively emotional approach with greater rationality. Mr. D. could be encouraged to balance his more rational and detached style with increased emotionality, which is often reflective of greater interest and investment in one's children. Displacement stories can be used as a nonthreatening medium to examine patterns relevant in one's own family (Nichols & Schwartz, 2001). Displacement stories involve narratives or media materials of family interactions that illustrate emotional reactivity outside of Mike's family, with the hope that D. family members will be better able to discuss dysfunctional interactions when patterns in their own family are not being scrutinized (with heightened defensiveness).

PROMOTION OF DIFFERENTIATION OF SELF.   Development of differentiation, the skill of being simultaneously close to and separate from another person, is one of the central intervention techniques of Bowen's theory (Goodrow, 1997; Papero, 1988). Mike's family should be educated about the costs of parental failure to support individuation, including reactionary, rebellious adolescent separation responses and impaired adolescent independence. Family members could be taught to identify their own values and principles and to use the "I" position to clarify and state opinions that differ from other family members. Using this skill, members of the D. family can learn to adopt a removed, objective response in the context of high emotion.

TEACHING FAMILY MEMBERS TO BIND ANXIETY INDEPENDENTLY.   Once family members are taught about the role of anxiety in precipitating unhealthy dynamics in the family (i.e., pressures for fusion), the stage is set for this family to take responsibility for managing it (Nelson, 2003). The therapist can help members of the family to recognize anxiety and patterns of management in past generations. Using process questions, they can then be encouraged to identify the need to take responsibility for containing their own anxiety when family's levels of anxiety rise, rather than resolving it by anxiously attaching with others to diffuse it.

PROMOTE INSIGHT INTO INFLUENCE OF PAST GENERATIONAL PATTERNS.   As noted earlier, the genogram is a tool commonly used to examine intergenerational patterns of relating and emotional functioning (Springer et al., 2003; Young, 1991). In exploring family patterns, Mr. D. and Ms. D. could be encouraged to contact other relatives to gain perspective on familial patterns. Interviews with family members could focus on patterns in the family and perceptions of how and why these patterns emerged. Mr. D. and Ms. D. could interview relatives about family dynamics such as alliances, triangles, subsystem functioning, substance abuse, physically abusive behavior, and limit setting. The function of these family patterns with respect to maintenance of family homeostasis should be explored. Specifically, family roles of scapegoating (a pattern reflective of Mike's role), enabling (a pattern suggested by Ms. D.'s nonconfrontational stance), and family hero (a pattern reflected by hints of Mike's sister overachieving behaviors) could be examined. Mr. D. and Ms. D. could then be asked to examine how these patterns from past generations are similar to those in their own family.

INDIVIDUATION FROM FAMILY OF ORIGIN.   For many families, the inability to manage family-of-origin anxiety has resulted in geographical cutoff through a physical move away from one's family of origin (Oehrle, 1997). Unfortunately, this move gives the family member who leaves an artificial sense of independence; in reality, the abrupt and absolute split from family typically leaves the family member unprepared for dealing with future conflict (Goodrow, 1997; Nelson, 2003). Changing one's role in families from that of past generations depends on recognizing patterns in the multigenerational transmission process. Mr. D. and Ms. D. can be encouraged to use information from the genogram to break the cycle of multigenerational transmission by identifying and changing unwanted patterns played out from their family of origin. A Bowenian therapist would encourage Mike's parents to revisit and resolve central conflicts with members of their family of origin. Such experiences give family members the opportunity to resolve emotional conflicts by substituting emotional reactivity with objectivity and separateness. Without the opportunity to develop skills in differentiation in the context of family-of-origin anxiety, Mr. D. and Ms. D. are at risk for repeating disturbed family relations in their family of procreation (Oehrle, 1997).

DETRIANGULATING.   In restructuring a family, a Bowenian family therapist would attend to dysfunctional groupings involving a third party (Nelson, 2003; Sayger, 1992). Triangulation noted across parent and child subsystems should be addressed through blocking of third party involvement in dyadic interactions. The therapist might first encourage the sibling dyad to independently manage tension without involving their mother, unless safety became a threat. Likewise, Ms. D. should be supported in breaking patterns involving arguments with her ex-husband, which result in her attempts to triangulate her children into the conflict. Ms. D. could be asked about how she might be using the children as a way to perpetuate the conflict and how this relates to past intergenerational patterns. In therapy, recent conflicts involving Mike's father's threats to withdraw child support might be enacted, with the therapist blocking Ms. D.'s involvement of members of the child subsystem. The therapist could use such an enactment to illustrate successes in broaching and resolving conflicts between two parties when the option of involving a third party was removed.

OUT-OF-SESSION TASKS.   Kerr (2003) noted that families learn family therapy concepts best by practicing them, rather than having them explained. In fact, much of the insight-raising work initiated in sessions is intended to serve as a stimulus for out-of-session practice (Freeman, 1992; Kerr, 2003). One out-of-session task might be to have Ms. D. record significant changes that have occurred in the family from the point of separation until the present. The therapist can use this exercise as a basis for inquiring about how certain transitions associated with changes might have been associated with heightened anxiety and preoccupations with closeness. The therapist could also give Mr. D. an assignment to record significant changes in his involvement in work across a certain number of years. The therapist might use this exercise to inquire about how family anxiety might have been associated with periods in his life in which work was made more time-consuming. The therapist can use this as a basis for making inquiries about how this family distancing pattern related family-of-origin patterns in work investment, especially during periods of stress.

Mechanisms for Change

For the structural family therapist, the key to change lies in having the family interact and experience one another differently (Fishman & Fishman, 2003; Freeman, 1992). If family members change the way that they interact, the therapist assumes that they will think differently about the problem. The process can be thought of as disconnecting automatic responses in a family that are linked together (Minuchin & Nichols, 1998). Underlying any sustained progress is the family's understanding of how altered transactions are preferable to old, automatic patterns. Embracing the notion of boundaries serving the function of "membranes" of autonomy (Guerin & Chabot, 1992, p. 254) is the key to family members being able to carry out many important family therapy tasks successfully (e.g., conceptualizing family cohesion levels as enmeshed or disengaged; recognizing the need for modified hierarchies).

An important mechanism of change in the Bowenian model is curiosity—an interest in how current behavior can possibly be influenced by people who are not members of one's current family. This curiosity can energize families to transform intergenerational roles adopted automatically into more conscious ways of behaving, which are reflective of their own personal values and principles. A second key underlying mechanism for change in this model is the ability to develop an enthusiasm for separateness (Kerr, 2003). One must possess a desire to decrease his/her sense of emotional interdependence with the family in order to successfully reach the point of binding one's own anxiety. Members of the D. family must also be able to recognize that family members who do not successfully reduce or bind their own anxiety will not change. If Ms. D. failed to develop skills in reducing her currently high levels of anxiety, the need to bind it through patterns of conflict with her ex-husband and son will prevail.

Medical and Nutritional Issues

Family functioning has been noted as a significant influence of individual health; likewise, the entire family is typically impacted by the compromised health of one of its members (Cox, 2003a). Structural therapy actually has its roots in the examination of family structure in context of family health issues. Early work in structural therapy with eating disorders and psychosomatic problems has revealed the significant impact that family member illness can have on family structure (Nichols & Schwartz, 2001). A family that has faced a medical crisis in the past may have made significant adjustments in family structure, perhaps successfully (Cox & Anderson, 2003). In cases of chronic illness, the adjustment process for the family may be ongoing. Understanding how Mike's family has had to reorganize around any such critical events can be important in understanding how certain dysfunctional patterns have developed. For example, information on family members' health may allow the therapist to appraise how family members have organized structure around sick role(s) in the family (Cox & Anderson, 2003). Given the potential, negative impact of chronic worry and anxiety about family illness, the therapist working with Mike's family should inquire about present and past health struggles for all family members (Cox, Keltner, & Hogan, 2003).

A number of studies have documented the problematic, low nutritional intake of adolescents and the consequences of such patterns, including impaired learning (Bull, 1992; Contento, 1999; Rees & Trahms, 1989; Walker, Grantham-McGregor, Himes, Williams, & Duff, 1998). Unstructured adolescent diets consisting of high fat and refined carbohydrates often leave them without adequate vitamins and minerals, particularly iron (Bull, 1992). Low energy levels associated with low iron intake in any family member could negatively affect that family member's motivation. These issues are particularly relevant for Mike, whose academic functioning has declined since his family's divorce. The chaotic organization that characterizes Mike's mother's home post-divorce suggests that foundations for family routines, such as meals, are absent. Results from the Family Unpredictability Scale can be examined to identify the degree to which routines exist around family meals, which are typically healthier than eating patterns of youths. Interestingly, in an examination of 7th and 8th grader responses to 30 health-related topics, nutrition was identified as one of the top four health topics for which adolescents expressed concern (Sobal, 1987). This suggests that the sibling subsystem (Mike and his sister) in this family may be open to structuring family meal routines to increase health habits.

Potential Pitfalls

With any approach used with families, the therapist must learn to map out the mine fields of family work to guard against stepping into therapeutic failures. Early in the structural therapy process, the therapist should emphasize that the entire family will need to be present. The therapist's honoring of a parent request to see Mike individually for therapy would likely result in parental withdrawal from the system so that the therapist can fix the problem family member (Kerr, 2003). Also, therapeutic conceptualizations that ignore the developmental processes that the family is facing may create blind spots for the therapist. In this case, the mounting need for autonomy for Mike and his sister as part of normal, adolescent developmental processes should be recognized throughout therapy.

Structural family therapists respond to what a family does versus what a family says (Papero, 1988). However, at times, therapists may become drawn into the content of family stories and overlook the more important focus on process (Freeman, 1992). This mistake can result in a therapist focusing on the presenting problems, the biases that the family brings to therapy, rather than how the family is dealing with those specific problems. Unfortunately, without appropriate attention to *how* the family deals with issues, the therapist is unable to appropriately discern restructuring that is needed. Also, the focus of therapy is narrowed to resolving specific conflict issues versus problematic *patterns* that pervade multiple family problems.

Therapists who fail to devote sufficient time to the critical task of joining may also encounter problems throughout therapy. They may intervene (e.g., restructure) too early, risking heightened defensiveness and failed treatment outcomes (Carpenter & Treacher, 1982). The therapist's tendency to rush therapy could also result in the family being asked to complete a task outside of the session that is too difficult. Without adequate preparation, the family cannot complete a task that requires creation of novel structures (Stanton, O'Reilly, & Speck, 1990). For example, in-session preparation of an out-of-session task involving Ms. D. strengthening the parental subsystem boundary by preventing interruptions should involve session practice through enactments until sources of interference to the newly established structure are eliminated.

A number of strategies have been noted as important in the facilitation of effective enactments. Therapists' failure to follow these strategies may result in less productive outcomes in enactments. Pitfalls of effective enactments can include (a) failure to provide a specific topic to discuss; (b) allowing the family members to talk to the therapist, rather than to one another; (c) intervening too much in enactment dialog; and (d) failure to provide direction about how to improve transactions observed in an enactment (Cowan, 2001).

In structural therapy, the therapist's focus on one subsystem exclusively, while ignoring others, can also be problematic. For example, a therapist working with the D. family could focus on clarifying boundaries between the parental and child subsystems, while ignoring opportunities to strengthen boundaries around Mike's sibling subsystem. Family members also frequently attempt to pull the therapist into a coalition against other family members. If a therapist establishes a coalition with one particular family member it should be strategically motivated, rather than a product of emotionally reactive siding with a family member. Even strategic alignments should be developed cautiously, given the risk of alienating the nonaligned family members (Alexander et al., 1990). Also, confrontation of particular family members in context of these coalitions should always be coupled with support (Friedman, 1990). With this family, the therapist's formation of a coalition with Ms. D. to support the parental subsystem, for example, might alienate Mike and his sister. Therapist initiation of family discussions of how taking sides with a family member affected others are important to not only reinforce the lessons learned by experimentation within the family system, but also decrease anxiety of family members with whom the therapist did not align temporarily.

In practicing Bowenian therapy, the treatment provider can sometimes get stuck in the problems of the nuclear family, neglecting to examine how family patterns are part of that legacy. When therapists do prompt an intergenerational focus, the therapist should take care not to pathologize family members of past generations (Brown, 1991). Doing so might result in an excessive focus on the negative characteristics of family members and prolonged anger toward family, impeding the development of positive relationships. Instead, therapists should encourage family members to take a more benign view of family dysfunctional patterns. After all, one's parents' responding may be characterized by the same limitations brought about by the intergenerational transmission process as the clients that are working with the therapist.

Kerr (2003) has noted patterns whereby, in an effort to reduce anxiety, family members often shift anxiety around to different family members. A Bowenian therapist's failure to consider all family members as potential stabilizing forces of family anxiety may result in a therapist overestimating a family's level of functioning. If a Bowenian therapist notes decreases in anxiety in one particular family member in response to treatment, s/he could assume that family functioning has improved. However, without appropriate attention to how this anxiety plays a role in interactions throughout the entire family, the therapist could miss the fact that anxiety has not been reduced; it has simply been directed to another family member.

Termination and Relapse Prevention
It can be argued that there is always some degree of subjective judgment associated with a decision to terminate, even when objective measures of

family functioning are used to guide this decision. Karrer and Schwartzmann (1985) have noted structural family therapists' failure to develop clear guidelines for termination as a weakness of this model. Indeed, this matter becomes particularly complex when considering progress and levels of functioning of many different family members. One guiding criterion for termination using both models is that family members become independent experts in thinking in terms of systems (Sayger, 1992). Beyond this, signals of termination in either model of family therapy can be reduced to two criteria—spontaneity and independence (Alexander et al., 1990).

When considering termination of structural family therapy, the family will likely be transformed such that family rules are more explicit, boundaries are clearer, and the family members are equipped with skills in spontaneously recognizing and altering transactions that are problematic (Cox, 2003b). This will be reflected in the family's ability to spontaneously change transactions, rather than merely respond to a therapist's redirection (Alexander et al., 1990). With both forms of family therapy, the goal is to collaborate with families and, eventually, have them adopt the role of experts of their own family and replace the therapist (Brown, 1991). Fishman and Fishman (2003) likened the active roles of both therapists and families in sessions to that of co-therapists. To the extent that the therapist has gradually and successfully involved all members of the D. family in newly developed structures, this family will have become skilled in independent initiation and maintenance of new structures.

Spontaneity and independence also serve as useful criteria for Bowenian therapists' termination planning. The decision to terminate can be based on a therapist's assessment that family members have enough of a working concept for differentiation that they can continue to develop skills in individuating without the assistance of therapy (Papero, 1988). To do so, at a minimum, family members should be able to independently recognize problems related to inappropriate levels of differentiation in their own family. While participation in therapy might create initial changes with respect to autonomous functioning, individuation is expected to be mastered across time. To the extent possible, Mr. D. and Ms. D. would be encouraged to make more spontaneous, versus planned, contacts with their nuclear and extended family (Sayger, 1992).

In terminating therapy, members of the D. family would be given instructions to return during periods in which family members experience difficulties in separating from patterns of reactivity in the family (Brown, 1991). The therapist would gradually schedule sessions farther apart, from once per week to twice per month for structural therapy and from twice per month to monthly for Bowenian therapy. During this phase, the therapist would focus more on family strengths and gains, encouraging family members to continue using transactional or insight building skills that have been successfully implemented in therapy.

SUMMARY

This chapter has highlighted two models of family therapy with a number of congruencies. Structural therapy assumes that family members form patterns of behaving that become so habitual that they end up becoming unspoken rules of family interaction (Cox, 2003b). This model of family therapy assumes that family members have options for rearranging themselves available to them that are not considered because of these family rules or structures. The therapist changes how family members behave, altering structures that are dysfunctional and replacing them with transactions that are more appropriate. Ideally, the D. family will leave therapy learning to be critical of its own structure so that it can adapt to accommodate the many demands and life adjustments that most families face.

Bowenian therapy also ascribes importance to boundaries in the family system, but uses a slightly different organizational framework to conceptualize why maladaptive boundaries exist. The Bowenian therapist assumes that the family members have natural tendencies toward both separation and togetherness, and that family dysfunction results from an imbalance of these two forces. Bowenian therapists assume that families have options for separating or becoming more autonomous that are limited because of patterns of responding that repeat across generations. Ideally, the D. family will leave Bowenian-guided therapy having made some progress in creating new patterns related to healthy separation, both within one's family of origin and one's family of procreation. With both approaches, successful therapy is characterized by transformations in family, transformations that go beyond the family's initial, narrow definition of truth.

REFERENCES

Abelsohn, D., & Saayman, G. S. (1991). Adolescent adjustment to parental divorce: An investigation from the perspective of basic dimensions of structural family therapy theory. *Family Process, 30,* 177–191.

Alexander, J., Waldon, H. B., Newberry, A. M., & Liddle, N. (1990). The functional family therapy model. In A. S. Friedman, & S. Granick (Eds.), *Family therapy for adolescent drug abuse* (pp.184–199). Lexington, MA: Lexington Books.

Bartle-Haring, S., Rosen, K. H., & Stith, S. M. (2002). Emotional reactivity and psychological distress. *Journal of Adolescent Research, 17*, 568–585.

Bowen, M. (1978). *Family therapy in clinical practice.* New York: Aronson.

Bray, J. H., Williamson, D. S., & Malone, P. E. (1984). Personal authority in the family system: Development of a questionnaire to measure personal authority in intergenerational family processes. *Journal of Marital and Family Therapy, 10*, 167–178.

Brown, F. H. (1991). *Reweaving the family tapestry.* New York: W. W. Norton.

Bull, N. L. (1992). Dietary habits, food consumption, and nutrient intake during adolescence. *Journal of Adolescent Health, 13*, 384–388.

Callapinto, J. (1988). Teaching the structural way. In H. A. Liddle, D. C. Breunlin, & R. C. Schwartz (Eds.), *Handbook of family therapy training and supervision* (pp. 17–37). New York: Guilford Press.

Carpenter, J., & Treacher, A. (1982). Family therapy in context: Working with child focused problems. *Journal of Family Therapy, 4*, 15–34.

Chamberlain, P., & Rosicky, J. G. (1995). The effectiveness of family therapy in the treatment of adolescents with conduct disorders and delinquency. *Journal of Marital and Family Therapy, 21*, 441–459.

Clarkin, J. F., & Carpenter, D. (1995). Family therapy in historical perspective. In B. Bongar, & L. E. Beutler (Eds.), *Comprehensive textbook of psychotherapy theory and practice* (pp. 205–227). New York: Oxford University Press.

Coco, E. L., & Courtney, L. J. (2003). A family systems approach for preventing adolescent runaway behavior. *Family therapy, 30*, 39–50.

Contento, I. R. (1999). Nutrition and food choice among children and adolescents. In A. J. Goreczny, & M. Hersen (Eds.), *Handbook of pediatric and adolescent health psychology* (pp. 249–273). Needham Heights, MA: Allyn & Bacon.

Cowan, J. A. (2001). Maximizing the effectiveness of enactments in structural family therapy: A qualitative analysis of productive and unproductive variables in the therapeutic process (Doctoral dissertation, Virginia Consortium Program in Clinical Psychology). *Dissertation Abstracts International, 63*(2-B), 1018.

Cox, R. P. (2003a). The Individual-family connection. In R. P. Cox (Ed.), *Health related counseling with families of diverse cultures* (pp. 1–16). Westport, CT: Greenwood Press.

Cox, R. P. (2003b). Transcultural family counseling: A Case Study. In R. P. Cox (Ed.), *Health related counseling with families of diverse cultures* (pp. 193–204). Westport, CT: Greenwood Press.

Cox, R. P., & Anderson, H. (2003). Theories and concepts: How to understand families and health. In R. P. Cox (Ed.), *Health related counseling with families of diverse cultures* (pp. 73–115). Westport, CT: Greenwood Press.

Cox, R. P., Farr, K., & Parish, E. (2003). Family health counseling, counseling of disasters, health interventions, and reimbursement with families of diverse cultures. In R. P. Cox (Ed.), *Health related counseling with families of diverse cultures* (pp. 169–191). Westport, CT: Greenwood Press.

Cox, R. P., Keltner, N., & Hogan, B. (2003). Family assessment tools. In R. P. Cox (Ed.), *Health related counseling with families of diverse cultures* (pp. 145–167). Westport, CT: Greenwood Press.

Daroff, L. H., Marks, S. F., & Friedman, A. S. (1990). The parents' predicament. In A. S. Friedman, & S. Granick (Eds.), *Family therapy for adolescent drug abuse* (pp. 85–108). Lexington, MA: Lexington Books.

DeMaria, R., & Hannah, M. T. (2003). *Building intimate relationships: Bridging treatment, education, and enrichment through the PAIRS program.* New York: Brunner-Routledge.

Diamond, G., & Siqueland, L. (1995). Family therapy for the treatment of the depressed adolescent. *Psychotherapy, 32,* 77–90.

Doherty, W. J., & Carroll, J. S. (2002). The citizen therapist and family-centered community building: Introduction to a new section of the journal. *Family Process, 4,* 561–569.

Edmonson, C. R. (2001). Differentiation of self and patterns of grief following the death of a parent (Doctoral Dissertation, Texas Women's University, Denton Texas). *Dissertation Abstracts International, 62*(12-B), 5960.

Edwards, M., & Steinglass, P. (1995). Family therapy treatment and outcomes for alcoholism. *Journal of Marital and Family Therapy, 21,* 475–509.

Fishman, H. C., & Fishman, T. (2003). Structural family therapy. In G. P. Sholevar, & L. D. Schwoeri (Eds.), *Textbook of family and couples therapy* (pp. 35–54). Washington, D.C.: American Psychiatric Press.

Framo, J. L. (1990). Intergenerational family therapy. In J. K. Zeig, & W. M. Munion (Eds.), *What is psychotherapy?* (pp. 257–261). San Francisco: Jossey-Bass.

Frankel, L. (1990). Structural family therapy for adolescent substance abusers and their families. In A. S. Friedman, & S. Granick (Eds.), *Family therapy for adolescent drug abuse* (pp. 129–266). Lexington, MA: Lexington Books.

Freeman, D. S. (1992). *Multigenerational family therapy.* New York: Haworth Press.

Friedman A. S. (1990). The adolescent drug abuser and the family. In A. S. Friedman, & S. Granick (Eds.), *Family therapy for adolescent drug abuse* (pp. 3–22). Lexington, MA: Lexington Books.

Friedman, A. S., Utada, A., & Morissey, M. R. (1990). Families of adolescent drug abusers are "rigid": Are these families either "disengaged" or "enmeshed," or both? In A. S. Friedman, & S. Granick (Eds.), *Family therapy for adolescent drug abuse* (pp. 145–168). Lexington, MA: Lexington Books.

Goldberg, L. J. (1994). Family therapists' conceptualizations and treatment of adolescent suicidality (Doctoral dissertation, Pacific Graduate School of Psychology, Palo Alto, CA). *Dissertation Abstracts International, 56,* 2325.

Goodrow, K. K. (1997). Bowenian Theory and its application: A case study of a couple intending to marry. *Journal of Family Psychotherapy, 8,* 33–42.

Gordon-Rabinowitz, B., & Rabinowitz, M. D. (2003). PAIRS and family systems. In R. DeMaria, & M. T. Hannah (Eds.), *Building intimate relationships* (pp. 115–130). New York: Brunner-Routledge.

Guerin, P. J., & Chabot, D. R. (1992). Development of a family systems theory. In D. K. Freedheim (Ed.), *History of psychotherapy* (pp. 225–260). Washington, D.C.: American Psychological Association.

Gurman, A. S., & Kniskern, D. P. (1981). *Handbook of family therapy*. New York: Brunner/Mazel.

Haley, J. (1976). *Problem solving therapy*. San Fransisco, CA: Jossey-Bass.

Henderson, A. D., Sayger, T. V., & Horne, A. M. (2003). Mothers and sons: A look at the relationship between child behavior problems, marital satisfaction, maternal depression, and family cohesion. *The Family Journal: Counseling and Therapy for Couples and Families, 11*, 33–41.

Horne, A. M. (1993). Family-based interventions. In A. P. Goldstein, & C. R. Huff (Eds.), *The gang intervention handbook* (pp. 189–218). Champaign, IL: Research Press.

Hovestadt, A., Anderson, W., Piercy, F., Cochran, S., & Fine, M. (1985). A family-of-origin scale. *Journal of Marital and Family Therapy, 11*, 287–298.

Jordan, C., & Franklin, C. (1999). Mental Research Institute (MRI), Strategic, and Milan family therapy. In C. Franklin, & C. Jordan (Eds.), *Family practice: Brief systems methods for social work* (pp. 45–72). Pacific Grove, CA: Brooks/Cole.

Kaplan, S. L. (1977). Structural family therapy for children of divorce: Case Reports. *Family Process, 16*, 75–83.

Karrer, B. M., & Schwartzmann, J. (1985). The stages of structural family therapy. *Family Therapy Collections, 14*, 41–50.

Kaslow, N. J., Dausch, B. M., & Celano, M. (2003). Family therapies. In A. S. Gurman, & S. B. Messer (Eds.), *Essential psychotherapies* (pp. 400–462). New York: Guilford Press.

Kaufman, E. (1990). Adolescent substance abusers and family therapy. In A. S. Friedman, & S. Granick (Eds.), *Family therapy for adolescent drug abuse* (pp. 47–61). Lexington, MA: Lexington Books.

Kerig, P. K. (1995). Triangles in the family circle: Effects of family structure on marriage, parenting, and child adjustment. *Journal of Family Psychological, 9*, 28–43.

Kerr, M. (2003). Multigenerational family systems theory of Bowen and its application. In G. P. Sholevar, & L. D. Schwoeri (Eds.), *Textbook of family and couples therapy* (pp. 35–54). Washington, D.C: American Psychiatric Press.

Kerr, M. E., & Bowen, M. (1988). *Family evaluation: An approach based on Bowen theory*. New York: W. W. Norton.

Knauth, D. G. (2003). Family secrets: An illustrative clinical case study guided by Bowen Family Systems Theory. *Journal of Family Nursing, 9*, 331–344.

Kolevzon, M. S., & Green, R. G. (1983). Practice and training in family therapy: A known group study. *Family Process, 22*, 179–1990.

Larson, J. H., & Wilsoon, S. M. (1998). Family of origin influences on young adult career decision problems: A test of Bowenian theory. *American Journal of Family Therapy, 26*, 39–53.

Liddle, H. A. (1983). Diagnosis and assessment in family therapy: I. A comparative analysis of six schools of thought. *Family Therapy Collections, 4*, 1–33.

Lindah, K. M., & Malik, N. M. (1999). Observations of marital conflict and power: Relations with parenting triad. *Journal of Marriage and the Family, 61*, 320–321.

Matusi, W. T. (1988). The process of structural family therapy: Level of experience makes a difference. *Family Therapy Collections, 24*, 1–20.

Minuchin, S. (1974). *Families and family therapy*. Cambridge, MA: Harvard University Press.

Minuchin, S., & Fishman, H. C. (1981). *Family therapy techniques*. Cambridge, MA: Harvard University Press.

Minuchin, S., & Nichols, M. P. (1998). Structural family therapy. In F. M. Dattilio (Ed.), *Case studies in couple and family therapy* (pp. 108–131). New York: Guilford Press.

Nelson, T. S. (2003). Transgenerational family therapies. In L. L. Hecker, & J. L. Wetchler (Eds.), *An introduction to marriage and family therapy* (pp. 255–293). New York: Haworth Clinical Practice Press.

Nelson, T. S., & Utesch, W. E. (1990). Clinical assessment of structural family therapy constructs. *Family therapy, 18*, 233–249.

Nichols, M. P., & Schwartz, R. C. (2001). *Family therapy: Concepts and methods*. Boston: Allyn and Bacon.

Oehrle, N. (1997). Toward a better utilization of sibling relationships in adult therapies (Doctoral Dissertation, California School of Professional Psychology, Alameda, CA). *Dissertation Abstracts International, 58*(9-B), 5135.

Olson, D. H., Bell, R., & Postner, J. (1978). *FACES manual and item booklet*. St. Paul, MN: Family Social Science.

Olson, D. H., Russell, C. S., & Sprenkle, D. H. (1983). Circumplex model VI: Theoretical update. *Family Process, 22*, 69–83.

Panichelli, S. M., & Kendall, P. C. (1995). Therapy with children and adolescents. In B. Bongar, & L. E. Beutler (Eds.), *Comprehensive textbook of psychotherapy theory and practice* (pp. 336–358). New York: Oxford University Press.

Papero, D. V. (1988). Training in Bowen Theory. In H. A. Liddle, D. C. Breunlin, & R. C. Schwartz (Eds.), *Handbook of family therapy training and supervision* (pp. 62–77). New York: Guilford Press.

Parr, P., & Zarski, J. (2002). Before you can conquer the beast you must first make it beautiful. In R. E. Watts, & J. Carlson (Eds.), *Techniques in marriage and family counseling* (Vol. 2, pp. 89–91). Alexandria, VA: American Counseling Association.

Partridge, K. (2000). Family problems. In L. Champion, & M. Power (Eds.), *Adult psychological problems* (pp. 175–230). Philadelphia: Taylor & Francis.

Peck, J. D., & Brown, F. H. (1991). Families in the divorce and post-divorce process. In F. H. Brown (Ed.), *Reweaving the family tapestry: A multigenerational approach to families* (pp. 191–218). New York: W. W. Norton.

Powell, J. Y., & Dosser, D. A. (1992). Structural family therapy as a bridge between "helping too much" and empowerment. *Family Therapy, 19*, 243–256.

Protinsky, H., & Shilts, L. (1990). Adolescent substance abuse and family cohesion. *Family Therapy, 17*, 173–175.

Rees, J. M., & Trahms, C. M. (1989). Nutritional influences on physical growth and behavior in adolescence. In G. R. Adams, & R. Montemayor (Eds.), *Biology of adolescent behavior and development* (pp. 195–222). Thousand Oaks, CA: Sage.

Ross, L. T., & Hill E. M. (2000). The family unpredictability scale: Reliability and Validity. *Journal of Marriage and Family Therapy, 62*, 549–562.

Sand-Pringle, C., West, J. D., & Bubenzer, D. L. (1991). Family counseling rituals: A case study. *Journal of Mental Health Counseling, 13*, 500–505.

Santisteban, D. A., Coatsworth, J. D., Perez-Vidal, A., Mirrani, V., Jean-Gilles, M., & Szapocznik, J. (1997). Brief structural/strategic family therapy with African American and Hispanic high-risk youth. *Journal of Community Psychology, 25*, 453–471.

Sayger, T. V. (1992). Family psychology and therapy. In C. E. Walker, & M. C. Roberts (Eds.), *Handbook of clinical child psychology* (2nd ed., pp. 783–807). Oxford, UK: John Wiley.

Sholevar, G. P. (1995). Family interventions. In G. P. Sholevar (Ed.), *Conduct disorders in children and adolescents* (pp. 193–368). Washington, DC: American Psychiatric Press.

Skowron, E. A., & Friedlander, M. L. (1988). The differentiation of self inventory: Development and initial validation. *Journal of Counseling Psychology, 45*, 235–246.

Sobal, J. (1987). Health concerns for young adolescents. *Adolescence, 22*, 739–750.

Springer, D. W., McNeece, C. A., Arnold, E. M. (2002). *Substance abuse treatment for criminal offenders*. Washington, D.C.: American Psychological Association.

Stanton, M. D., O'Reilly, D. M., & Speck, R. V. (1990). Three responses to Frankel's report on structural family therapy and the "Miller" case. In A. S. Friedman, & S. Granick (Eds.), *Family therapy for adolescent drug abuse* (pp. 267–277). Lexington, MA: Lexington Books.

Todd, T. C., & Selekman, M. (1974). A structural-strategic approach for treating the adolescent who is abusing alcohol and other drugs. In W. Snyder, & T. Ooms (Eds.), *Empowering families, helping adolescents: Family-centered treatment of adolescents with alcohol, drug abuse, and mental health problems* (Publication series 6, pp. 79–89). Rockville, MD: U.S. Department of Health and Human Services, Center for Substance Abuse Treatment.

Utada, A., & Friedman, A. S. (1990). The family scene when a teenager uses drugs: Case vignettes and the role of family therapy. In A. S. Friedman, & S. Granick (Eds.), *Family therapy for adolescent drug abuse* (pp. 47–61). Lexington, MA: Lexington Books.

Vetere, A. (2001). Structural family therapy. *Child Psychology and Psychiatry, 6*, 133–139.

Wagner, B. M., Silverman, M. A. C., & Martin, C. E. (2003). Family factors in youth suicidal behaviors. *American Behavioral Scientist, 46*, 1171–1191.

Waldron, H. B. (1997). Adolescent substance abuse and family therapy outcome: A review of randomized trials. *Advances in Clinical Child Psychology, 19,* 199–234.

Walker, S. P., Grantham-McGregor, S. M., Himes, J. H., Williams, S., & Duff, E. M. (1998). School performance in adolescent Jamaican girls: Associations with health, social, and behavioral characteristics, and risk factors for drop out. *Journal of Adolescence, 21,* 109–122.

Watzlawick, P. (1990). Psychotherapy of "As If." In J. K. Zeig, & W. M. Munion (Eds.), *What is psychotherapy* (pp. 266–305). San Fransisco: Jossey-Bass.

Wells, K. C. (1988). Family therapy. In J. L. Matson (Ed.), *Handbook of treatment approaches in childhood psychopathology. Applied clinical psychology* (pp. 45–61). New York: Plenum Press.

Wetchler, J. L. (2003). Primary and secondary influential theories of family therapy supervisors: A research note. *Family Therapy, 15,* 69–74.

Wiener, D. J. (2003). Creating a participating role for adolescents in group and family therapy. In C. F. Sori, & L. L Hecker (Eds.), *The therapist's noteboook for children and adolescents* (pp. 180–184). New York: Haworth Clinical Practice Press.

Young, P. (1991). Families with adolescents. In F. H. Brown (Ed.), *Reweaving the family tapestry* (pp. 131–148). New York: W. W. Norton.

CHAPTER 5

Cognitive-Developmental Treatment of Conduct Disorder

Mark A. Reinecke

TREATMENT MODEL

Conduct disorder (CD) is both common and complex, exacting significant costs on individuals, families, communities, institutions, and society. A defining characteristic of CD is a persistent pattern of behavior in which the rights of others and social rules are violated. Youths with CD often have a history of oppositional-defiant disorder (ODD), which is characterized by a repetitive pattern of disobedient, defiant, and negativistic behavior; and attention deficit hyperactivity disorder (ADHD), which is characterized by impulsivity, motoric overactivity, inattention, and deficits in planning or executive function. CD has a prevalence rate of 6–16% for males and 2–9% for females (American Psychiatric Association, 2000a; Lahey, Miller, Gordon, & Riley, 1999; Offord, Alder, & Boyle, 1986), and is associated with significant morbidity. It is an enduring form of psychopathology and is associated with a range of behavioral, social, and emotional difficulties, including an increased risk of alcohol and substance abuse and antisocial personality disorder (APD; Frick, 1998; Loeber, Green, & Lahey, 2003). Rates of CD increase dramatically over the course of childhood and adolescence, with the rate in boys exceeding that in girls during childhood and approximately equal rates during adolescence (Hinshaw & Lee, 2003). CD is associated with significant social, academic, and vocational impairment as well as an increased risk of suicidal behavior. Taken together, these findings suggest that CD among children and adolescents is common, and that it represents a significant public health concern.

Interest in biological, environmental, social, and cognitive factors associated with CD among children and adolescents has grown during recent years as clinicians and researchers have attempted to understand factors associated with the risk for developing the disorder, develop means for identifying children who are most vulnerable, and test treatment and prevention strategies. The purpose of this chapter is to present a cognitive-developmental model for understanding the development of this disorder and to describe how it may be used in conceptualizing and treating the condition. The model represents an extension of standard cognitive and schema-focused models. It is developmental in that it postulates that CD stems from: (a) biological and genetic propensities toward affect dysregulation; (b) deficits in the acquisition of emotion regulation skills; and (c) the establishment of maladaptive tacit beliefs about oneself, others, and of the adaptiveness of destructive, oppositional, and aggressive behavior. The cognitive-developmental model is similar, in many respects, to existing cognitive-behavioral models (Dodge & Pettit, 2003; Lochman & Dodge, 1994; Reid, Patterson, & Snyder, 2002) in that it emphasizes the central role of cognitive and perceptual processes in the development and maintenance of the disorder. It is conceptually broader than traditional cognitive-behavioral approaches in that it incorporates insights from the developmental psychopathology literature (DeKlyen & Speltz, 2001; Loeber et al., 2003; Pettit, 2004; Rutter, 2003; Tremblay, 2000). Specifically, it postulates that CD may be understood from a developmental-systems perspective, that factors associated with risk for the condition transactionally influence one another over time in contributing to vulnerability, that there may be several developmental pathways or trajectories leading to this disorder, and that prevention and treatment strategies should be directed toward ameliorating cognitive, behavioral, social, and affective risk factors. In this chapter links are proposed between early experience, attachment security, the development of maladaptive beliefs and coping strategies, and the emergence of symptoms of CD. It is a biopsychosocial model insofar as it attends to the broad range of factors implicated in the etiology of the disorder, and provides a framework for generating testable hypotheses regarding the development of the condition and for treatment.

A Heterogeneous Condition

In the beginning of our discussion on CD, it is worth acknowledging that it has been conceptualized in a number of ways: (a) diagnostic criteria have changed substantially over the years, (b) it overlaps with a number of conditions and problems, and (c) youths who meet criteria for CD present with an array of behaviors and comorbid conditions. Not every youngster who is aggressive, for example, manifests CD (a child who is violent toward a sibling may, for example, be otherwise reasonably well-adjusted) and not every individual who manifests CD is aggressive (e.g., a teen who is frequently truant, steals, and engages in vandalism, but is not violent or aggressive toward others). CD is a complex condition, in terms of its developmental psychopathology, course, and clinical presentation. Any integrative model of CD must attend to developmental and gender differences in the disorder, and to variations in symptoms and patterns of comorbidity (Costello & Angold, 1993).

With these considerations in mind, what can be said with confidence regarding the development of this condition? First, although children with CD are heterogeneous with regard to clinical presentation and course, there appear to be common or shared mechanisms or processes. Second, although early adverse experiences may place individuals at risk for developing CD, there is a great deal of diversity in how children respond to these events. Vulnerability factors appear to act in a cumulative manner. The greater the number, range, severity, and duration of risk factors, the greater the likelihood that a child will develop the disorder. It is the accumulation of events, and the effects that these experiences have on subsequent coping, that render children vulnerable. Adverse experiences appear to contribute to the development of CD by interfering with normative developmental processes. Over time, vulnerable children may fail to acquire the skills needed to cope with life's challenges and frustrations, engendering feelings of anger, resentment, and sadness. Third, the ways in which individuals think about their experiences matters. What children learn about themselves and their relationships with others can influence the ways in which they process information and understand later relationships and events. Experiences which lead to reduced feelings of efficacy, control, or worth, and that lead individuals to perceive aggressive or oppositional behavior as reasonable and adaptive, make it more likely that the child will act in ways that elicit a negative reaction from others.

Definition and Scope

"Conduct disorder" is a term that refers to behaviors that reflect the inability of an individual to conform to social norms, authority figures, or to respect the rights of others. These behaviors can range from the simply annoying to the explosively violent. Individuals with CD are often irritable, provocative, or argumentative, and may engage in stealing, vandalism, and physical harm to others. Emotionally, youths with CD often experience feelings of resentment, frustration, and anger. Affect regulation is often poor. They appear to lack effective cognitive, behavioral, and emotional skills for attending to internal emotional states and for managing feelings of anger and frustration. Individuals with CD are, as a consequence, often described as moody or emotionally labile; relationships frequently are conflicted, particularly with parents, teachers, and other authority figures.

To be sure, some amount of aggression is to be expected, particularly among younger children, and some level of resistance to authority figures is normative among adolescents. CD, then, represents a deviation from a normative developmental course. These are youths who are *excessively* aggressive, antisocial, oppositional, destructive, or provocative, and who demonstrate these behaviors in socially inappropriate ways.

Youths with CD can manifest a varied range of social and behavioral problems. That said, few children with CD demonstrate only one type of behavior problem in the absence of others (Frick et al., 1993). The fact that associations have been observed between these behaviors suggests that they may reflect a single psychological dimension and that shared etiological factors may be at play.

Insofar as CD is a clinical syndrome with a broad list of symptoms, it is not surprising that a great deal of heterogeneity is found among youths who receive the diagnosis. It is possible, as well, that different subtypes of the disorder exist, each of which may be associated with a different constellation of vulnerability factors, course, prognosis, and response to treatment (NICHD Early Child Care Research Network, 2004). There is little consensus, however, as to the most appropriate scheme for classifying subtypes. The *Diagnostic and Statistical Manual of Mental Disorders-IV-TR* (DSM-IV-TR; American Psychiatric Association, 2000b) classification system distinguishes children who begin showing conduct problems in early childhood from those who first demonstrate symptoms during adolescence. Early-onset CD is typically associated with aggressive behavior, whereas adolescent-onset CD is more often associated with socialized, delinquent behavior (such as vandalism).

CD is characterized by labile affect, feelings of frustration, resentment and anger, conflicted relationships, and aggressive behavior. These difficulties are often long-standing, recurrent, and seriously impair relationships, academic performance, and work. Whereas there appears to be a number of developmental pathways culminating in the emergence of CD (Nagin & Tremblay, 1999), they appear to share at least two factors—(a) deficits in the development of affect regulation capacities, and (b) the establishment of beliefs about the reasonableness of behavior that violates the norms of the larger society.

Development of Conduct Disorder

Although the causes of CD are not known, a number of biological and psychosocial variables have been associated with the risk for developing this disorder (Lahey, Waldman, & McBurnett, 1999; Loeber & Farrington, 2000; Pettit, 2004; Rutter, 2003; Tremblay, 2000). Risk factors include conditions, events, experiences, or variables that are associated with an increased likelihood of developing a disorder. They need not, however, be causally related to the development of the condition. Although low socioeconomic status (SES) and a chaotic home environment, for example, have been associated with an increased risk of developing this condition, they appear to be neither necessary nor sufficient for developing the disorder. Rather, they may be seen as "predictive markers" or "contributory factors" in that they are associated with increased incidence. Therefore, it is important not only to identify relationships among factors that predict the emergence of CD, but also to clarify *how* they contribute to the development of the condition. Moreover, it is necessary to distinguish factors that are associated with an increased risk (i.e., predictors of onset) from those that are associated with severity, course, and treatment response. It is important, as well, to determine whether there are "critical" or "sensitive" periods during which exposure to a vulnerability factor will have a more deleterious effect. Models should attend to whether risk factors must persist for a specific duration in order to exert their effects (i.e., Does, for example, the length of time a child is exposed to a risk factor matter? Is there a dose–outcome relationship?). Finally, it is necessary to determine whether there are protective factors or buffers that moderate the effects of risk factors and which may serve as a source of resilience (Rutter, 1985).

Predictors of CD include biological vulnerabilities, the child's behavior and adaptive capacities, characteristics of their home and social environments, parental discipline practices, and parental emotions. Understanding relationships between these factors is important for at least two reasons. First, they serve as a foundation for understanding the developmental psychopathology of this condition. As importantly, they may allow us to identify youths who are most at risk, and serve as a focus for preventative efforts. Specific factors associated with vulnerability for the developing CD, as well as protective factors, can be found in Table 5.1.

Findings from the Developmental Trends Study (Loeber et al., 2003) indicate that low SES, a history of ODD and parental substance abuse are strongly associated with the risk for developing CD. Youths with a history of early physical fighting or recurrent aggression are at particularly high risk. Moreover, a significant number of youths with CD also report histories of conflict with parents and peers as children, as well as histories of punitive, inconsistent parental discipline. Studies suggest, as well, that biological factors

TABLE 5.1
Factors Associated with Vulnerability for CD

Risk factors	Protective factors
Low SES; neighborhood poverty	No familial history of psychiatric illness
History of ADHD or ODD	No apparent genetic vulnerability
Parental substance abuse and/or antisocial behavior	No prenatal alcohol or drug exposure; no maternal smoking
Difficult temperament type	Easy temperament type; easy to soothe as an infant
Punitive parenting, neglect	Positive parents (responsive, reliable, supportive, nonpunitive, models of effective affect regulation, and conflict management)
Childhood victimization	
Negative peer group; rejection by peers	Supportive relationships with prosocial peers
Poor social skills	Social skills
	Empathy, social perspective taking
	Effective social problem solving
	Family stability
	Secure attachment
	Positive relationship with an adult outside the family
	Limited exposure to violent media, games

may be implicated in the development and maintenance of CD. Specifically, systems involved in the regulation of attention and arousal may be affected in individuals with externalizing behavior problems (Caspi et al., 2002). How is it that these factors interact in contributing to the development of CD? It can be argued that each of these factors may be associated with difficulties in the acquisition of emotion regulation skills and that aggressive, oppositional behavior is modeled and reinforced.

It appears that CD, like other psychiatric conditions, is multiply determined. CD may be understood as stemming from transactional relations between genetic, biological, social, and psychological vulnerability factors over the course of development (Dodge & Pettit, 2003; Pettit, 2004).

Toward an Integrated Cognitive-Developmental Model

The question, then, arises—how does this constellation of risk and protective factors contribute to the emergence of symptoms of CD? What are the mechanisms by which early experience, familial psychopathology, genetic factors, cognitive variables, and environmental variables interact in contributing to risk? Although a number of models have been proposed (Deater-Deckard, Dodge, Bates, & Pettit, 1998; Dodge & Pettit, 2003; Kazdin, 1993; Lahey & Loeber, 1994; Lahey et al., 1999), a consensus has not yet emerged for understanding how these variables influence one another in the etiology and maintenance of the disorder. No individual risk factor or set of factors has been found to be necessary or sufficient for the development of CD. Rather, findings from prospective longitudinal studies are consistent with a hierarchical model of development (Lahey & Loeber, 1994; Loeber, Green, Keenan, & Lahey, 1995). At this point, then, it may be best to acknowledge that risk factors tend to co-occur, that the development of the disorder is predicted by a convergence of risk factors rather than by one or two variables, and that individual factors might best be viewed as "contributory" rather than "causal" (Rutter, 2003). With this in mind, we hypothesize that

1. Parents who do not provide a consistent, supportive, nurturant, and responsive home environment place their children at risk for the development of CD;
2. Early-onset CD may be characterized by failures in the development of affect regulation skills;
3. Genetic and biological vulnerabilities related to temperament, sociability, impulsivity, and affective dysregulation interact with parenting style to contribute to the development of an insecure or avoidant attachment style;
4. Insecure or avoidant attachment style is a nonspecific predictor of several forms of psychopathology, including CD. Insecure or avoidant attachment places the individual at risk for the development of maladaptive schemata regarding self-worth, security within relationships, and impaired perceptions of self-efficacy;
5. Punitive, inconsistent discipline is associated with the development and consolidation of oppositional and aggressive patterns of social behavior;
6. Maladaptive tacit beliefs or schema regarding control and personal worth, when activated by specific life events, serve as proximal risk factors for behavioral and emotional symptoms of CD.

Individuals may manifest a genetic or biological vulnerability in that they may be temperamentally impulsive, labile, or aggressive. Genetic and biological factors may exert their effects indirectly, as well, contributing to the "activation" of social or environmental factors that are also associated with vulnerability. A temperamentally impulsive, labile, or inconsolable child, for example, may frustrate their parents, eliciting punitive discipline. As Pettit (2004, p. 195) succinctly notes, "Life experiences… may be the means through which inherited dispositions exert an impact on later antisocial outcomes."

Inconsistent or punitive parenting may exacerbate these emerging behavioral and emotional problems in several ways. They interfere with the development of affect regulation skills and contribute to the establishment of maladaptive belief systems and problem-solving styles. Social factors, such as a punitive or stressful environment, also may act indirectly by interacting with genetic factors in contributing to risk. Genetic vulnerabilities may tend to be expressed under conditions of environmental stress (Caspi et al., 2002). Genetic and biological factors, from this perspective, may contribute to the establishment of high-risk environments. Punitive, inconsistent discipline and poor monitoring, as well as breakdowns in the development of adaptive problem solving, social, and affect regulation skills may mediate associations between larger, contextual risk factors (such as SES and community cohesion) and the development of CD.

Beliefs, expectations, and attributions that characterize CD, as well as patterns of oppositional and aggressive social behavior, may be modeled and reinforced by family members and peers. Patterson (1982) argues that impulsive, difficult children who grow up with parents who readily become frustrated and who attempt to discipline them in harsh, punitive ways learn that, if they escalate their angry oppositionality, their parents will ultimately relent. This, in turn, reinforces the escalation of their anger and their oppositionality. When interacting with other adults, such as teachers, who wish for children to behave in a calm, compliant manner, these behavioral approaches can lead to confrontation. As they have not learned adaptive social and affect regulation skills, they may seek out other children who, like themselves, have had less success academically and socially. These negative peer groups will tend to model, encourage, and support further oppositional and aggressive behavior.

Emotional factors (including the activation of feelings of shame, anger, frustration, or resentment) may interact with cognitive factors (such as the perception of malicious intent on the part of others and beliefs about the value and appropriateness of aggressive behavior) in mediating associations between social experiences and the emergence of symptoms of CD. It is not adverse social experiences, per se, that are associated with risk so much as the meanings the child attaches to them. Cognitive factors are postulated to mediate between early experiences and the development of this condition. Temperament, early experience, and social context contribute to the development of CD by facilitating the development of maladaptive beliefs and by impeding the acquisition of more adaptive beliefs and the development of more effective social skills. Cognitive, social, and affect regulation skills, then, become the focus of therapy and prevention efforts.

For all of us, knowledge structures serve as a link between early experience and later behavior. We learn from our experiences and use this knowledge to guide us in responding to novel, fluidly changing social situations. For the child or adolescent with CD, tacit beliefs, attitudes, expectations, and perceptual biases influence the interpretation of social events and guide their behavior. Through practice and reinforcement, these beliefs and attitudes become consolidated, leading to characteristic ways of interpreting social events and "scripts" for responding to them.

Based on their early experiences (i.e., insecure or avoidant attachment), youths with CD come to anticipate that others will be inconsistent, unreliable, unsupportive, and potentially harsh or punitive. When placed in an unfamiliar or threatening social setting, they will be attentive to cues suggestive of risk (such as facial expressions or hand gestures). They are perceptually wary. When a cue is observed, this is compared with memories of similar situations in the past. Memory processes of youths with CD may be biased such that they are more likely to recall instances of threat or conflict. They then interpret the event as benign or threatening. Should an appraisal be made that the event is threatening, the child will quickly access behavioral response "scripts" of alternative courses of action. Based on beliefs they hold about the appropriateness of these courses of action (e.g., "One has to be strong," "Never back down," "People only respect you if you're tough," "They have it coming"), the child selects a course of action. Social scripts often are associated with emotional states. They are not simply intellectual plans, but carry an emotional valence. These associated emotions serve both an organizing and motivational function. Once initiated, these scripts typically run to completion. The child or adolescent may later report that he "couldn't stop" himself. Cognitive processing, then, occurs in a sequential manner, with the opportunity for maladaptive processing at each of the fives stages (attention, perception, script selection, belief activation, and organization/motivation). Processing at each step is necessary for an individual to respond in an oppositional, aggressive, or antisocial manner. Conversely, interfering with this process at any of the stages will disrupt the behavior of the child. The cognitive-developmental model of CD is presented in Figure 5.1.

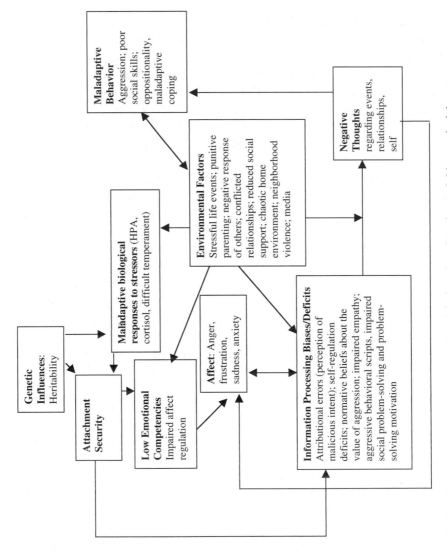

FIGURE 5.1 Cognitive-developmental model of conduct disorder in children and adolescents.

Treatment Implications

A number of approaches have been developed for treating children with behavioral problems, including CD (for reviews see Baer & Nietzel, 1991; Brosnan & Carr, 2000; Dumas, 1989; Durlak, Fuhrman, & Lampman, 1991; Fonagy & Kurtz, 2002; Kazdin, 2001). Brestan and Eyberg (1998), for example, reviewed findings from 82 controlled treatment studies of psychosocial interventions for children and adolescents with CD. From this literature, 12 different approaches have received empirical support and might be characterized as "well established" or "probably efficacious." Of these, four stand out as the most promising (Nock, 2003). Parent management training (PMT; Dishion & Andrews, 1995; Dishion, Patterson, & Cavanaugh, 1992; Graziano & Diament, 1992; Long, Forehand, Wierson, & Morgan, 1994), Cognitive Problem-Solving Skills Training (PSST; Fiendler & Ecton, 1986; Kazdin, 1997), Functional Family Ttherapy (FFT; Alexander, Barton, Schiavo, & Parsons, 1976; Alexander & Parsons, 1982) and Multisystemic Therapy (MST; Henggeler & Borduin, 1990; Henggeler et al., 1986; Henggeler, Schoenwald, Borduin, Rowland, & Cunningham, 1998). These treatment approaches have been found to yield durable, clinically important improvement in randomized controlled trials with clinically referred youths. What characteristics do these effective treatments for CD share?

First, like many empirically supported forms of therapy, they are intensive, highly structured, and problem focused. Interventions for each are described in treatment manuals, and each explicitly attempts to address problematic behavior. In PMT, for example, parents meet with a therapist who instructs them in specific procedures for altering coercive, negativistic interactions with their children. Similarly, in PSST children are systematically taught how to approach problematic interpersonal situations. Adaptive, prosocial behavior and cognitive skills are modeled and reinforced. Second, each of these therapies includes psychoeducational components. A rationale is developed and shared with the child and his parents. This rationale provides them with an understanding of factors that may be contributing to their difficulties, and so may develop their motivation for interacting in a more constructive manner. Third, each of these approaches explicitly attends to the social contexts in which children function. Treatment, from this perspective, is multimodal, behavioral, and skills oriented. They do not explicitly focus on providing the child or adolescent with insight into motivations or intrapsychic defenses, or emphasize the interpretation of emergent processes within the therapeutic relationship. Rather, an emphasis is placed on understanding and changing problematic behavior as they occur in children's day-to-day relationships with their parents, teachers, and peers. Fourth, each of these treatments encourages the active involvement of the child's parents. This involvement is most apparent in PMT, FFT, and MST. Finally, each of these treatments specifically addresses a behavioral, social, and cognitive factor associated with vulnerability for CD. PMT, for example, explicitly encourages parents to identify and address behavioral problems in new ways. Parent–child interaction problems are directly discussed and rectified. In a similar manner, PSST focuses upon cognitive factors, including problem-solving skills, associated with the disorder. An explicit focus is placed on assisting the child to more adaptively generate alternative solutions, appreciate how others may feel, identify the consequences of their actions, and develop more reasonable attributions about the behavior of others. Cognitive-developmental psychotherapy shares these characteristics.

Cognitive-developmental interventions focus on: (a) directing attention away from threatening cues (or toward indicators that others might respond in a kind, supportive manner); (b) encouraging benign interpretations of others' behavior (rather than viewing others as malicious); (c) developing and rehearsing alternative, more adaptive social scripts; (d) rectifying maladaptive beliefs, expectations, and schema regarding self-worth and the appropriateness of aggressive or antisocial behavior, and (e) developing affect regulation skills.

The notion that attachment theory and research may have implications for psychotherapy is not new (Belsky & Nezworski, 1988; Bowlby, 1944; Holmes, 1993). How might the treatment of CD be improved by attention to the role of attachment and affect regulation? First, it directs our attention to early parent–child interaction patterns and their role in the development of children's beliefs, social skills, and emotion regulation abilities. Avoidance, resistance, and oppositional behavior are understood from this perspective as reflecting learned strategies for coping with difficulties in relationships with parents and other key figures in the child's life, and as serving an adaptive function for the child. Second, findings from the attachment literature may guide the identification of subgroups of children with CD, and so may assist with case formulation. We do not presume, for example, that all youths with CD manifest an insecure, avoidant, or disorganized attachment style. Some children and parents may have a secure attachment, which would bode well for collaborative forms of therapy. For parents who experience difficulty responding reliably to the needs of their child, who respond inconsistently and punitively, or who are emotionally unresponsive, a therapeutic focus might be placed on understanding their perceptions, expectations, and attributions about their child's behavior. Consistent with cognitive-behavioral models of psychopathology, attachment theory emphasizes the importance of understanding how children, adolescents, and parents understand their experiences and construct meanings, and focuses our attention on the importance of developing parent–child relationships that are responsive, reliable, nurturing, consistent, caring, and predictable. Cognitive-developmental therapy explicitly assists caretakers in developing more effective, positive parenting skills, and so facilitates the development of more secure attachment relationships.

Cognitive-developmental psychotherapy interventions are directed toward: (a) developing children's emotion regulation skills; (b) addressing beliefs that aggressive and oppositional behavior is reasonable, appropriate, and adaptive; (c) improving social problem-solving skills and motivation; (d) enhancing children's perceptions of efficacy and control; (e) addressing tacit beliefs that others are unreliable, punitive, and uncaring; and (f) improving the quality of the parent–child relationship. Strategies can include training in positive parenting practices, parent support groups, developing reasonable parental expectations for children's behavior, and anger management sessions.

Developing a more secure parent–child relationship is an important focus in cognitive-developmental psychotherapy. With younger children, this therapy may take the form of teaching parents how to engage their child in a warm, nonpunitive, and nondirective manner. They are encouraged to play together on a regular basis, to respond to their child in a predictable, nurturing manner. Quite often, parents of children with CD are exasperated by their child's behavior. This can lead them to feel a reduced sense of competence, efficacy, and worth as a parent. Their child appears, in many ways, to be "out of control," and they view their child's oppositional or aggressive behavior as intentional or malicious. Therapy sessions may focus, at least in part, on understanding parents' thoughts and feelings about their child's behavior, and the attributions they are making about its causes. As in other forms of cognitive therapy, maladaptive beliefs, expectations, and attributions are directly addressed through psychoeducation, rational disputation, and behavioral experiments.

Adolescents with CD typically have conflicted relationships with their parents. In cognitive-developmental therapy we work directly to address this problem. We begin by asking the teenager and his parents to think back to a point in time when they had a closer, warmer relationship. Most families are able to do this, and recount a time (typically during early childhood) when they enjoyed each other's company and had a close, more affectionate relationship. They are asked to describe their relationship at that time in some detail, to recall their feelings toward one another at that time, and to discuss how this leads them to feel about themselves. Most families report wishing that they could have better relationships and are able to discuss their frustration and disappointment with the current state of affairs.

Developing a clear memory of a positive past parent–child relationship (or, at least, more positive than their current relationship) allows adolescents and their parents to begin to develop an image of a closer, more secure future relationship—a *possible* relationship—that they can work toward. The adolescent and his parents are next asked what they have done to bring about this more positive relationship. Given the conflicted, often coercive, nature of their interactions, most families acknowledge that they have done little to accomplish this. Working collaboratively, behavioral strategies are then developed to improve the quality of their relationship at home. This may include simple behavioral techniques, such as increasing random, kind gestures (which we refer to as "gives") and showing appreciation for what others have done for you (referred to as "gets"). We work with parents and teenagers to reduce the frequency of critical, demanding statements, and to increase the frequency of empathic reflective statements. Modeling and role-plays are regularly used in session, and we review their success in implementing these approaches at home.

Prevention

Given its focus on the importance of early parent–child relationships for understanding CD, the cognitive-developmental model may have implications for prevention efforts. A number of multicomponent prevention programs have been developed during recent years. As a group, they tend to focus upon developing cognitive, social, and affect regulation skills, and on addressing parental child rearing skills (Beelman, Pfingsten, & Losel, 1994; Catalano, Arthur, Hawkins, Berglund, & Olson, 1998; Farrington & Welsh, 1999; Lipsey & Wilson, 1998; Tremblay, LeMarquand, & Vitaro, 1999). Early intervention programs such as Fast Track developed by the Conduct Problems Prevention Research Group (1992, 1999) are promising.

Although several of these programs have focused on developing affect regulation, problem solving, and social skills, it is worth acknowledging that there have not, to our knowledge, been controlled studies examining whether improving parent–child relationships and developing a secure parent–child attachment will reduce the likelihood developing CD. Research into prevention of externalizing behavior problems, although promising, is quite limited. Methodological shortcomings center on the types of control groups used, sample sizes and power, demonstrations of the integrity of the interventions, and generalizability of findings. Moreover, processes by which these interventions reduce the risk of developing behavioral problems are not well understood. It has not been demonstrated, for example, that prevention efforts that focus upon developing affect regulation skills and improving children's social problem-solving abilities exert their effects by enhancing these important skills.

Directions for Research

As Kazdin (2000) and Nock (2003) have noted, progress in psychotherapy research tends to follow identifiable steps. Cognitive-developmental models are new, and treatment strategies based on them are largely untested. A study of 391 children between 10 and 17 years of age found that attachment-based interventions were effective in reducing the severity CD behavior, and that gains were maintained at 18 months, with both children and caregivers reporting decreased behavioral problems. (Holland, Moretti, Verlaan, & Peterson, 1993; Moretti, Holland, & Peterson, 1994). The lack of a control group however represents an important shortcoming. Cognitive-developmental therapy does not yet stand, then, as an empiricallysupported form of psychotherapy. Treatment manuals have not been developed, and initial randomized controlled efficacy trials have not been completed. At this point, then, it may be more appropriate to view cognitive-developmental therapy as an empirically informed paradigm for understanding processes of change in different forms of psychotherapy, rather than as an independent therapeutic school of thought. Attachment-based strategies might be viewed as "adjuncts" that may enhance the effectiveness and generalizability of other forms of therapy (such as PSST, PMT, FFT, and MST) across conditions, settings, and populations. As we have seen, effective forms of psychotherapy for CD share a number of features. The active components of therapy may be present, in different amounts, in different forms of therapy. Attachment theory may provide a paradigm for understanding these commonalities, and for identifying shared mechanisms of change across therapeutic models. This, in turn, may allow us to refine our techniques and to develop more powerful prevention strategies.

Research on the treatment of CD is, in many ways, a young endeavor. As we have seen, several forms of therapy have been found to be efficacious in randomized controlled trials. Research is needed, however, into moderators and predictors of improvement. We have not yet addressed the important question: "Which treatment is most effective for which child under which conditions?" The effects of severity, age of onset, and comorbity on treatment outcome are largely unexplored. At the same time, our understanding of processes of change in psychotherapy for CD is limited. Dismantling studies to identify therapeutic strategies and techniques most associated with clinical improvement are needed, as are studies of mediators of change. Given the range of cognitive, social, environmental, and biological factors implicated in the etiology and maintenance of the disorder, much remains to be done. At the same time basic research into the nature of attachment during later childhood and adolescence is warranted. There are, for example, no well-validated techniques for assessing attachment security during adolescence (Goldberg, 1997). Outcome and process research is an iterative process. Research into the developmental psychopathology of CD, including the role of attachment security will, over time, inform the development of more effective interventions.

Attachment theory was developed as a means of understanding relations between parent–infant interactions and the development of psychopathology in at risk children. Although based on observations of parents and their children in clinical settings, it has received its fullest explication as a framework for understanding normal social and emotional development. At the same time, cognitive therapy has emerged as powerful model for understanding behavioral and emotional disorders and their treatment. Studies indicate that associations may exist between attachment security, neuroendocrine function, and the establishment of maladaptive beliefs. The ways in which these systems influence social behavior during later childhood and adolescence, however, is not clear.

Relatively little prospective research has been completed on the social and emotional consequences of insecure, avoidant, and disorganized attachment, and of factors influencing the stability of attachment styles over time. Although insecure-avoidant and disorganized attachment styles during infancy appear to be associated with an increased risk of developing externalizing behavior problems during early childhood (Erickson, Sroufe, & Egeland, 1985; Goldberg, 1997; Lewis, Feiring, McGuffog, & Jaskir, 1984; Lyons-Ruth, Alpern, & Repacholi, 1993; Renken, Egeland, Marvinney, Mangelsdorf, & Sroufe, 1989), links between attachment security and vulnerability for psychopathology during later childhood and adolescence have not yet been demonstrated.

THE CASE OF "MIKE"
Conceptualization, Assessment, and Treatment Planning
Additional Information

Following the cognitive-developmental model, the therapist will want to assess factors that may be contributing to or maintaining Mike's difficulties. As can be seen in Table 5.2, Mike appears to manifest a number of factors

TABLE 5.2
Risk and Protective Factors for Mike

Risk factors	Case example—Mike
A. Low SES; neighborhood poverty	No, though financial stress
B. History of ADHD or ODD	Possible
C. Parental substance abuse	Paternal alcohol abuse
D. Parental antisocial behavior	Unclear, Possible
E. Difficult temperament type	Yes, likely
F. Punitive parenting, neglect	Yes, likely
G. Childhood victimization	No, None reported
H. Negative peer group; rejection by peers	Yes
I. Poor social skills	Variable
Protective factors	
J. No familial history of psychiatric illness	No
K. No apparent genetic vulnerability	No
L. No prenatal alcohol or drug exposure	Unknown
M. No maternal smoking	Unknown
N. Easy temperament type	No
O. Family stability	No
P. Positive parents	No
Q. Secure attachment	No, Unlikely
R. Positive relationships with adults	No, none reported
S. Empathy, social perspective taking	Unknown
T. Social skills	Variable
U. Effective social problem solving	No, poor motivation
V. Supportive, prosocial peers	No
1. Limited exposure to violent media, games	No, unlikely

associated with risk for developing CD, and has been exposed to relatively few protective factors.

The therapist will want to evaluate each of these domains, paying particular attention to understanding how Mike manages his feelings of anger, frustration, and resentment, his beliefs regarding the value and appropriateness of his behavior, the attributions he is making about the behavior of others, and his views of his relationships with his parents. Both objective and subjective approaches may be used. Our goal is to maintain an objective stance, and to balance this with an appreciation of Mike's subjective experience.

It is quite common for adolescents who are brought to therapy by their parents to remain "defiantly silent" when they first come to our offices. I typically begin by having the family join me in the office and by asking a parent to describe his or her motivation for seeking treatment for their child. I would invite Mike to participate in the discussion, and would let him know that it is entirely all right for him to sit and listen. Most often, as parents recite their litany of concerns, the teen will become agitated, and will feel a need to defend himself. After Mike's parents have developed a problem list, described the development of his problems, and discussed their fears for his future, I will ask if they feel I have understood their concerns (at least in broad brush strokes), and if there is anything else that may be important for me to know. It will be important for Mike's parents (particularly Ms. D.) to feel understood and validated, as she will be responsible for bringing Mike to therapy. I would then ask them to leave the room so that I might talk with Mike in private. Turning to Mike, I would acknowledge how broad and significant the problem list is and invite him to "share his side of the story." By patiently addressing each of the issues his parents have discussed, as well as life events that are associated with risk for CD, Mike will be able to share his views of his life and his relationships with his parents.

Objective rating scales and semistructured diagnostic instruments are often used in cognitive-developmental psychotherapy. It may be helpful, for example, to complete the Schedule for Affective Disorders and Schizophrenia for School-Aged Children (K-SADS), a structured diagnostic interview (Puig-Antich & Chambers, 1978) with Mike and his mother to clarify his diagnosis. It will be important to know if he has any history of major depression, bipolar disorder, ADHD, or ODD, and to confirm the diagnosis of CD. It will also be important to clarify his history of cannabis use, and to rule out other substance abuse or alcohol use.

It appears there may be a family history of psychopathology. His father, for example, has a history of explosive rage and alcohol use. It would be interesting to know how Ms. D. has felt, and if she has any history of depression, anger, or substance use. It would not be surprising, for example, to find that she has felt depressed, anxious, or overwhelmed since her separation from Mr. D. Her family has come under increasing financial stress, and she appears to feel overmatched by her son's behavioral problems. Feelings of depression and anxiety would be understandable, and might make her less emotionally available to her son.

Objective rating scales, such as the parent and teacher versions of the Child Behavior Checklist (CBCh; Achenbach, 1991) can be useful for identifying behavioral problems at home and school, and for monitoring treatment gains.

Therapeutic Goals

When working with adolescents and their parents it is critically important to identify therapeutic goals that all can share. It may be helpful to have both Mike and his mother independently list their goals for treatment and how they would know if they have been accomplished. Ms. D. is concerned by her son's shoplifting, anger, argumentativeness, poor school performance, oppositional behavior, and cannabis abuse. Although Mike denies seeing any need for therapy, he acknowledges that he does not like being viewed as the "black sheep" of the family, that he does not like demands being placed on him, and that he does not like visiting his father. Mike stated that he may be interested in completing high school and in joining the military. His desire to pursue these vocational goals may allow us to engage him in talking about other, shorter-term goals. Although Mike does not believe that he is in need of therapy, he would, I suspect, readily acknowledge that he is frustrated with much in his life. Simply asking, "Is your life *perfect*? What could be *better* for you at home? At school?" may allow him to discuss his frustrations, anxieties, resentments, insecurities, and goals. Although he is at least nominally supportive of the therapeutic process, Mr. D.'s goals for treatment are not clear.

Reasonable primary goals would include: (a) reducing the frequency of Mike's shoplifting and theft from home, (b) improving class attendance, (c) reducing his feelings of anger and frustration, (d) reducing the frequency and severity of conflict with his sister, (e) reducing the frequency and severity of oppositional behavior toward his mother and teachers, and (f) reducing or eliminating his cannabis use. At the same time secondary goals for treatment might be to (a) develop Mike's emotion regulation skills, (b) improve the quality of his relationship with his parents, (c) improve his social problem-solving skills, and (d) address maladaptive beliefs he may have about the reasonableness and adaptiveness of his oppositional, aggressive, and antisocial behavior.

Length of Treatment

Treatment duration can vary depending on a number of factors, including Mike's motivation to participate, specific goals, and the presence of comorbid conditions. Parental motivation and support from Mike's teachers and school officials also can influence the course of treatment. Cognitive-developmental therapy, like other forms of CBT, is active, problem oriented, and strategic. As noted, the techniques of cognitive-developmental therapy can be used as "augmentation strategies" with other, empirically supported forms of psychotherapy. Problem Solving Skills Training, for example, consists of 12–20 weekly therapy sessions with the child, which may be supplemented with additional sessions if the child requires further assistance. The core interventions in Parent Management Training are provided over the course of 12–16 weekly sessions with parents and teachers. Cognitive-developmental interventions may be incorporated into PSST or PMT sessions, or may be included as supplementary sessions. For patients with moderate to severe CD, sessions are held weekly for approximately 6 months. Sessions are held more frequently if needed.

Case Conceptualization

As noted, a number of biological, environmental, social, and cognitive factors appear to contribute to Mike's behavioral and emotional problems. It appears as though biological and temperamental factors were present and served as a substrate for his difficulties. Mike was a colicky, difficult infant, and his parents may have found him frustrating as an infant and toddler (Did they draw comparisons with a "perfect" older sister?), and so may have responded to him in a less than optimally consistent, reliable, and supportive manner. The possibility exists that he demonstrated an insecure, avoidant, or disorganized attachment to one or both of his parents. This pattern would serve as a template for the development of tacit beliefs about relationships with others.

Mike's father reportedly was a harsh, unpredictable disciplinarian. He is affectively labile and has a history of alcohol abuse. The possibility exists that Mike felt unsure of how to maintain a close, supportive relationship with his father. This sense of uncertainty—not knowing whether to turn to his father for support, or to avoid him due to fear of his angry outbursts—sets the stage for his ambivalent relationship with his father and with other authority figures. It is postulated that he came to view others as like his father—unreliable, uncaring, critical, and rejecting. Mike has become vigilant, anticipating that others will behave in a harmful manner, and may inappropriately attribute other's behaviors to malicious intent. Youths with CD frequently view their behavior as reasonable and adaptive. Mike acknowledges that it is important to be viewed as a "tough guy"—strong, invincible, and in control.

Mike's affect regulation and problem-solving skills appear to be poorly developed. His mood is labile and his behavior is impulsive. It is likely that Mike's father neither modeled nor reinforced calm, reflective problem solving, or helped Mike to calm himself when he became upset. Emotion regulation skills, like other adaptive capacities, are learned in a social context. It is not clear that Mike was able to learn these important skills from his parents.

As Patterson (1982) suggests, coercive family interaction patterns may contribute to the development of CD among children. We do not have information regarding how conflicts were resolved between Mike and his parents during his childhood. It is plausible to suggest that, given his father's punitive discipline style, a coercive pattern may have emerged. Mike's mother reportedly manifests an air of resignation, which may stem from a history of being unable to influence her son's increasingly oppositional behavior.

Although Mike was inattentive and somewhat oppositional as a child, his conduct problems did not emerge until 11 years of age when parents decided to separate and divorce. It is plausible to suggest that the change in Mike's behavior may have stemmed from feelings of insecurity and anger regarding the loss of an organized (albeit somewhat chaotic) family. Mike's father has not consistently been supportive or available, exacerbating Mike's feelings of insecurity. As Ms. D. remarked, Mike often shoves his sister so that she "has to get involved." Indeed. Mike's aggressive, oppositional behavior may serve an adaptive function in that it re-establishes and maintains an attachment to his mother. This hypothesis is consistent with Ms. D.'s comment that, since the divorce she has taken a position as a secretary, and so has been less available to her children.

Children begin, during early adolescence, to identify with peer groups (most often of the same sex). This identification with peers (referred to during years past as "chums") serves a developmental function in that it facilitates the development of social skills and provides support as the child becomes autonomous from their family. Unfortunately, Mike has been drawn toward a group of peers who, like himself, are experiencing behavioral and emotional challenges. They appear to both model and support his oppositional, aggressive, and antisocial behavior.

The Therapeutic Relationship

Cognitive-developmental psychotherapy emphasizes the importance of therapeutic warmth, responsiveness, reliability or consistency, nurturance, and predictability as a foundation for therapeutic progress. As in CBT, nonspecific therapeutic factors are seen as necessary but not sufficient for change. Studies indicate that effective parents provide "frames" or "scaffolds" to guide their child's development. These frames take several forms and serve several functions. Effective parents are nurturing in that they are emotionally warm and appropriately affectionate, and provide for the child's basic needs. They are protective in that they take steps to ensure the child's safety, and prevent the child from engaging in activities that may harm themselves or others. They have clear and reasonable expectations, and place clear limits on inappropriate or dangerous behavior. They provide instrumental support for developing important skills (often by challenging the child within the zone of proximal development). They provide feedback on the child's performance, and consistently reinforce their efforts and their successes. They model and rehearse adaptive behavior and more advanced skills. Often this modeling takes the form of failure with a task, persistence in attempting to solve it, flexibility in attempting various solutions, and patiently developing a skilled solution, and practicing the newly acquired skill. They encourage reciprocity within relationships and facilitate the development of social perspective taking skills. Finally, they serve a memory function in that they direct the child to reflect on past experiences that may inform their understanding of current problems. The therapeutic relationship functions in a similar manner. From this perspective the processes of change in psychotherapy and in normative development are essentially similar. The therapist guides the child's development by actively attempting to provide "frames" for addressing behavioral and emotional difficulties within the therapy session, and by assisting parents to employ child rearing practices that are warm, responsive, reliable, consistent, nurturant, and predictable.

Areas to Avoid
There are no specific problems or topics that, if raised by Mike or his parents, we would want to avoid. Certain clinical problems, however, might be better addressed with other clinical strategies. If, for example, Mike began to experiment with other drugs, such as cocaine or hashish, a referral for a consultation with a specialist in substance abuse would be appropriate. Along the same lines, if it became apparent that Mike represented a clear and imminent risk to his sister (e.g., by threatening to kill her once again), more intensive interventions, such as an inpatient hospitalization or a residential placement, might be warranted. The ways in which his increased drug use or threatening behavior are related to deficits in affect regulation, attachment security, and the consolidation of maladaptive beliefs would be carefully explored in therapy.

Patient Strengths
Mike has a number of strengths that may be called upon over the course of therapy. We may think of strength as existing within the individual and their environment. These might include adaptive coping skills, cognitive and social abilities, family support, and community resources. Mike is reasonably intelligent, and has, in the past, done fairly well academically. He may, as a consequence, be able to benefit from verbally based interventions. Moreover, Mike's verbal abstraction capacities appear to be developing normally. It is interesting to note that, at the outset of their first appointment, Mike

impressed his therapist as being a "handsome and capable" 13-year-old. Mike appears, in many ways, to be sociable and attractive—characteristics that may be of use therapeutically. What, though, led the therapist to view him as "capable?" Was it simply that he is attractive, and so creates a favorable first impression, or does he, in some ways, exude a sense of confidence and control? Do others view him as capable, and is this a valid perception? Does Mike view himself as capable? These are important questions insofar as perceptions of self-efficacy can be an important prognostic indicator. If Mike is, in fact, a capable young man, and others perceive him as such, this would be a personal strength. Mike might be encouraged to identify additional strengths and capacities. Has he, for example, ever coped successfully with a challenge, or learned a difficult skill? Has he ever tactfully resolved a social problem *without* arguing, starting a fight, or simply leaving? How did he accomplish this? Has he ever behaved in a kind and generous manner to others? What brought this about and how did it lead him to feel? Has he ever empathized with someone in distress and worked to assist him?

It also may be helpful to identify other family or community resources for Mike. Are there other relatives Mike can turn to for support and guidance? Are there clubs or teams he might join that would provide a sense of accomplishment and social connection (and that might be a bit of fun as well)? Although Mike is only 13 years of age, are there family members or individuals in the community who might offer him a part-time job? Developing additional personal strengths and community resources may be helpful to Mike and may play an invaluable role in changing his developmental path.

Limits and Boundaries

In addition to difficulties with managing negative moods, children and adolescents with CD often believe that they are entitled to behave as they wish and that it is essential for them to maintain their autonomy from others. They tend, as a group, to believe that "no one should be able to control me." Maintaining clear and appropriate therapeutic limits and expectations can be helpful in addressing each of these concerns.

Children's beliefs, coping capacities, and information processing skills are acquired—they are learned in a social context. By maintaining appropriate limits, and by modeling effective affect regulation skills, the therapeutic relationship can serve as a model for how one can manage stressful situations. The rules and guidelines that the therapist places on the therapeutic relationship—limit setting—would be openly discussed with Mike and his parents and, over time, internalized. With younger adolescents, such as Mike, we typically have four "rules of the room": (a) this is their hour, so they should feel free to say anything they wish; (b) verbal and physical aggression is not permitted—they cannot destroy objects in the room or threaten anyone in it; (c) if they wish to draw, write, or play with objects in the office, that is fine, so long as they put them back at the end of the hour; and (d) they can not run out of the office. If, for example, Mike became upset that his therapist did not allow him to use the office computer to go online and surf violent Web sites, this would become a topic for discussion. His thoughts, feelings, and attributions about the limit that has been placed on his behavior would be discussed. We would acknowledge his feelings of frustration and resentment and would explore the validity of his belief that the limit was unfair, that the therapist did not understand or support him, and that limits on his behavior are, in and of themselves, bad. We would discuss ways of managing his feelings of anger and resentment toward the therapist, and explore how these skills might be used to cope with his feelings of resentment toward his sister and his teachers. As in standard cognitive therapy, the therapy relationship itself becomes a laboratory for testing maladaptive beliefs and for developing adaptive skills. The therapeutic relationship serves as a scaffold, organizing and guiding the process of treatment. Therapeutic limits and boundaries are an important part of this scaffold. For children and adolescents who lack the ability to regulate their moods and behavior, and who view close relationships as unpredictable and potentially dangerous, maintaining consistent therapeutic limits becomes an important part of the treatment process.

Treatment Implications and Outcome
Therapeutic Techniques

Many of the techniques of cognitive-developmental therapy are similar to those used in standard cognitive-behavioral therapy with adolescents. The therapist begins by developing a problem list with the child and his or her parent. It is not uncommon for children and parents to have very different views of the primary problems. With this difference in mind, a patient approach must be taken in developing a problem list that all agree upon. This patience is essential if we are to engage Mike and his parents in the treatment process. Ms. D., for example, is concerned by her son's shoplifting, anger, and argumentativeness, whereas Mike does not like being viewed as the "black sheep" of the family. Is there a point of contact between them? Perhaps. What, for example, leads Mike to believe that his parents view him as a "black sheep," and why is this important to him? One suspects that his parents are, in fact, quite frustrated and disappointed in him, and have been for some time. One suspects, as well, that they have conveyed this to him in ways both explicit and subtle. What Mike wants is reliable and consistent approval and support. He would like a secure and reliable attachment to his parents, but anticipates rejection, criticism, and disapproval. Working together, Mike and his mother may be able to develop a shared therapeutic goal of developing a less conflicted relationship.

We next present a cognitive-developmental rationale for the therapy to Mike and his parents. Using material they have presented regarding his early development, as well as life experiences that may have contributed to his current situation, we would share the case formulation with them and describe a proposed treatment program.

Initial interventions typically are directed toward reducing conflict at home and toward improving Mike's affect regulation skills. We would begin by asking Mike to identify recent problematic situations (such as a conflict with his sister or a teacher) and discussing how he would approach them. We would be interested in understanding his thoughts, feelings, and goals in the situations, how he feels others will react to him, and whether he has considered alternative courses of action. Given the importance of establishing a trusting rapport with Mike, we would acknowledge his feelings of resentment, anxiety, and frustration in these situations, as well as the strength of his beliefs (e.g., that he has to "be strong," that others are unfair, that he cannot be controlled or pushed around). We would work with Mike to recognize relations between these thoughts and changes in his mood, and ask him to discuss evidence supporting these beliefs. Although our approach to rational disputation is similar in many ways to that used with adults, it is imperative that it be presented in a collaborative, nonconfrontational manner. Children with CD tend to react negatively to direct confrontation. Maintaining a gentle, Socratic stance is nowhere more important than when working with children with CD and their families. Mike might be encouraged to develop simple, adaptive self-statements that he can use in frustrating situations. These might include (a) "What's really my goal here?" (encouraging him to reflect on his motives); (b) "Relax... it's no big deal" (leading him to practice relaxation exercises and to maintain a more reasonable view of the significance of the situation); and (c) "Is there another way to handle this? What's the best solution?" (encouraging him to engage in active social problem solving).

Children with CD often manifest difficulties with rational problem solving and demonstrate low problem-solving motivation. They may experience difficulty identifying problematic situations, generating alternative solutions, evaluating their relative strengths and weaknesses, selecting the most appropriate course of action, and evaluating the effectiveness of their solutions.

In addition, they tend to approach problems in an impulsive manner (i.e., "just do anything to get it over") or attempt to avoid the situation altogether (as when Mike cuts class to visit his friend's home). A problem-solving workbook, including simple vignettes, might be shared with Mike. Working together, we would practice developing solutions for problems described by teenagers in the book. As his level of problem-solving competence improves, we would begin discussing examples that are increasingly similar to experiences he has had at home (e.g., argument with his mother about grades, conflict with a sibling). We would conclude by asking Mike to prepare a list of his "top ten" problems. Working together, we would develop solutions for each of the problems, evaluate them, and plan a course of action. Teenagers typically find this exercise quite helpful. We are acknowledging their view that these situations are problematic, and are working directly with them to resolve them.

The development of emotion regulation skills plays a central role in cognitive-developmental therapy. As noted, affect regulation may be seen as an integrated set of cognitive, perceptual, and social capacities that allow an individual to maintain a level of affective arousal that is appropriate for effective coping with stressful situations. These component skills include attention control, mood monitoring, cue identification, and implementation of cognitive and behavioral regulation strategies. If an individual is able to maintain a stable level of arousal when confronted with stressful events, he will be better able to use more sophisticated skills, such as rational problem solving, or assertive communication, to resolve the problems.

The first step in assisting Mike to more effectively regulate his emotions is for him to recognize that affective lability may, in fact, be a problem. Like many adolescents, Mike may view his reactions toward his sister, his parents, and his teachers as entirely reasonable, adaptive, and appropriate. He may view his shoplifting as "no big deal," feel that his sister "made me shove her," and view his teachers as "deserving what they get." We will begin by encouraging him to recount a recent event that led him to feel angry, frustrated, or resentful, then to reflect on the strength of his reaction. The question is not, "Was your reaction reasonable?" (he will say it was), but "Was it stronger than it needed to be?" (he may acknowledge that he did not need to react so strongly). Insofar as strong feelings of anger and resentment are uncomfortable, we would like for Mike to acknowledge that a goal of therapy is to reduce them. It is worth acknowledging that angry, resentful adolescents often feel morally justified in their rage. They believe they have been unfairly and maliciously harmed, and feel, with a sense of righteous indignation, that they are entitled to feel resentful. We can acknowledge the depth of these feelings.

One can understand, for example, how Mike might resent his father's angry outbursts and how he has failed to support his family. At the same time, we would like for Mike to come to appreciate how this sense of resentment may influence his perceptions of others. Unfortunately, as Mike's psychologist noted, he appears to demonstrate "limited insight" into himself or his motivations. A slow, patient approach, as such, will be needed.

As Mike comes to recognize that his labile mood may, in fact, be a problem, we can begin to introduce cognitive-behavioral affect regulation strategies. These may include traditional anger management skills, relaxation training, and attention control strategies.

As Patterson (1982) has observed, parents often become entangled in a coercive struggle to manage their child's behavior. In an attempt to rectify this, Mike's parents might be taught how to monitor their son's problematic behavior and use positive reinforcement to increase the frequency of his adaptive, prosocial behavior. Specific coercive behaviors—such as yelling, threatening physical punishment, and swearing—would be monitored and addressed. An explicit goal would be to immediately reduce the frequency of these three behaviors by both Mike and his parents. Working together, we would practice noncoercive, consistent, and appropriate approaches to discipline to address Mike's aggressive, disrespectful behavior. Sessions might also focus on teaching Mike's parents how to use social problem-solving strategies (described previously), relaxation and attention control exercises, and negotiation strategies to reduce conflict at home. Parenting skills might be taught using handouts, modeling, and in-session role-plays.

Significant Others and Homework

Parent–child relationships appear to play a critical role in the etiology of CD and in the maintenance of symptoms. With this in mind it can be quite helpful to include parents and other family members in the therapy process. The level of parental involvement in the therapy process can vary depending upon their motivation and the quality of their relationship with their child. At a minimum, parents and other family members can provide important information about the patient's developmental history, symptom severity, and therapeutic progress. Children with CD often minimize the severity of their difficulties, or deny problems all together. Caregivers can provide useful information about symptoms of CD and associated conditions.

Parents can also provide support for their child completing therapeutic homework assignments. This may take the form of organizing a contingency management program, reviewing problem-solving or anger management exercises, or supervising their child's participation in after-school activities.

Inasmuch as relationships between children with CD and their parents often are conflicted, parents can be taught specific therapeutic strategies, and enlisted as "co-therapists" to administer and supervise treatment components at home. Parents would, for example, play an active role in interventions designed to reduce coercive parent–child interactions and in practicing negotiation exercises. Finally, parents whose beliefs and emotional reactions to their child may contribute to their child's difficulties might themselves be the focus of clinical interventions. Mr. D., for example, believes that physical punishment, threats, and yelling are appropriate discipline strategies, and that Mike should not be "protected" from physical discipline. It is likely that Mr. D.'s unpredictable, episodic anger and coercive approach to discipline contributes to his son's current behavioral problems. Mr. D.'s thoughts and feelings about his son, as well as his beliefs and expectations about child rearing, are worthy of careful discussion. Mr. D. may benefit, as well, from anger management therapy.

Homework plays a central role in cognitive-developmental therapy for CD. Every session concludes with a review of the tasks and strategies discussed during the hour, and the collaborative development of a homework assignment. Frequently used homework assignments include relaxation training, mood monitoring, affect regulation exercises, assertive communication, family negotiation, social problem solving, anger management, pleasant activities scheduling, "give and get," and adaptive self-statements. Whenever possible, homework assignments are practiced during the session, and possible cognitive, behavioral, and environmental impediments are identified and resolved. If, for example, Mike firmly believes that "It'll do no good" to try to talk calmly with his father, it is unlikely that he will make the attempt. We will want, then, to carefully examine the evidence for this belief and, if possible, put the validity of the belief to test. We might, for example, develop criteria for "doing no good," then test to see if this actually occurs. Our goal is to develop homework assignments with a high likelihood of success. We want for Mike to leave each session with a clear sense of a strategy he can use to improve the quality of his life and his relationships, and be confident in his ability to implement it.

Mechanisms of Change

Cognitive-developmental therapy of CD is believed to promote behavioral and emotional change by: (a) supporting the development of affect regulation skills, (b) changing maladaptive beliefs about the appropriateness and value of aggressive and oppositional behavior, (c) changing maladaptive tacit beliefs or schema about relationships with others, (d) improving social problem-solving skills and problem-solving motivation, and (e) improving the quality of parent–child relationships.

Medical and Nutritional Issues

Medications can, in some circumstances, play a role in the treatment of CD. Antidepressant medications, such as SSRIs, may be helpful if conduct problems are due to depression or if there are high levels of impulsivity. Stimulants may be used when there is significant inattention or motoric overactivity, which is suggestive of comorbid ADHD, and mood stabilizers can be useful with children who exhibit explosive, unprovoked episodes of rage.

Potential Pitfalls

Treatment of CD is, in many ways, a challenging and potentially unrewarding endeavor. Teenagers rarely are self-referred, and are not motivated to participate in treatment. Parents often seek immediate solutions for long-standing behavioral problems, and have difficulty implementing therapeutic strategies at home. Moreover, teachers typically view children with CD as disruptive nuisances (which, admittedly, they can be), rather than as youths in need of their assistance. A potential pitfall exists in therapists' natural tendency to empathize with their patients' experiences, and to respond to positive feedback from their patients. Positive feedback from adolescents with CD is rare. Although it is important to validate the legitimacy of Mike's emotional experience, and so to have him feel understood and reliably supported, it is essential to maintain an objective, critical stance with regard to the meanings he attaches to them. Our therapeutic goal is to acknowledge the depth of his feelings of anger toward his teachers, and yet readily not accept the perception that they are malicious, that it is adaptive to cut class, and that that it is essential to maintain one's autonomy at all costs. It is possible, as well, to acknowledge Mike's feelings of resentment and loss toward his father, yet not accept the validity of his belief that others will behave toward him as his father has.

A second potential pitfall centers on Ms. D.'s comment that she is "frustrated and upset." How does she express her feelings of frustration toward her son? What are her expectations regarding his behavior? What attributions does she make about the causes of his difficulties? Does she view his behavior as intentional? Malicious? Genetically based (he's just like his father)? Directed at her? The meanings she attaches to Mike's behavior are potentially important in that they will influence both her emotions and her behavioral reactions to him. It may be helpful to clarify her thoughts about her son's difficulties, and how this leads her to feel about herself as a mother, and about her son. This will allow us to help her to respond to him in a more effective, proactive, and nurturing manner. Ms. D.'s feelings of hopelessness also are of concern. She reportedly feels a lack of control over her son's behavior, and presents with "an air of helplessness and ineptness." These feelings of helplessness may lead her to withdraw from her son emotionally and to respond to him in an inconsistent manner. As noted earlier, the effective parent is protective, and provides clear, consistent support and guidance. We will want to assist Ms. D. to become a more effective (and confident) parent.

Mr. D.'s apparent lack of investment in the treatment process is a potential concern. Both he and Ms. D. continue to play a role in his upbringing, and Mr. D. remains an important figure in Mike's life. Mr. and Ms. D. approach child rearing in very different ways. Although Mr. D.'s punitive discipline style (including yelling and threatening physical contact) appears to be effective in the short term, it also may be exacerbating his son's feelings of resentment and maintaining his behavioral difficulties. If possible, it would be helpful to engage Mr. D. as a participant in his son's treatment.

A final potential pitfall may be Mike's peer group. Mike openly acknowledges that he smokes cannabis with his friends on the weekends and when they skip school, raising questions about parental supervision. It will be important to more closely supervise Mike's activities and, if possible, to have him become involved in other activities (such as sports or clubs) with other peers.

Prognosis

It can be difficult to predict adolescents' response to psychotherapy. Research indicates that long-term outcomes for youths with CD are guarded, and that a significant percentage of youths with this disorder experience ongoing social and vocational problems. That said, research also indicates that adolescents can benefit from active, intensive treatment. Adolescents' response to CBT for depression *may* be predicted by their age, family income, level of functional impairment, the presence of suicidality, the number of comorbid diagnoses, level of cognitive distortions, level of hopelessness, their expectation of treatment outcome, and how they were referred to the clinic. With this in mind, Mike's prognosis may be improved if we are able to address factors that are associated with long-term outcome. This approach might include seeking community services to reduce financial stress on Mike's family, actively working to reduce the functional impact of Mike's behavior, addressing comorbid problems (such as his cannabis abuse), rectifying cognitive distortions, enhancing his sense of efficacy and control over important outcomes, developing clearer vocational and social goals, and improving his expectation of a positive treatment outcome.

Termination and Relapse Prevention

Inasmuch as children with CD rarely wish to participate in treatment, one might suspect that they would have little difficulty separating from their therapist and that they would, if given the chance, wish to terminate treatment as quickly as possible. To be sure, it can be difficult for children with CD, like Mike, to establish a close and trusting therapeutic rapport. Once a relationship is established, however, children can come to appreciate it. Based upon early experiences, children with CD often anticipate that others will be unreliable, unpredictable, unsupportive, uncaring, inconsistent, and punitive. A close and trusting therapeutic rapport, however, violates each of these expectations. It is not uncommon, then, for children with CD to come to value this relationship.

Given their concerns with control, trust, and rejection, children with CD may react strongly to an impending termination. Their reactions can vary, ranging from dependency and neediness to indifference or anger. As such, termination may activate tacit beliefs that play a central role in CD. Mike, for example, might come to believe that "you're just like all the others. . . I knew sooner or later you'd give up on me. . . you think I'm a loser, don't you?" Termination, then, offers an opportunity to understand and rectify beliefs that may be contributing to Mike's difficulties. The child's (and parents') thoughts and feelings about termination are worthy of careful exploration.

Termination can be difficult for patients with CD, yet, it can be useful to taper sessions slowly, to offer the child and his family booster sessions as needed, to coordinate family and community resources for the child, to practice the skills learned, and to recommend that medications be maintained after therapy has been completed.

As in CBT, relapse prevention in cognitive-developmental therapy involves consolidating newly acquired cognitive and behavioral skills, and identifying potentially problematic situations. Mike might be encouraged to identify situations that may lead him to feel frustrated, angry, or resentful. Mike's thoughts and feelings when he meets his father, has a disagreement with his mother or sister, or receives an unexpected assignment from a teacher all might be discussed. Mike would then be assisted in developing a list of strategies and techniques (which we refer to as "tools in the toolbox") that have been most effective for regulating his mood. The ways these might be used in coping with these situations would then be practiced. Our goal is to provide Mike and his parents with skills that will allow them to cope more effectively with frustrating situations and interpersonal conflicts that may emerge, and so to improve the quality of their relationship.

CONCLUSIONS

Research on the developmental psychopathology of CD and its treatment has advanced at a rapid pace during recent years. CD is a complex condition and, like many forms of behavior, appears to be multiply determined.

Genetic, biological, social, cognitive, and environmental factors all are implicated in the development and maintenance of the disorder. These factors appear to interact transactionally in placing youths at risk. Different subtypes of the disorder may exist, each associated with different risk factors and developmental trajectories. There appear, in short, to be a number of paths to CD.

That said, CD is characterized by a number of cognitive, social, and emotional deficits. These include deficits in attention and emotional regulation, perceptual biases, maladaptive beliefs or schema, maladaptive social scripts, and organizational–motivational factors. Given the heterogeneity of the condition and individual differences in course, two questions come to mind— what are the defining characteristics of the disorder, and what are underlying mechanisms or processes that mediate its development? Evidence indicates that behavioral impulsivity, deficits in executive function and planning, social problem-solving deficits, lack of regard for social expectations, and impaired empathy all may play a role. Beliefs and behaviors that characterize CD can be learned from parents, peers, and the larger community. At the same time, CD also may be viewed as stemming from failures in the acquisition of adaptive cognitive, affective, and social skills. The cognitive-developmental model suggests that there are two critical mediating factors—affect regulation and the consolidation of maladaptive beliefs about relationships with others and the appropriateness of aggressive or oppositional social behavior—and that these may serve as a focus for treatment and prevention. Attachment theory and research in developmental psychopathology provide a framework for understanding relationships between biological, social, and cognitive risk factors, and may guide the development of effective interventions.

Social learning and attachment-based approaches to understanding the development of psychopathology have, for many years, been seen as inconsistent. A cognitive-developmental model offers the opportunity of a rapprochement between these schools of thought, and suggests that they may mutually inform and augment each other. Attachment theory provides a paradigm for understanding the development of cognitive and behavioral vulnerabilities for psychopathology. Cognitive-behavioral theory provides a means of understanding how nonsecure patterns of attachment may lead to specific forms of psychopathology, as well as therapeutic techniques that may be useful for addressing these problems. Admittedly, much of this model is speculative. Although research is consistent with this approach, longitudinal studies of interactions between biological, cognitive, social, and emotional factors associated with psychopathology among both normal and at-risk youths are needed. It will be necessary to refine our models of attachment during adolescence and to develop techniques for assessing attachment styles among older children and adolescents. Important questions regarding the stability of attachment patterns over the course of development, and how nonsecure attachment styles may serve an adaptive function, have not been answered. Finally, controlled studies are needed to demonstrate the efficacy and effectiveness of attachment-based cognitive-behavioral strategies for preventing and treating externalizing behavior problems among youths. Although integrative models, such as the cognitive-developmental model of CD, are intriguing, much work remains to be done.

There is, nonetheless, reason for guarded optimism. We should not accept the easy belief that CD cannot be prevented or treated, or that youths who grow up in vulnerable environments are beyond our help. To be sure, CD is a significant, complex, and challenging social and psychological problem. By directing our prevention and treatment efforts toward ameliorating factors that have been demonstrated to be associated with risk, we may be able to assist children who are most in need.

REFERENCES

Achenbach, T.M. (1991). *Manual for the Child Behavior Checklist and 1991 profile.* Burlington, VT: University of Vermont, Department of Psychiatry.

Alexander, J., Barton, C., Schiavo, R., & Parsons, B. (1976). Systems-behavioral intervention with families of delinquents: Therapist characteristics, family behavior, and outcome. *Journal of Consulting and Clinical Psychology, 44,* 656–664.

Alexander, J., & Parsons, B. (1982). *Functional family therapy.* Monterey, CA: Brooks/Cole.

American Psychiatric Association. (2000a). *Diagnostic criteria from DSM-IV-TR.* Washington, DC: American Psychiatric Press.

American Psychiatric Association. (2000b). *Diagnostic and statistical manual of mental disorders* (4th ed., text rev.). Washington, DC: American Psychiatric Press.

Baer, R., & Nietzel, M. (1991). Cognitive and behavioral treatment of impulsivity in children: A meta-analytic review of the outcome literature. *Journal of Clinical Child Psychology, 20,* 400–412.

Beelman, A., Pfingsten, U., & Losel, F. (1994). Effects of training social competence in children: A meta-analysis of recent evaluation studies. *Journal of Clinical Child Psychology, 23,* 260–271.

Belsky, J., & Nezworski, T. (Eds.). (1988). *Clinical implications of attachment.* Hillsdale, NJ: Erlbaum.

Bowlby, J. (1944). Forty-four juvenile thieves: Their characteristics and home life. *International Journal of Psycho-Analysis, 1,* 19–52, 107–27.

Brestan, E., & Eyberg, S. (1998). Effective psychosocial treatments of conduct-disordered children and adolescents: 29 years, 82 studies, and 5272 kids. *Journal of Clinical Child Psychology, 27,* 180–189.

Brosnan, R., & Carr, A. (2000). Adolescent conduct problems. In A. Carr (Ed.), *What works with children and adolescents? A critical review of psychological interventions with children, adolescents, and their families* (pp. 131–154). London: Routledge.

Caspi, A., McClay, J., Moffitt, T., Mill, J., Martin, J., Craig, I., Taylor, A., & Poulton, R. (2002). Role of genotype in the cycle of violence in maltreated children. *Science, 297,* 851–854.

Catalano, R., Arthur, M., Hawkins, J., Berglund, L., & Olson, J. (1998). Comprehensive community- and school-based interventions to prevent antisocial behavior. In R. Loeber, & D. Farrington (Eds.), *Serious and violent juvenile offenders: Risk factors and successful interventions* (pp. 248–283). Thousand Oaks, CA: Sage.

Conduct Problems Prevention Research Group. (1992). A developmental and clinical model for the prevention of CD: The FAST Track program. *Development and Psychopathology, 4,* 509–527.

Conduct Problems Prevention Research Group. (1999). Initial impact of the FAST Track prevention trial for conduct problems: I. The high-risk sample. *Journal of Consulting and Clinical Psychology, 67,* 631–647.

Costello, E., & Angold, A. (1993). Toward a developmental epidemiology of the disruptive behavior disorders. *Development and Psychopathology, 5,* 91–101.

Deater-Deckard, K., Dodge, K., Bates, J., & Pettit, G. (1998). Multiple risk factors in the development of externalizing behavior problems: Group and individual differences. *Development and Psychopathology, 12,* 23–45.

DeKlyen, M., & Speltz, M. (2001). Attachment and CD. In J. Hill, & B. Maughan (Eds.), *CDs in children and adolescents* (pp. 320–345). Cambridge: Cambridge University Press.

Dishion, T., & Andrews, D. (1995). Preventing escalation in problem behaviors with high risk young adolescents: Immediate and 1-year outcomes. *Journal of Consulting and Clinical Psychology, 63,* 538–548.

Dishion, T., Patterson, G., & Cavanaugh, K. (1992). An experimental test of the coercion model: Linking theory, measurement, and intervention. In J. McCord, & R. Tremblay (Eds.), *Preventing antisocial behavior* (pp. 253–282). New York: Guilford Press.

Dodge, K., & Pettit, G. (2003). A biopsychosocial model of the development of chronic conduct problems in adolescence. *Developmental Psychology, 39,* 189–190.

Dumas, J. (1989). Treating antisocial behavior in children: Child and family approaches. *Clinical Psychology Review, 9,* 197–222.

Durlak, J., Fuhrman, T., & Lampman, C. (1991). Effectiveness of cognitive-behavioral therapy for maladapting children: A meta-analysis. *Psychological Bulletin, 110,* 204–214.

Erickson, M.E., Sroufe, L.A., & Egeland, B. (1985). The relationship between quality of attachment and behavior problems in a preschool high-risk sample. In I. Bretherton, & E. Waters (Eds.), *Growing points of attachment theory and research. Monographs of the Society for Research in Child Development* (Vol. 50(1–2), pp. 147 166, Serial 209).

Farrington, D., & Welsh, B. (1999). Delinquency prevention using family-based interventions. *Children and Society, 13,* 287–303.

Fiendler, E., & Ecton, R. (1986). *Adolescent anger control: Cognitive-behavioral techniques.* Elmsford, NY: Pergamon.

Fonagy, P., & Kurtz, A. (2002). Disturbance of conduct. In P. Fonagy, M. Target, D. Cottrell, J. Phillips, & Z. Kurtz (Eds.), *What works for whom? A critical review of treatments for children and adolescents* (pp. 106–192). New York: Guilford Press.

Frick, P. J. (1998). CDs. In T. Ollendick, & M. Hersen (Eds.), *Handbook of child psychopathology* (3rd ed., pp. 213–234). New York: Plenum Press.

Frick, P. J., Lahey, B., Loeber, R., Tannenbaum , L., VanHorn, Y., Christ, M.A.G., Hart, E. L., & Hansen, K. (1993). Oppositional defiant disorder and CD: A meta-analytic review of factor analyses and cross-validation in a clinic sample. *Clinical Psychology Review, 13,* 319–340.

Goldberg, S. (1997). Attachment and childhood behavior problems in normal, at-risk, and clinical samples. In L. Atkinson, & K. Zucker (Eds.), *Attachment and psychopathology* (pp. 171–195). New York: Guilford Press.

Graziano, A., & Diament, D. (1992). Parent behavior training: An examination of the paradigm. *Behavior Modification, 16,* 3–38.

Henggeler, S., & Borduin, C. (1990). *Family therapy and beyond: A multisystemic approach to treating the behavior problems of children and adolescents.* Pacific Grove, CA: Brooks/Cole.

Henggeler, S., Schoenwald, S., Borduin, C., Rowland, M., & Cunningham, P. (1998). *Multisystems treatment of antisocial behaviour in children and adolescents.* New York: Guilford Press.

Hinshaw, S., & Lee, S. (2003). Conduct and oppositional defiant disorders. In E. Mash, & R. Barkley (Eds.), *Child psychopathology* (2nd ed., pp. 144–198). New York: Guilford Press.

Holland, R., Moretti, M., Verlaan, V., & Peterson, S. (1993). Attachment and CD: The response programme. *Canadian Journal of Psychiatry, 38,* 420–431.

Holmes, J. (1993). Attachment theory: A biological basis for psychotherapy? *British Journal of Psychiatry, 163,* 430–438.

Kazdin, A. (1993). Treatment of CD: Progress and directions in psychotherapy research. *Development and Psychopathology, 5,* 277–310.

Kazdin, A. (1997). Psychosocial treatments for CD in children. *Journal of Child Psychology and Psychiatry, 38,* 161–178.

Kazdin, A. (2000). *Psychotherapy for children and adolescents: Directions for research and practice.* New York: Oxford University Press.

Kazdin, A. (2001). Treatment of CDs. In J. Hill, & B. Maughan (Eds.), *CDs in childhood and adolescence* (pp. 408–448). Cambridge, England: Cambridge University Press.

Lahey, B., & Loeber, R. (1994). Framework for a developmental model of oppositional-defiant disorder and CD. In D. Routh (Ed.), *Disruptive behavior disorders in childhood: Essays honoring Herbert C. Quay* (pp. 139–180). New York: Plenum Press.

Lahey, B., Miller, T., Gordon, R., & Riley, A. (1999). Developmental epidemiology of disruptive behavior disorders. In H. Quay, & A. Hogan (Eds.), *Handbook of disruptive behavior disorders* (pp. 23–48). New York: Plenum Press.

Lahey, B., Waldman, I., & McBurnett, K. (1999). The development of antisocial behavior: An integrative causal model. *Journal of Child Psychology and Psychiatry, 40*, 669–682.

Lewis, M., Feiring, C., McGuffog, C., & Jaskir, J. (1984). Predicting psychopathology in six-year-olds from early social relations. *Child Development, 55*, 123–136.

Lipsey, M., & Wilson, D. (1998). Effective intervention for serious juvenile offenders: A synthesis of research. In R. Loeber & D. Farrington (Eds.), *Serious and violent juvenile offenders* (pp. 313–345). Thousand Oaks, CA: Sage.

Lochman, J., & Dodge, K. (1994). Social-cognitive processes of severely violent, moderately aggressive, and nonaggressive boys. *Journal of Consulting and Clinical Psychology, 62*, 366–374.

Loeber, R., & Farrington, D. (2000). Young children who commit crime: Epidemiology, developmental origins, risk factors, early interventions, and policy implications. *Development and Psychopathology, 12*, 737–762.

Loeber, R., Green, S., Keenan, K., & Lahey, B. (1995). Which boys will fare worse? Early predictors of the onset of CD in a six-year longitudinal study. *Journal of the American Academy of Child and Adolescent Psychiatry, 34*, 499–509.

Loeber, R., Green S., & Lahey, B. (2003). Risk factors for adult antisocial personality. In D. Farrington, & J. Coid (Eds.), *Early prevention of adult antisocial behavior* (pp. 79–108). Cambridge: Cambridge University Press.

Long, P., Forehand, R., Wierson, M., & Morgan, A. (1994). Does parent training with young noncompliant children have long-term effects? *Behaviour Research and Therapy, 32*, 101–107.

Lyons-Ruth, K., Alpern, L., & Repacholi, B. (1993). Disorganized infant attachment classification and maternal psychological problems as predictors of hostile-aggressive behavior in the preschool classroom. *Child Development, 64*, 572–585.

Moretti, M., Holland, R., & Peterson S. (1994). Long-term outcome of an attachment-based program for CD. *Canadian Journal of Psychiatry, 39*, 360–369.

Nagin, D., & Tremblay, R. (1999). Trajectories of boys' physical aggression, opposition, and hyperactivity on the path to physically violent and nonviolent juvenile delinquency. *Child Development, 70*, 1181–1196.

NICHD Early Child Care Research Network. (2004). Trajectories of physical aggression from toddlerhood to middle childhood. *Monographs of the Society for Research in Child Development.* Serial No. 278, Vol. 69, No. 4.

Nock, M. (2003). Progress review of psychosocial treatment of child conduct problems. *Clinical Psychology: Science and Practice, 10*, 1–28.

Offord, D., Alder, R., & Boyle, M. (1986). Prevalence and sociodemographic correlates of CD. *American Journal of Social Psychiatry, 4,* 272–278.

Patterson, G. (1982). *Coercive family process.* Eugene, OR: Catalia.

Pettit, G. (2004). Violent children in developmental perspective: Risk and protective factors and the mechanisms through which they (may) operate. *Current Directions in Psychological Science, 13*(5), 194–197.

Puig-Antich, J., & Chambers, W. (1978). *The Schedule for Affective Disorders and Schizophrenia for School-Aged Children (Kiddie-SADS).* New York: New York State Psychiatric Institute.

Reid, J., Patterson, G., & Snyder, J. (2002). *Antisocial behavior in children and adolescents: A developmental analysis and model for intervention.* Washington, DC: American Psychological Association.

Renken, B., Egeland, B., Marvinney, D., Mangelsdorf, S., & Sroufe, L. (1989). Early childhood antecedents of aggression and passive-withdrawal in early elementary school. *Journal of Personality, 57,* 257–281.

Rutter, M. (1985). Resilience in the face of adversity: Protective factors and resistance to psychiatric disorder. *British Journal of Psychiatry, 147,* 598–611.

Rutter, M. (2003). Commentary: Causal processes leading to antisocial behavior. *Developmental Psychology, 39,* 372–378.

Tremblay, R. (2000). The development of aggressive behavior during childhood: What have we learned in the past half century? *International Journal of Behavioral Development, 24,* 129–141.

Tremblay, R., LeMarquand, D., & Vitaro, F. (1999). The prevention of ODD and CD. In H. C. Quay, & A. E. Hogan (Eds.), *Handbook of disruptive behavior disorders* (pp. 525–555). New York: Kluwer/Plenum.

CHAPTER 6

Behavioral Treatment for Youth with Conduct Disorder

Janet R. Schultz

THE TREATMENT MODEL

The behavior therapy approach to conduct problems rests on the belief that all behaviors, deviant or not, are acquired according to the same principles. Learning principles emphasize the importance of social context, especially the interactions of children with people in their environment. For treatment purposes, the social context typically includes the family, school, and peers. Social context can be analyzed in terms of stimulus control, modeling, and contingencies. The contingencies, in turn, can be considered from the perspective of patterns and relative rates of positive and negative reinforcement, punishment, and absence of contingent responses which could alter a child's conduct problems. Learning principles also hold that treatment success, defined as acquiring, maintaining, and generalizing new positive behaviors to replace those constituting the conduct problem, is dependent on mutual exchange of reinforcement between the child and those in the environment.

As the empirical literature regarding the development of conduct problems has evolved, three findings that are now taken as obvious were established: First, not all families are equally likely to have children who develop conduct disorder (CD). Second, not all children are equally likely to develop CD. Third, the development of CD is related to the interplay between family (especially parent) variables and child variables.

Family Variables

There are identifiable risk factors associated with the families of children with CD, although it is not yet clear how much of the transmission of the disorder is genetic as opposed to environmental. Regardless of the cause, most studies have identified familial behavior patterns. For example, in families with parents and grandparents with antisocial behaviors, there is considerably increased likelihood of offspring with CD (Huesmann, Eron, Lefkowitz, & Walder, 1984), and parental antisocial personality has been strongly and specifically related to childhood CD (Faraone, Biederman, Keenan, & Tsuang, 1991). Parental diagnosis of antisocial personality disorder also predicted the persistence of CD over a 4-year period (Lahey et al., 1995). This pattern can be understood as a function of learning, as parents who display antisocial attitudes or behaviors are likely to model and reinforce different behaviors than those who do not. Patterson, Reid, and Dishion (1992) found that the parenting practices of mothers and fathers were less effective and more problem engendering when parents showed antisocial behaviors. Parental substance abuse also affects the child through parenting practices. For example, observation studies indicated that parental alcohol abuse was associated with diminished engagement with the children and less pleasantness in the family (Fitzgerald & Zucker, 1995). Diminished engagement often leads to reduced supervision and fewer reliable consequences for both desirable and undesirable child behaviors. Substance use changes the user's mood, thoughts, and actions, in turn affecting the likelihood that the child's world is reliable and predictable.

Parents of children with conduct problems have been found to have more emotional problems, such as depression, than parents of children without conduct problems. Dumas and Serketich (1994) and Forehand, Lautenschlager, Faust, and Graziano (1986) found that mothers' depressed mood altered their parenting behaviors and contributed to a negative mindset regarding her children, perhaps increasing criticism and punitive actions. If a mother is difficult to engage with prosocial, age-typical behavior, significant misconduct can sometimes evoke a response. Depression's irritability or lack of responsiveness (or the combination) can lead to inconsistent limit setting, rewards, and punishment.

Marital dissatisfaction and divorce are also associated with an increased incidence of conduct problems in offspring. Marital dissatisfaction can contribute to depression or irritability. Divorce contributes to family disruption through change of access to parents (both through custody arrangement and a parent's return to work), change of mood of caregivers, access to money, and relative distribution of particularly powerful reinforcers between the parents (e.g., "Disneyland Dad"). However, the effects of divorce on child behavior can be mediated through parental discipline and problem solving, as found by Forgatch, Patterson, and Ray (1996).

Parenting style is also related to the development of CD. In general, parents of delinquents tend to fall at the extremes of the permissive-restrictive dimension of parenting style, often with unpredictable variation. Parents of seriously conduct-disordered children do not supervise their children as closely as other parents. At the same time, these parents are more likely to be hostile and rejecting, show more inconsistency in discipline, use physical discipline, and display higher rates of antisocial behaviors themselves (Moore & Arthur, 1983; Snyder & Patterson, 1987). Ge, Best, Conger, and Simons (1996) found that later onset (teen) antisocial behavior was associated with the parental hostility and emotional distance they had measured a few years earlier. From a learning perspective, the issues of modeling and parent contributions to coercive family process are raised. Coercion (using aversive behaviors to control the behavior of others) appears to be an especially important feature of the family interaction patterns of children with CD, and it will be described in more detail in the text that follows.

Just as parents of children with conduct problems have higher rates of personal problems, they also have higher rates of interpersonal difficulties with those outside the family than parents of typical children. Jennings, Stagg, and Connors (1991) identified a pattern of parental insularity with low social support among families of children with CD. Interactions with the world outside the family have also been found to be characterized by a high level of negatively perceived coercive interchanges and a low level of positively perceived supportive interchanges (Dumas & Wahler, 1983). Insularity is positively associated with negative parent behavior directed toward children and oppositional child behavior directed toward parents (Dumas & Wahler, 1985). Insular mothers also repeatedly modeled negative, frequently contentious interactions with people outside the family. Further, Dumas and Wahler (1983) found that treatment effects for the child did not persist well in insular families.

Child Variables

Temperament is often viewed as a predisposition to the development of certain styles of interacting with the environment, related to "constitutionally based individual differences in reactivity and self regulation" (Rothbart, Posner, & Hershey, 1995). The children that Thomas, Chess, and Birch (1968) called "temperamentally difficult" are high intensity, hard to soothe, and not very adaptable, with unpredictable rhythms. These children, in particular, have been seen to be at higher risk of developing conduct problems over time, because of the increased likelihood of disrupted, negative interactions between parents and children. Difficult temperament has been repeatedly found to have a moderate association with development of conduct problems in early and middle childhood (e.g., Bates, Bayles, Bennett, Ridge, & Brown, 1991; Webster-Stratton & Eyberg, 1982).

Quay (1987) reviewed a large body of research that showed a reliable, inverse relationship between a child's level of arousability and antisocial behaviors, suggesting that some infants and toddlers are less responsive to environmental contingencies. These may be the children clinicians hear about from parents who report they had disciplined their child like their other children, but that the particular child's behavior remained unresponsive to their efforts. In the 1960s, Patterson and his colleagues carried out a number of laboratory-based studies that found that compared to typical children, children with conduct problems were less responsive than typical children to both the responses of people in their environment and attempts at punishment (Patterson, 1965; Patterson & Fagot, 1967; Patterson, Jones, Whittier, & Wright, 1965). Children who are less responsive to contingencies are likely to evoke more intense and negative reactions from their parents as they attempt to have an impact on the behavior of their offspring.

Risk taking or sensation seeking is another variable that has been linked to antisocial behaviors in teenagers. Johnson and Fennell (1992) defined this as a tendency to engage in a variety of exciting, stimulating, and novel behaviors that are assumed to result in increased arousal. It is hypothesized that sensation seekers are attempting to engage in behaviors that will raise their level of stimulation or arousal to a preferred level. Certainly some of the behaviors that define CD can be seen as quite stimulating (breaking into a house, for instance), and numerous studies have found differences in sensation seeking when comparing CD (or delinquent) youth to a nonaffected group (e.g., Farley & Sewell, 1976; Zuckerman, 1979). In a related vein, Satterfield, Schell, and Backs (1987) found that teenagers who had been in trouble with the law showed smaller autonomic reactions and slower responses to stimulation than typical age mates. Although sensation seeking does not apply to all juveniles with CD, it appears to serve as a risk factor, as these youths respond differently to experiences and environmental contingencies. This may be especially true for those youths whom Frick, O'Brien, Wootten, & McBurnett (1994) labeled "psychopathic," that is, youths who have not only superficial charm but also a lack of concern for people or guilt for hurting them. O'Brien and Frick (1996) demonstrated that psychopathic young people have a different response to contingencies than others, being motivated more by positive reinforcement than the avoidance of punishment.

The temperament and behavioral style literature suggests that some of the differences between those who engage in conduct problems and those who do not may be neurologically based. There is consistent evidence that prematurity and/or birth complications are related to antisocial behaviors (Brennan & Mednick, 1997; Brown et al., 1991). There have also been repeated findings that conduct-disordered or delinquent teenagers score lower on IQ tests than typical age mates by about a half a standard deviation. Moffitt and Lynam (1994) contended, however, that early-onset CD is found in boys with an average of a full standard deviation lower on IQ tests that cannot be explained by motivation, race, socioeconomic level, or school failure. They speculated that these boys might have a broad-based neuropsychological dysfunction. Similarly, in a study of almost 2000 adolescent boys, Keilitz and Dunivant (1986) found learning disabled males to be violent more frequently and involved with the courts more often than those without learning disabilities. Neither the direction of the link between learning disabilities and CD is clear nor is there a clear distribution of disability subtypes among various offender subgroups. In a review, Crick and Dodge (1994) presented studies that found that children with conduct problems process social information less effectively than their typical peers. Examples of such differences are relative inattention to social cues and poor problem solving. These learning differences set the stage for misbehavior (Weiss, Dodge, Bates, & Pettit, 1992) and altered, less appropriate social interactions that can lead to a cycle of rejection and hostility. In short, there are converging lines of research that suggest neurologically related risk factors for CD, insofar as IQ, learning disabilities, and cognitive processing are believed to be related to central nervous system functioning.

Attention deficit hyperactivity disorder (ADHD) is also thought to have a neurological basis, primarily resulting from impaired executive functions (Barkley, 1997a, 1997b), and ADHD is the condition most commonly found to be comorbid with CD. In juvenile offenders, estimates of incidence of ADHD reach 30% (Taylor & Watt, 1977) as compared to the 3–5% expected in the general population (Rapport, 1987). Some researchers have suggested that ADHD may be an important component of boys' development of early-onset conduct problems (Coie & Dodge, 1998; Loeber & Keenan, 1995; Morrell & Murray, 2003). The review by Hinshaw, Lahey, and Hart (1993) found that boys with comorbid CD and ADHD have a poorer outcome in comparison to both boys with CD alone, or those with CD and other psychological symptoms. The CD/ADHD boys engaged in more frequent physical aggression, more persistent antisocial activity, poorer academic achievement, and they experienced higher rates of peer rejection. Of the symptoms of ADHD, it appears to be the behavioral impulsivity that predicts later antisocial behavior (Barkley, 1994). Whereas ADHD alters the likelihood that the child will engage in certain classes of behaviors, environmental response may reinforce opportunities for learning antisocial or unpleasant ways of reaching one's goals.

Interaction

Despite the clear direct effect of child and adult variables, there is evidence that the development of CD is related to the interplay between family (especially parent) variables and child variables. Child and family characteristics alter the likelihood of certain behaviors, affecting learning history through reinforcement patterns, modeling, and stimulus control. For example, child characteristics such as age and gender appear to moderate the relationship of parental marital adjustment to the development of conduct problems (Katz & Gottman, 1993). In the Dunedin Multidisciplinary Heath Study, age of the child interacted with risk factors for the development of conduct problem behaviors. Pre-existing family adversity and lower IQ were not related to later onset conduct problems, although they were associated with conduct problems in younger children (Moffitt, Caspi, Dickson, Silva, & Stanton, 1996). The mechanisms are not yet clear but the difference appears related to the patterns of interaction and the reinforcement that result from the interactions. Obviously by the teen years, early-onset behaviors are well practiced and patterns more deeply established than new behaviors, offering some explanation for the repeated finding that children with early-onset CDs have a poorer prognosis than those with adolescent onset.

Cadoret, Yates, Troughton, Woodworth, and Stewart (1995) demonstrated the importance of the interaction of parental environment with child characteristics. They studied the offspring of parents with adjudicated antisocial behavior who had given up their infants at birth. Although having a birth parent with antisocial behaviors was related to CD in teenagers, so was the adoptive home environment. The findings suggested that the disrupted family relations and parenting interacted with genetic background to produce teens with CD. Whatever genetic predisposition was present in the child was not as important in the absence of problematic parenting. This view is in keeping with the suggestion of Rutter (1972) that delinquent behavior is not inherited as such, but rather, that inherited temperament in association with family discord, negativity, and disruption are of greater influence in the development of antisocial problems in childhood.

Ge et al. (1996) also studied biological and adoptive parents and the adopted children, using multiple sources of information. Fifty teenaged adoptees were classified by whether they had a biological parent with substance abuse/dependency or antisocial personality or neither. Offspring with birth parents with the problem behaviors showed greater antisocial/hostile behaviors, especially if the birth parent abused substances and had an antisocial personality. What was more unusual in this study was that the authors also looked for and found significant associations between biological parents' disorders and the behavior of the adoptive parents. Both the affective tone and the dimension of behavioral control (harsh/inconsistent and nurturant/involved discipline) of the adoptive parents were associated with birth parents' psychiatric status. This finding was explained by the inherited characteristics of the children shaping and evoking certain kinds of responses in the adoptive parents, which in turn molded the responses of the children. These teens were generally not experiencing serious disorders as much as impulsiveness, anger, and problems with controlling their own emotional expressions. As Caspi, Elder, and Bem (1987) demonstrated in their study of explosive children, the child acts, the environment reacts, and the child reacts again in a mutually interlocking interaction. The experiences of children who derive from environmental reactions to their biological propensities may result in a developmental trajectory that increases the risk for further maladaptive behaviors.

COERCION THEORY

Oregon Research Institute has been the home of one of the most comprehensive, programmatic, and long-running research programs regarding conduct problems and CD. Beginning in the 1960s, research was carried out by Patterson, Reid, Dishion and their colleagues. Early in his career, Gerald Patterson was running an outpatient child guidance clinic for the Psychology Department. He had been well trained in psychodynamic play therapy and was teaching that model to graduate students when it became increasingly clear that there were childhood problems for which that method was not effective. One of those areas of failed treatment was conduct problems (Patterson, Reid, & Eddy, 2002). The failures led to the beginning of the research that resulted in what is now called coercion theory, the central model used in understanding CD from a behavioral perspective.

In the course of the 1970s and 1980s, much work was done by the Oregon Research Institute team and other researchers interested in conduct problems to explicate the pathways by which a child develops a CD. Two major paths have been identified, each has been referred to by several names.

One path is characterized by conduct problems that become evident in the preschool or early school ages. The problems show a high degree of continuity throughout childhood, adolescence, and often into adulthood. The other pathway has been described more variably but there is consensus that the conduct problems begin in adolescence and generally do not extend into adulthood. This second pathway is generally seen as resulting in less serious forms of CD (not involving as much violence). On the other hand, this second pathway is more common with as many as a quarter of children involved (Moffitt et al., 1996).

Early Starters

The first pathway has been called "the early starter" (Patterson, Capaldi, & Bank, 1991), "life-course persistent" (Moffitt, 1993), and "childhood onset" (Hinshaw et al., 1993). The pathways are acknowledged by those researchers who use perspectives other than behavioral. However, the behavioral approach has developed an understanding of the mechanisms and microinterchanges that will be addressed in the text that follows. Affecting about 7% of children, mostly boys (Moffitt et al., 1996), the path reliably leads from early conduct problems and oppositional behaviors, to more serious overt conduct problems and precocious arrests. Later, CD behaviors expand the children's behavioral repertoire rather than replacing earlier problem behaviors (Frick & Jackson, 1993), and the settings where the behaviors emerge broaden to include places outside the home or school (Lahey & Loeber, 1994). Often, antisocial personality disorder and other serious diagnoses follow in adulthood (Robins, 1966, 1978).

Patterson (2002a, 2002b) described the early-starter pathway as likely to begin in infancy. Infants are seen as active in the shaping of their own environments. Their temperamental and developmental qualities are important in this process. There is a connection between parents and infants that is inevitably linked to the concept of contingency. Infants, despite their immaturity, have powerful rewards and punishments available to them. One can observe this in grocery stores. People of all ages greet and interact with babies, trying to get a smile or other positive acknowledgment. A baby's crying has a uniquely aversive quality that evokes a similar physiological response in most adults but most strongly in his or her parent. Parents try a range of responses until they find the one for which they are rewarded, with the quiet of a satisfied baby. A parent responds to what the infant does and the infant in turn, responds to the parent. This mutually contingent pattern is a normal and important context of human development.

Temperament plays a central role in the beginning of the coercive pathway (Shaw & Winslow, 1997). Difficult-to-soothe children are slower to reinforce their caregivers. Those children who are easily upset by change or who have trouble with transitions in the day have more occasions in which to behave in an aversive fashion. In turn, their irritability may be related to a distant or depressed mother or underinvolved parenting style. As a result, the dyad most at risk for developing a coercive process would be a child with a difficult temperament being raised by a caregiver of marginal competence. The bidirectional nature contributes to the possibility of rapidly developing mutual aversion or coercion (Patterson, 2002a, 2002b).

It is often in the toddler years that a large proportion of children who are later diagnosed with ADHD are identified as hyperactive (Barkley & Biederman, 1997). This identification is related to overactivity, but also to intrusive and, at times, out-of-control behavior. Parents of these children often feel that their limit setting and consequence providing are generally ineffective, even before the child has attended school. Patterson, DeGarmo, and Knutson (2000) using structural equation modeling, found that the relationship between hyperactivity and antisocial behavior was mediated by the ways parents attempted to manage their son's behavior. The presence of parents who are antisocial themselves helps to determine which children with ADHD move on to CDs (Biederman et al., 1996).

Siblings can be an important influence too. Tremblay et al. (1992) asked mothers to report on hitting and kicking by their toddlers. They found that boys with brothers and sisters were twice as likely to engage in those kinds of aggression than only children. It appears that some forms of aggression were under the stimulus control of the presence of siblings. Modeling has also been considered as a possible explanation as well as the reinforcing value of defending one's turf. Patterson and Stouthamer-Loeber (1984) found that brothers and sisters of children with conduct problems were more coercive than the siblings of normally developing children, suggesting that they also learn the coercive pattern and use it in their interactions with their family members. Their more prosocial skills are not as delayed, allowing fewer and less extreme negative interactions with peers and teachers. He found that the siblings were "intimately involved in mutual coercive interactions with each other" and felt that this might be part of the basic training of CDs. In most families, the mother's relationship with the identified patient was more conflicted than with the siblings, but siblings were often just as coercive. Bank, Patterson, and Reid (1996) used structural equation modeling to demonstrate that negative sibling interactions contributed to future behaviors. The boys who were arrested most often by the end of high school generally had clearly negative interchanges with their siblings in the context of ineffective parenting years earlier.

From a learning perspective, then, the process of developing conduct problems is inherently dyadic (at the least). The process is between or among people, not within one person, rooted in the behaviors of individuals in a connected system. Prevention studies have shown, however, that even early in the process the outcome can be changed. For example, van den Boom (1995) intervened with mothers who lived in poverty, had multiple stressors, and also had irritable infants. Reasoning that low maternal responsiveness was often shown by mothers from lower socioeconomic groups with children with behavior problems, van den Boom developed a program to train the mothers to respond sensitively to the needs and cries of their babies. Not only did the predicted reduction in irritability occur, but differences in relationship and behavior held up at 3-year follow-up.

The actual mechanism of the coercive process depends on the stimuli present, positive reinforcement, and, most powerfully, negative reinforcement, which is avoidance or escape from a situation, demand, or interaction that is aversive. Moment by moment changes in undesirable behavior by the child were found largely to be under stimulus control (Patterson & Fagot, 1967). That is, for example, who else is there and what are they doing? (The child cannot pester the dog if the dog is outside, out of range, but when the dog comes in, the probability of pestering the dog changes dramatically.) Positive reinforcement was found to be part of the process for some dyads. For example, a parent who gives in and buys the candy bar that the child is having a tantrum about, positively reinforces the behavior of having a tantrum, increasing the likelihood that the child will have a tantrum again on another, similar occasion.

Most central to the coercive process is negative reinforcement. In coercion, members of the family use aversive reactions to control the actions of the other(s). These aversive behaviors allow the child to avoid or escape from a demand or situation. They may operate in the three-step operant perspective that boils down to the parent acting in a way that is aversive to the child (perhaps giving the command to turn off the television); then the child reacts with aversive behaviors such as whining or stomping. The parent backs down; the child is reinforced, and more likely to whine and stomp in the face of the next unpleasant request. Most children cooperate or if not, use social skills to neutralize or deflect the request. However, children on the trajectory to conduct problems generally become more skilled at aversive responses at the cost of their developing prosocial options (Fagot & Pears, 1996). Parents may also have limited repertoires and rely heavily on coercion too. As a dyad, they learn that escalating the amplitude of the aversive responses works better, so that stomping moves to throwing things and parental scolding moves up a notch or two to yelling, insulting, or spanking. This escalation is generally a mutual function and eventually the household is characterized by loud, nasty, and defiant interchanges that reflect high levels of intensity and sometimes reach the point of violence. Snyder, Schrepferman, and St. Peter (1997) showed that aggressive boys whose families were observed both initiated and reciprocated aggression with parents and siblings. Their behavior was found to follow the patterns predicted by coercion theory; aggressive behavior was used to the extent it terminated conflict with family members (negative reinforcement model).

Sometimes the chain of events is a little longer with negative reinforcement still playing an important role. Here, a parent still makes a request that is undesirable to the child, the child behaves aversively, and then the parent backs down from the command. When the parent drops the request and talks of something else, the child calms down and behaves in a neutral or occasionally positive way. This in turn terminates the aversive event (child's undesirable behavior) for the parent, increasing the likelihood that he or she will back down the next time. Patterson found this to be the case in a series of field observations in the homes of those seeking treatment. He and his colleagues also noticed that these interactions become so well practiced that they appear to have the same automatic, overlearned qualities as the driving of someone who has been operating a motor vehicle for many years. The interactions are frequent, develop and escalate rapidly, and occur with little deliberation or thought (Patterson, 2002a, 2002b). They are most likely to occur during family conflicts. The aversiveness of interactions may also contribute to increased parent–child distance and reduced supervision. Parents sometimes say that it is just not worth it to get into a big argument with the child and the child has greater freedom from supervision than his typical siblings or agemates. Parents say that they have no impact anyway because the child may ignore their rules and limits and go on about their own desired activities, sometimes in an ostentatious fashion.

The form of conduct problems changes with age and development. Shaw and Winslow (1997) found that for preschool boys the progression begins with disobedience, and then moves to other forms. Patterson (1992) studied 59 preschool boys. The majority were considered by their mothers to be disobedient but half of the disobedient children progressed to temper tantrums and about 60% of those with tantrums went on to physical attacks, sometimes with parents as the desired target. Although there were a few exceptions to the progression, the direction was clear and one way. Follow-up showed that the boys who had engaged in temper tantrums and hitting in preschool were the ones likely to be identified by their second grade teachers as stealing and fighting. The escalation had continued.

Part of the progression of the conduct problems is the expansion of the coercive patterns to settings outside the family. Behavior in school and relationships with peers are both affected. As early as preschool, peers sometimes positively reinforce the conduct problem behaviors of their peers (Patterson, Littman, & Bricker, 1967), even as they reject as a friend-candidate the child who is aggressive or socially unskilled in interacting with them (Vitaro, Temblay, Gagnon, & Bouvin, 1992). Even in the preschool years, children who spent considerable time with aggressive peers showed reliable increases in their own aggression as recorded by observers and rated by teachers (Snyder, Horsch, & Childs, 1997). Snyder et al. interpreted their findings to mean that aggressive children are more able to shape the behavior of their companions than the reverse. In grade school, coercive behaviors progressively become more likely to be used with teachers. Overt defiance, angry outbursts, and demonstrative pushing of furniture can shape the demands teachers make on the children, just as they help to shape the demands of parents. Poor academic achievement may also make school work punishing, so avoidance is a desirable outcome. Tremblay et al. (1992) found, however, that school achievement problems were neither necessary for the development of antisocial behaviors nor helpful in predicting them but that early disruptiveness was a good predictor of later aggression. Repetti (1996) found that after children had failure experiences at school, they often behaved more aggressively and aversively at home, setting the stage for possible additional mutual coercion. In the primary grades, when children do not change classes frequently, they have a limited selection of people with whom to interact. Because the development of coercive behaviors is generally at the expense of developing alternative ways of interacting, skills for cooperation and relationship formation with peers are impaired. Thus, there are repeated opportunities for avoidance through coercion and rejection.

As children grow and progress in school, there is greater freedom to move among social groups and to choose people with whom to associate. Those choices usually rely on mutual positive reinforcement for maintenance. At this level, coercion and negative reinforcement contribute to rejection by prosocial children. Patterns of reinforcement are one source of the power of peers. Typical peers often reinforce prosocial behaviors like studying or avoiding fights (e.g., Kindermann, 1993). On the other hand, they can also reinforce antisocial behaviors such as physical aggression (Dishion, Patterson, & Griesler, 1994). As deviant children affiliate, they support aggression-based talk, such as, "I'm going to kick his butt after school" (Hayes & Wu, 1998). The reaction to verbalized intentions, in turn, can alter the likelihood of actually carrying out the behaviors. Conversation about engaging in conduct problem behaviors is not just talk, but has diverse developmental effects that last for years. Dishion and colleagues have termed this "peer deviancy training," which they have found to predict arrests, violent behavior, drug use, and sexual actions for at least the next 2 years (Dishion, Capaldi, Spacklen, & Li, 1995; Dishion, Eddy, Haas, Li, & Spracklen, 1997). By 4th grade, boys with early conduct problems have significantly higher rates of skipping school, sometimes with peers, and experimenting with substances (Patterson, 1993).

With peer support and reduced parental monitoring, preadolescents and adolescents with conduct problems may coerce their way into the habit of "running the streets," or being in a group of peers with antisocial behaviors for extended periods of time without adult supervision. This type of freedom is related to the further escalation of conduct problems and illegal activities (Dishion & Medici Skaggs, 2000; Stoolmiller, 1994). Patterson and Stouthamer-Loeber (1984) studied the behavior of junior high and high school boys, relating behavior to parenting variables. Monitoring by parents accounted for the greatest variance with regard to delinquency. Monitoring also differentiated moderate from persistent offenders. Monitoring is particularly important in neighborhoods occupied by adults and older teens and conduct problem peers who model and reinforce these kinds of behaviors. They provide a disproportionate number of opportunities for the child with the developing CD to try the antisocial activities. This constitutes further "deviancy training" and Dishion, McCord, and Poulin (1999) warned that it can be the unintended effect of some group treatments for conduct disordered youth, in addition to occurring in the natural environment.

Eddy, Leve, and Fagot (2001) enrolled over 500 boys and girls living in two-parent families in a longitudinal study that began when the children were 18 months old. Self-report of structured data, the Achenbach Child Behavior Checklist, and home observations were used. In general, 5-year olds were found to be a very compliant, nonaggressive group. There were exceptions, however. Using structural equation modeling, the authors found the relationship between what they termed "inept" parenting and conduct problems by the time the participants were 5 years old to be very similar to Patterson's model. The process was seen as applying to both boys and girls, although girls were somewhat less severe than boys in their behaviors.

There is clear consensus that the children who follow the early-onset pathway are the ones at greatest risk for serious criminal outcomes in adolescence and adulthood (Farrington, 1995; Rutter, Harrington, Quinton, & Pickles, 1994). They also are at highest risk for antisocial personality disorder and other mental health diagnoses; and they further show generally poorer adjustment, relationship problems, and poor vocational outcomes.

Late-Starter Pathway

The late-starter pathway has been proposed but the evidence for it is less well developed than for the early-starter pathway. The Dunedin Multidisciplinary Health Study (Moffitt et al., 1996) found that 24% of children are involved in this pathway, while only 7% are early starters. According to that epidemiologic study and others (e.g., McGee, Feehan, Williams, & Anderson, 1992), there is a major upswing in nonaggressive conduct problems during the preteen and early teen years (11 through 14). Both boys and girls are involved in this increase. In contrast to the early starters, the late starters had not had conduct problems at younger ages and there were no signs of verbal IQ deficits. Learning disabilities were not nearly as common, and temperamental differences were not as striking. Fewer late starters had been arrested for violent crimes. Overall the family resources and histories were more positive too.

Patterson et al. (1991) described families of late starters as "marginally effective," as they have somewhat stronger parenting skills than early-starter families. With the onset of a significant family stressor or change (e.g., divorce) or even the typical growing strains of teenage rebellion, these families no longer parent as well. Supervision drops off and the teens affiliate themselves with a group of peers who are engaging in conduct problems. However, because these young people had a longer period of social skills development and more personal and family resources, they are seen as less likely to persist in conduct problems over time. As in the younger starting cohort, late starters engage in conduct problems to the extent that relative rates of pay-off (support of peers or negative reinforcement from adults, etc.) in their lives make it worthwhile.

Simons, Wu, Conger, and Lorenz (1994) followed 169 boys for 4 years beginning when they were in seventh grade, with multiple data collection points. They corroborated the early- and late-starter groupings. For the early starters, parenting quality was a major predictor of conduct problems. For late starters, parenting quality had more to do with the choices the children made about friends and associates. In turn, those choices predicted the juvenile justice records of the teens. These investigators used structural equation modeling to test which of several theoretical perspectives best predicted the pattern of associations among social variable and police records. Their findings supported Patterson's view that there are two different paths to delinquency and that peer influences are more directly involved in outcome for late starters. Quality of parenting has an indirect role, serving to predict who would affiliate with peers who have already been in trouble with the law. They suggested that affiliation with deviant peers is the way adolescents learn to engage in conduct problems and/or break laws.

The behavioral conceptualization of CD is that it is the result of a fairly lengthy training process that involves the youthful offender and his family and other people in his environment. This dyadic process mutually shapes the behaviors of the participants so that aversiveness and avoidance become key aspects determining actions. Family and peers are important in this process but other adult systems such as school can also play a role in the problem or its treatment. In light of this conceptualization, behavioral treatment focuses on changing the specific consequences of behaviors, especially the avoidance and escape that negatively reinforce many coercive behaviors. Further, these contingencies must be altered for an indefinite period to prevent relapse. This can be facilitated by creating a new cycle of mutual reinforcement for prosocial or neutral behaviors. The conceptualization also suggests that multiple parts of the environment need to be involved, especially with older children, so that contingencies are altered at home, in free time with peers, and at school. Especially with early starters, basic social skills may need to be addressed because for most children, those skills suffer as the antisocial ones flourish.

Family-Based Interventions

Given the evidence that parenting skills deficits are at least in part responsible for the development and maintenance of CDs, the behavioral approach involves family members of the identified patient. Kazdin (1996) pointed out that parent training is the most well researched of all the interventions for CD. Kazdin (1995) outlined core elements of parent training. First, treatment is conducted primarily with the parents, with relatively less emphasis on therapist–child interaction. Second, treatment emphasizes prosocial goals and removes some of the focus from the undesirable conduct. Third, the treatment reflects the underlying learning theory. This means that defining, monitoring, and tracking the child's behavior are the focus of the parent training. Another central aspect is teaching parents methods of reinforcement that involve positive parent attention and extinction/punishment methods such as ignoring, response cost, and time out. Instruction in giving clear commands and in problem solving are commonly included in parent training. Last, the methods of teaching are behavioral in nature with frequent use of modeling, role playing, and structured homework. The intention is to disrupt the longstanding moment-by-moment parent–child interactions, replacing the old pattern with a less coercive and more positive set.

The effectiveness of parent training methods have been repeatedly evaluated and the behavioral approach to this training is considered to have reached criteria to be called empirically supported (Christophersen & Mortweet, 2002; Kazdin, 1995). Because noncompliance with parental commands and requests is a central feature, programs often focus on that symptom as one of the behavior sets to be changed. In Forehand's program *Helping the Noncompliant Child* (Forehand & McMahon, 1981), parents were taught to change their patterns of interaction in the "here-and-now" of the clinic by the use of the "bug in the ear" mechanism. Skills were taught didactically, then rehearsed, then coached during practice with the child. Ways of creating a more positive, mutually rewarding relationship were introduced first, followed by learning to give clear commands and use time out when they are not obeyed. Progression through the program was based on a competency model with criteria for passing. Generalization to the home environment was demonstrated (Peed, Roberts, & Forehand, 1977), and long-term effectiveness was tested in multiple studies from 6 months to as long as 14 years after treatment (Baum & Forehand, 1981; Long, Forehand, Wierson, & Morgan, 1994).

Eyberg and Matarazzo (1980), working from the same perspective as Forehand, evaluated Parent–Child Interaction Training for young children with disruptive behavior. Compared to a didactic approach and a wait list control, this method was most helpful. In a follow-up study (Eyberg & Robinson, 1982) parents were taught to alter their way of interacting with their children in play and command situations. Not only did this behavioral method improve the relationship of the mother and child, but it also increased rates of compliance in children who were less compliant than their siblings. Interestingly, treatment effects also generalized to the sibling's behaviors, and parent satisfaction was high.

There have been many variations on parent training as put forth by Forehand, most of which showed good outcomes. The videotape modeling and discussion program of Webster-Stratton (1981) used vignettes and a parents-only group format, augmented by homework of practicing newly presented parenting skills. Both short-and long-term behavior changes in the offspring with conduct problems were noted (Webster-Stratton, 1990). Webster-Stratton has since developed a second phase of treatment, designed to follow the first, that produces documented improvements in communication and problem solving. She also developed a series for the children that is designed to focus on social skills and classroom behaviors, also using videos as a core component (Webster-Stratton, 1997). Including teachers to address consistent goals in classroom behavior management was also found to facilitate behavior change in childhood conduct problems (Webster-Stratton, 1996).

Similarly, Patterson and his colleagues developed programs of intervention using the classic *Living with Children* and *Families* books as the core (Patterson, 1975). These books can be used preventively or remedially. The books, which are in programmed learning format, teach tracking of the problem behaviors or concerns, and a simple token economy based on points with back-up reinforcers. In keeping with his research that identified the need for punishment to change the behaviors of children with CDs, the program introduces response cost and chores for use with older children. The basic program and many variants have been repeatedly evaluated. Changes reflecting major decreases in noncompliance and improvements in adjustment that last for at least 2 years have been reliably found (Arnold, Levine, & Patterson, 1975; Patterson, 1974; Patterson & Forgatch, 1995; Patterson & Reid, 1973) although there have been exceptions (e.g., Eyberg & Johnson, 1974). The parent training program also produced better behavior change outcomes than either "eclectic" or family therapy (Patterson & Chamberlain, 1988; Patterson, Chamberlain, & Reid, 1982).

Sells (2001) has written one of the more detailed books for parents wanting to change the way their teenagers act. It is written for parents whose offspring are exhibiting problem behaviors or who are "out-of-control." There is no empirical evaluation of these methods but they are generally consistent with contingency management. Sells instructs parents to take control back by making their offspring accountable for their behaviors with "ironclad" behavior contracts. The method for writing these contracts is spelled out and includes considerable input from the teens themselves. The book also points out the need for parents to design a "Plan B" and have it ready to implement even while implementing "Plan A." He endorses involving the wider community of adults, and sometimes peers, in the interventions. Sells is explicit about the importance of parents working to develop more positive relationships with the teens, even when they are furious with their teen's behaviors.

The Oregon parent training programs have been modified to meet the needs of adolescents with CD and their families. Parents can include any undesirable behavior they think places the teenager at risk for further delinquency and include that behavior as a target. There is also considerable emphasis on teaching parental monitoring, especially as it relates to school. Specifics of rewards and punishments are altered and may include court proceedings as punishment. There is also greater involvement of the adolescent particularly in developing mutually agreed upon behavior contracts with parents (Bank, Marlowe, Reid, Patterson, & Weinrott, 1991). Some contracts reached the complexity of simple token economies. During treatment, teenagers in the groups whose parents received behavioral training had fewer arrests and fewer nonstatus arrests but those differences did not hold at 1 year. Nonetheless, the teens who were in the parent training condition were institutionalized for shorter times, which resulted in financial gain. Dishion and Andrews (1995) divided families with preteen and early teenage children with behavior problems into four groups. One group had interventions with the parents only to address behavior management, one focused on the teens only to address prosocial skill development, one had the therapist meet with both parents and teens, and the other was a self-directed change control group. The parent only group had rapid effects on school behaviors. However, they found that adolescents who met in groups with other teens with behavior problems showed persistent post-treatment escalations in problem behavior and smoking, suggesting an iatrogenic affect.

Behavioral methods also have been found to be useful for the treatment of youths with CDs who are living in foster care. One such example is the Teaching Family model (TFM), which has been evaluated many times (Blase, Fixsen, Freeborn, & Jaeger, 1989). This model uses detailed contingency management for both positive and negative behaviors. Fewer offenses were committed by adolescents in the program compared to those in control group homes but no lasting effect was found. Behavior has been found to improve in the TFM homes but once the teens return to their original environments, the effect diminishes rapidly (e.g., Kirigin, Braukmann, Atwater, & Wolf, 1982). Behavioral theory would call for changing the contingencies at home too, because the behavior is embedded in a social context.

To address some of these issues, Chamberlain and her colleagues developed and evaluated a similar program known as "treatment foster care" in which adolescents with conduct problems were placed in foster homes where the parents had received training in learning-based parenting skills (Chamberlain, 1994; Chamberlain & Reid, 1994). The system also has support for the foster parents, including 24-hour on call consultation and weekly meetings. Foster parents were taught how to advocate in the schools and support academics with home report cards. Individual skills training for teens was also provided. Simultaneously, the teen's family of origin was engaged in treatment to teach them the same parenting principles so that there a successful transfer home could occur. Compared to typical foster parents, those with training reported fewer major teen behavior problems, fewer changes in residence for the teens, and improved behavior management (Chamberlain,

Moreland, & Reid, 1992). A separate evaluation found similar increases in foster parent competence to manage behavior, reduced behavior problems, and a shorter time until the child returned home (Chamberlain & Reid, 1991).

Since the 1960s, behavior management in the classroom has been the topic of considerable research. Despite teacher beliefs that they often praise their students, classroom observations have shown low rates of positive attention for prosocial behaviors (Martens & Hiralall, 1997; White, 1975). Strategies that help the teacher to arrange classroom contingencies to favor prosocial behaviors and reduce classroom disruption are especially helpful with children with mild-to-moderate conduct problems (Walker, Hops, & Fiegenbaum, 1976). Token reinforcement systems have been used with success for classroom management of disruptive behaviors, especially to increase the prosocial behaviors that are incompatible with conduct problem behaviors. Abramowitz and O'Leary (1991) reviewed the use of token systems in schools and report consistent decreases in aggressive and disruptive behaviors along with an increase in more desirable classroom behavior. Fading the token system needs to be carried out carefully and strategically so that more naturally occuring environmental contingencies can maintain the newly developed behaviors.

There is a more recent body of research that indicates that combining positive and punitive approaches to contingency management in the classroom results in better outcomes than either alone (Pfiffner & O'Leary, 1987; Walker, Hops, & Greenwood, 1993). Several school programs that rely heavily on contingency management have been designed for younger children with conduct problems. The Center at Oregon for Research in Behavioral Education of the Handicapped (CORBEH) plan (Hops & Walker, 1988), the Contingencies for Learning Academic and Social Skills (CLASS) program (Walker & Hops, 1979), and Reprogramming Environmental Contingencies for Effective Social Skills (RECESS) intervention (Walker et al., 1993), all of which rely on skills training and contingency management, have been found to be effective in the short term. CORBEH and CLASS both showed treatment gains relative to controls at least 3 years after completion of the program.

THERAPIST SKILLS AND ATTRIBUTES

Working with any family in therapy requires knowledge of family function, normal and abnormal development, and, obviously, competence in the therapeutic modality being used. It also requires the clinical skill to carry out therapy with a stressed and distressed family, and the empathy to relate to the teenager and important adults in his or her life. Ethical awareness and practice are also assumed, but working with teenagers who break the law can readily challenge a therapist in this regard. When using a behavioral approach, assuming a collaborative stance that recognizes the various areas of expertise of all involved in the process is typically preferable. The role of the therapist, then, is not that of one more person telling everyone what to do; instead, the therapist is a facilitator and coworker. Working collaboratively also helps in managing the family's hopelessness, and can assist the therapist in understanding the family's perspective on the situation, which can be very different from that of the therapist's. Collaboration also helps the therapist (and family) manage the blocks to progress that inevitably emerge. Collaboration is also a useful approach for working with professionals in schools or other systems. Cultural sensitivity, while necessary in all cases, is often particularly important in working with youths with CD because the backgrounds, habits, and beliefs of these families are often different from those of the therapist, even when the clients otherwise "look like" the therapist. There are significant and, to some extent, predictable differences among parents from different backgrounds regarding beliefs about tasks of parents, the role of children, and methods of socializing offspring (Forehand & Kotchick, 1996).

Working with families who have a child with CD can call for other more specific therapist characteristics. The work can be a draining, frustrating experience. One of the important characteristics of the clinicians carrying out therapy with these families is patience. Because part of the family functioning that contributed to the development of a CD is the use of coercion, the therapist must be able to identify when he or she too is being coerced by a family member, while remaining able to respond to it differently than the family members have over the years. This often requires being "tuned into" one's own emotional and even physical reactions to the coercive cycle so that the coercion can be recognized. Therapists who work effectively with families with CD are also able to keep the therapy on course regardless of the multitude of events that may cloud the direction and provide distraction from the real issues. This characteristic may require both confidence and firmness. In addition, easy access to consultation or being part of a team is often helpful for that purpose. A sense of humor can be helpful in normalizing events and relieving tension when there is yet another return to former functioning. Last, the therapist must ensure that participants know how to reach him or her in a crisis. The intent is not to breed dependency, but to offer an alternative to the current behavior patterns of conflict and impulsive, aggressive actions.

THE CASE OF "MIKE"

Conceptualization, Assessment, and Treatment Planning

Additional Information

From a behavioral perspective, much of the information that is most relevant for treatment planning for Mike and his family is not included in the provided information. In particular, the provided history related to Mike's behavior seems to indicate that he is a "late starter," which has implications for treatment (Frick, 2004). A more detailed history related to the onset of his conduct problems would be necessary to confirm this impression, however. Given the early difficult temperament, his teachers' concerns over the years, and his mediocre to poor grades since fifth grade, it also would be important to determine whether or not Mike has an attention deficit hyperactivity disorder (ADHD) or a specific learning disability. The Wechsler Intelligence Scale for Children—IV (WISC-IV, Wechsler, 2003) and Wide Range Achievement Test—3 (WRAT-3; Wilkinson, 1993) scores suggested that he is not having significant difficulty with academic learning, although as acknowledged, the WRAT is useful only as a screening device here. Review of Mike's performance on standardized and proficiency tests might save any need for further testing. I would also ask his teacher to complete a teacher's report form of the Achenbach Child Behavior Checklist (Achenbach, 1991b), the School Situations Questionnaire (Barkley, 1997a, 1997b), and the Conners Rating Scale (Conners, 1990), and Ms. D. would be asked to complete the parent version of the Conners, the ADHD Rating Scale (DuPaul, 1991), to provide additional information about ADHD symptoms. If the results of the scales suggest that ADHD is part of the clinical presentation, I would ask for permission to communicate with Mike's physician to discuss whether he or she felt a trial of medication might be helpful, in which case parent and teacher could be used to track drug effects, one of the best uses of that scale.

Ms. D. would also be asked to complete the Eyberg Child Behavior Inventory (Eyberg, 1992) to assess disruptive behaviors, and she would also be asked to keep a log regarding Mike's problem behaviors. This log would track oppositional, aggressive, and antisocial behaviors by time, place, persons involved, behaviors involved, events that preceded the problem behavior, and what happened afterward. This log would help elucidate patterns of behavior, serving as a functional analysis. If I could enlist Mike in the process, I would ask him to keep a similar log so that I could see events from his perspective, as well as gain information about events that occurred outside of his mother's presence. If I had a staff member who could economically carry out a school visit and a home visit, I would arrange for behavior observations, using frequency counts of target behaviors distributed across small segments of time or the direct observation form of the Child Behavior Checklist (Achenbach, 1991a). If no such person were available, I would ask the family to leave a video camera running during whatever 2–3-hour period was noted to have the most frequent conflicts and to bring in a film of one of their altercations. This approximates a field observation and allows the interchange among family members to be viewed without having to rely on each participant's memory and viewpoint.

The question of substance use is also important. Mike has admitted to marijuana use and it appears supported by his peers. Monitoring the frequency of Mike's marijuana use and what other drug use is occurring should be an ongoing aspect of treatment. If drug use continues, it needs to be addressed in individual sessions and in parent training sessions that occur with Ms. D. and perhaps Mr. D. as well.

Finally, an assessment of what constitutes meaningful consequences for Michael would be helpful. The list could constitute things to work for as well as things to work to avoid. They should include both tangible rewards, such as money, CDs, or certain kinds of clothes, and intangibles like time interacting with parents in a desired setting or certain privileges. It is also important to assess meaningful punishments such as fines, keeping belongings from his use, or banning him from activities with friends (grounding). Modeling further aggression through corporal punishment would not be recommended, even if Ms. D. were physically capable of doing so.

Therapeutic Goals

In working with this family, it would be critical to have input from Ms. D. and Mike regarding their goals for treatment. It could be useful to involve Mr. D. (separately from Ms. D.) and Mike's sister in that endeavor. Based on the history, testing, and interview material, my primary goals in the short term would be to improve the relationship between Michael and his mother and reduce both their conflicts and Mike's conduct problems. In the longer term, improving Mike's prosocial behaviors and skills to promote responsible behaviors, altering his peer affiliation, eliminating drug use, and improving academic achievement would be important.

Length of Treatment

Treatment for CD is not brief therapy. Previous behavioral literature suggests that involvement with the family for a year is common, although the number of sessions per month may diminish over time. With parent training, 45 hours of treatment, some perhaps by phone, is not unusual. Because Mr. D. is not living in the home, has sporadic contact with Michael, and is not likely to make a major commitment to therapy, Ms. D. would receive the parent training. It could be readily carried out in a group setting with occasional individual consultations, probably to address the arguments between Michael and his sister and other situations in need of rapid problem solving. The group would also provide Ms. D. with support and, perhaps, perspective as other parents discuss their situations. There would be occasions when I would try to enlist Mr. D., in treatment, primarily to get his backing for some plans or to involve him as a reinforcer for Mike. A similar arrangement would be made with Mike's sister, with occasional meetings with her, Mike, and Ms. D. Several hours of consultation with the school personnel would be required to address ADHD (if found), remediate his academic weaknesses, and deal with truancy. Individual sessions for developing Mike's skills and promoting prosocial behaviors would require an additional 20–40 hours. Ideally, contact would also occur with Mike's probation officer, probably by phone, to let him know about the family's follow-through and to assess the program's effectiveness in terms of new legal issues.

Case Conceptualization

Michael has had a challenging temperament but there is no history of early disciplinary problems. If no such history were to emerge with deliberate inquiry, Michael would qualify as a late starter, suggesting that until the disruption of having his father leave the family and his mother return to work full time, many aspects of his functioning were probably in the typical range. Other features of his adjustment, such as academic achievement and classroom behavior, have been at times marginal. The possible ADHD may account for these problems. The divorce and disruption in his family and the resulting change in Ms. D.'s availability, self-efficacy, and monitoring interacted with the typical developmental increase in peer importance in early teen years to lead to undesirable peer affiliations and conduct problems. The significant change in the availability of Mr. D. constituted a loss for Mike and a further disruption in parenting. It has also diminished Ms. D.'s ability to monitor and supervise Mike's activities, alone and with his peers. Mike's sister, like most siblings of teens with CD, knows how to "push his buttons" and how to activate her mother's involvement, even if she is also legitimately scared and upset.

Prognostication is limited by the absence of the supplementary data, but it appears that Mike exemplifies the late-starter category of conduct problems, which means he has a better prognosis than if he had been an early starter. His mother's caring and cooperation are strengths and his father's failure to obstruct the process is at least neutral rather than an obstacle. With some effort, Mr. D. might become involved in the therapeutic process, if only to prove he can handle Mike. Another positive indication, if accurate, is his mother's belief that Mike is worried about the outcome of his court hearing. This suggests that there could be remorse and if not, at least the worry that there may be a punishment that is meaningful to him. In some respects, his willingness to interrupt his mother, even rudely, to indicate he has another view of what she is saying also suggests he has not become entirely apathetic to the process. His anger, perhaps, his sense that his friends left him to take the blame, might also be harnessed in the name of progress.

There were no indications of suicidal ideation that would point to self-endangerment. On the other hand, his impulsivity, drug use, and thoughts of running away suggest that there is a lower level of possible danger to himself that could result from poor judgment and lack of forethought. Because increased monitoring would be one of the earliest goals, it is likely that the danger from impulsive actions might decrease, but Mike's anger at perceived restrictions could lead to a crisis for which Mr. and Ms. D. would each need to be prepared. Although Mike has pushed and shoved his sister (as his father modeled for him with his mother) and indicated he could "really hurt her" (or, perhaps, the mother fears, kill her), he has shown the ability to inhibit himself, at least when angry at his mother. In the interim, his sister clearly provides stimulus control for the worst of his outbursts. Keeping her away from Mike and addressing their fighting and arguing early in the treatment (involving all three family members) should be enough to protect them all.

The Therapeutic Relationship

A behavior therapist working on a child also works with the family, and must wear many hats. The therapist must be able to form relationships with difficult teens, and angry, frustrated, sometimes frightened parents. As with any therapy, the clinician will be more successful if the "common factors" of various approaches, empathy, positive regard, and genuineness, are evident. Good listening skills and clarifying the statements of clients are important to the relationship. The discussion of confidentiality and therapist behavior that lives up to what is promised is important to build trust and facilitate communication. The therapist could use play or play-like activities to engage Mike and relieve tension. Although Mike is apparently trying to be tough, games or puzzles that allow cooperative efforts can help the relationship by creating a nonconfrontational, pleasurable time, similar to the ones he and his mother can come to enjoy together. The relationship, however, is not formed as an end in itself, but is a means to establishing trust, creating useful communication, and perhaps, establishing the reinforcing qualities of the therapist.

One of the most useful roles for a therapist working with families with CD from a behavioral perspective is to be a collaborator. More specifically, the expertise of all participants, including Mike, should be acknowledged and brought into the problem-solving process. The therapist has one type of expertise, but family members bring a useful, if different, expertise. Although Ms. D. should be supported in her role as adult authority for the family, all family members have an equal contribution to the therapeutic process and all are involved in the problem. Collaboration creates another role for the therapist, that of model. Collaboration is the antithesis of coercion and thus, serves an alternative to the pattern that the family maintains. The therapist models and teaches problems solving, negotiating and compromising (through behavior contracts), holding people accountable for their actions, and reacting in a thoughtful fashion rather than an impulsive one. Being a collaborator is also different from being an authority, a figure to whom many families with CD have strong, negative responses. Some well-chosen self-disclosure can be useful as a way to emphasize the collaborative nature of the relationship. Collaboration also calls for the family members to be active evaluators of sessions and specific interventions, and to provide their opinions on whether something worked and can be maintained.

A subtext of being willing to be a collaborator in addressing family problems is the communication that the therapist believes there is hope for change. The expression of optimism and recognition of the strengths and positive actions of family members is a message that can help people tolerate discomfort, struggle, and temporary set backs. Similarly, backing and coaching the parents (or to use the common psychological parlance, "empowering parents"), rather than taking over or doing for them is part of this message of belief in change.

Another "hat" worn by therapists is consultant to schools. Forming a collaborative relationship with school professionals will be helpful in obtaining information about the school's view of the situation and Mike's progress toward better behavior and achievement. If some session time will be held during school hours, it provides a good point for joint planning and collaboration to minimize the work and content to be missed. More important, if new actions are being requested of teachers, collaboration to reach shared goals is more effective than an authority figure calling to make demands, especially in the context of an ongoing relationship.

A therapist is also a consultant to representatives of other systems such as the probation officer, pediatrician, or medicating psychiatrist. Collaboration is key, coupled with perseverance because all involved are likely to be difficult to reach by phone. Having a therapist who is fully informed of what is happening in the treatment of the client and family and what they are doing in and out of therapy is important for establishing credibility. Confidentiality, as negotiated with the family, needs to be maintained, of course.

It is often difficult for one person to work with the parent, the teen, various family members, and outside systems. In situations where staffing arrangements allow, dividing relationships and tasks among more than one therapist is recommended. That way, there is less perceived conflict of interest and if joint sessions are held, each individual involved can have a professional as an advocate.

Treatment Implications and Outcome

One of the first steps in any therapy is to address expectations of the participants and to clarify the match between what is planned and what is anticipated. (For example, many parents expect the therapist to "fix" the child. Mr. D. may fall in this category.) This exploration also opens the door to discussion of procedural necessities such as frequency of meetings, who will be involved in what ways, and how the process will unfold. The second aspect is to address any concerns about differences between the therapist and the family. These may include race, age, gender, or ethnicity. Discussion of these differences can model openness and allows any concerns to be voiced as a way to reduce anxiety and encourage mutual trust.

Therapeutic Techniques and Strategies

Many parents expect and dread that they will be blamed for the problems in their families. Interestingly, they may do this at the same time they blame their offspring for their antisocial behavior. An important strategy to manage this issue is to reduce blame, which often translates into two phases: educating the family in the learning model and then using it to refocus the problem and its solutions. In the first phase, the model is explained and then the observation notes or videotape is used to illustrate the sequence and the mutuality of the process. This helps to shift the focus from there being one improperly behaving teenager, to a whole family with problematic interactions and "autopilot" habits that lead to repeated conflicts. Many families find that they can accept a learning model explanation for family problems (Gordon, Arbuthnot, Gustafson, & McGreen, 1988). Accepting the learning model means that the solution is no longer for Mike to stop being the problem, but rather for all to change the nature of their behaviors toward each other. An analysis of the consequences of antisocial behavior (part of a functional analysis), especially the role of negative reinforcement, is key for guiding what happens next in therapy. Accountability is increased and blame decreased.

For Mike, an important intervention will be to increase the supervision and monitoring of his activities, in and out of the home. Although parent training could certainly address the skill aspect and expand Ms. D.'s options, it is likely that someone outside of the family will need to be recruited, given Mr. D.'s job demands and attitudes, and Ms. D.'s work hours. Although at 13, Mike is too old for most after-school child care programs, there are in many cities, recreation centers, Boys' clubs, church groups, and similar activities that he could be expected to attend. If those are not viable options, jobs, sitting in the break room of his mother's work, going to the home of a friend or neighbor, being tutored, or volunteering can all be considered as alternatives to Mike spending time without adult supervision. If lack of supervision is a common problem in Mike's neighborhood, community action could also be helpful in starting some supervised but "cool" and fun activities for people in that age range.

Many techniques are routinely used for the mastery of skills, including parental monitoring. These include explicit teaching, sometimes with illustrative video footage (e.g., Webster-Stratton, 1996). Didactics are often followed by modeling, role-play, and coached behavioral rehearsal. During coached behavioral rehearsal, a scenario or task is set for the parent(s) and child(ren). Ideally the resulting interactions are observed by live video feed or through an observation window. The therapist can call into the room, declare breaks to process, or communicate to at least one parent through a bug in the ear. Homework assignments are routine, often accompanied by sheets of instructions to prompt the parents and avoid misunderstanding. It is crucial to follow up on assignments and demonstrate their importance in the process. Problem solving, relaxation training, and assertiveness skills may be taught to parents in addition to specific parenting skills. Teens like Michael may need to learn anger management, study, relaxation, assertion, problem solving, and social skills.

Another commonly used technique is behavioral contracting. This involves a carefully crafted agreement between the teenager and parent(s). Each participant in the contract spells out the agreed-upon behavior change (not nagging, not swearing, not acting disrespectfully) with careful definition of what the behaviors mean in detailed behavioral terms. An example would be defining disrespect as mumbling under one's breath, imitating the person's statements in an unflattering way, or rolling one's eyes when asked to carry out a task. It requires the clearest description possible to avoid disagreements about whether the promised actions have been carried out. The consequences for both success and failure to carry them out are specified equally transparently. Consequences can be presented hierarchically: for the first violation a consequence occurs but the consequences escalate with each offense of that category that follows. A common error in implementing this strategy is the failure to evaluate the value the child places on the consequences. That is, does Mike find confinement to his room or loss of computer access an event he would work to avoid, or are these only minor inconveniences? Is earning a new game for his PlayStation desirable, or will his grandparents purchase him one, even if his behavior problems continue? Although it can take some time (and, sometimes, trial and error) to identify meaningful contingencies, that time is well spent in the behavior change outcome it can provide.

Careful design of a back-up strategy is useful because often teens with CD find ways around the original plan. Patterson found that the use of punishment was necessary to establish changes in teens with conduct problems. Mild ignoring or absence of positive reinforcement did not bring about change. Similar results seem highly likely in Mike's situation too. Punishment such as response cost, extra work, additional school time, loss of privileges, or removal of a valued object (e.g., his cell phone, the TV, or computer in his room) are likely to be necessary to produce rapid behavior change. With Mike and his mother, there would be many possibilities for such contracts, but they should not all be included in one, huge document. Rather, choosing a few behaviors to address first would keep the behavior contract from overwhelming all of them.

Breaking the coercive cycle with humor or absurdity can also be effective. Sells (2001) gave the example of responding to a coercive act by having family members dance around the room while singing a children's song. On the other hand, he emphasized that a back-up plan would need to be in place in case that did not work. Retreating from Mike's presence, then calling male relatives Mike respects who had been prepared ahead of time to come over and show their views of his behavior was one of the possible back-up plans.

The previous caveat not withstanding, it is important to use positive reinforcement. In tense and distressed families, praise and statements of appreciation are rare, primarily because of family member's anger and the coercive interaction cycle. When people are feeling hurt and angry, or put upon and ill-treated, it is not likely that they naturally reinforce each other for desirable actions. Instead, desirable acts tend to be unnoticed, treated suspiciously, or greeted with some variant of "it's about time." It is critical in a family with CD to start to rebuild some of the positive aspects of the parent–child relationship. Although finding things to praise and making positive statements are helpful, often parents do not want to risk taking the first step and being rejected. Obstacles to parents' being able to take the first step need to be considered with the parent. It is a long-established finding that differential attention to desirable behaviors has been shown to increase the likelihood of those behaviors occurring again.

Positive time together that is not contingent on behavior is also helpful even if often very difficult at first. "Compulsory fun" such as going out to eat once a week, going to the mall for 2 hours, or going fishing, carried out on a routine basis, has been found to be a way to start to alter the microinterchanges. Mike and each of his parents could develop scheduled, predictable times for doing something together. Something similar may be useful to help him develop a positive relationship with his older sister.

Identifying stimuli that seem to control the antisocial behavior is important (part of a functional analysis). Patterson (1982) found that about a third of all aggression by boys with conduct problems was "counterattack" rather than initiation. Certain people and situations are particularly associated with violent or verbally abusive outbursts. Some of these can be avoided or changed through interventions such as contingency contracting with the other person. This feature of intervention demonstrates the role of siblings, and it is important to show siblings that they are also expected to be actively engaged in behavior change when they are involved as instigators.

Mechanism of Change
The mechanism of change is the intervening in the coercive cycle through altering stimuli and contingencies. The therapist's collaborative and supportive stance is what may make the changes possible for parents, siblings, or the identified patient. Changing contingencies in several settings (home, school, the community) is the one hope for aiding in generalization.

Medical and Nutritional Issues
If Mike has been receiving ongoing physicals and medical care over the year, it could be useful to contact the physician to rule out concerns that parents did not communicate. From the parents' reports, there are no apparent medical issues regarding Mike, with the exception of possible ADHD and/or effects of substance abuse, as described earlier. The use of medication for ADHD, if present, could be helpful, and this will require some ongoing communication with the prescribing physician. There is no information provided as to Mike's nutrition, but assuming there is no eating disorder present, I would have no nutritional intervention in mind for Mike.

Potential Pitfalls

Just about anyone attempting behavior change experiences obstacles to accomplishing that goal. One of the major pitfalls could turn out to be Mr. D.; he may be threatened by any progress that his former wife makes regarding Mike' behavior, as he seems to see himself as the "successful" disciplinarian. Depending on his contact with Mike, he could sabotage the effort. To prevent this pitfall, it would be important to enlist him as one of the treatment team, if at all possible. Having the parents together in one room is not likely to be helpful due to other issues that could lead to arguments and blaming. But seeing Mike with each parent and/or each parent alone would be more likely to be productive. Another potential pitfall is the ever-present possibility that Mike could escalate his behaviors as the rule and contingencies change. An extinction burst might well be expected, which could bring more aggression or higher levels or criminal action. Moving Mike to affiliate with peers who are not in trouble with the law will be difficult as well. Parents are often successful in limiting contacts, but finding new contacts with nondeviant boys can be a challenge, especially if Mike has begun to have a reputation as a "bad" boy in the neighborhood. That is, other parents may be hesitant to allow their sons to affiliate with someone who may have a negative influence on them. Therefore, involvement in structured activities such as sports teams, clubs, or other activities may allow new friendships to form, and to give parents an opportunity to see Mike's strengths as a potential friend. Along these lines, I would recommend working with Mike alone rather than seeing him in a group with other boys with CD because of the risk of his becoming more skilled and more socialized in that direction.

Termination and Relapse Prevention

Termination should be determined by two factors: improvement and consensus. Specifically, improvement would be defined by well-reduced or eliminated antisocial behaviors, academic achievement at least to the average level, improved relationships among family members, and reduction or cessation of drug use. Although Mike's self report would be an important measure, observations of interactions with his parents and sister, teachers' reports, grades, and the parents' reports of his substance use and behavior in the home would be confirmatory. Consensus has to do with the agreement of family members that they were ready to terminate. Given the nature of CD, length of time required for treatment, and the intensity of some of the relationships that are likely to develop, a gradual decrease in frequency of sessions, with booster sessions at scheduled intervals would be the preferred mode. Relapse prevention would involve reiteration of the signs of the cycle of coercion and recognition of upcoming challenges with successful planning by the family to manage them, with minimal therapist input. His peer affiliations will be one sentinel sign. Relapse prevention would also involve deliberate challenges in the office for Ms. D. and Mike to work out in the here and now while the therapist watches from another room, if possible. Predicting occasional relapses to the family and developing a written plan to remind them how to approach them would be the final relapse prevention activity.

REFERENCES

Abramowitz, A. J., & O'Leary, S. G. (1991). Behavioral interventions for the classroom: Implications for students with ADHD. *School Psychology Review, 20*, 220–234.

Achenbach, T.M. (1991a). *Manual for the Revised Child Behavior Profile and the Child Behavior Checklist*. Burlington, VT: University of Vermont, Department of Psychiatry.

Achenbach, T. M. (1991b). *Manual for the Teacher's Report Form and 1991 Profile*. Burlington, VT: University of Vermont, Department of Psychiatry.

Arnold, J. E., Levine, A. G., & Patterson, G. R. (1975). Changes in sibling behavior following family intervention. *Journal of Consulting and Clinical Psychology, 43*, 683–688.

Bank, L., Marlowe, J., H., Reid, J., B., Patterson, G. R., & Weinrott, M. R. (1991). A comparative evaluation of parent training interventions for families of chronic delinquents. *Journal of Abnormal Child Psychology, 19*, 15–33.

Bank, L., Patterson, G.R., & Reid, J.B. (1996). Negative sibling interaction patterns as predictors of later adjustment problems in adolescent and young males. In G.H. Brody (Ed.) *Sibling relationships: Their causes and consequences* (pp. 197 229). Norwood, NJ: Ablex publishing.

Barkley, R. A. (1994). Impaired delayed responding: A unified theory of attention deficit hyperactivity disorder. In D. K. Routh (Ed.), *Disruptive behavior disorders: Essays in honor of Herbert Quay* (pp.11–57). New York: Plenum Press.

Barkley, R. A. (1997a). *Defiant children: A clinician's manual for assessment and parent training* (2nd ed.). New York: Guilford Press.

Barkley, R. A. (1997b). Behavioral inhibition, sustained attention, and executive functions: Constructing a unifying theory of ADHD. *Psychological Bulletin, 121*, 65–94.

Barkley, R. A., & Biederman, J. (1997). Toward a broader definition of the age-of-onset criterion for attention-deficit hyperactivity disorder. *Journal of American Academy of Child and Adolescent Psychiatry, 36*, 1204–1210.

Bates, J. E., Bayles, K., Bennett, D. S., Ridge, B., & Brown, M. M. (1991). Origins of externalizing behavior problems at eight years of age. In D. J. Pepler, & K. H. Rubin (Eds.), *The development and treatment of childhood aggression* (pp. 93–120). Hillsdale, NJ: Erlbaum.

Baum, C. G., & Forehand, R. (1981). Long-term follow-up assessment of parent training by use of multiple-outcome measures. *Behavior Therapy, 12*, 643–652.

Biederman, J., Faraone, S. V., Milberger, S., Jetton, J. G., Garcia, J., Chen, L., Mick, E., Greene, R. W. & Russell, R. W. (1996). Is childhood oppositional defiant disorder a precursor to adolescent conduct disorder? Findings from a four-year follow up study of children with ADHD. *Journal of American Academy of Child and Adolescent Psychiatry, 35*, 1193–1204.

Blase, K. A., Fixsen, D. L., Freeborn, K., & Jaeger, D. (1989). The behavioral model. In R. D. Lyman, S. Prentice-Dunn, & S. Gabel (Eds.), *Residential and inpatient treatment of children and adolescents* (pp. 43–59). New York: Plenum Press.

Brennan, P. A., & Mednick, S. A. (1997). Medical histories of antisocial individuals. In D. M. Stoff, J. Breiling, and J. D. Maser (Eds.), *Handbook of antisocial behavior* (pp. 269–279). New York: Wiley.

Brown, R. T., Coles, C. D., Smith, I. E., Platzman, K. A., Silverstein, J., Erickson, S., & Falek, A. (1991). Effects of prenatal alcohol exposure at school age: II. Attention and behavior. *Neurotoxicology and Teratology, 13*, 369–376.

Cadoret, R., Yates, W. R., Troughton, E., Woodworth, G., & Stewart, L. (1995). Adoption study demonstrating two genetic pathways to substance abuse. *Archives of General Psychiatry, 52*, 42–52.

Caspi, A., Elder, G. H., Jr., & Bem, D. J. (1987). Moving against the world: Life-course patterns of explosive children. *Developmental Psychology, 23*, 308–313.

Chamberlain, P. (1994). *Family connections.* Eugene, OR: Castalia.

Chamberlain, P., Moreland, S., & Reid, J. B., (1992). Enhanced services and stipends for foster parents: Effects on retention rates and outcomes of children. *Child Welfare, 71*, 387–401.

Chamberlain, P., & Reid, J. B. (1991). Using a specialized foster care community treatment model for children and adolescents leaving the state mental health hospital. *Journal of Community Psychology, 19*, 266–276.

Chamberlain, P., & Reid, J. B. (1994). Differences in risk factors and adjustment for male and female delinquents in treatment foster care. *Journal of Child and Family Studies, 3*, 23–39.

Christophersen, E. W., & Mortweet, S. L. (2002). *Treatments that work with children: Empirically supported strategies for managing childhood problems.* Washington, DC: American Psychological Association.

Coie, J. D., & Dodge, K. A. (1998). Aggression and antisocial behavior. In W. Damon (Ed.), *Handbook of child psychology: Social, emotional, and personality development* (Vol. 3, 5th ed., pp. 779–862). New York: Wiley.

Conners, C. K. (1990). *Conners rating scales manual.* North Tonawanda, NY: Multi-Health Systems.

Crick, N. R., & Dodge, K. A. (1994). A review and reformulation of social information-processing mechanisms in children's social adjustment. *Psychological Bulletin, 115*, 74–101.

Dishion, T. J., & Andrews, D. W. (1995). Preventing escalation in problem behaviors with high-risk young adolescents: Immediate and 1-year outcomes. *Journal of Consulting and Clinical Psychology, 63*, 538–548.

Dishion, T. J., Capaldi, D., Spacklen, K. M., & Li, F. (1995). Peer ecology of male adolescent drug use. *Developmental and Psychopathology, 7*, 803–824.

Dishion, T. J., Eddy, J. M., Haas, E., Li, F., & Spracklen, K. (1997). Friendshps and violent behavior during adolescence. *Social Development, 6*, 207–223.

Dishion, T. J., McCord, J., & Poulin, F. (1999). When interventions harm: Peer groups and problem behavior. *American Psychologist, 54*, 755–764.

Dishion, T. J., & Medici Skaggs, N. (2000). An ecological analysis of monthly bursts in early adolescent substance use. *Applied Developmental Science, 4*, 89–97.

Dishion, T. J., Patterson, G. R., & Griesler, P. C. (1994). Peer adaptation in the development of antisocial behavior: A confluence model. In L. R. Huesmann (Ed.), *Current perspectives on aggressive behavior* (pp. 61–95). New York: Plenum Press.

Dumas, J. E., & Serketich, W. J. (1994). Maternal depressive symptomology and child maladjustment: A comparison of three process models. *Behavior Therapy, 25*, 161–181.

Dumas, J. E., & Wahler, R. G. (1983). Predictors of treatment outcome in parent training: Another insularity and socioeconomic disadvantage. *Behavioral Assessment, 5*, 301–313.

Dumas, J. E., & Wahler, R. G. (1985). Indiscriminate mothering as a contextual factor in aggressive-oppositional child behavior: "Damned if you do and damned if you don't." *Journal of Abnormal Child Psychology, 13*, 1–17.

DuPaul, G. J. (1991). Parent and teacher rating of ADHD symptoms: Psychometric properties in a community-based sample. *Journal of Clinical Child Psychology, 20*, 245–253.

Eddy, J. M., Leve, L. L., & Fagot, B. I. (2001). Coercive family processes: A replication and extension of Patterson's coercion model. *Aggressive Behavior, 27*, 14–25.

Eyberg, S. M. (1992). Parent and teacher behavior inventories for the assessment of conduct problem behaviors in children. In L. VandeCreek, S. Knapp, & T. L. Jackson (Eds.), *Innovations in clinical practice: A source book* (Vol. 11, pp. 261–270). Sarasota, FL: Professional Resource Exchange.

Eyberg, S. M., & Johnson, S. M. (1974). Multiple assessment of behavior modification with families: Effects of contingency contracting and order of treated problems. *Journal of Consulting and Clinical Psychology, 42*, 594–606.

Eyberg, S. M., & Matarazzo, R. G. (1980). Training parents as therapists: A comparison between individual parent child interaction training and parent group didactic training. *Journal of Clinical Psychology, 36*, 492–499.

Eyberg, S. M., & Robinson, E. A. (1982). Parent-child interaction training: Effects on family functioning. *Journal of Clinical Child Psychology, 11*, 130–137.

Fagot, B. I., & Pears, K. C. (1996). Changes in attachment during the third year: Consequences and predictions. *Developmental Psychopathology, 8*, 325–344.

Farley, F., & Sewell, T. (1976). Test of an arousal theory of delinquency: Stimulation seeking in delinquent and nondelinquent black adolescents. *Criminal Justice and Behavior, 3*, 315–320.

Faraone, S. V., Biederman, J., Keenan, K., & Tsuang, M. T. (1991). Separation of DSM-III Attention Deficit Disorder and Conduct Disorder: Evidence from a family genetic study of American child psychiatry patients. *Psychological Medicine, 21*, 100–121.

Farrington, D. P. (1995). The development of offending and antisocial behaviour from childhood: Key findings from the Cambridge study in delinquent development. *Journal of Child Psychology and Psychiatry, 36*, 929–964.

Fitzgerald, H. E., & Zucker, R. A. (1995). Socioeconomic status and alcoholism: The contextual structure of developmental pathways to addiction. In H. Fitzgerald & B. M. Lester (Eds.), *Children of poverty: Research, health, and policy issues*. New York: Garland.

Forehand, R., & Kotchick, B. A. (1996). Cultural diversity: A wake-up call for parent training. *Behavior Therapy, 27*, 187–206.

Forehand, R., Lautenschlager, G. J., Faust, J., & Graziano, W. G. (1986). Parent perceptions and parent–child interactions in clinic-referred children: A preliminary investigation of the effects of maternal depressive moods. *Behaviour Research and Therapy, 24*, 73–75.

Forehand, R., & McMahon R. J. (1981). *Helping the noncompliant child: A clinician's guide to parent training*. New York: Guilford Press.

Forgatch, M. S., Patterson, G. R., & Ray, J. A. (1996). Divorce and boys' adjustment problem: Two paths with a single model. In E. M. Hetherington, & E. A. Blechman (Eds.), *Stress, coping and resiliency in children and families* (pp. 67–105). Mahwah, NJ: Erlbaum.

Frick, P. J. (2004). Developmental pathways to conduct disorder: Implications for serving youth who show severe aggressive and antisocial behavior. *Psychology in the Schools, 42*, 823–835.

Frick, P. J., & Jackson, Y. K. (1993). Family functioning and childhood antisocial behavior: Yet another reinterpretation. *Journal of Clinical Child Psychology, 22*, 410–419.

Frick, P. J., O'Brien, B. S., Wootten, J. M., & McBurnett, K. (1994). Psychopathy and conduct problems in children. *Journal of Abnormal Psychology, 103*, 700–707.

Ge, X., Best, K. M., Conger, R, D., & Simons, R. L. (1996). Parenting behaviors and the occurrence and co-occurrence of adolescent depressive symptoms and conduct problems, *Developmental Psychology, 32*, 717–731.

Ge, X., Conger, R. D., Cadoret, R. J., Neiderhiser, J. M., Yates, W., Troughton, E., & Stewart, M. A. (1996). The developmental interface between nature and nurture: A mutual influence model of child antisocial behavior and parent behaviors. *Developmental Psychology, 32*, 574–589.

Gordon, D. A., Arbuthnot, J., Gustafson, K. E., & McGreen, P. (1988). Home-based behavioral systems family therapy with disadvantaged juvenile delinquents. *American Journal of Family Therapy, 16*, 243–255.

Hayes, S. N., & Wu, W. (1998). The applied implications of rule-governed behavior. In W. O'Donohue (Ed.), *Learning and behavior therapy* (pp. 374–391). Needham Heights, MA: Allyn & Bacon.

Hinshaw, S. P., Lahey, B. B., & Hart, E. L. (1993). Issues of taxonomy and comorbidity in the development of Conduct Disorder. *Development and Psychopathology, 5,* 31–49.

Hops, H., & Walker, H. M. (1988). *CLASS: Contingencies for learning academic and social skills.* Seattle, WA: Educational Achievement Systems.

Huesmann, L. R., Eron, L. D., Lefkowitz, M. M., & Walder, L. O. (1984). Stability of aggression over time and generations. *Developmental Psychology, 20,* 1120–1134.

Jennings, K. D., Stagg, V., & Connors, R. E. (1991). Social networks and mothers' interactions with their preschool children. *Child Development, 62,* 966–978.

Johnson, J. H., & Fennell, E. B. (1992). Aggressive, antisocial, and delinquent behavior in childhood and adolescence. In C. E. Walker, & M. C. Roberts (Eds.), *Handbook of clinical child psychology* (2nd ed.). New York: Wiley.

Katz, L. F., & Gottman, J. M. (1993). Patterns of marital conflict predict children's internalizing and externalizing behavior. *Developmental Psychology, 29,* 940–950.

Kazdin, A. E. (1995). Child, parent, and family dysfunction as predictors of outcome in cognitive-behavioral treatment of antisocial children. *Behaviour Research and Therapy, 33,* 371–281.

Kazdin, A. E. (1996). *Conduct disorders in childhood and adolescence* (2nd ed.). Thousand Oaks, CA: Sage.

Keilitz, I., & Dunivant, N. (1986). The relationship between learning disability and juvenile delinquency: Current state of knowledge. *RASE: Remedial and Special Education, 7*(3), 18–26.

Kindermann, T. A. (1993). Natural peer groups as contexts for individual development: The case of children's motivation at school. *Developmental Psychology, 29,* 970–977.

Kirigin, K. A., Braukmann, C. J., Atwater, J. D., & Wolf, M. M. (1982). An evaluation of teaching-family (Achievement Place) group houses for juvenile offenders. *Journal of Applied Behavior Analysis, 15,* 1–16.

Lahey, B. B., & Loeber, R. (1994). Framework for a developmental model of Oppositional Defiant Disorder and Conduct Disorder. In D. K. Routh (Ed.), *Disruptive behavior disorders in childhood* (pp. 139–180). New York: Plenum Press.

Lahey, B. B., Loeber, R., Hart, E. L., Frick, P. J., Applegate, B., Zhang, Q., Green, S. M., & Russo, M. F. (1995). Four-year longitudinal study of Conduct Disorder in boys: Patterns and predictors of persistence. *Journal of Abnormal Psychology, 104,* 83–93.

Loeber, R. & Keenan, K. (1995). Interaction between Conduct Disorder and its comorbid conditions: Effects of age and gender. *Clinical Psychology Review, 14,* 497–523.

Long, P., Forehand, R., Weirson, M., & Morgan, A. (1994). Does parent training with young noncompliant children have long-term effects? *Behaviour Research & Therapy, 32*(1), 101–107.

Martens, B. K., & Hiralall, A. S. (1997). Scripted sequences of teacher interaction. *Behavior Modification, 21,* 308–323.

McGee, R., Feehan, M., Williams, S., & Anderson, J. (1992). Disorders from age 11 to age 15 years. *Journal of the American Academy of Child and Adolescent Psychiatry, 31*, 50–59.

Moffitt, T. E. (1993). "Adolescence-limited" and "life-course persistent" antisocial behavior: A developmental taxonomy. *Psychological Review, 100*, 674–701.

Moffitt, T. E., Caspi, A., Dickson, N., Silva, P., & Stanton, W. (1996). Childhood-onset versus adolescent-onset antisocial conduct problems in males: Natural history from ages 3 to 18 years. *Development and Psychopathology, 8*, 399–424.

Moffitt, T. E., & Lynam, D. (1994). The neuropsychology of conduct disorder and delinquency: Implications for understanding antisocial behavior. In D. C. Fowles, P. Sutker, & H. Goodman (Eds.), *Progress in experimental and psychopathology research* (pp. 233–262). New York: Springer Publishing Co.

Moore, D. R., & Arthur, J. L. (1983). Juvenile delinquency. In T. Ollendick, & M. Hersen (Eds.), *Handbook of child psychopathology.* New York: Plenum Press.

Morrell, J. & Murray, L. (2003). Parenting and the development of conduct disorder and hyperactive symptoms in childhood: A prospective, longitudinal study from 2 months to 8 years. *Journal of Child Psychology and Psychiatry and Allied Disciplines, 44*, 489–509.

O'Brien, B. S., & Frick, P. J. (1996). Reward dominance: Associations with anxiety, conduct problems, and psychopathy in children. *Journal of Abnormal Child Psychology, 24*, 223–240.

Patterson, G. R. (1965). Responsiveness to social stimuli. In L. Krasner, & L. P. Ullmann (Eds.), *Research in behavior modification* (pp. 157–178). New York: Holt, Rinehart and Winston.

Patterson, G. R. (1974). Interventions for boys with conduct problems: Multiple settings, treatments and criteria. *Journal of Consulting and Clinical Psychology, 42*, 471–481.

Patterson, G. R. (1975). *Families: Applications of social learning to family life* (rev. ed.). Champaign, IL: Research Press.

Patterson, G. R. (1982). *A social learning approach: Coercive family process* (Vol. 3). Eugene, OR: Castalia.

Patterson, G. R. (1992). Developmental changes in antisocial behavior. In R. D. Peters, R. J. McMahon, & V. L. Quinsey (Eds.), *Aggression and violence throughout the life span* (pp. 52–82). Newbury Park, CA: Sage.

Patterson, G. R. (1993). Orderly change in a stable world: The antisocial trait as a chimera. *Journal of Consulting and Clinical Psychology, 61*, 911–919.

Patterson, G. R. (2002a). A brief history of the Oregon Model. In J. B. Reid, G. R. Patterson, & J. Snyder (Eds.), *Antisocial behavior in children and adolescents: A developmental analysis and model for intervention.* Washington, DC: American Psychological Association.

Patterson, G. R. (2002b). The early development of coercive family process. In J. B. Reid, G. R. Patterson, & J. Snyder (Eds.), *Antisocial behavior in children and adolescents: A developmental analysis and model for intervention.* Washington, DC: American Psychological Association.

Patterson, G. R., & Chamberlain, P. (1988). Treatment process: A problem at three levels. In L. C. Wynne (Ed.), *The state of the art in family therapy research: Controversies and recommendations* (pp. 189–223). New York: Family Process Press.

Patterson, G. R., Chamberlain, P., & Reid, J. B. (1982). A comparative evaluation of a parent training program. *Behavior Therapy, 13*, 638–650.

Patterson, G. R., DeGarmo, D. S., & Knutson, N. (2000). Hyperactive and antisocial behaviors: Comorbid or two points on same process? *Development and Psychopathology, 12*, 91–106.

Patterson, G. R., & Fagot, B. I. (1967). Selective responsiveness to social reinforcers and deviant behavior in children. *Psychological Record, 17*, 359–368.

Patterson, G. R., & Forgatch, M. S. (1995). Predicting future clinical adjustment from treatment outcome and process variables. *Psychological Assessment, 7*, 275–285.

Patterson, G. R., Jones, R., Whittier, J., & Wright, M. A. (1965). A behavior modification technique for the hyperactive child. *Behaviour Research and Therapy, 2*, 217–226.

Patterson, G. R., Littman, R. A., & Bricker, W. (1967). Assertive behavior in children: A step towards a theory of aggression. *Monographs of the Society for Research in Child Development, 32*, 1–43.

Patterson, G. R., & Reid, J. B. (1973). Intervention for families of aggressive boys: A replication study. *Behaviour Research and Therapy, 11*, 383–394.

Patterson, G. R., Reid, J. B., & Dishion, T. J. (1992). *Antisocial boys*. Eugene, OR: Castalia.

Patterson, G. R., Reid, J. B., & Eddy, J. M. (2002). A brief history of the Oregon Model. In J. B. Reid, G. R. Patterson, & J. Snyder (Eds.), *Antisocial behavior in children and adolescents: A developmental analysis and model for intervention*. Washington, DC: American Psychological Association.

Patterson, G. R., & Stouthamer-Loeber, M. (1984). The correlation of family management practices and delinquency. *Child Development, 55*, 1299–1307.

Peed, S., Roberts, M., & Forehand, R. (1977). Evaluation of the effectiveness of a standardized parent training program in altering the interaction of mothers and their noncompliant children. *Behavior Modification, 1*, 323–350.

Pfiffner, L. J., & O'Leary, S. G. (1987). The efficacy of all-positive management as a function of the prior use of negative consequences. *Journal of Applied Behavior Analysis, 20*, 265–271.

Quay, H. C. (1987). Patterns of delinquent behavior. In H. C. Quay (Ed.), *Handbook of juvenile delinquency* (pp. 118–138). New York: Wiley.

Rapport, M. (1987). Attention deficit disorder with hyperactivity. In M. Hersen, & V. Van Hasselt (Eds.), *Behavior therapy with children and adolescents*. New York: Wiley.

Repetti, R. L. (1996). The effects of perceived daily social and academic failure experiences on school-age children's subsequent interactions with parents. *Child Development, 67*, 1467–1482.

Robins, L. N. (1966). *Deviant children grown up*. Baltimore: Williams & Wilkins.

Robins, L. N. (1978). Sturdy childhood predictors of adult antisocial behavior: Replications from longitudinal studies. *Psychological Medicine, 8*, 611–622.

Rothbart, M. K., Posner, M. I., & Hershey, K. L. (1995). Temperament, attention, and developmental psychopathology. In D. Cicchetti & D. J. Cohen (Eds.), *Developmental psychopathology. Theory and methods* (Vol. 1, pp. 315–340). New York: Wiley.

Rutter, M. (1972). Parent-child separation: Psychological effects on the children. *Journal of Child Psychology and Psychiatry, 12*, 233–260.

Rutter, M., Harrington, R., Quinton, D., & Pickles, A. (1994). Adult outcome of Conduct Disorder in childhood: Implications for concepts and definitions of patterns of psychopathology. In R. D. Ketterlinus, & M. E. Lamb (Eds.), *Adolescent problem behaviors: Issues and research* (pp. 57–80). Hillsdale, NJ: Erlbaum.

Satterfield, J. H., Schell, A. M., & Backs, R. W. (1987). Longitudinal study of AERP's in hyperactive and normal children: Relationship to antisocial behavior. *Electroencephalography and Clinical Neurophysiology, 67*, 531–536.

Sells, J. N. (2001). Purpose, process, and product: A case study in marital intervention. *Family Journal: Counseling & Therapy for Couples, 9*(2), 186–190.

Shaw, D. S., & Winslow, E. B. (1997). Precursors and correlates of antisocial behavior from infancy to preschool. In D. M. Stoff, J. Breiling, & J. D. Maser (Eds.), *Handbook of antisocial behavior* (pp. 148–158). New York: John Wiley & Sons.

Simons, R. L., Wu, C., Conger, R. D., & Lorenz, F. O.(1994). Two routes to delinquency: Differences between early and late starters in the impact of parenting and deviant peers. *Criminology, 32*, 247–275.

Snyder, J., & Patterson, G. R. (1987). Family interaction and delinquent behavior. In H. C. Quay (Ed.), *Handbook of juvenile delinquency*. New York: Wiley.

Snyder, J., Horsch, E., & Childs, J. (1997). Peer relationships of young children: Affiliative choices and the shaping of aggressive behavior. *Journal of Cllinical Child Psychology, 26*, 145–156.

Snyder, J., Schrepferman, L., & St. Peter, C. (1997). Origins of antisocial behavior: Negative reinforcement and affect dysregulation of behavior as socialization mechanisms in family interaction. *Behavior Modification, 31*, 187–215.

Stoolmiller, M. (1994). Antisocial behavior, delinquent peer associations, and unsupervised wandering for boys: Growth and change from childhood to early adolescence. *Multivariate Behavioural Research, 29*, 263–288.

Taylor, T., & Watt, D. C. (1977). The relation of deviant symptoms and behavior in a normal population to subsequent delinquency and maladjustment. *Psychological Medicine, 7*, 163–169.

Thomas, A., Chess, S., & Birch, H. C. (1968). *Temperament and behavior disorders in children*. New York: New York University Press.

Tremblay, R. E., Masse, B., Perron, D., Leblanc, M., Schwartzman, A. E., & Ledingham, J. E. (1992). Early disruptive behavior, poor school achievement, delinquent behavior, and delinquent personality: Longitudinal analyses. *Journal of Consulting and Clinical Psychology, 60*, 64–72.

van den Boom, D. C. (1995). Do first-year interventions effects endure? Follow-up during toddlerhood of a sample of Dutch irritable infants. *Child Development, 66*, 1798–1816.

Vitaro, F., Tremblay, R. E., Gagnon, C., & Bouvin, M. (1992). Peer rejection from kindergarten to grade 2: Outcomes, correlates and predictions. *Merrill Palmer Quarterly, 38,* 382–400.

Walker, H. M., & Hops, H. (1979). The CLASS program for acting out children: R&D procedures, program outcomes, and implementation issues. *School Psychology Digest, 8,* 370–381.

Walker, H. M., Hops, H., & Fiegenbaum, E. (1976). Deviant classroom behavior as a function of combinations of social and token reinforcement and cost contingency. *Behavior Therapy, 7,* 76–88.

Walker, H. M., Hops, H., & Greenwood, C. R. (1993). *RECESS: A program for reducing negative-aggressive behavior.* Seattle, WA: Educational Achievement Systems.

Webster-Stratton, C. (1981). Modification of mothers' behaviors and attitudes through videotape modeling group discussion program. *Behavior Therapy, 12,* 634–642.

Webster-Stratton, C. (1990). Long-term follow-up of families with young conduct problem children: From preschool to grade school. *Journal of Clinical Child Psychology, 19,* 14–149.

Webster-Stratton, C. (1996). Early intervention with videotape modeling: Programs for families of children with Oppositional Defiant Disorder or Conduct Disorder. In E. S. Hibbs, & P. S. Jensen (Eds.), *Psychosocial treatments for child and adolescent disorders: Empirically based strategies for clinical practice* (pp. 435–474). Washington, D.C.: American Psychological Association.

Webster-Stratton, C. (1997). From parent training to community building. *Families in Society, 78*(2), 156–171.

Webster-Stratton, C., & Eyberg, S. M. (1982). Child temperament: Relationship with child behavior problems and parent-child interactions. *Journal of Clinical Child Psychology, 11,* 123–129.

Wechsler, D. (2003). *The Wechsler Intelligence Scale for Children—Fourth edition.* San Antonio, TX: Psychological Corporation.

Weiss, B., Dodge, K. A., Bates, J. E., & Pettit, G. S. (1992). Some consequences of early harsh discipline: Child aggression and a maladaptive social information processing style. *Child Development, 63,* 1321–1335.

White, M. A. (1975). Natural rates of teacher approval and disapproval in the classroom. *Journal of Applied Behavior Analysis, 8,* 367–372.

Wilkinson, G.S. (1993). *Wide Range Achievement Test—3.* Wilmington, DE: Jastack Associates.

Zuckerman, M. (1979). *Sensation seeking: Beyond the optimal level of arousal.* Hillsdale, NJ: Erlbaum.

CHAPTER 7

Cognitive-Behavioral Psychotherapy for Conduct Disorder

The Coping Power Program

John E. Lochman, Nicole R. Powell, Melissa F. Jackson, and Wendy Czopp

THE TREATMENT MODEL

Once established, aggressive behavior in childhood is a stable behavior pattern and a high level of impulsive, uncontrolled aggression in childhood serves as a predictor for substance use, delinquency, and other negative outcomes during adolescence and adulthood (Lochman & Wayland, 1994; Miller-Johnson, Coie, Maumary-Gremaud, Lochman, & Terry, 1999). Conduct problems may be one of the most enduring forms of psychopathology in children (Frick, 1998). The timing of the initiation of aggressive behavior problems in children affects outcomes. Youths who engage in the most persistent, severe, and violent antisocial behavior are most likely to initiate their delinquent behavior in childhood rather than adolescence (Lahey, Waldman, & McBurnett, 2001). As a result, interventions that are designed to interrupt this developmental trajectory toward progressively more serious antisocial behavior can be developed for aggressive children based on developmental models of risk factors for aggression (Tolan, Guerra, & Kendall, 1995) and on evolving knowledge about evidence-based cognitive behavioral and behavioral interventions for aggressive children (Farmer, Compton, Burns, & Robertson, 2002; Leff, Power, Manz, Costigan, & Nabors, 2001).

Contextual Social-Cognitive Model

Many of the most recent interventions for disruptive behavior disorder are based on cognitive-behavioral theories of antisocial and delinquent behavior. The premise behind most of these approaches is that cognitions or thoughts influence the behavior that an individual displays in various situations; the interventions aim to alter both an individual's general response (behavioral) patterns and the cognitions that accompany or precede the behaviors. Cognitive-behavioral interventions with aggressive children are thus designed to have an impact on social behavior and related cognitive processes.

Existing research suggests that a contextual social-cognitive model can account for the development of substance use and delinquency during the preadolescent and early adolescent years, and can serve as the conceptual framework for cognitive-behavioral intervention (Lochman & Wells, 2002a). This model indicates that two relevant sets of potential mediators of adolescent antisocial behavior include: (a) child-level factors (e.g., Tremblay & LeMarquand, 2001), including poor social-cognitive and decision-making skills, poor self-regulation, perceived peer context, and poor ability to resist peer pressure; and (b) contextual factors, including poor parental caregiver involvement with, and discipline of, the child (e.g., Wasserman & Seracini, 2001). It is assumed that broader contextual risk factors, such as the level of neighborhood violence (Luthar, 1999), impact these mediational processes and children's subsequent behavior.

Child-Level Factors

Anger Arousal Model

An early form (the Anger Control Program) of our current cognitive-behavioral intervention program was based on an Anger Arousal model (Lochman, Nelson, & Sims, 1981), which was primarily derived from Novaco's (1978) work with aggressive adults. In this conceptualization of anger arousal, which stressed sequential cognitive processing, the child responded to problems such as interpersonal conflicts or frustrations with environmental obstacles (i.e., difficult schoolwork). However, it was not the stimulus event itself that provoked the child's response, but rather the child's cognitive processing of and about that event. This first stage of cognitive processing was similar to Lazarus' (Smith & Lazarus, 1990) primary appraisal stage, and consisted of labeling, attributions, and perceptions of the problem event. The second state of processing, similar to Lazarus' secondary appraisal, consisted of the child's cognitive plan for his or her response to the perceived threat or provocation. This level of cognitive processing was accompanied by anger-related physiological arousal. The Anger Arousal model indicated that the child's cognitive processing of the problem event and his or her planned response led to the child's actual behavioral response (ranging from aggression to assertion, passive acceptance, or withdrawal) and to the positive or negative consequences that the child experienced as a result.

Coping Power Model: Social Information Processing

The Anger Arousal model was amplified as research and theories of social information processing progressed (Crick & Dodge, 1994). The contextual social-cognitive model (Lochman & Wells, 2002a) stresses the reciprocal interactive relationships among the initial cognitive appraisal of the problem situation, the cognitive appraisal of the problem solutions, the child's physiological arousal, and the behavioral response. In this model, there is greater emphasis on the recursive nature of the different elements in the model with all processing steps/components having some influence on all other elements. The level of physiological arousal will depend on the individual's biological predisposition to become aroused, and will vary depending on the interpretation of the event (Williams, Lochman, Phillips, & Barry, 2003). The level of arousal will further influence the social problem solving, operating either to intensify the fight or flight response, or to interfere with the generation of solutions. Because of the ongoing and reciprocal nature of interactions, it may be difficult for children to extricate themselves from aggressive behavior patterns.

Aggressive children have cognitive distortions at the appraisal phases of social-cognitive processing because of difficulties in encoding incoming social information, and in accurately interpreting social events and others' intentions. They also have cognitive deficiencies at the problem solution phases of social-cognitive processing shown by their generating maladaptive solutions for perceived problems and having nonnormative expectations for the usefulness of aggressive and nonaggressive solution to their social problems. At the first step of information processing, aggressive children have been found to recall fewer relevant cues about events (Lochman & Dodge, 1994), base interpretations of events on fewer cues (Dodge, Pettit, McClaskey, & Brown, 1986), selectively attend to hostile rather than neutral cues (Gouze, 1987), and recall the most recent cues in a sequence with selective inattention to earlier presented cues (Milich & Dodge, 1984). MacKinnon, Lamb, Belsky, and Baum (1990) have suggested that these biases at the encoding phase, which involve selective attention to particular cues in the environment, are a direct result of prior negative or aggressive interactions with the parent and others in the environment.

At the next stage, or the interpretation stage, aggressive children have been shown to have a hostile attributional bias, as they tend to excessively infer that others are acting toward them in a provocative and hostile manner (Dodge et al., 1986; Feldman & Dodge, 1987; Lochman & Dodge, 1994). These attributional biases tend to be more prominent in reactively aggressive children than in proactively aggressive children (Dodge, Lochman, Harnish, Bates, & Pettit, 1997), which offers support for the need for a subclassification of aggressive children, as the particular social-cognitive deficits may be different in differentially aggressive children (Crick & Dodge, 1996).

The problem-solving stages of information processing begin when the child accesses the goal that she/he chooses to pursue; in turn this will affect the responses generated for resolving the conflict, which occurs in the next processing stage. Aggressive children have been found to have social goals that are more dominant and revenge oriented, and less affiliation oriented, than is the case for nonaggressive children (Lochman, Wayland, & White, 1993). The fourth information-processing stage involves a generative process whereby potential solutions for coping with a perceived problem are recalled from memory. At this stage, aggressive children demonstrate deficiencies in both the quality and the quantity of their problem-solving solutions. These differences are most pronounced for the quality of the solutions offered, with aggressive children offering fewer verbal assertion solutions (Joffe, Dobson, Fine, Marriage, & Haley, 1990; Lochman & Lampron, 1986), fewer compromise solutions (Lochman & Dodge, 1994), more direct action solutions (Lochman & Lampron, 1986), a greater number of help-seeking or adult intervention responses (Rabiner, Lenhart, & Lochman, 1990), and more physically aggressive responses (Pepler, Craig, & Roberts, 1998; Waas & French, 1989) to hypothetical vignettes describing interpersonal conflicts. In terms of the quantity of solutions offered by aggressive children, there is little evidence in general that they offer fewer responses (Bloomquist, August, Cohen, Doyle, & Everhart, 1997), although the most severely aggressive and violent youths do have a deficiency in the number of solutions they can generate to resolve social problems (Lochman & Dodge, 1994). The nature of the social problem-solving deficits for aggressive children can vary depending on their diagnostic classification. Boys with conduct disorder diagnoses produce more aggressive/antisocial solutions in vignettes about conflicts with parents and teachers, and fewer verbal/nonaggressive solutions in peer conflicts, in comparison to boys with oppositional defiant disorder (Dunn, Lochman, & Colder, 1997). Thus, children with conduct disorder have broader problem-solving deficits in multiple interpersonal contexts, in comparison to children with oppositional defiant disorder.

The fifth processing stage involves a two-step process: first, identifying the consequences for each of the solutions generated; and second, evaluating each solution and consequence in terms of the individual's desired outcome. In general, aggressive children evaluate aggressive behavior as more positive (Crick & Werner, 1998) than children without aggressive behavior difficulties. Children's beliefs about the utility of aggression and about their ability to successfully enact an aggressive response can operate to increase the likelihood of aggression being displayed, as children who hold these beliefs will be more likely to also believe that this type of behavior will help them to achieve the desired goals, which then influences response evaluation (Lochman & Dodge, 1994; Perry, Perry, & Rasmussen, 1986). Deficient beliefs at this stage of information processing are especially characteristic for children with proactive aggressive behavior patterns (Dodge et al., 1997) and for youths who have callous, unemotional traits consistent with early phases of psychopathy (Pardini, Lochman, & Frick, 2003). Recent research has found that beliefs about the acceptability of aggressive behavior lead to deviant processing of social cues, which in turn lead to children's aggressive behavior (Zelli, Dodge, Lochman, Laird, & The Conduct Problems Prevention Research Group, 1999), indicating that these information-processing steps have recursive effects rather than strictly linear effects on each other.

The final information-processing stage involves behavioral enactment or displaying the response that was chosen in the above steps. Aggressive children have been found to be less adept at enacting positive or prosocial interpersonal behaviors (Dodge et al., 1986). This interpretation would suggest that improving the ability to enact positive behaviors may influence aggressive children's belief about their ability to engage in more prosocial behaviors and thus functions to change the response evaluation.

Role of Schemas

Recent revisions of social-cognitive models have more explicitly introduced the role that children's cognitive schemas have on their information processing (Crick & Dodge, 1994; Lochman, Magee, & Pardini, 2003; Lochman, Whidby, & FitzGerald, 2000). Schemas account for how individuals actively construct their perceptions and experiences, rather than merely being passive receivers and processors of social information (Ingram & Kendall, 1986). Schemas have been defined in somewhat different ways by various theoreticians and researchers, but they are commonly regarded as consistent, core beliefs, and patterns of thinking (Lochman & Lenhart, 1995). These underlying cognitive structures form the basis for individuals' specific perceptions of current events (DeRubeis & Beck, 1988). Similar to Adler's (1964) concept of "style of life" (Freeman & Leaf, 1989), schemas are cognitive blueprints or master plans that construe, organize, and transform peoples' interpretations and predictions about events in their lives (Mischel, 1990). Schemas have certain basic attributes. First, a distinction can be made between *active* schemas, which are often conscious and govern everyday behavior, and *dormant* schemas, which are typically out of individuals' awareness and emerge only when the individuals are faced with specific events or stressors. The dormant schemas are in a state of "chronic accessibility" (Higgins, King, & Marvin, 1982; Mischel, 1990) or state of potential activation, ready to be primed by minimal cues. Thus, individuals' beliefs and expectations, which emerge when they are intensely stressed or aroused, may not be at all apparent when they are calm and not aroused. Second, existing schemas can be either compelling or noncompelling (Freeman & Leaf, 1989).

Noncompelling schemas are not strongly held by a person, and can be given up easily. In contrast, compelling schemas are strongly entrenched in the person's way of thinking. They promote more filtering and potential distortions of the person's perceptions of self and others (Fiske & Taylor, 1984). The compelling schemas lead to more rapid judgments about the presence of schema-related traits in self and others, and they often operate outside of conscious awareness (Erdley, 1990). Third, schemas can be more or less permeable. Permeable schemas permit individuals to alter their interpretation of events through successive approximations, a process identified as "constructive alternativism" by Kelly (1955). A person with relatively permeable schemas can readily adapt schemas to the specific situations and conditions he or she encounters, thereby adding new elements and complexity. Schemas are typically more permeable and situational as individuals develop and have experiences in a variety of situations (Mischel, 1990; Rotter, Chance, & Phares, 1972). Relatively nonpermeable schemas are preemptive, and promote rigid black–white thinking (Kelly, 1955).

Schemas Within the Social-Cognitive Model

Schemas have been proposed to have a significant impact on the information-processing steps within the contextual social-cognitive model underlying cognitive-behavioral interventions with aggressive children (Lochman et al., 2003; Lochman & Wells, 2004). Schematic propositions include information both in semantic memory (general knowledge that has been acquired and learned) and in episodic memory (personal information gleaned through one's experiences in the world). Schematic propositions are those beliefs, ideas, and expectations that can have direct and indirect effects on the social-cognitive products. Schematic propositions include information stored in memory about individuals' beliefs, general social goals, generalized expectations, and their understanding of their competence and self-worth.

Direct Effects of Schemas on Social Information Processing

Schemas can influence the sequential steps of information processing in different ways. Early in the information-processing sequence, when the individual is perceiving and interpreting new social cues, schemas can have a clear direct effect by narrowing attention to certain aspects of the social cue array (e.g., Lochman et al., 1981). A child who believes it is essential to be in control of others and who expects that others will try to dominate him or her, often in aversive ways, will attend particularly to verbal and nonverbal signals about someone else's control efforts, easily missing accompanying signs of the other person's friendliness or attempts to negotiate. Schemas about control and aggression will also heavily influence the second stage of processing, as the child interprets the malevolent meaning and intentions in others' behavior.

Indirect Effects of Schemas on Information Processing

Schemas can also have indirect or mediated effects on information processing through the influence of schemas on children's expectations for their own behavior and for others' behavior in specific situations, through the associated affect and arousal when schemas are activated, and through schemas' influence on the style and speed of processing. Schemas about attributes of self and others (such as aggressiveness or dominance) produce expectations about the anticipated presence or absence of these attributes as individuals prepare to interact with people in specific situations. Research by Lochman and Dodge (1998) found that aggressive boys' perceptions of their own aggressive behavior was primarily affected by their prior expectations, while nonaggressive boys relied more on their actual behavior to form their perceptions. These results indicate that the schemas of aggressive boys about their aggressive behavior are strong and compelling, leading the aggressive boys to display cognitive rigidity between their expectations and perceptions. The aggressive boys' perceptions of their behavior, driven by their schemas, were relatively impermeable to actual behavior, and instead were heavily governed by the boys' preconceptions.

Parent-Level Factors

There is a wide array of factors in the family that can affect child aggression, ranging from parenting practices to parental psychopathology, stressors, and discord within the family. Starting as early as the preschool years, marital conflict likely causes disruptions in parenting and these disruptions can contribute to children's high levels of stress and consequent aggression (Dadds & Powell, 1992). The contextual social-cognitive model emphasizes the role of parenting processes in the development and escalation of problem behaviors.

As articulated by Patterson (Patterson, Reid, & Dishion, 1992), child aggressive behavior arises most fundamentally out of early contextual experiences with parents who provide harsh or irritable discipline, poor problem solving, vague commands, and poor monitoring and supervision of children's behavior. In an extensive review of the risk factors for adolescent antisocial behavior, Hawkins, Catalano, and Miller (1992) identified several parental risk factors that are also directly linked to childhood aggression, including deficient family management practices involving lack of maternal involvement and inconsistent parenting (e.g., Kandel & Andrews, 1987). Irritable, ineffective discipline has been found in families with children displaying overt (oppositional behavior, arguing, and physical aggression) and covert (stealing, lying, and truancy) antisocial behavior (Patterson & Stouthamer-Loeber, 1984). Capaldi and Patterson (1991) have found that low parental involvement with children predicted poor adjustment for boys 2 years later. Severity of parental discipline has been found to be positively correlated with teacher ratings of aggression and behavior problems and with children's poorer social information processing, even when controlling the possible effects of socioeconomic status (SES), marital discord, and child temperament (Weiss, Dodge, Bates, & Pettit, 1992). It is important to note that although such parenting factors are associated with childhood aggression, child temperament and behavior also affect parenting behavior. Such evidence indicates the bidirectional relation between child and parent behavior.

Peer and Community Factors

Children with disruptive behaviors are at risk for being rejected by their peers. Childhood aggressive behavior and peer rejection independently predict delinquency and conduct problems in adolescence (Lochman & Wayland, 1994). Aggressive children who are also socially rejected tend to exhibit more severe behavior problems than children who are either only aggressive or only rejected. As children with conduct problems enter adolescence, they tend to associate with deviant peers. It is believed that many of these teens have been continually rejected from more prosocial peer groups because they lack appropriate social skills and, as a result, they turn to antisocial cliques as their only means for social support (Miller-Johnson et al., 1999). The relation between childhood conduct problems and adolescent delinquency is at least partially mediated by deviant peer group affiliation (Vitaro, Brendgen, Pagani, Tremblay, & McDuff, 1999).

Neighborhood and school problems and low SES have also been found to be risk factors for aggression and delinquency over and above the variance accounted for by family characteristics (Kupersmidt, Griesler, DeRosier, Patterson, & Davis, 1995). For example, early onset of aggression and violence has been associated with neighborhood disorganization and poverty partly because children who live in lower SES and disorganized neighborhoods are not well supervised and engage in more risk-taking behaviors. The density of aggressive children in classroom settings can also increase the amount of aggressive behavior emitted by individual students (Barth, Dunlap, Dane, Lochman, & Wells, 2004).

Evidence Base for Cognitive-Behavioral Intervention with Aggressive Children
The Coping Power Program: Efficacy Study

The Coping Power Program described in this chapter was derived from earlier research on an Anger Coping Program (Larson & Lochman, 2002; Lochman, 1992) and from the social-cognitive contextual model. In an initial efficacy study of the Coping Power Program, Lochman and Wells (2002a, 2004) randomly assigned 183 aggressive boys (60% African American, 40% white non-Hispanic) to one of the three following conditions: a cognitive-behavioral coping power child component, combined coping power child and behavioral parent training components, and an untreated cell. The two intervention conditions took place during 4th and 5th grades or 5th and 6th grades, and intervention lasted for 1.5 school years. Screening of risk status took place in 11 elementary schools, and was based on a multiple-gating approach using teacher and parent ratings of children's aggressive behavior. The at-risk boys were in the top 20% according to teacher ratings of their classrooms.

Analyses of outcomes at the time of the 1-year follow-up indicated that the intervention cells (child component only; child plus parent components) had produced reductions in children's self-reported delinquent behavior and parent-reported alcohol and marijuana use by the child, and improvements in their teacher-rated functioning at school during the follow-up year, in comparison to the high-risk control condition (Lochman & Wells, in press). Results indicated that the Coping Power intervention effects on lower rates of parent-rated substance use and delinquent behavior at the 1-year follow-up, in comparison to the control cell, were most apparent for the children and parents who received the Coping Power Program with both child and parent components. In contrast, boys' teacher-rated behavioral improvements in school during the follow-up year appeared to be primarily influenced by the coping power child component. Mediation analyses, using path-analytic techniques, indicate that the intervention effect for both of the intervention cells on the delinquency, parent-reported substance use, and teacher-rated improvement outcomes at the 1-year follow-up were mediated by intervention–produced improvements in children's internal locus of control, their perceptions of their parents' consistency, children's attributional biases, person perception, and children's expectations that aggression would not work for them (Lochman & Wells, 2002a).

Coping Power Program: Effectiveness Studies

Given these positive findings from the prior efficacy study, the next research questions examined whether Coping Power has similar positive effects in other settings and with personnel who are more equivalent to typical school and agency staff. Several types of effectiveness and dissemination studies have been conducted with Coping Power, indicating intervention effects on children's aggressive behavior and problem-solving skills among aggressive deaf children (Lochman et al., 2001) and among children with conduct disorder and oppositional defiant disorder in Dutch outpatient clinics (van de Wiel, Matthys, Cohen-Kettenis, & van Engeland, 2003).

In a more extensive effectiveness study, the Coping Power Program (the combined child and parent components) was evaluated as an indicated preventive intervention directed at high-risk children. The efficacy of the program was examined along with the effects of a universal, classroom-level preventive intervention (Lochman & Wells, 2002b). A total of 245 male and female aggressive 4th-grade students were randomly assigned to one of four conditions. Children were selected from 17 elementary schools, and the study had a greater proportion of schools from inner-city, high-poverty areas than was the case for the prior efficacy study. Intervention began in the fall of the 5th-grade year, and was delivered by personnel more equivalent to counselors and social workers in school settings, with higher case loads and less opportunity for home visits. At postintervention, the three intervention conditions (Coping Power alone, Coping power plus classroom intervention, classroom intervention alone) produced lower rates of substance use than did the control cell (Lochman & Wells, 2002b). Children who received both interventions displayed improvements in their social competence with peers, and their teachers rated these children as having the greatest increases in problem-solving and anger-coping skills. The Coping Power Program also produced reductions in parent-rated and teacher-rated proactive aggressive behavior, and increases in teacher-rated behavioral improvement. A 1-year follow-up of this sample replicated the findings of the prior efficacy study. Coping Power children were found to have lower rates of self-reported substance use and delinquency, and lower levels of teacher-rated aggressive social behavior at school, in comparison to the control children (Lochman & Wells, 2003).

THERAPIST SKILLS AND ATTRIBUTES

Intervention staff for the Coping Power Program has consisted of clinicians at the master's degree level of professional training (e.g., school counselors, Master's of Social Work) and psychologists at the early doctoral level. These individuals conduct both the child component within the school setting and the parent component generally at the child's school or at an accessible community center during a convenient time for parents. An interest and prior experience in working with children and families within a cognitive-behavioral framework is essential for a clinician who chooses to implement this program.

Adequate training and consultation are also critical for successful implementation of the Coping Power Program (Lochman, Wells, & Murray, in press). Clinicians should begin their training by reading the two intervention manuals (child and parent components), which contain the session-by-session outlines of the objectives and the process of each of the major components of the program. Attendance at a Coping Power training workshop is the second stage recommended for any clinician using this program. During the workshop clinicians will become familiar with the background and rationale of the Coping Power Program and they will review individual sessions to discuss the relevance of the session objectives to the overall objectives of the program. Once the clinician begins implementing the program, it is essential that the clinicians have access to an experienced Coping Power Program interventionist or another supervisor with cognitive-behavioral specialty training with children and families, with whom to consult regularly throughout the process.

The clinician's ability to identify social problems or negative group process issues and treatment flexibility are essential in implementing the Coping Power Program. For example, when the child or any group member (if using a group format) begins discussing a social problem that has recently occurred, the clinician should respond by immediately shifting the agenda for the session to the presented problem, rather than rigidly adhering to the planned activities for the session. The clinician can thus take advantage of the naturally presented opportunity to model and reinforce problem-solving skills. It is critical that clinicians are mindful of the overall objectives of the program so that the clinicians' flexible responses to children's problems and to group process issues can still have a direct impact on the targeted social-cognitive difficulties of aggressive children.

Basic skills essential to all practicing clinicians should also be noted because of the impact these skills have on treatment compliance and discontinuation of treatment (i.e., by caregivers). The clinician's ability to build therapeutic alliances with the patient, relevant school personnel, and caregivers is an important component of the Coping Power Program because of the facets of the program. Failure to build rapport with pertinent people may interfere with effectual implementation of the program. Also, a clinician's ability to empathize with the child (Poal & Weisz, 1989) and the parents of the child is essential to treating children with externalizing problems.

Strict adherence to ethics should be practiced by the clinician, which can become somewhat complicated with the different therapeutic alliances that may potentially be created, particularly if the clinician chooses to use a school-based group format for the sessions (i.e., clinician–child, clinician–teacher, clinician–caregiver). Some potential conflicts that may arise that should be considered by clinicians from an ethics standpoint are: a parent having concerns of confidentiality and fears about his or her child attending a group and possibly being "labeled" at school; a parent (with a strained relationship with a teacher) sharing information in confidence that the clinician *knows* would be helpful for the teacher; or the child sharing information with the clinician during an individual session that the clinician feels would be useful for group discussion. Clinicians with multiple, intertwined therapeutic relationships must inform all parties of the limits of confidentiality and the clinicians should not violate these rules of confidentiality set within the clinician–group, clinician–child, clinician–school personnel, or clinician–caregiver relationships. Also, proper documentation of group sessions, individual sessions, and other related contacts (i.e., IEP meetings) is essential and should be practiced.

THE CASE OF "MIKE"
Additional Information, Assessment
The psychological evaluation conducted by the county juvenile court and the interview conducted by the private practitioner were fairly thorough and sound. Multiple informants and multiple, well-accepted techniques were

used to assess Mike's presenting problems, his developmental history, and overall psychological functioning. The results of the assessment procedures strongly suggest that diagnoses of conduct disorder and cannabis abuse are warranted. Mike's aggressive, rule-breaking behavior has become a pattern over at least the past 2 years, and it is significantly interfering with his family relationships and school progress. The interviews and test results indicate that Mike is easily angered and often responds aggressively to conflict situations. Specific examples of Mike's problematic aggression include the following: trying to intimidate peers in the neighborhood by "presenting himself as a tough guy," fighting in the neighborhood, frequent arguing (and nearly fighting) with peers at school, shoving and slapping his sister, and threatening to hurt his mother and kill his sister. He also frequently engages in serious rule-breaking behavior, such as staying out past curfew and truancy. Theft has started to emerge as another problem behavior. Although the items he has taken from home and from the convenience store have been of only trivial value, the stealing behavior may reflect an increasingly risky antisocial behavior pattern. With regard to cannabis abuse, Mike admitted in the interview and on the SASSI to marijuana use since age 11, and he endorsed attitudes and beliefs that reflect susceptibility to substance abuse.

The diagnosis of conduct disorder is further supported by the fact that the evaluation's broad scope allows for ruling out alternative explanations for Mike's behavioral problems. Mike's Wechsler Intelligence Scale for Children— IV (WISC-IV; Wechsler, 2003) and Wide Range Achievement Test—3 (WRAT-3; Wilkinson, 1993) scores indicate that his intelligence and achievement are within average range. Therefore, his aggressive behavior is not likely to be attributable to frustration over cognitive limitations or a learning disorder. Interview and rating scale data suggest that Mike does not have an internalizing disorder or an attention problem like ADHD, which if present, might help explain his conduct problems. He has no physical complaints and there is no history of major health/medical problems that might complicate normal development.

Conduct problems are associated with an increased risk of physical harm to self and others. At the present time, Mike's behavior seems to reflect conduct disorder of a relatively mild to moderate severity. The physical altercations he has been involved in have not resulted in serious harm to anyone. He did not hurt or threaten to hurt the clerk in the convenience store theft incident. However, Mike could be on a path of escalating physical danger toward others. The clinician should try to ascertain whether his aggression is primarily proactive, reactive, or both. He or she should also assess Mike's access to weapons and his intent to cause serious harm to others in conflict situations, particularly his sister, whom he has threatened to kill. Careful and continual monitoring of the level of threat Mike poses to others will be an important part of treatment. Depending on state laws, a duty to warn a potential victim may also come into play.

Mike's risk of harm to himself is tentatively estimated to be low. His mother has apparently not observed significant depressive symptoms in Mike, based on her responses to the Achenbach Child Behavior Checklist (CBCL; Achenbach, 1991). Mike denied depressive symptoms and suicidal ideation on the Children's Depression Inventory (CDI; Kovacs, 1992) and during the interview. On the other hand, Mike was quite guarded during the evaluation process, and his current relationship with his mother does not seem to be one in which he shares his feelings openly. This kind of general defensiveness may mask feelings of depression and thoughts of self-harm. Because internalizing problems are highly comorbid with conduct disorder, the clinician should periodically reassess this area of functioning as he or she develops a relationship with Mike in the course of intervention.

The evaluation would probably yield a more complete understanding of Mike if it included additional information across several domains. For example, finding out more about Mike's social behavior during elementary school might help in determining whether his conduct problems are truly of the *Adolescent-Onset* subtype. Timing of onset of conduct problems has a significant impact on treatment and prognosis, so it may be worthwhile to spend time assessing this more thoroughly. In the current evaluation, Mr. and Ms. D. reported that Mike's rule-breaking, aggressive behavior started 2 years ago, coinciding with his parents' divorce and the onset of adolescence. However, there is evidence that a negative developmental trajectory may have started much earlier for Mike. Ms. D. described Mike as having a difficult temperament from birth. He cried a great deal as an infant, followed by severe temper tantrums as a toddler. He reportedly did "OK" in elementary school, although his mother acknowledged restlessness and a tendency for getting into trouble. To get a better sense of whether Mike may have the more severe *Childhood-Onset* form of conduct disorder, his mother could be asked more specific questions about his functioning during elementary school. She could be queried about symptoms from the four categories of conduct disorder symptoms: aggression to people or animals, destruction of property, deceitfulness or theft, and serious violations of rules.

Conceptualization and treatment planning would also be facilitated by obtaining more information about the way Mike processes social information. We know, from his Minnesota Multiphasic Personality Inventory—Adolescent (MMPI-A; Butcher et al., 1992) results, that Mike is distrustful and that he tends to assume the worst of others, so addressing his attribution style will be important for treatment. Less is known about Mike's underlying goals in social situations, or about his problem-solving abilities. Also, how well has Mike learned to take different people's perspectives in conflict situations and empathize with their feelings? The Problem Solving Measure for Conflict (PSM-C) could be used to assess these features of Mike's thinking about social encounters (Dunn et al., 1997; Lochman & Lampron, 1986). The PSM-C presents the child with an ambiguous situation or story and asks the child to describe what would happen next and about the intentions of the characters in the stories. Mike's responses to an instrument such as the PSM-C could help determine which social-cognitive processes to target for remediation in the course of therapy.

Another area of interest for further assessment of Mike would be social contextual factors, such as the school and neighborhood environments and his parents' psychological functioning. By making telephone contact with one of Mike's current teachers or with his school counselor, the clinician might be able to gather useful data about school climate and school-level norms, while also gaining yet another perspective on Mike's behavior. The current evaluation provides very little information about the quality of Mike's neighborhood environment. Ms. D. stated that she and the children continued living in the family's "middle-class home" after her divorce. The only other reference to neighborhood context was Ms. D.'s report that Mike gets in frequent fights in the neighborhood. Additional information that might be helpful includes: How much unsupervised time does Mike spend in the neighborhood? Where, in the neighborhood, does he go, and how does he get there? What is the level of criminal activity in the neighborhood? Is it a cohesive neighborhood—do the adults look out for each others' children and communicate with one another about neighborhood problems? Answers to these types of questions could help determine if increasing parental monitoring and decreasing time spent in the neighborhood should be treatment targets.

As the primary attachment figures, role models, and managers of behavioral contingencies for Mike, the evaluation could benefit from a more thorough assessment of Mr. and Ms. D.'s psychological functioning. From the interviews with them, it is clear that their relationship with each other is chronically conflicted, and that Mr. D. is not very engaged in his parenting role and is prone to substance use and aggressive behavior himself. But beyond these generalities, we know very little about his parents' level of functioning. A relatively brief but broad screening instrument such as the Symptom Checklist-90-Revised (SCL-90-R; Derogatis & Lazarus, 1994) or the Brief Symptom Inventory (BSI; Derogatis & Melisaratos, 1983) and/or a stress measure such as the Parenting Stress Index (PSI; Abidin, 1983) could be used for this purpose. Also, a frank discussion about the extent to which Mr. and Ms. D. are willing to be involved in Mike's treatment would be an appropriate addition to the assessment procedures.

Last, this evaluation is very problem focused and neglects to assess Mike's psychological strengths and positive characteristics. It is worthwhile to assess for prosocial behavior and positive personality characteristics for two main reasons. First, in terms of providing Mike and his parents with evaluation feedback, it is important to model for them having a balanced view of Mike—that he is an individual with both strengths and weaknesses. Second, knowing his strengths, interests, and what things he finds reinforcing can help tremendously during the intervention phase.

Therapeutic Goals

The primary, long-term therapeutic goals we would have for Mike are to reduce his conduct problems and substance use to normative levels for a child of his age, and to increase his engagement with prosocial activities and interests. The route we would propose for reaching these goals includes individual and/or group therapy with Mike using the Coping Power curriculum, individual or group parent training using the Coping Power parent component with Mr. and Ms. D., and occasional consultation with school personnel.

Length of Treatment

Mike would be asked to attend weekly, hour-long sessions that teach anger management and social problem-solving skills. He would probably need to participate in approximately 20–33 sessions over the course of 15–18 months. Mike's parents would be asked to participate in a 10–16-session course of parent training, in which they would learn effective stress reduction, behavior management, communication, and negotiation techniques. Finally, occasional contact with Mike's school counselor would be used to facilitate the generalization of skills learned in therapy to the school setting.

Case Conceptualization

Given known risk factors for the development of conduct problems and given the current evaluation of Mike, one can speculate about how he may have developed an aggressive, defiant behavior pattern. One possible factor is that Mike may have had a genetic predisposition for irritability. His mother reported that he had a difficult temperament from birth and that, with regard to anger and temper problems, Mike is "just like his father" (although the latter observation may also reflect the effects of modeling). In the present evaluation, Mike's MMPI-A test results suggest that he has basic tendencies for impulsivity, cynicism, pessimism, and is easily bored or restless. Substance use, fighting, and theft could all be impulsive activities that provide a kind of excitement and stimulation that Mike seeks.

Several features of Mike's family environment certainly placed him at risk for developing behavior problems. His parents' marriage was troubled for a long time, and, 2 years after their divorce, Mr. and Ms. D. continue to be in conflict with each other. Mr. D. reportedly threatened his wife and even shoved her from time to time during their marriage. Witnessing chronic parental conflict and aggression may have led Mike to develop dysfunctional beliefs about relationships and ways of resolving problems. For example, Mike may have learned that arguing and aggression are the most reliable ways of getting attention and getting one's way. Mr. D. may have also modeled substance abuse for Mike; in the interview, Mike stated that his father used to drink heavily, although he has cut back recently.

Another risk factor for aggression to which Mike was probably exposed during childhood is poor parenting practices. It appears that Mr. D. may have been overly strict with the children, issuing harsh punishments and "raging" at the children when angry. In fact, Ms. D.'s fear that her husband might seriously harm the children with physical punishment was the ultimate reason she cited for the break-up of the marriage. Mr. D.'s lack of monitoring of, and involvement with, Mike would also be considered risk factors for the development of conduct disorder in Mike. If Mr. D. has not developed a warm, supportive, involved relationship with his son, Mike may not feel very motivated to please his father by "getting on the right track."

Other potential parenting problems could include inconsistency in rules and consequences between the two homes; possible permissiveness on the part of Ms. D.; and a possible decrease in Ms. D.'s availability to her children since the divorce, due to her having to work. If she has decreased her monitoring of Mike's activities, it has probably been easier for him to engage in deviant activities without experiencing punishment. If she feels she no longer has the time to engage in enjoyable, relationship-enhancing activities with Mike very often, the overall quality of their relationship may be suffering, which puts him at risk for externalizing behavior problems. Another aspect of Mike's family life that could contribute to his current difficulties is possible resentment of his sister's apparent perfection; he might feel like there is little incentive to follow rules and get along with others if his family has already determined that his sister is "the good child" and he is "the bad child."

Mike's experiences at school also may have played a role in the development of his conduct problems. Mike probably has a history of not feeling very successful in school. Although his grades were good throughout most of elementary school, he may have received considerable attention and punishment for his negative behaviors. An identity as a "bad kid" may have been established and reinforced from early on. Because of his behavior problems, he may have experienced peer rejection from an early age, which could have resulted in his failure to develop good social skills and in his meeting affiliation needs by associating with deviant peers. In the last 2 years, Mike may have received more negative attention, which is warranted for the drop in his grades from A's and B's to mostly C's. This change could simply be attributable to the fact that academic material becomes considerably more complex by about the 5th grade. His current testing suggests that his academic achievement is within the average range, and only slightly below what would be expected for his average intelligence level. Now that he is a 7th grader, Mike "cuts" classes frequently and there is a treat of truancy charges. The accumulated negative feedback he has received about his school performance over the years may have resulted in a weak bond to school, which is a risk factor for the development of aggression and delinquency.

We feel guardedly optimistic that this course of therapy would be at least moderately effective for Mike. Previous intervention research using Coping Power with children with conduct problems indicates that the average child responds with a meaningful improvement in his or her behavior by the end of the intervention (approximately 15 months). There are several reasons to think that Mike would make at least "average" progress in the course of treatment. First, his intellectual abilities and developmental level suggest that he can participate appropriately in a cognitive-behavioral therapy. Children with below-average intelligence and children under age 10 typically do not benefit as much from training in social-cognitive skills. Second, although Mike has some serious behavior problems, he is not yet entrenched in a severely, chronically antisocial behavior pattern. Coping Power has been used as a prevention program for high-risk children, as well as a treatment program in outpatient clinics. On a related note, Mike's case appears relatively uncomplicated by other problems that are often seen with conduct disorder, such as learning or internalizing disorders, ADHD, or the hardships of family poverty. These factors bode well for Mike.

Other positive treatment indicators for Mike include his possible fear of negative consequences for the theft incident, his prosocial goals for his future, and his mother's commitment to her parenting responsibilities. The clinician reported that, although Mike expressed no remorse for stealing from the convenience store, Ms. D. was confident that Mike is, in fact, worried about punishment from the court. This is a good sign because it suggests that there are negative consequences the court could impose that would be aversive to Mike, which might deter him from engaging in theft in the future. He has not yet become a "hardened criminal," unresponsive to punishment. On a related note, optimism is warranted because Mike does not yet view himself in purely antisocial terms. When asked about his future, he cited prosocial goals, such as joining the military or becoming a professional football player. The clinician's impressions of Ms. D. were also encouraging. Although the family certainly has its difficulties and Ms. D. is not perfect, she seems appropriately concerned about Mike and willing to cooperate with treatment. This is of critical importance because she will probably be the person responsible for bringing Mike to his therapy appointments regularly, and because her participation in parent training is an extremely important component to Mike's treatment.

On the other hand, the cause for "guarded" optimism stems from the possibility that Mike may have the more severe, chronic form of conduct disorder (childhood onset) and from the negative influences of his father. If further assessment results in a change of diagnosis to childhood-onset conduct disorder, we would modify our expectations somewhat. Treatment might take longer and be less effective. Also, based on Mr. D.'s lack of involvement with Mike and his long pattern of ineffective parenting behavior, we predict that he probably will not become as engaged in treatment as would be necessary for Mike to make maximum gains.

The Therapeutic Relationship

The therapeutic relationship established within any treatment program is an important factor, because of the effect on compliance and termination of treatment. As discussed in a previous section of this chapter, clinician skills and attributes are essential in the clinician's ability to establish and maintain effectual relationships between the client and other significant contributors within the therapeutic "network." Other factors, such as confidentiality and limit setting, are also important. In the case of Mike, the clinician using the Coping Power Program group format would find it necessary to consider therapeutic factors within four relationship sets: (a) the clinician–school personnel relationship, (b) the clinician–group relationship, (c) the clinician–child (Mike) relationship, and (d) the clinician–caregiver(s) relationship. If the clinician chooses to treat Mike individually, only the last two mentioned relationship sets, and possibly the first set (clinician–school personnel), would be relevant.

The Clinician–School Personnel Relationship

If the school environment is the chosen location for treatment, whether administered to a group of similar students or individually to Mike, collaborative relationships with Mike's teachers will be critical to effectively implement the program within the school setting. Because Mike would likely have to miss class time to attend the 45–60 minute sessions, it would be beneficial for the clinicians to briefly meet with Mike's teacher(s) and other interested personnel (i.e., principal, school counselor) prior to scheduling the sessions, to discuss potential barriers and to work toward establishing positive relationships early in the process. During this initial meeting, topics of discussion should include an overview of the program (i.e., specific goals of the Coping Power Program), the teacher's role in program implementation, and a schedule for the weekly sessions, preferably during a relatively convenient day and time for the teachers but not during a class that Mike enjoys (e.g., physical education). From the start, the clinicians will emphasize a collaborative treatment approach and will demonstrate to the teacher that his or her input is valued (encouraging him or her to continually communicate with the clinicians). Also, teachers may assist the clinicians in deriving short-term weekly goals, related to Mike's current school problems (e.g., nonparticipation in class, disruptive behavior).

The Clinician–Group Relationship

As a member of a group, Mike will be in a unique situation in which he will not only learn from the clinicians but may also gain from interactions with peers who are working through similar problems. Of course, inherent in the benefits of group therapy are risks related to maintaining group confidentiality, recognizing and intervening during deviant peer interactions, and problems caused by ability disparities between group members. During the first session the clinician will discuss confidentiality and the importance of having a group rule to maintain confidentiality (e.g., "What's said in group, stays in group"). Any breaches of this rule should be dealt with firmly within group and/or during the individual sessions. If Mike or other group members have difficulty with maintaining confidentiality, it may be necessary for the clinician to encourage Mike to discuss personal situations during individual sessions if he has concerns of personal information being shared outside of group. The clinicians should also follow rules of confidentiality and should not share any group-related information (e.g., group videos presented at the parent group) without the consent of all child group members.

The clinician's ability to recognize and intervene during deviant group processes (i.e., group members reinforcing aggressive behavior by laughing about an aggressive act) and his or her ability to maintain control during the group sessions will have a major impact on the nature of the clinician–group relationship. Establishing rules for acceptable (and unacceptable) behavior during the first session will help to clarify clinician expectations. Intervening during apparent deviant processes during group may limit the effects of the acts on the group. Maintaining control through a contingency system (e.g., "three strikes" = lose a point) is also essential to creating a positive clinician–group relationship.

Ability disparities (e.g., reading level, ease of "understanding") between Mike and other group members should also be taken into account because low self-efficacy (Mash, 1998) and/or norm comparisons may affect whether Mike attempts certain assignments or whether he actively participates during group. With Mike's apparent aversion to school, probably a result of negative experiences within the school environment, it would be essential for the clinician to attempt to make the group experience an accomplishable, learning experience for Mike (i.e., begin with goals of low difficulty) to improve the likelihood of his active participation during the group sessions.

During the course of group sessions, the clinicians should attempt to enhance a positive group process by including positive feedback from all group members at the end of group sessions by including group-wide contingencies for earning group reinforcements, which promote cooperative behavior among group members; and by encouraging group members to plan prosocial group activities that can positively impact others outside the group (e.g., creating "resisting peer pressure" posters, which can be mounted in their school). If disagreements or conflicts develop between Mike and another group member during sessions or when a group member begins discussing a recent social problem outside of group, clinicians using the Coping Power Program would view the "true life" problem as an opportunity to directly model and reinforce the social-cognitive skills that are the focus of the program. In this situation, the clinician would direct Mike and/or the other group member(s) in problem solving and ways to cool down, to listen to the other person's interpretation of the event, and to use verbal assertion and negotiation skills to effectively deal with the situation.

The Clinician–Client Relationship

Children with the same disorder often have variations in the presentation of the disorder (Mash, 1998) and/or in the factors that appear to maintain the symptoms. Because of possible individual treatment issues and the potential added benefit of focusing on Coping Power objectives individually, approximately eight individual sessions (or more, if necessary) will be conducted with Mike, concurrent with the group sessions. This gives one of the clinicians an opportunity to form a clinician–client relationship with Mike. Rules of confidentiality should again be stressed, specifically how they relate to information shared during the individual sessions. Always, it is important for the clinician to share with Mike any information from the individual sessions he or she plans to disclose to Mike's parents and/or his teachers. This will not only demonstrate respect for Mike (and hopefully encourage communication) but also allow him an opportunity to discuss alternatives (e.g., Mike asks to disclose the information himself) or to problem solve (e.g., how to handle the situation when confronted by his teacher/parent). The individual sessions are less structured than the group sessions and can be used as a means to allow for client-directed discussions, in relation to personal issues/concerns or Coping Power-related objectives.

As with any individual therapy client, the clinician will need to use basic therapeutic skills to encourage participation from Mike during the sessions and to enhance the effects of the individual session. Therapeutic skills related to rapport-building (i.e., empathy, positive regard, minimal directive commands) and occasional disclosure are two skills that may lead to a degree of comfort in Mike and to trust. Games (e.g., checkers or therapeutic games) could also be used during individual sessions if Mike has problems discussing certain issues, due to the fact that play can at times reverse inhibitive behaviors in child and adolescent therapy clients. The clinician would need to be responsive to Mike's verbal and nonverbal behavior throughout the implementation of the program and should document his reactions and behaviors during individual sessions. The clinician may also benefit from documenting relevant clinical impressions resulting from the interactions and behaviors during the individual sessions. Clinical impressions may aid in creating treatment objectives or may suggest a need for a different approach during Mike's individual meetings.

The Clinician–Caregiver(s) Relationship

Collaborative relationships with caregivers and their active engagement in the parent component of the Coping Power Program greatly enhances the effects of the program on target children (Lochman et al., in press). The clinicians would benefit from establishing a relationship with Ms. D., and with Mr. D. if he expresses an interest. Visiting the caregiver(s) prior to the first session (i.e., during the consent stage, clerical process stage) gives the clinicians an opportunity to discuss the child and parent components of the program and to encourage the caregiver to attend the sessions (e.g., discuss incentives such as childcare, if provided). This contact gives Ms. and Mr. D. a chance to ask questions and discuss problems they presently have with Mike. The clinicians could discuss how the parent sessions will focus on some of their concerns (e.g., discipline strategies, academic support, monitoring) and how they could use the sessions to discuss issues and learn from other parents who may have experienced similar situations. A list of the scheduled parent meetings (including time and place) would be left with Ms. and Mr. D., along with contact information for the clinicians. Prior to each parent meeting, the clinicians will send home a flier to remind Ms. and Mr. D. of the approaching session and one of the clinicians would call them the evening prior to the scheduled meeting date.

During the parent groups the clinicians will establish rules of confidentiality (first session) and will encourage parents to discuss personal situations related to the session objectives. The clinicians will also share the objectives that the children are learning, being careful not to disclose any personal, child-specific information, in order to encourage the parents to help facilitate and reward the new skills when noticed at home (Lochman & Wells, 1996). If Ms. D. or Mr. D. attend the parent sessions and implement the behavioral management strategies taught during the sessions, Mike's chances of benefiting from the program will be significantly enhanced.

Treatment Implications and Outcome
Therapeutic Techniques and Strategies
Mike's evaluation identified a number of concerning behaviors consistent with diagnoses of conduct disorder and cannabis abuse. These diagnoses are not an unexpected outcome at this stage of his life given that his early history included significant risk factors such as severe temper tantrums, overactivity, and behavior problems at school. Though Mike's problems may have reached a more pronounced level of severity, his history and current presentation are, in fact, consistent with those of many children who have participated in the Coping Power Program. Coping Power was originally designed as a prevention program to inhibit further escalation of existing problem behaviors, but it also has been effectively used as a treatment program in outpatient clinics.

Coping Power was designed to target deficits in social competence, self-regulation, school bonding, and positive parenting, all of which are present in Mike's situation in varying degrees. However, given that Mike has already engaged in substance abuse and antisocial behaviors, some modifications to the standard protocol may be necessary, specifically with regard to the intensity of treatment and monitoring of target behaviors. This would likely include the more active involvement of parents, school personnel, and legal representatives, such as Mike's probation officer, in his treatment.

What follows is a session-by-session description of the standard, group-format coping power child component as applied to the case of Mike. Ideally, Mike would join a group of similarly aged peers, also presenting with disruptive behaviors and social skills deficits. Of course, group leaders would need to carefully monitor group interactions to prevent deviancy training among the boys (Dishion & Andrews, 1995; Poulin, Dishion, & Burraston, 2001). It appears that Mike's treatment could be enhanced through a group experience in several ways. First, immersion in a group context might help to catalyze Mike's engagement and participation in treatment. He presented at the first meeting with his mother and therapist as sullen and minimally communicative. Inclusion in a group of peers might lower Mike's defenses making him more accepting of the intervention and, in turn, more motivated to participate. Second, Mike was reported to have friends and he appears to enjoy the company of his peers. Group treatment might therefore be a more positive and rewarding experience than individual sessions, and may increase the probability of his continued attendance. Third, although Mike acknowledged that he had a "bad temper," he was resistant to the idea that he had a problem with anger management. If others in his group are willing to acknowledge their problems with anger management, Mike might also follow suit. In addition, Mike might recognize how anger causes problems for others and may become more receptive to his own problems with anger management. Fourth, the group context would afford Mike opportunities to learn from the experiences and ideas of others. It is likely that peer reports would be more salient to Mike than those of adult group leaders.

The Coping Power child component.   In the first session, typically held around the beginning of the school year, Mike will be introduced to his fellow group members and will work with them on a collaborative activity designed to foster group cohesion. For example, the group might generate ideas and vote on a group name, or might create a group banner or flag. The group will also work together to generate the group rules, which should outline basic safety requirements (e.g., no fighting) and govern respectfulness to leaders and one another. The purpose of the group will be articulated as will the behavioral point system that will be used for the remaining sessions to reward adherence to the rules, positive participation in group activities, and progress toward individually selected goals (explained in Sessions 2 and 3).

In addition, group members will be told that they will have monthly individual meetings with one of their group leaders. These meetings are an essential part of the program in monitoring and providing reinforcement for behavioral goals and for maintaining rapport and bonding between the participants and leaders. The monthly meetings also allow group leaders to individualize the material to participants' current problems (e.g., using coping power material as a framework for discussing recent conflicts with peers).

In Sessions 2 and 3, the importance of setting and working toward goals will be discussed and members will identify long-term and short-term goals for themselves. In Mike's evaluation, he identified several long-term goals, including completing high school, playing professional football, and joining the armed forces. During these sessions, the necessity of breaking such long-range ambitions into more manageable steps will be explained, and members will be challenged to recognize how their current choices influence the likelihood that they will attain their goals. For example, leaders might work with Mike on his goal of completing high school by having him develop a list of the things that this requires, including adequate grades, regular attendance, and appropriate behavior. With Mike's input, the leaders could then break these smaller goals down even further, to set daily goals such as completing assignments, attending his classes, and treating school staff respectfully. As Mike experiences success in these smaller goals, he may become more hopeful and optimistic about his ability to achieve additional, more challenging goals. If Mike's treatment occurs in a school-based setting, teachers will provide daily feedback on Mike's progress toward his goals using a coping power "Goal Sheet." If Mike's treatment occurs in a clinic or private practice setting, the procedure can be modified to include home-based goals monitored by a parent.

Sessions 4 and 5 focus on the physiological reactions corresponding to anger and frustration. Group members learn to recognize their internal cues to anger, such as muscle tension and elevated heart rate, and they are introduced to the concept that anger occurs at varying levels (e.g., annoyance, irritation, rage). Group members also identify the different types of problems that lead them to experience different levels of anger. For Mike, these sessions will be particularly important in addressing his self-described bad temper. If he can meet the objectives of these sessions and develop an awareness of his physiological cues to anger and the circumstances that trigger his anger, he will be primed for the next major unit in the program, anger management skills.

In Sessions 6 through 8, group members learn several techniques to manage their angry feelings including distraction, breathing techniques, and positive self-statements. Activities are designed to give students practice with the techniques and to help students memorize the positive self-statements so that they are cognitively accessible. Sessions 10 and 11 will further build on these skills (see below).

Session 9 focuses on the organizational and study skills required for adequate school progress, with an emphasis on the importance of these skills in middle school. In this session, group members participate in several activities designed to highlight the importance of being organized, and to give students practice using the organizational techniques. For Mike, who appears to have been disengaged from school since his parents' divorce 2 years ago, practice in organizational and study skills will likely provide needed remediation for time lost in these areas since fifth grade. Gaining competence in organizational and study skills will help Mike to achieve goals related to his academic performance, such as completion of assignments and improved grades.

In Sessions 10 and 11 members participate in a series of activities designed to elicit actual feelings of anger, during which they are coached in using the anger management skills they learned in previous sessions. Initial exercises are conducted with puppets and role-plays, allowing group members to gain experience with the techniques in a very controlled manner. Later activities are more realistic and personally relevant. For example, in one activity, each child is taunted by the group and uses anger management skills to control and reduce resulting feelings of anger.

The descriptions of Mike's angry outbursts suggest that he does not deal effectively with the physiological surges in anger resulting from provocation or frustration. Skills learned in these sessions will help him to manage these feelings and to restore a state of calm after an anger-inducing experience. He will then be able to refocus and use the cognitive problem-solving strategies that form the next major unit of the program.

In Session 12, students learn the first step of coping power's Problem Identification, Choices, Consequences (PICC) model, which they will employ for the remainder of the program to address problems in an adaptive manner. The Problem identification step is first taught with concrete examples (e.g., a car that would not run; a Nintendo game that would not work). Problem identification is extended to interpersonal situations in Sessions 13 through 15. These sessions focus on perspective taking by teaching group members to consider the various motivations and circumstances underlying social problems. Cognitive errors such as the hostile attribution bias, in which threat is perceived in others' neutral or even positive actions, are challenged in these sessions to improve the accuracy of participants' social problem identification. For Mike, who, as stated in his evaluation, displays "cynicism and distrust of others, and a tendency to assume the worst of others," these will be particularly relevant and important sessions.

The remaining two steps of the PICC model, Choices and Consequences, are taught in Sessions 16 through 22. First, group members participate in a number of "brain-storming" exercises in which they generate multiple solutions to a given problem. These exercises address common deficits of aggressive children in the quality of their problem-solving solutions. Mike's tendency to "respond to problem situations with ready anger, including verbal and occasional physical aggression," may be a result of such a deficit. The Consequences step requires participants to think through the results of each possible choice, and to evaluate whether the results are helpful, harmful, or neutral. To increase the salience of the PICC model, group members create a videotape over several sessions in which they portray a problem, then act out various solutions with resulting consequences.

Session 23 is generally held after students return from their summer break and serves as a reintroduction to the program and review of topics already covered. In Sessions 24 through 27, the PICC model is applied to relationships with teachers, peers, and siblings. Mike's history indicates that he has difficulties with each of these groups, and could benefit from coaching and modeling in resolving problems with them. Peer relations, in particular, will be an important area to emphasize with Mike, given his history of engaging in delinquent behaviors with peers. In these sessions, Mike might be given a scenario such as being pressured by peers to vandalize property, from which he would generate several choices (e.g., go along with it; try to get them interested in doing something else) and the resulting consequences (e.g., could be caught and arrested; could avoid trouble). Working through situations like this in treatment will help Mike transfer the problem-solving skills when he encounters difficult situations in his daily life.

In addition to applying the PICC model to peer conflicts, Sessions 25 and 26 highlight positive social relationships and attempt to steer participants away from deviant peer groups. Participants complete activities in which they identify important friendship qualities (both what they look for in a friend and what they can bring to a friendship) and practice entering a new group of peers. The sessions have a self-esteem enhancing component as participants identify their strengths and unique personal attributes. Further, group members participate in role-plays, allowing them to gain practice with introducing themselves and making assertive requests, which will increase their chances of peer acceptance.

Peer pressure is the theme of Sessions 28 and 29, particularly covering pressure to engage in substance abuse. Group members view a video and participate in role-plays and discussions that highlight effective coping strategies to deal with peer pressure. In Session 30, group members participate in awareness-building exercises about their neighborhoods and how the environments in which they live may contain both dangers and positive resources.

Sessions 31 and 32 are also focused on peer relations, specifically leading group members to identify the various groups or "cliques" in their schools and communities and to classify them as positive or problematic. Group members participate in exercises helping them to identify their own place in their groups and how they can become more involved in prosocial groups of peers. These concepts are relevant to Mike's case, in that he presents as a social boy who enjoys being in the company of peers, though he has aligned himself in the past with deviant groups. Through exercises such as those in Sessions 31 and 32, Mike might identify groups he would like to join, and he might work with his session leaders to develop a plan on how to incorporate himself into the group's activities. For example, Mike might like to become a part of an athletic group of boys and could set goals of trying out for a sports team, attending practices, and later, participating in social activities with his teammates. The final session in the Coping Power Program encompasses a review of the entire treatment package, games, and closure activities.

Adaptation for clinic settings.   Although the preceding summary of the coping power child component describes the program in its original school-based group intervention format, Coping Power can also be adapted for use in clinic settings. A clinical trial of the Coping Power Program has been conducted in an outpatient setting in Utrecht, The Netherlands, and Coping Power's precursor, anger coping, has also been implemented in clinic settings. Adapting the program for use in clinic settings requires only minor changes to selected activities (e.g., weekly goals will likely be home-based rather than school-based) and will not alter the content of the program.

In the current outpatient treatment climate, Coping Power may be more likely to be implemented on an individual basis, rather than in a group format. With minor modifications, the program can be used with individual clients. Modifications will primarily require the clinician to make up for the absence of peers by taking a more active role in some activities (e.g., being involved in role-plays) and provoking discussion with examples and questions that other group members might have raised. More often than in a group setting, clinicians may need to incorporate appropriate self-disclosures and hypothetical case examples (e.g., "I once worked with a boy your age who . . .") to bring salience to the program content. Using Coping Power in a one-on-one setting may also afford several advantages, such as allotting time to topics based on the client's mastery of the material, and allowing clinicians to individualize activities to target issues relevant to the particular client's treatment plan. For example, Mike's therapist might incorporate problems related to truancy and substance abuse when working with him on the PICC model.

Adaptation for adolescents.   Coping Power has most often been used with children in the fourth through sixth grades, but can be adapted for an older population. In describing use of Anger Coping Program with adolescents, Lochman, FitzGerald, and Whidby (1999) describe several modifications which are also relevant to Coping Power. For example, clinicians might allow adolescents more opportunities to choose topics that are relevant to them, and clinicians may be less directive during discussions. Problems with attendance, which are likely to be heightened with adolescent groups, may require clinicians to be more flexible in covering session material and in setting program end dates. Readers are referred to Lochman et al. (1999) for additional details for making program adaptations for adolescents.

The Coping Power parent component.   Our experience and research indicate that working with parents will enhance the treatment effects of the Coping Power Program. The coping power parent component was developed to involve parents of referred children in their treatment in a systematic manner. The complete parent component consists of 16 sessions, spread over a 15–18-month period. The sessions focus on building parenting skills, including positive reinforcement, discipline, and improving the parent–child relationship. Mike's history suggests that family relationships are currently strained, and are unlikely to improve without intervention. Ideally, Mike's mother *and* father would attend the sessions, although in our experience, noncustodial parents do not typically attend, and even in two-parent families it is the mother who most often comes to the meetings. What follows is a session-by-session review of the Coping Power parent component as it applies to Mike and his family.

The first session focuses on rapport-building and introducing parents to the educational program. Basic principles of social learning are reviewed and parents are introduced to the Antecedent-Behavior-Consequence (ABC) model as a framework for evaluating behaviors. The use of praise and consequences, as they relate to behavior change, is also discussed.

In Session 2, the topic of academic support in the home is reviewed, which is an area of substantial interest for most parents. In this session, Mike's mother will be given information on how to support Mike's completion of homework, including using structure and supervision to ensure the work is done properly. In addition, the session includes a section on working effectively with school personnel, which will also be important for Mike's mother in enlisting the support of teachers and administrators to help Mike improve his academic and behavioral performance at school.

The next three sessions focus on a proactive approach to parenting. Skills addressed include ignoring minor disruptive behaviors, giving clear instructions, and developing clear and consistent rules and expectations for behavior. In these sessions, leaders might work with Ms. D. to develop a set of house rules (e.g., no swearing or threats) and expectations (e.g., that children attend school; that children inform parents of their whereabouts after school) that she can present to Mike and his sister. The use of "good" instructions (i.e., delivered in a manner that will elicit compliance) should also be helpful to Ms. D. in asserting her role as the parent in the family and in avoiding power struggles with Mike.

In Sessions 6 and 7, the focus shifts to discipline techniques that are age-appropriate and effective. There is a discussion of physical punishment and its limitations, and alternatives such as work chores and privilege removal are presented. It would be particularly helpful for Mike's father to attend this session, given the history of physical punishment used in the family and Mr. D.'s continued use of threats. Ideally, both parents would discuss punishment procedures together and jointly decide upon the procedures they will use with Mike. Such consistency would likely improve Mike's response to discipline procedures and reduce the likelihood of him "splitting" his parents when he is being punished.

Stress management techniques are presented in Sessions 8 and 9, with a particular emphasis on stress related to parenting. Topics include the importance of parents taking time to "take care of themselves," time management, active relaxation, and cognitive reframing of stressful events. These sessions are generally very well received by parents and would likely be relevant for Ms. D., given the number of recent significant stressors in her life. Improvements in her ability to manage stress might result in increased energy to parent Mike and cope effectively with his behaviors.

Sessions 10 through 12 are geared toward improving family relations. Several strategies are presented toward this end, including planning positive family activities to promote cohesiveness, using the PICC problem-solving model to resolve family conflict, and enhancing family communication through structure (e.g., family meetings, writing notes). In Mike's family, family turmoil over the previous years has likely disrupted communication and the flow of positive feelings among Ms. D. and her two children. The material presented in these sessions may help to restore family closeness and help them to deal with difficult issues in an effective manner.

The remaining sessions focus on planning for the future, including preparing for middle school, and identifying prosocial activities for the summer and beyond. At the time of referral, Mike was not reported to be involved in extracurricular activities and was spending a large amount of unsupervised time in problem activities (e.g., truancy, substance abuse). In these sessions, Ms. D. will be presented with a variety of age-appropriate, prosocial activities that Mike might become involved in, and the immediate and long-term benefits to his development will be discussed. Additional discussions will center around how parents can remain involved in their children's lives as they approach and progress through adolescence, including the ongoing importance of parents' roles as behavior managers and community/school advocates.

Mechanisms of Change

Through this course of intervention, we would expect behavioral improvement in Mike to occur via several mechanisms. Anger-management training with Mike would be aimed at helping him to identify situations that make him angry, to identify anger at various levels of intensity, and to develop ways of calming himself down. Training Mike in problem-solving skills would help him learn to evaluate problem situations more accurately (i.e., with less of a hostile, pessimistic, cynical bias), to reduce his impulsivity, and to improve his ability to generate prosocial alternative choices. Direct intervention with Mike would also feature instruction in setting prosocial goals and monitoring his own progress toward those goals.

Parent training could be expected to reduce Mike's conduct problems in several ways. Mike's parents would receive instruction and support in the consistent use of effective discipline techniques. They would be helped to increase their monitoring of Mike and their positive involvement with him. Intervention would also focus on ways of reducing their own personal stress and the conflict within their relationship with each other. Furthermore, they would be given information about the skills Mike is learning in his individual and/or group coping power sessions, so that they can better assist Mike with generalizing those skills to the home and community environments.

The mechanisms of change for Mike's behavior will include child-level factors and parenting factors. Research on the Coping Power Program has demonstrated that the Coping Power child component alone is effective in producing change in child behavior problems and substance abuse rates, but that the addition of the parent component further enhances treatment effects and produces even better sustained outcomes (Lochman, Wells, & Murray, in press). These results suggest that, together, the Coping Power child and parent components will be the most important mechanisms of change for Mike.

The Coping Power child component was designed to target a range of social problem-solving deficits typically exhibited by aggressive children, all of which are likely to be helpful to Mike. Given his presenting problems, it appears that anger-management training, problem-solving training, and skills to deal with peer pressure will most closely target his treatment needs. In addition, the goal-setting procedures will help to generalize treatment effects.

Within the Coping Power parent component, an important goal for Ms. D. will be to gain confidence in her parenting skills so that she can feel in charge and in control of her son. Improving the mother–son relationship should help her to earn credibility with Mike and will hopefully initiate a pattern of increased communication and effective problem solving. Another objective that will be particularly relevant for Ms. D. will be the ability to supervise and monitor Mike's activities. She will further need to have the skills to hold him accountable for rule violations and to enforce her punishments.

Medical and Nutritional Issues

Other than encouraging Ms. D. to schedule a physician's appointment for Mike to rule out any medical causes for his irritability and subclinical attention problems, medical and nutritional issues would not be a focus of this treatment program.

Potential Pitfalls

Our experience in implementing the Coping Power Program has taught us that attendance problems represent a major potential pitfall to the success of the program. When the program is implemented in the school setting, various school activities, including field trips, assemblies, and testing, can interfere with group members' attendance. Our experience also indicates that teachers often have difficulties with excusing students from class because the students may miss instructional time that cannot be made up. We have dealt with such implementation difficulties in various ways, including meeting with teachers prior to the start of intervention to identify the best times of day for groups and checking in with teachers on a regular basis to ensure the time is working out. This continued contact also serves to keep teachers involved, maintaining their interest and commitment to support students' participation in the program. Other methods we have used to improve attendance include meeting with children during after-school programs and meeting with children at their homes. Clinician flexibility is key in addressing the difficulties with scheduling and attendance.

Attendance at parent groups has also been a limiting factor in Coping Power implementation. Our research group has come up with a number of ways to encourage parental attendance including scheduling the sessions after 5 PM to accommodate working parents' schedules; providing childcare with fun activities for the Coping Power child and any siblings; and providing dinner and/or snacks to parents and children. In addition, reminder letters are sent home with the group participant prior to each parent meeting and reminder telephone calls are made before the meetings. However, even with these strategies, attendance at parent groups is typically less than 50% (Lochman & Wells, 1996).

Termination and Relapse Prevention

The Coping Power Program is time-limited and is designed to be completed in 20–33 sessions, spread over a 15–18-month period. Participants are prepared for termination during sessions through review and closure activities. Participants in both the child and parent components are provided with notebooks in which to keep the various handouts and worksheets that are used during the program, and they are encouraged to keep and refer to their notebooks after the program's termination.

Relapse prevention is built into the program through an emphasis on skill-building and generalization activities. The skills are taught using real-life examples, and participants in both the child and parent components are encouraged to discuss the application of these skills to their personal experiences. In addition, the goal sheets used in the child component allow for daily application and feedback of Coping Power concepts and skills. Also, the delivery of Coping Power in the school setting promotes generalization because students have many opportunities at school throughout the day to practice newly learned skills in an environment that has likely presented multiple challenges for them. Working with this system over an extended period of time should help to maintain the skills addressed even after the program is completed.

ACKNOWLEDGMENTS

The preparation of this chapter has been supported by grants from the Centers for Disease Control and Prevention (R49/CCR418569), the Center for Substance Abuse Prevention (KD1 SP08633; UR6 5907956), the National Institute on Drug Abuse (R01 DA08453; R01 DA16135), and the U.S. Department of Justice (2000CKWX0091).

REFERENCES

Abidin, R. R. (1983). *Parenting stress index—Manual*. Charlottesville, VA: Pediatric Psychology Press.

Achenbach, T. M. (1991). *Manual for the Child Behavior Checklist and 1991 profile*. Burlington, VT: University of Vermont, Department of Psychiatry.

Adler, A. (1964). *Social interest: A challenge to mankind*. New York: Capricorn.

Barth, J. M., Dunlap, S. T., Dane, H., Lochman, J. E., & Wells, K. C. (2004). Classroom environment influences on aggression, peer relations, and academic focus. *Journal of School Psychology, 42*, 115–117

Bloomquist, M. L., August, G. J., Cohen, C., Doyle, A., & Everhart, K. (1997). Social problem solving in hyperactive—Aggressive children: How and what they think in conditions of automatic and controlled processing. *Journal of Clinical Child Psychology, 26*, 172–180.

Butcher, J. N., Williams, C. L., Graham, J. R., Archer, R. P., Jellegen, A., Ben-Porath, Y. S., & Kaemmer, B. (1992). *MMPI—A (Minnesota Multiphasic Personality Inventory—Adolescent): Manual for administration, scoring and interpretation*. St. Paul, MN: University of Minnesota Press.

Capaldi, D. M., & Patterson, G. R. (1991). Relation of parental transitions to boys' adjustment problems: Mothers at risk for transitions and unskilled parenting. *Developmental Psychology, 27*, 489–504.

Crick, N. R., & Dodge, K. A. (1994). A review and reformulation of social-information processing mechanisms in children's social adjustment. *Psychological Bulletin, 115*, 74–101.

Crick, N. R., & Dodge, K. A. (1996). Social information-processing mechanisms on reactive and proactive aggression. *Child Development, 67*, 993–1002.

Crick, N. R., & Werner, N. E. (1998). Response decision processes in relational and overt aggression. *Child Development, 69*, 1630–1639.

Dadds, M. R., & Powell, M. B. (1992). The relationship of interparental conflict and global marital adjustment to aggression, anxiety, and immaturity in aggressive and nonclinic children. *Journal of Abnormal Child Psychology, 19*, 553–567.

Derogatis, L. R., & Lazarus, L. (1994). SCL-90-R, Brief Symptom Inventory, and matching clinical rating scales. In M. E. Maruish (Ed.), *The use of psychological testing for treatment planning and outcome assessment* (pp. 217–248). Hillsdale, NJ: Erlbaum.

Derogatis, L. R., & Melisaratos, N. (1983). The Brief Symptom Inventory: An introductory report. *Psychological Medicine, 13*, 595–605.

DeRubeis, R. J., & Beck, A. T. (1988). Cognitive therapy. In K. S. Dobson (Ed.), *Handbook of cognitive-behavioral therapies* (pp. 85–135). New York: Guilford Press.

Dishion, T. J., & Andrews, D. W. (1995). Preventing escalation in problem behaviors with high risk young adolescents: Immediate and 1-year outcomes. *Journal of Consulting and Clinical Psychology, 63*, 538–548.

Dodge, K. A., Lochman, J. E., Harnish, J. D., Bates, J. E., & Pettit, G. (1997). Reactive and proactive aggression in school children and psychiatrically impaired chronically assaultive youth. *Journal of Abnormal Psychology, 106*, 37–51.

Dodge, K. A., Pettit, G. S., McClaskey, C. L., & Brown, M. M. (1986). Social competence in children. *Monographs of the Society for Research in Child Development, 51,* 1–85.

Dunn, S. E., Lochman, J. E., & Colder, C. R. (1997). Social problem solving skills in boys with Conduct and Oppositional Defiant Disorders. *Aggressive Behavior, 23,* 457–469.

Erdley, C. A. (1990). *An analysis of children's attributions and goals in social situations: Implications of children's friendship outcomes.* Unpublished manuscript, University of Illinois.

Farmer, E. M. Z., Compton, S. N., Burns, B. J., & Robertson, E. (2002). Review of the evidence base for treatment of childhood psychopathology: Externalizing disorders. *Journal of Consulting and Clinical Psychology, 70,* 1267–1302.

Feldman, E., & Dodge, K. A. (1987). Social information processing and sociometric status: Sex, age, and situational effects. *Journal of Abnormal Child Psychology, 15,* 211–227.

Fiske, S. T., & Taylor, S. E. (1984). *Social cognition.* Reading, MA: Addison-Wesley.

Freeman, A., & Leaf, R. C. (1989). Cognitive therapy applied to personality disorders. In A. Freeman, K. M. Simm, L. E. Beutler, & H. Arkowitz (Eds.), *Comprehensive handbook of cognitive therapy* (pp. 403–433). New York: Plenum Press.

Frick, P. J. (1998). *Conduct disorders and severe antisocial behavior.* New York: Plenum Press.

Gouze, K. R. (1987). Attention and social problem solving as correlates of aggression in preschool males. *Journal of Abnormal Child Psychology, 15,* 181–197.

Hawkins, J. D., Catalano, R. F., & Miller, J. Y. (1992). Risk and protective factors for alcohol and other drug problems in adolescence and early adulthood: Implications for substance abuse prevention. *Psychological Bulletin, 112,* 64–105.

Higgins, E. T., King, G. A., & Marvin, G. H. (1982). Individual construct accessibility and subjective impressions and recall. *Journal of Personality and Social Psychology, 43,* 35–47.

Ingram, R. E., & Kendall P. C. (1986). Cognitive clinical psychology: Implications of an informational processing perspective. In R. E. Ingram (Ed.), *Information processing approaches to clinical psychology* (pp. 3–21). New York: Academic Press.

Joffe, R. D., Dobson, K. S., Fine, S., Marriage, K., & Haley, G. (1990). Social problem solving in depressed, conduct-disordered, and normal adolescents. *Journal of Abnormal Child Psychology, 18,* 565–575.

Kandel, D. B., & Andrews, K. (1987). Processes of adolescent socialization by parents and peers. *International Journal of Addictions, 22,* 319–342.

Kelly, G. A. (1955). *The psychology of personal constructs.* New York: W. W. Norton.

Kovacs, M. (1992). *Children's Depression Inventory.* Los Angeles, CA: Western Psychological Services.

Kupersmidt, J. B., Griesler, P. C., DeRosier, M. E., Patterson, C. J., & Davis, P. W. (1995). Childhood aggression and peer relations in the context of family and neighborhood factors. *Child Development, 66,* 360–375.

Lahey, B. B., Waldman, I. D., & McBurnett, K. (2001). The development of antisocial behavior: An integrative causal model. *Journal of Child Psychology and Psychiatry, 40*, 669–682.

Larson, J., & Lochman, J. E. (2002). *Helping schoolchildren cope with anger: A cognitive-behavioral intervention.* New York: Guilford Press.

Leff, S. S., Power, T. J., Manz, P. H., Costigan, T. E., & Nabors, L. A. (2001). School-based aggression prevention programs for young children: Current status and implications for violence prevention. *School Psychology Review, 30*, 344–363.

Lochman, J. E. (1992). Cognitive-behavioral interventions with aggressive boys: Three-year follow-up and preventive effects. *Journal of Consulting and Clinical Psychology, 60*, 426–432.

Lochman, J. E., & Dodge, K. A. (1994). Social cognitive processes of severely violent, moderately aggressive, and nonaggressive boys. *Journal of Consulting and Clinical Psychology, 62*, 366–374.

Lochman, J. E., & Dodge, K. A. (1998). Distorted perceptions in dyadic interactions of aggressive and nonaggressive boys: Effects of prior expectations, context, and boys' age. *Development and Psychopathology, 10*, 495–512.

Lochman, J. E., FitzGerald, D. P., Gage, S., Kanaly, K., Whidby, J., Barry, T. D., Pardini, D.A., & McElroy, H. (2001). Effects of a social-cognitive intervention for aggressive deaf children: The Coping Power Program. *Journal of the American Deafness and Rehabilitation Association, 35*, 39–61.

Lochman, J. E., FitzGerald, D. P., & Whidby, J. M. (1999). Anger management with aggressive children. In C. E. Schaefer (Ed.), *Short-term psychotherapy groups for children: Adapting group processes for specific problems* (pp. 301–349). Northvale, NJ: Aronson.

Lochman, J. E., & Lampron, L. B. (1986). Situational social problem solving skills and self-esteem of aggressive and nonaggressive boys. *Journal of Abnormal Child Psychology, 14*, 605–617.

Lochman, J. E., & Lenhart, L. (1995). Cognitive behavioral therapy of aggressive children: Effects of schemas. In H. P. J. G. Van Bilsen, P. C. Kendall, & J. H. Slavenburg (Eds.), *Cognitive behavioral approaches for children and adolescents: Challenges for the next century* (pp. 145–166). New York: Plenum Press.

Lochman, J. E., Magee, T. N., & Pardini, D. (2003). Cognitive behavioral interventions for children with conduct problems. In M. Reinecke, & D. Clark (Eds.), *Cognitive therapy over the lifespan: Theory, research and practice* (pp. 441–476). Cambridge, UK: Cambridge University Press.

Lochman, J. E., Nelson, W. M., & Sims, J. P. (1981). A cognitive behavioral program for use with aggressive children. *Journal of Clinical Child Psychology, 13*, 146–148.

Lochman, J. E., & Wayland, K. K. (1994). Aggression, social acceptance, and race as predictors of negative adolescent outcomes. *Journal of the American Academy of Child and Adolescent Psychiatry, 33*, 1026–1035.

Lochman, J. E., Wayland, K. K., & White, K. J. (1993). Social goals: Relationship to adolescent adjustment and to social problem solving. *Journal of Abnormal Child Psychology, 21,* 135–151.

Lochman, J. E., & Wells, K. C. (1996). A social-cognitive intervention with aggressive children: Prevention effects and contextual implementation issues. In R. D. Peters, & R. J. McMahon (Eds.), *Prevention and early intervention: Childhood disorders, substance use and delinquency* (pp. 111–143). Thousand Oaks, CA: Sage.

Lochman, J. E., & Wells, K. C. (2002a). Contextual social-cognitive mediators and child outcome: A test of the theoretical model in the Coping Power Program. *Development and Psychopathology, 14,* 971–993.

Lochman, J. E., & Wells, K. C. (2002b). The Coping Power Program at the middle school transition: Universal and indicated prevention effects. *Psychology of Addictive Behaviors, 16,* S40–S54.

Lochman, J. E., & Wells, K. C. (2003). Effectiveness study of Coping Power and classroom intervention with aggressive children: Outcomes at a one-year follow-up. *Behavior Therapy, 34,* 493–515.

Lochman, J. E., & Wells, K. C. (2004). The Coping Power program for preadolescent aggressive boys and their parents: Outcome effects at the one-year follow-up. *Journal of Consulting and Clinical Psychology, 72, 571–578.*

Lochman, J. E., Wells, K. C., & Murray, M. (in press). The Coping Power Program: Preventive intervention at the middle school transition. In P. Tolan, J. Szapocznik, & S. Sambrano (Eds.), *Preventing substance abuse: 3 to 14.* Washington, DC: American Psychological Association.

Lochman, J. E., Whidby, J. M., & FitzGerald, D. P. (2000). Cognitive-behavioral assessment and treatment with aggressive children. In P. C. Kendall (Ed.), *Child and adolescent therapy: Cognitive-behavioral procedures* (2nd ed., pp. 31–87). New York: Guilford Press.

Luthar, S. S. (1999). *Poverty and children's adjustment.* New York: Sage.

MacKinnon, C. E., Lamb, M. E., Belsky, J., & Baum, C. (1990). An affective-cognitive model of mother–child aggression. *Development and Psychopathology, 2,* 1–13.

Mash, E. J. (1998). Treatment of child and family disturbance: A behavioral systems perspective. In E. J. Mash, & R. A. Barkley (Eds.), *Treatment of childhood disorders* (2nd ed.). New York: Guilford Press.

Milich, R., & Dodge, K. A. (1984). Social information processing in child psychiatric populations. *Journal of Abnormal Child Psychology, 12,* 471–490.

Miller-Johnson, S., Coie, J. D., Maumary-Gremaud, A., Lochman, J., & Terry, R. (1999). Relationship between childhood peer rejection and aggression and adolescent delinquency severity and type among African American youth. *Journal of Emotional and Behavioral Disorders, 7,* 137–146.

Mischel, W. (1990). Personality disposition revisited and revised: A view after three decades. In L. Pervin (Ed.), *Handbook of personality: Theory and research* (pp. 111–134). New York: Guilford Press.

Novaco, R. W. (1978). Anger and coping with stress: Cognitive behavioral interventions. In J. P. Foreyet, & D. P. Rathjen (Eds.), *Cognitive behavioral therapy: Research and application*. New York: Plenum Press.

Pardini, D. A., Lochman, J. E., & Frick, P. J. (2003). Callous/unemotional traits and social-cognitive processes in adjudicated youths. *Journal of the American Academy of Child and Adolescent Psychiatry, 42*, 364–371.

Patterson, G. R., Reid, J. B., & Dishion, T. J. (1992). *Antisocial boys*. Eugene, OR: Castalia.

Patterson, G. R., & Stouthamer-Loeber, M. (1984). The correlation of family management practices and delinquency. *Child Development, 55*, 1299–1307.

Pepler, D. J., Craig, W. M., & Roberts, W. L. (1998). Observations of aggressive and nonaggressive children on the school playground. *Merrill Palmer Quarterly, 44*, 55–76.

Perry, D. G., Perry, L. C., & Rasmussen, P. (1986). Cognitive social learning mediators of aggression. *Child Development, 57*, 700–711.

Poal, P., & Weisz, J. R. (1989). Therapists' own childhood problems as predictors of their effectiveness in child psychotherapy. *Journal of Clinical Child Psychology, 18*, 202–205.

Poulin, F., Dishion, T. J., & Burraston, B. (2001). 3-Year iatrogenic effects associated with aggregating high-risk adolescents in cognitive-behavioral preventive interventions. *Applied Developmental Science, 5*, 214–224.

Rabiner, D. L., Lenhart, L., & Lochman, J. E. (1990). Automatic vs. reflective problem solving in relation to children's sociometric status. *Developmental Psychology, 71*, 535–543.

Rotter, J. B., Chance, J. E., & Phares, E. J. (1972). *Applications of a social learning theory of personality*. New York: Holt, Rinehart, and Winston.

Smith, C. A., & Lazarus, R. W. (1990). Emotion and adaptation. In L. Previn (Ed.), *Handbook of personality: Theory and research* (pp. 609–637). New York: Guilford Press.

Tolan, P. H., Guerra, N. G., & Kendall, P. C. (1995). Introduction to special section: Prediction and prevention of antisocial behavior in children and adolescents. *Journal of Consulting and Clinical Psychology, 63*, 515–517.

Tremblay, R. E., & LeMarquand, D. (2001). Individual risk and protective factors. In R. Loeber, & D. P. Farrington (Eds.), *Child delinquents: Development, intervention, and service needs* (pp. 137–164). Thousand Oaks, CA: Sage.

van de Wiel, N. M. H., Matthys, W., Cohen-Kettenis, P., & van Engeland, H. (2003). Cost effectiveness of the Coping Power Program with conduct disorder and oppositional defiant disorder children. *Behavior Therapy, 34*, 421–436.

Vitaro, F., Brendgen, M., Pagani, L., Tremblay, R. E., & McDuff, P. (1999). Disruptive behavior, peer association, and conduct disorder: Testing the developmental links through early intervention. *Development and Psychopathology, 11*, 287–304.

Waas, G. A., & French, D. C. (1989). Children's social problem solving: Comparison of the open middle interview and children's assertive behavior scale. *Behavioral Assessment, 11*, 219–230.

Wasserman, G. A., & Seracini, A. M. (2001). Family risk factors and interventions. In R. Loeber, & D. P. Farrington (Eds.), *Child delinquents: Development, intervention, and service needs* (pp. 165–189). Thousand Oaks, CA: Sage.

Wechsler, D. (2003). *Wechsler Intelligence Scale for Children—Fourth Edition.* San Antonio, TX: Psychological Corporation.

Weiss, B., Dodge, K. A., Bates, J. E., & Pettit, G. S. (1992). Some consequences of early harsh discipline: Child aggression and maladaptive social information processing style. *Child Development, 63,* 1321–1335.

Wilkinson, G. S. (1993). *The Wide Range Achievement Test—3. Wilmington, DE: Jastak Associates.*

Williams, S. C., Lochman, J. E., Phillips, N. C., & Barry, T. D. (2003). Aggressive and non-aggressive boys' physiological and cognitive processes in response to peer provocations. *Journal of Clinical Child and Adolescent Psychology, 32,* 568–576.

Zelli, A., Dodge, K. A., Lochman, J. E., Laird, R. D., & The Conduct Problems Prevention Research Group. (1999). The distinction between beliefs legitimizing aggression and deviant processing of social cues: Testing measurement validity and the hypothesis that biased processing mediates the effects of beliefs on aggression. *Journal of Personality and Social Psychology, 77,* 150–166.

CHAPTER 8

Multisystemic Therapy in the Treatment of Adolescent Conduct Disorder

Lisa Saldana and Scott W. Henggeler*

TREATMENT MODEL

Multisystemic therapy (MST) is a well-specified and empirically supported approach to treating youths who have serious clinical problems and their families. Extensive descriptions of the MST model are provided in comprehensive clinical volumes pertaining to the treatment of antisocial behavior (Henggeler, Schoenwald, Borduin, Rowland, & Cunningham, 1998) and serious emotional disturbance (Henggeler, Schoenwald, Rowland, & Cunningham, 2002) in adolescents and their families.

Theoretical Basis
Theory of Social Ecology
MST is based largely on a social–ecological theory of development and behavior (Bronfenbrenner, 1979). Key features of this theory are that behavior is multidetermined and bidirectional in nature. Children are nested within multiple systems (i.e., family, peer, school, neighborhood) that have reciprocal influences on their behavior. As presented in Figure 8.1, the closer in proximity that a nested system is to the child, the greater influence the system

*Scott W. Henggeler is a board member and stockholder of MST Services, LLC, the Medical University of South Carolina-licensed organization that provides training in MST.

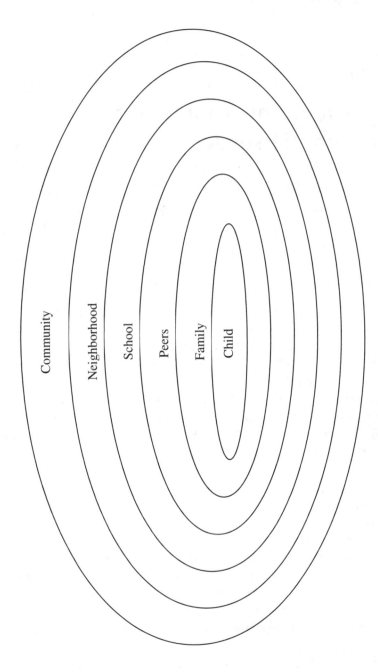

FIGURE 8.1   Social–ecological model of the child environment.
From Bronfenbrenner, U. (1979). *The ecology of human development*. Cambridge, MA: Harvard University Press. Reprinted with permission.

has on child behavior. Thus, the family generally has the maximum influence over child behavior; and the community, where service providers are positioned, has the least amount of influence. Given this underlying conceptual framework, MST interventions generally target, in descending order of priority, the relationship between the child and his or her family, peers, school, and neighborhood. Caregivers, therefore, are viewed as the keys to achieving favorable clinical outcomes, and, on an individualized basis, interventions might be applied to multiple aspects of the youth's social ecology that are associated with the identified problems.

It is important to note that findings from decades of research on the correlates and determinants of antisocial behavior in adolescents are highly consistent with the social–ecological framework. The correlates of antisocial behavior in children and adolescents include factors at the level of family and caregivers (e.g., conflictual marital relations, parental psychopathology, use of harsh or permissive discipline, poor parental monitoring, parental substance abuse, high level of family stressors, poor communication), the individual child (e.g., attributional bias, impulsivity), peers (e.g., association with deviant peers, poor social skills, high levels of peer rejection), school (e.g., low grades, truancy, poor teacher relations, dropout), neighborhood (e.g., dangerous, opportunity for involvement with criminal activity), and community systems (e.g., adversarial contact with service providers) (Elliott, 1994; Henggeler, 1998; Kazdin, 2003). A central assumption of the MST model, therefore, is that the antisocial behavior of a particular youth is associated with some combination of these factors as well as others that are idiosyncratic to the youth and his or her ecology. As discussed subsequently, MST practitioners intervene with the most proximal and potent of the identified determinants, while concomitantly building youth and family protective factors and competencies.

Pragmatic Family Therapies
In practice, the MST model also draws on strategic (Haley, 1976) and structural (Minuchin, 1974) theories of family therapy. Both theories conceptualize irresponsible behavior as being multidetermined, with interventions designed to address multiple levels of client needs. From within these models, behavior problems are viewed as developing out of normal life stressors or crises that were not handled well by family members. Problematic behaviors are assumed to (a) be related to patterns of family interaction, (b) occur as a result of difficulty in the management of developmental transitions and life stressors, and (c) have a functional component that is somehow reinforced. Both strategic and structural family therapies are compatible with the MST model in (a) the use of problem-focused and change-oriented interventions; (b) the

recognition that multiple paths can be followed to achieve desired outcomes; (c) the belief that therapists should be problem focused and action oriented; (d) the development of interventions that conceptualize the problem in the context of the current environment; and (e) the view of long-term behavior change being dependent on changing interactions between individuals across multiple systems.

Empirical Support for MST

MST has been identified by several federal entities (National Institute on Drug Abuse, 1999; President's New Freedom Commission on Mental Health, 2003; U.S. Department of Health and Human Services, 1999) as an effective treatment of youth antisocial behavior and substance abuse. MST effects are summarized in a recent meta-analysis (Curtis, Ronan, & Borduin, 2004). The Surgeon General (U.S. Public Health Service, 2001) reported MST to be one of the only three empirically supported treatments for juvenile offenders. In comparison with control conditions, MST has consistently achieved significant reductions in rates of rearrest and conduct problems (Borduin, Henggeler, Blaske, & Stein, 1990; Borduin et al., 1995; Henggeler et al., 1986, 1991; Henggeler, Melton, & Smith, 1992; Henggeler, Melton, Brondino, Scherer, & Hanley, 1997; Henggeler, Pickrel, & Brondino, 1999; Ogden & Halliday-Boykins, 2004) with follow-ups ranging from 1.7 to 13.7 years (Henggeler et al., 1997; Schaeffer & Borduin, 2005). MST has also been highly successful at reducing rates of out-of-home placement, which has led the Washington State Institute on Public Policy to conclude that MST can produce more than $130,000 per youth in savings in placement, criminal justice, and crime victim costs (Aos, Phipps, Barnoski, & Lieb, 2001).

In addition to showing effectiveness in the treatment of criminal behavior, outcomes from MST randomized clinical trials have demonstrated promising results in the treatment of adolescent alcohol and marijuana abuse (McBride, VanderWaal, Terry, & VanBuren, 1999; Stanton & Shadish, 1997). These are important findings because one of the strongest correlates of juvenile offending is substance abuse (Howell, 2003). Indeed, the National Institute on Drug Abuse (1999) and the Center for Substance Abuse Prevention (2001) have included MST as one of the few empirically supported treatments for adolescent substance abuse. Two randomized clinical trials examined the effectiveness of MST in the treatment of substance abuse within the context of chronic juvenile offenders, with results indicating significant reductions in marijuana and alcohol use at post-treatment and in substance-related arrests at 4-year follow-up (Borduin et al., 1995; Henggeler et al., 1991). More recently, a randomized trial has been completed with juvenile offenders meeting diagnostic criteria for substance abuse or dependence (Henggeler et al., 1999). Findings favoring the MST condition have been observed for out-of-home placement (Schoenwald, Ward, Henggeler, Pickrel, & Patel, 1996) and school attendance (Brown, Henggeler, Schoenwald, Brondino, & Pickrel, 1999); and at a 4-year follow-up, young adults in the MST condition evidenced increased rates of marijuana abstinence and reduced rates of violent criminal activity.

The MST Clinical Structure

Initiatives to transport evidence-based treatments to community settings have come to place considerable emphasis on the promotion of treatment fidelity (Schoenwald & Henggeler, 2003). In the case of MST, such emphasis is reinforced by findings from several studies (Henggeler et al., 1997, 1999; Henggeler & Schoenwald, 1999; Huey, Henggeler, Brondino, & Pickrel, 2000; Schoenwald, Henggeler, Brondino, & Rowland, 2000) linking therapist adherence to MST treatment principles to youth outcomes. That is, high therapist adherence to MST treatment protocols has been associated with favorable outcomes, whereas poor treatment adherence has not. Consequently, considerable support is provided to practitioners, supervisors, administrators, and organizations providing MST programs. Indeed, licensed MST programs are operating in 30 states across the United States and seven countries around the world—treating approximately 10,000 youths with serious antisocial behavior annually. Maintenance of an MST operating license is based, partially, on demonstrated adherence to the model and program. Although multiple layers to the MST quality assurance infrastructure have been specified (Henggeler & Schoenwald, 1999), for the purposes of the present chapter, attention focuses primarily on the therapeutic team rather than organizational factors and system level factors (Strother, Swenson, & Schoenwald, 1998).

THERAPIST SKILLS AND ATTRIBUTES

MST Team

The MST therapist works as a member of a therapeutic team. Each team is typically comprised of three to four therapists, a half-time supervisor, and an expert consultant. The majority of therapists are masters' level clinicians, many of whom are social workers with experience working in the juvenile justice system. Caseloads are low, ranging from four to six families per therapist. As a member of the team, at least one therapist is on call 24 h a day, 7 days a week, to provide immediate assistance to all families being served by the team when needed. Although not a prerequisite, many MST supervisors gain experience within the MST model as a therapist prior to advancing into the supervisory role. The supervisor provides weekly supervision with the entire team and is also available on call 24 h a day to provide additional supervision when needed. Furthermore, the supervisor is available to attend sessions with the therapist to assess barriers to behavior change when progress is limited, or during particularly challenging or potentially dangerous situations. He or she is the immediate, onsite representative of MST and, as such, is responsible for promoting treatment fidelity and achieving targeted clinical outcomes for each case. The consultant is an MST expert who provides consultation on active cases, at least once a week, to the entire team. The consultant is responsible for promoting favorable outcomes by enhancing treatment fidelity and building the competencies of the therapists and supervisor. In addition, the consultant provides quarterly booster training for the team on topics that are posing particular challenges with the population being served. The MST therapist, therefore, must be willing to work as a member of a team and accept the assistance of the supervisor and consultant in meeting the needs of the families.

Session Arrangement

MST assessment and treatment processes take full advantage of the youth and family's social ecology. Conducting sessions within a typical office setting presents attendance barriers for some family members (including extended members if deemed necessary) as well as for peers, teachers, and other individuals who are important within the multiple systems of the child. Furthermore, the typical outpatient session limits the therapist's ability to assess the child's environment, witness maladaptive interactions as they occur in their natural context, and coach the involved members toward more adaptive functioning. MST assessments and interventions therefore occur in the natural settings of the participants. Most often sessions are in the family home; however, they also may occur with teachers at the school, coaches on the practice field, or any other place that provides a direct route to obtaining client information and promoting behavior change.

In addition to being flexible with session location, the MST therapist is accommodating in scheduling sessions. Sessions are held during times that are convenient for families, including weekends, mornings, and in the evening. The MST therapist is not bound by the typical 50-min session, but meets the families for as little or as long as needed to complete the goals of the session, and for as many or as few times during the week as needed. In addition, as noted previously, a member of the MST team is available on call at all times. In the event that a family experiences a crisis or challenging situation with the youth, the on call therapist is available to coach the family over phone, or if necessary, to meet at their home. This *in vivo* strategy allows interventions to occur "in the moment" and when they are most salient to participants.

Flexibility with session arrangement and time not only increases the efficiency of treatment but also offers advantages from a services' perspective. First, arranging sessions at convenient times for families facilitates engagement between caregivers and the therapist. When caregivers feel that the therapist is respectful of the family's schedule, particularly when caregivers work non-traditional hours and the therapist conducts sessions in the home, barriers to service access are less of a challenge. Moreover, conducting sessions in the environment in which the family lives increases the validity of assessment information and provides the opportunity for more valid evaluation of inter-vention outcomes. The flexibility of MST session arrangement, therefore, is advantageous from both the provider and consumer perspectives.

Although many MST therapists have extensive experience conducting psychotherapy, their advanced degree or years of experience do not appear to significantly predict client outcomes (Schoenwald, Letourneau, & Halliday-Boykins, 2005). Rather, adhering to the MST model is the most significant predictor of positive behavior change in antisocial youths and families (Huey et al., 2000). Therapist qualifications, therefore, are not necessarily measured by degree. Most MST therapists are Masters level clinicians who are flexible in their approach to treatment (i.e., not wedded to an individual model), competent in conducting empirically based interventions such as cognitive-behavioral and behavioral interventions, and comfortable working in a wide array of environments (e.g., low-income housing projects, mobile home neighborhoods, suburban neighborhoods). Moreover, strong MST therapists are energetic in their efforts to engage and work with families, positive in their conceptualization of case characteristics, and creative in finding ways to use family strengths to develop interventions. Because the MST model is an ecological method to intervention that is strength focused, present focused, and culturally and developmentally sensitive, successful MST therapists ap-proach work with families from this perspective. In doing so, therapist ac-tivities are monitored by other members of the therapeutic team to ensure adherence to the MST protocols.

Quality Assurance

The overarching goal of the quality assurance protocol developed for MST teams is to help obtain positive clinical outcomes for referred youths and fami-lies (Henggeler & Schoenwald, 1999). The brokering of MST programs is over-seen by MST Services (MSTS), which has the license for the transport of MST technology and intellectual property through the Medical University of South Carolina. When stakeholders are interested in developing MST programs in their agencies, a contract is developed through MSTS to obtain an MST operating license. MSTS is predominantly staffed with doctoral level individuals who are expert in the areas necessary to run a successful MST program.

Prior to beginning an MST program, several steps are taken to aid in the development of successful quality assurance. First, a site assessment is conducted to promote organizational and ecological conditions that are in agreement with the establishment of an MST program (e.g., agreement of agencies to small caseloads for therapists). Following this "start-up" period, training is provided to the therapeutic team that includes an initial 5-day orientation training, followed by quarterly booster sessions designed to address the strengths and needs of the particular team. As previously noted, each team receives weekly consultation from an MST expert who is often a part of MSTS. However, for states (e.g., Ohio, Connecticut, Hawaii, Colorado) and nations (e.g., Norway) with major MST initiatives, local MST infrastructures have been developed to serve the functions of MSTS. Each component of the quality assurance process is supported by a manualized protocol developed for clinicians (Henggeler et al., 1998), supervisors (Henggeler & Schoenwald, 1998), consultants (Schoenwald, 1998), and organizations (Strother et al., 1998).

Each component of the MST infrastructure is held accountable for adhering to the principles of the MST model. As part of the quality assurance protocol, therapist adherence to the MST principles is monitored monthly through standardized client ratings of therapist behaviors and, at times, coding of session audio tapes. Furthermore, the adherence of supervisors and consultants is monitored through standardized assessments completed by therapists to assure that delivery of services fits within the MST model (Henggeler & Schoenwald, 1999).

Principles of MST

In light of the flexible structure of MST sessions and interventions, principles have been developed to operationalize the nature of interventions. These nine principles are used to guide the MST therapist in decision-making when working with families. Adherence to these principles defines fidelity to the MST model.

Principle 1. The Primary Purpose of Assessment Is to Understand the Fit Between the Identified Problems and Their Broader Systemic Context

A key component of case conceptualization involves the use of "fit" assessments. As shown in Figure 8.2, a target behavior is identified and each of the

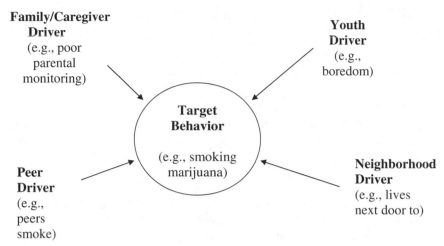

FIGURE 8.2 Simple fit assessment. The target behavior represents the conduct to be addressed as an overarching goal. The "drivers" indicate factors that are conceptualized as influencing the maintenance of the irresponsible target behavior.

potential "drivers" or correlates from multiple systems in the ecology related to the problem is considered. Because youths and families have different strengths and needs, fit assessments are individualized. Drawing from the empirical literature, correlates that have been identified as being associated with particular deviant behaviors are considered first in the fit assessment and are included in hypothesis testing. Furthermore, assessment is viewed as an ongoing process, and therefore, the fit assessment usually changes during the course of treatment as more information is gathered and as needs are addressed.

Principle 2. Therapeutic Contacts Emphasize the Positive and Use Systemic Strengths as Levers for Change

Interventions are tailored to maximize the strengths identified from within and between systems. Drawing on such characteristics, skills, and relationships enables caregivers and youths to feel that they are capable of increasing responsible behavior. Focusing on strengths also assists family members to recognize and take ownership of their roles in positive change. Most importantly, by developing interventions that draw on existing strengths, the amount of change required for a family to experience success is reduced. Thus, the MST therapist should find what is "working well" within the family and make modifications to these skills to address the target behavior change.

Members of the MST team not only must recognize systemic strengths, but must also be able to focus on these strengths during challenging times. To assist in this process, the therapist is encouraged to use strength-focused language when discussing the families in supervision, when writing case notes, and when interacting with the family directly. Furthermore, the supervisor, consultant, and other members of the MST infrastructure are trained to use language that capitalizes on family strengths. Finally, efforts are made to provide an organizational environment that supports strength-focused conceptualizations of problems.

Principle 3. Interventions Are Designed to Promote Responsible Behavior and Decrease Irresponsible Behavior Among Family Members

Similar to the use of strength-oriented interventions, MST therapists do not focus on diagnoses and psychopathology—they are not deficit oriented. Rather, treatment focuses on increasing rates of responsible behavior. Such behavior might include, for example, attending school and helping around the house for the youth; and modeling healthy behavior and providing appropriate family structure by the caregivers. Treatment also aims to decrease rates of irresponsible behavior (e.g., adolescent temper tantrums, caregiver substance use). Depathologizing behavior problems and treatment goals facilitates communication with lay stakeholders, and sets the stage more effectively for behavior change (e.g., increasing child compliance with caregiver requests is easier to change than treating "oppositional defiant disorder").

Principle 4. Interventions Are Present Focused and Action Oriented, Targeting Specific and Well-Defined Problems

MST interventions focus on the "here and now." Family members are encouraged to target change in their present lives as a route for creating a more responsible and positive future. Although present problems might be conceptualized as originating from historical challenges (e.g., difficult child temperament in infancy), the past cannot be altered, and a focus on the past does not address the current factors that are maintaining present problems. Relevant aspects of family members' histories, therefore, are not ignored, but interventions do not rely on detailed analyses of the past.

Moreover, MST interventions typically are action-oriented and target-discrete problems. Given the MST focus on treatment with multineed families referred for serious youth externalizing behavior, swift action toward change often is required to prevent serious consequences (e.g., expulsion, residential care, incarceration). Hence, interventions are implemented quickly and their success is monitored continuously. Consistent with behavior therapy perspectives, targets for change are well operationalized and subject to verification (e.g., urine screens to detect marijuana use, teacher reports to assess school attendance). Identifying and measuring well-defined problems adds clarity to the goals of treatment for all parties and enables an unambiguous determination of goal attainment.

Principle 5. Interventions Target Sequences of Behavior Within and Between Multiple Systems That Maintain the Identified Problems

MST interventions focus on interpersonal relationships and interactions as the mechanism for achieving behavior change. Repeated sequences of interactions within and between each of the ecological systems (See Figure 8.1) that maintain the identified problem are identified and targeted in the treatment. Hence, interventions are individualized to attenuate problematic relationships specific to the family that contribute to the referral behavior. For example, when a youth's deviant peer group has been identified in the maintenance of marijuana use, the MST therapist will assist parents in weaning away the youth from these peers while concomitantly building more appropriate relationships with prosocial peers. Similarly, when it is learned that a permissive mother's boyfriend dictates how the mother spends her time, not allowing for appropriate parental monitoring, the MST therapist will empower the mother to assume her parenting role and to prioritize her child over her partner at appropriate times. This goal might be accomplished partially by facilitating relationships between the mother and other effective parents.

Principle 6. Interventions Are Developmentally Appropriate and Fit the Developmental Needs of the Youth

Holding unrealistic developmental expectations is a key correlate of the negative parent–child coercive cycle that promotes antisocial behavior in children (Azar, Robinson, Hekimian, & Twentyman, 1984). Inappropriate beliefs include both immature expectations of youth (e.g., not feeling an adolescent is old enough to engage in age-appropriate activities such as going out with friends) and overly mature expectations (e.g., believing an adolescent should support himself or herself). Drawing on the child development field, the MST therapist collaborates with caregivers to design interventions that are emotionally and cognitively appropriate for youths. Adolescents have varying learning abilities and emotional capacities, and thus interventions must be individualized to maximize youths' strengths.

Similarly, the therapist should consider the developmental functioning of caregivers when designing strategies to improve their parenting skills. For example, a caregiver's emotion-regulation abilities, intellectual functioning, and interpersonal relationship skills all must be considered when developing a plan for his or her delivery of sanctions to the youths. Thus, successful interventions will consider the developmental needs and levels of both caregiver and youth.

Principle 7. Interventions Are Designed to Require Daily or Weekly Effort by Family Members

Clinical progress is most likely to occur when consistent effort is put toward behavior change (Kazdin, 1994). When attempting to alter antisocial behaviors, the youths must be consistently engaged in self-monitoring and positive decision-making. Similarly, caregivers and other responsible members of the ecology must consistently put forth effort to create environmental change that supports decreased irresponsible behavior by the youths. In this endeavor, the therapist helps establish clearly defined expectations for family members, a method of monitoring participation and progress, and clearly defined positive and negative consequences for efforts made. Efforts toward behavioral change most often are implemented in the form of homework assignments to be completed outside of session. Homework assignments target individual behavior changes as well as interactional changes between members of the ecology (e.g., between parent and teacher, parent and youth, and both parents). Progress is monitored and plans for behavior change are fine tuned during therapy sessions. Substantive clinical progress occurs outside these sessions as plans are being implemented.

Principle 8. Intervention Effectiveness Is Evaluated Continuously from Multiple Perspectives with Providers Assuming Accountability for Overcoming Barriers to Successful Outcomes

As part of the MST analytical process (Figure 8.3), described subsequently, therapists monitor treatment progress and outcomes in an objective manner (e.g., monitoring charts, urine drug screens, teacher reports) consistently throughout treatment. Having multiple informants increases the reliability of information regarding the success of behavior change across settings. Importantly, methods of evaluating outcomes should be established that provide the therapist with relatively immediate feedback regarding intervention effectiveness. Thus, daily or weekly assessments provide the most direct information to the therapist who determines if interventions are successful or in need of alteration. Because

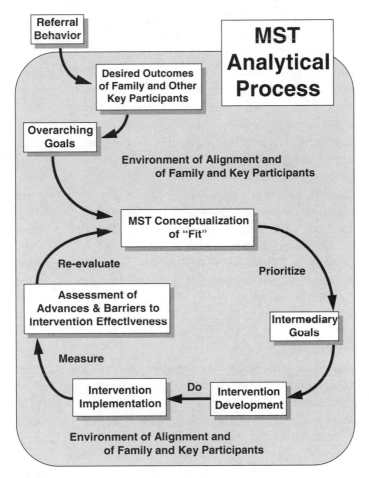

FIGURE 8.3   The MST analytic process, known as the "Do-Loop."

therapeutic goals can be accomplished through multiple avenues, when interventions are not successful, the therapist accepts the responsibility of reassess-
ing the fit of the problem and developing alternate intervention strategies that
capitalize on systemic strengths as levers for change.

*Principle 9. Interventions Are Designed to Promote Treatment Generalization
and Long-Term Maintenance of Therapeutic Change by Empowering Caregivers
to Address Family Members' Needs Across Multiple Systemic Contexts*
One of the most important roles that the therapist serves is that of a coach
to the caregivers. MST is time limited and therefore the therapist will only

be available for a finite period of time. Interventions are developed to teach caregivers how to recognize the connection between events (i.e., to conduct a functional analysis) across multiple systems, and to have the basic skills necessary to problem solve and address the concern. If the family is unable to carry out the intervention with the therapist serving only a peripheral role, the likelihood of the family maintaining use of the strategy in the absence of treatment is low, and therefore not useful for the future. To this end, one of the thrusts of MST is to empower caregivers to effectively and independently handle challenges related to raising youths. In this process, the naturally occurring social-support systems of families are drawn upon to assist caregivers in sustaining treatment gains. Examples of indigenous supports include extended family members, neighbors, church members, coworkers, and any other individuals who reinforce the caregivers' efforts for positive change. Thus, when implementing interventions, the therapist assesses the strengths and resources of the family and relevant systems, and assists them in carrying out the recommendations independently. Moreover, the therapist teaches the family to recognize similarities across problematic situations to reinforce the use of gained skills across settings.

Analytical Process

As noted previously, assessment is an ongoing process. As interventions are implemented and drivers are addressed, the therapist critically evaluates success and barriers to achieving treatment goals. This iterative analytical process, known as the "Do-Loop" (See Figure 8.3), is a key component of case conceptualization and the supervisory process. The MST therapist engages in hypothesis testing regarding barriers and advances to intervention effectiveness and changes his or her own behaviors and methods of interacting with the system to facilitate progress.

As shown in Figure 8.3, the first step in the Do-Loop is for the MST team to have clearly defined referral behaviors, followed by an understanding of the behavioral changes that are desired by the youth and members of his or her social ecology. Next, overarching goals (i.e., the ultimate objectives to be met by termination) for treatment are developed by the therapist and the members of the system (e.g., family members) during the initial assessment and engagement phases of treatment. As treatment enters the "Loop," the MST therapist begins the iterative cycle of (a) conceptualizing the fit of drivers and target behaviors, (b) developing a hierarchy of target behaviors, (c) developing intermediary goals that address these target behaviors, and (d) developing and implementing interventions that draw on the strengths of the youths and system and address their needs. After each point of intervention, the therapist measures its success and assesses any advances and barriers to intervention effectiveness. Depending on the outcome of this assessment, the MST team re-evaluates the case either to proceed with a successful intervention or to make adaptations to overcome barriers that hinder progress. The Loop, now completed, is reiterated beginning with the conceptualization of the fit of the next identified target behavior and step in treatment.

Summary

MST is based primarily on a social–ecological conceptual framework in which behavior is viewed as a product of the interplay among multiple aspects of the youth's social network. This view is consistent with the known determinants of antisocial behavior, and numerous randomized trials have supported the effectiveness of MST in treating serious antisocial behavior in children and adolescents. MST is specified in two extensive clinical volumes, and a home-based model of service delivery is used. Importantly, an intensive quality assurance system surrounds MST programs to support treatment fidelity and the attainment of desired clinical outcomes.

THE CASE OF "MIKE"

Conceptualization, Assessment, and Treatment Planning

As described, MST was developed for adolescents with severe clinical problems (e.g., chronic offending and substance abuse) at imminent risk of out-of-home placement. The case description provided for Mike is not indicative of a case that is "deep-end" or severe enough to meet the criteria for MSTS. Mike's shoplifting charge is his first contact with juvenile justice, and he is not at risk for out-of-home placement currently. His irresponsible behaviors do appear to be increasing in severity and, therefore, he and his family should receive services to improve his adaptive functioning. MST, however, would probably not be the treatment chosen for intervention. Nevertheless, the following case presentation assumes referral to an MST program.

Additional Information, Assessment Tools

The primary purpose of the assessment process is to determine the fit of what drivers are reinforcing problematic behavior (See Figure 8.2). Six areas of family functioning have been identified throughout the literature as key determinants of youth antisocial behavior: (a) family system interactions; (b) parenting styles, including beliefs, skills, and knowledge; (c) marital interactions; (d) individual parent characteristics; (e) social–ecological factors that influence parenting decisions; and (f) practicalities of the family ecology such as provisions of food and shelter (Henggeler et al., 1998). Each of these broad categories is evaluated during the assessment to identify specific characteristics to include in the fit assessment. Throughout the evaluation process, both strengths and needs are identified. Assessment strategies include interviews with key stakeholders and observations of within-system (e.g., family, school) and between-system interactions. Biological indices are obtained if substance problems are suspected, and standardized measurement instruments are used occasionally.

Interviews.   The assessment battery administered to Mike through the County Juvenile Court provides valuable data regarding Mike's specific symptomatology. One of the first steps for the MST therapist, however, is to conduct a more thorough assessment throughout the ecology. Although Mike's initial therapeutic contact was with his mother and an individual session was completed with his father, the MST therapist will prefer to have an assessment session with Mike and his father together. Mike's older sister will also be asked to participate in the assessment by describing her interactions with Mike, identifying what she views as the strengths in their relationship, noting her impressions of Mike's peer group, and discussing her impressions of the family system. In addition, the therapist will meet the school personnel to learn more about Mike's school behavior, interactions with peers and teachers, and academic strengths. Further, Mike and his family will be asked to identify other individuals in the ecology that are involved in Mike's care who can provide information, as well as potentially participate in interventions. Finally, the therapist will gather information about the neighborhood and community including level of crime, violence, and neighborhood cohesion.

Observations.   In addition to gathering verbal information, the MST therapist will develop hypotheses based on observations of transactions during the assessment process. Attention will be paid to how the family members position themselves during family meetings (e.g., far across the room from one another), the level of positive affect exchanged (e.g., smiles, physical touch), the tone of voice used when interacting, and other nonverbal cues that provide information about the dynamics of the system (Minuchin, 1974). The therapist will also note how family members respond to questions. That is, attention is paid to the roles that family members take during the interview (e.g., a child who is parentified). It is important to note that the therapist should empower caregivers by giving priority to their perceptions of problem behaviors and dynamics (Henggeler & Borduin, 1990).

Objective monitoring.   To assist in providing a reliable assessment of the youth and family, objective tools are also utilized to gather ongoing information. For a youth or caregiver who is abusing substances, such as Mike, random urine drug screens and/or breathalyzer screens will be used to provide an unbiased record of his behavior. School attendance and behavioral records will be examined to monitor school-related behavior and compliance. Moreover, for family members who are experiencing specific symptomatology (e.g., depression), standardized screening tools might be used during the ongoing assessment process to monitor change. Such objective measures do not substitute for cross-informant reports of youth and family behaviors, but are used concurrently with verbal reports and observations.

Assessment sheet.   Using the initial contact sheet completed by therapists (Figure 8.4), hypotheses can be developed regarding the drivers of the problems and foci of potential interventions. Based on the information provided thus far, the therapist can hypothesize that Mike has several areas of strength including athletic ability, feeling confident in peer interactions, average intellectual ability, and a clear goal for his future. Mike's parents also show strengths in their ability to obtain and maintain stable employment, their attempt to establish a visitation arrangement between Mr. D. and the children, and their expressed concern for Mike's problematic behaviors.

The information provided in the case summary, however, is incomplete from an MST perspective. As seen in Figure 8.4, the MST therapist will want to learn more about the strengths of the family and peer systems as well as both the strengths and needs in the school, neighborhood, and community systems. Again, these strengths will be used subsequently as levers for change. The following are examples of strengths that the therapist might identify: (a) Ms. D. is close to her sister (i.e., Mike's aunt) who comes to the house often. She has a flexible work schedule that allows her to help Ms. D. with childcare responsibilities. When Mike was younger and involved in sports, his aunt attended all of his ball games and enjoyed spending time with him. (b) Mike has a positive peer who lives on his street. The two used to be close until recently when Mike began associating with deviant peers. There is also a group of same-aged, prosocial peers who play basketball together on the weekends. Mike knows the boys from school and thinks that they are "alright." (c) The school has a strong athletic program with a coach who has spent time working with troubled youths. Tutoring is offered after school twice a week. Mike has a teacher who also taught at Mike's elementary school. This teacher has taken an interest in Mike's progress and acknowledges that Mike's behavior has not always been so unruly. (d) Mike's neighborhood is

Initial Contact Sheet

FAMILY NAME: Michael D   Therapist: Smalls   Date: Sept. 10, 2003

Reason for Referral

Mike was arrested for shoplifting at a convenience store with peers. This is his first contact with the Juvenile Office. He was referred by his probation officer following a psychological evaluation completed on September 6, 2003 when Mike was diagnosed with Conduct Disorder, Adolescent Onset Type with a rule out for Cannabis Abuse.

STRENGTHS	NEEDS

Individual

Athletic, above avg. grades through 4th grade, Mike reports ease in making friends, wants to finish HS, plans to join military, likes football, sleeps and eats well, cooperative with testing, avg. intelligence	Hx of temper tantrums, colic, restlessness dropping grades, truancy, disruptive behavior, smoking, not participating in school, verbal arguments with peers, suspensions, curfew violations, theft, gives up easily, substance abuse, low frustration tolerance

Family

Weekly visitation arrangement between dad and children; mother concerned about Mike; parents employed	Parental conflict-divorce 2 yrs ago; hx of paternal temper flairs, physical threat of cutting off child support, yelling, discipline, history of paternal alcohol abuse; high level of sibling conflict, inconsistent rules with limited consequences; daughter not participating in visitation with father; Mike acknowledges not liking home and that he tries to spend as much time as possible away; parents do not know peers

Peers

?	peers are truant, smoke marijuana

School

?	History of poor interactions between Mike and teachers; threats of filing truancy charges

Neighborhood/Community

?	?

FIGURE 8.4 Example of an Initial Contact Sheet used by an MST therapist. The strengths and needs of each of the systems are identified to be used when conceptualizing the fit assessment. In this example, data are missing regarding the strengths of the peer and school systems, as well as any information regarding the neighborhood/community.

relatively safe with limited criminal activity. A county park is within walking distance and provides structured activities for youths of all ages.

The therapist will also establish clearly defined goals, discussed subsequently, including all family members and key stakeholders in the process. For example, family members might agree that they would like Mike to attend school and not engage in truancy with his peers. Figure 8.5 shows how Mike's truant behavior is likely influenced by the behaviors of other family members. Interventions, therefore, will include all family members despite the initial individual referral focus. The drivers depicted in Figure 8.5 come from the information provided thus far in the psychological evaluation. This list of potential contributors to the behavior, however, is not exhaustive and should be expanded with further assessment. Critically, it is unclear from the information provided why Ms. D. is having such a difficult time monitoring Mike (i.e., the fit remains unclear). Further assessment is required regarding maternal characteristics (e.g., depression) and the ecological factors supporting Ms. D.'s apparent parenting difficulties.

Diagnosis. In light of the strength-focused emphasis of the MST model, formal diagnoses are usually not made unless necessary to accomplish an external goal (e.g., insurance payment). Nevertheless, given the framework of this case presentation, we will discuss diagnosis from an MST perspective. Mike's initial psychological report provides a diagnosis of Conduct Disorder, Adolescent Onset Type. Although Mike meets the *Diagnostic and Statistical Manual of Mental Disorders* (*DSM-IV*: American Psychiatric Association, 1994) criteria for Conduct Disorder, other critical systemic factors must be considered before labeling him with such a challenging diagnosis. Importantly, Mike's parents divorced 2 years ago after a long history of conflict. Empirical evidence suggests that interparental conflict can have distal and enduring negative effects on youths, including increased risk for poor academic performance, lower social competence, and the development of substance abuse and internalizing and externalizing difficulties (Ackerman & Kane, 1990; Doherty & Needle, 1991; Ducibella, 1995; McCabe, 1997; Roizblatt et al., 1997; Shaw, 1991; Silitsky, 1996). Youths not exposed to continued parental conflict generally have more positive adaptive functioning 2 years postdivorce relative to counterparts who continue to be exposed to parental discord (Shaw, 1991). Thus, although Mike's externalizing behaviors are problematic and will be addressed within the MST framework in the same manner as other antisocial behaviors, they likely stem from maladjustment to systemic stressors (i.e., Adjustment Disorder with Disturbance of Conduct). Interventions targeting systemic variables,

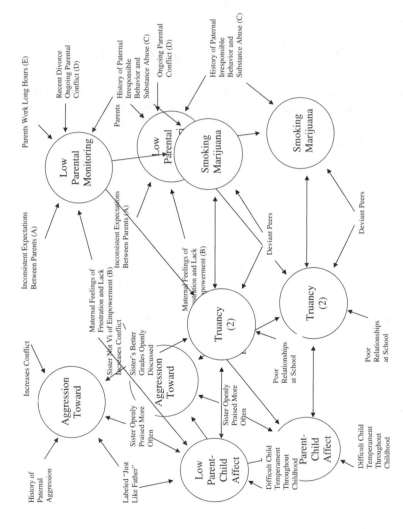

FIGURE 8.5   Fit assessment of the case of Mike. Target behaviors that are identified for the development of overarching goals are encircled. A hierarchy of goals is established (noted by numbers in parentheses), with many of the drivers conceptualized as influencing the target behaviors, overlapping.

predominantly focusing on parental behavior change, might be particularly effective in this case.

Therapeutic Goals

As depicted in Figure 8.5, a hierarchy of targeted goals can be established. In contrast with the notion of establishing primary and secondary goals, within the MST model, the therapist and family members determine the overarching goals of treatment (target behaviors in circles) followed by intermediary goals (targeting the drivers listed by arrows) that will create more responsible behavior. The overarching goals are defined as the outcome desired by the youth and members of the ecology at the end of treatment (e.g., pass the academic school year), whereas the intermediary goals are the steps and changes that are required to achieve the overarching outcomes (e.g., linking caregivers and school officials to develop a successful monitoring plan).

Hierarchy of overarching goals.   Although many of the treatment objectives are intertwined, addressing too many problems at one time can be overwhelming for multineed families and their therapists. Therefore, a hierarchy of goals should be established so that everyone in the system understands which goals are being addressed currently and which will be addressed in the future. In the case of Mike, the therapist might select low parental monitoring as the first goal. As indicated in Figure 8.5, addressing the drivers of low parental monitoring will reduce Mike's substance abuse and truancy. Furthermore, addressing "maternal feelings of frustration and lack of empowerment" will provide an opportunity to increase the level of positive affect between Mike and his mother. Similarly, once steps are taken to increase parental monitoring, with an emphasis on truancy (due to the high likelihood that truancy charges will be filed against Mike if he misses more days of school), key drivers of Mike's marijuana use will be addressed as well. During the course of addressing Mike's truancy, positive affect between family members will be targeted more closely, which, in turn, will begin to ameliorate drivers of Mike's aggression toward his sister. A possible scenario, therefore, for developing a hierarchy for overarching goals is (a) low parental monitoring; (b) truancy; (c) smoking marijuana; (d) low parent–child affect; and (e) aggression toward sister, keeping in mind that none of these goals are addressed in isolation and bidirectional relationships are evident among them.

Hierarchy of intermediary goals.   Intermediary goals can be conceptualized as the steps required on a daily or weekly basis to achieve the overarching goals. The therapist is responsible for developing strategies that use the strengths of the systems to accomplish these steps most efficiently. Assuming that the initial overarching goal is to improve "parental monitoring," steps toward altering the drivers in the fit assessment must be developed. Recalling that the information provided thus far does not support a strong fit for why Ms. D. is not monitoring Mike's activities effectively, the therapist will continue to assess maternal characteristics and circumstances that might shed light on this problem. The therapist will be most effective if she can work with both parents together, *assuming that Mr. D. is an active parenting figure for Mike.*

The following example illustrates the process of establishing intermediary goals toward achieving the overarching goal of increasing parental monitoring (see Figure 8.5). Because Mike's mother, Ms. D., is the primary caregiver, the therapist will meet her to devise a "plan" (step 1). During this meeting, the therapist will suggest that Mike's father, Mr. D., will need to be "on the same page" with Ms. D. and the therapist to ensure that expectations for Mike's behavior are consistent across environments (driver A). The therapist will empathize with Ms. D. regarding the challenges of being a single parent and will reinforce her position as primary caregiver (driver B), while simultaneously helping Ms. D. acknowledge the influence of Mr. D. Given the likelihood that Ms. D. will raise concerns regarding her and Mr. D.'s ability to engage in a cooperative dialog about their son, the therapist will be prepared to discuss the importance of putting her negative feelings about the marriage "on the shelf" to present a united parental front to Mike (drivers A and D). The therapist will, however, provide support and empathy toward Ms. D. regarding how difficult it will be emotionally to interact with her ex-husband.

Next, the therapist will meet Mr. D. and engage in a similar conversation (step 2). Given the observation made during the initial assessment that Mr. D. has a tendency to minimize the significance of Mike's irresponsible behavior (driver C), the therapist will be prepared to predict for Mr. D. the trajectory toward truancy charges, further delinquent behavior, and possible expulsion if he and Ms. D. do not begin to treat Mike's behavior seriously. The therapist will call on Mr. D. for assistance, explaining that his help is necessary to intervene successfully with his son. It should be noted, however, that such interventions will only be used if Mr. D. is an active parent for Mike. Should the therapist learn that Mr. D. has only a peripheral role in parenting, a different strategy (e.g., developing the mother's indigenous support system) that does not necessarily use Mr. D. as a support will be implemented to increase Ms. D.'s level of monitoring.

Next, the therapist will meet both Ms. D. and Mr. D. together (step 3). At the beginning of the session, strength-focused ground rules will be established to facilitate communication, cooperation, and agreement (driver D) toward establishing concrete rules and consequences for Mike (driver A). The therapist will recognize the obvious limitations in the ex-spousal relationship, yet will help the parents understand that renegotiation of their relationship is needed to strive toward the best interests of their children (Henggeler et al., 1998). Effort by both parents will be required to increase their parental monitoring of Mike and understand how their son uses his time. Because of Mike's risk for truancy charges, the therapist might focus initial parental monitoring efforts toward ensuring school attendance (step 4) and increasing the level of communication between Ms. D., Mr. D., and the school faculty (step 5).

Prognosis for adaptive change.   The level of overall behavior change expected from Mike in both the short- and long-term is very positive. Many youths who engage in antisocial behaviors during adolescence show a reduction in irresponsible behaviors as they mature, and are not necessarily life-course persistent delinquents (Moffitt, 1993). Moreover, although the irresponsible behaviors in which Mike is engaged have the potential to lead to more serious antisocial behaviors, interventions have been recommended at a relatively early stage of deviant behavior development. Mike's behaviors likely will become more responsible within a relatively short period of time with appropriate systemic interventions. As noted previously, MST has a well-documented capacity to reduce adolescent criminal behavior (Borduin et al., 1995; Henggeler et al., 1992, 1997) and substance use (Henggeler, Clingempeel, Brondino, & Pickrel, 2002; Henggeler et al., 1999; Schoenwald et al., 1996) in both the short- and long-term (Borduin et al., 1995; Henggeler et al., 2002; Schaeffer & Borduin, 2005).

In light of the established effectiveness of MST in the treatment of irresponsible and deviant youth behaviors, the many strengths identified across systems, lack of chronicity of the problems, and their relative lack of severity, Mike's externalizing symptoms should be reduced and more adaptive behaviors should be developed. Although Mike is expected to challenge his new structure and parental expectations initially, his parents likely have the resources to sustain the changes with guidance and support from the therapist. As Mike learns that his parents will maintain their consistency and follow-through with providing both positive and negative consequences for his behavior, he will be less likely to rebel, and positive behavioral change will occur more quickly.

Length of Treatment

The average length of MST treatment is between 3 and 5 months (Henggeler et al., 1998) depending on the seriousness of problems, the existing strengths within the system, and the success of achieving intermediary goals. The frequency of sessions varies with the interventions being employed, the family stability, and the amount of time the family has been involved in treatment. It is not unusual for the MST therapist to have contact with at least one system (e.g., family, school) each day in the immediate weeks following a referral. In the current example, within the first week, the MST therapist will meet Ms. D. and Mr. D., both individually and together, hold a school meeting with both caregivers, and hold at least one family meeting. In addition, the therapist might need to support Ms. D. on the phone each day to increase her feelings of empowerment and the likelihood of follow-through with plans made for parental monitoring. Such intensive involvement at the beginning of a case facilitates rapid change and progress, and promotes the engagement process by demonstrating to the members of the system that the therapist is motivated and interested in their individualized needs. As Mike and his parents' behaviors become more responsible, consistent, and stable, the MST therapist will titrate down the amount of weekly contact made with the systems. During this period, however, assistance will still be available to the family 24 h a day, if necessary. At the point of termination, the therapist might have reduced sessions to once a week with the goal of monitoring the maintenance of positive behavior change. The point of termination is determined once the overarching goals have been achieved.

Summary.   When working with a family similar to Mike's, the MST therapist will attend to aspects of multiple systems that are influencing the identified problems. A thorough assessment of the youth's social ecology is conducted, focusing on systemic strengths and needs. Therapeutic goals are discrete and well defined, with intermediary goals developed to help the therapist and systemic members make steady progress toward reaching overarching goals.

Case Conceptualization

Client strengths.   Referring to Figure 8.4, Mike has several strengths that can be used to facilitate favorable clinical outcomes. He is athletic, sociable, has academic potential, desires to complete high school, and aims for a career in the military. Mike appears to be quite likeable, and although somewhat aloof during his interview, his attitude was cooperative. Interventions will capitalize on each of these strengths to increase Mike's chance for success. For example, Mike's athletic ability might contribute to a choice for an extracurricular activity that will (a) develop relationships with nondeviant peers; (b) occupy his time when his parents are at work; (c) encourage academic efforts to maintain eligibility for the team; and (d) provide an opportunity to excel in a forum that his parents can observe and enjoy with other parents.

Client personality, behavior, affective state, and cognitions.   Although Mike did not endorse symptoms of depression, his responses and demeanor suggest that he is not happy in his current situation. His nonendorsement of problematic behaviors and emotions is likely a reflection of his mistrust of people and the well-protected defenses that he has established for himself. Furthermore, for youths with conduct problems, denial of problems and providing mistruths are expected by definition (American Psychiatric Association, 2000). Although Mike's report of his marijuana use was inconsistent, such reporting is not unusual for adolescents (Cunningham et al., 2003), particularly for those who believe they are "in trouble." Indeed, Mike reported that he did not feel the treatment was needed, and his attitude suggests that at the moment, he likely perceives treatment as a punishment.

Client functioning.   Mike's current level of functioning appears to be deteriorating as evidenced by his increase in maladaptive behaviors. Since the time of his parents' divorce, Mike began socializing with deviant peers, developed problematic behavior in the classroom, experienced decreased grades, and has been truant from school. Furthermore, he has started smoking marijuana with his friends and has had his first contact with the juvenile system for shoplifting. Within the home, Mike reportedly is aggressive toward his sister and has started to increase his unruly behavior. Mike acknowledged being unhappy in his home environment and wanting to find a means to escape. His deviant behavior is likely a reflection of his unhappiness, feeling of hopelessness and of responsibility regarding the interparental conflict, and feeling of being an imposition to his family (e.g., "he blurted out that he was sick and tired of being called the black sheep of the family"). His deviant behaviors also bring pleasure, excitement, and acceptance from peers, which serve to reinforce such behavior.

The behaviors of other members of Mike's social network must be considered when conceptualizing his decreased level of functioning. As noted previously, Mike's parents continue to engage in high levels of conflict. Some maternal characteristics, not identified at this time (e.g., depression or substance abuse), are likely contributing to Ms. D.'s lack of appropriate parenting. Furthermore, Mr. D. has a history of substance abuse, which is known by Mike. Mr. D. has also been physically and emotionally aggressive toward Ms. D., and has made verbal threats to the children in the past. These behaviors have not only modeled inappropriate interaction and communication for Mike, but have facilitated misattributions by Ms. D. regarding Mike's behavior. That is, Ms. D. stated that Mike's behavior is "just like his father's" and further reported that Mike's sister does not have any behavioral or emotional problems. Mike, therefore, has been identified as the problem by his mother and compared with her ex-spouse who engaged in substance abuse and aggression. Mike has a stronger relationship with his father than with his mother; thus, he might willingly accept the role that has been assigned to him by his mother. Moreover, although minimal data are provided regarding Mike's sister, the siblings should be observed together prior to making conclusions about their relationship. The sister might be excellent at provoking Mike's negative and aggressive exchanges with her.

Client dangerousness.   Currently, Mike denies all symptoms of emotional distress and will likely deny suicidal or homicidal ideation as well. Because of his level of unhappiness and the desire to be away from his environment (e.g., fantasizing about running away) as well as his passively aggressive gestures toward his mother and sister, dangerousness to self and others should be monitored throughout treatment. The therapist should help Mike's parents recognize signs of suicidal or homicidal ideation and gestures, especially as they begin to implement structure and rules that Mike might initially respond to negatively.

The Therapeutic Relationship

A fundamental assumption of the MST model is that caregivers are the keys to promoting and sustaining youth behavior change. Engaging caregivers in treatment, therefore, is primary and one of the initial goals of the therapist (see Figure 8.3). If caregivers are not engaged and involved in the treatment, interventions cannot be successful. Several indicators of family engagement within the MST model have been operationalized (Cunningham & Henggeler, 1999) and are monitored throughout quality assurance. Signs of engagement include: (a) high rates of attendance at sessions that are scheduled at convenient times for families; (b) completion of homework assignments—even if the intervention is not successful, the attempt and effort toward completing assignments is a sign of engagement; (c) emotional involvement in sessions, with family members actively engaging in discussions and activities with one another and the therapist; and (d) progress is being made toward meeting treatment goals. Similarly, signs of engagement problems have been operationalized and include: (a) difficulty scheduling appointments despite therapist flexibility and continued youth misbehavior; (b) missed appointments that were scheduled around the family's availability, or caregivers not showing up for appointments while making sure that the youth is present;

(c) intervention plans are not being followed; (d) goals of the family contain little substance and do not target the serious problems identified by the referral source or the therapist; (e) treatment progress is very uneven, suggesting ambivalence on the part of the family; and (f) family members are not candid about important issues regarding problematic youth and family functioning (Cunningham & Henggeler, 1999). Signs of both successful and problematic engagement with family members are constantly evaluated during treatment, as multineed families go through periods of more or less willingness to be involved in the treatment.

Roles in the Therapeutic Relationship

MST is a collaborative approach to intervening with youths and their families. As described previously, the therapist serves as a guide, coach, and educator as the caregivers develop the skills and resources needed to implement successful interventions on their own. Caregivers are active agents in treatment and are involved in all phases of the intervention strategies. Their roles are to accept the responsibility of parenting the youth, provide structure, and a supportive and healthy environment for the youth, and otherwise facilitate successful accomplishments for the family. The target youth's role is to increase his or her responsible behavior by following the rules that are established, make a reasonable effort in school, help around the home, and participate in family and community environments in socially acceptable ways.

The roles of other system members depend on the specific overarching goals of treatment. For example, because youths spend the majority of their time in school and are frequently experiencing behavioral and academic difficulties in that setting, teachers, principals, and guidance counselors often are included in intermediary treatment goals. The role of school officials might include: implementing a behavioral plan, agreeing to contact caregivers immediately when a child does not attend school, agreeing to contact the therapist when a behavioral problem has occurred on school property, or agreeing to hold a meeting with the caregivers prior to making a decision regarding disciplinary actions.

The role of juvenile justice personnel can vary significantly from case to case. If, for instance, a youth is at risk for incarceration, the juvenile officer might be kept continually informed of treatment goals and progress in preparation for court appearances as well as help monitor offending behavior and deliver external consequences (e.g., weekend detention). On the other hand, the juvenile officer might serve simply as leverage for working toward treatment goals. Youths having repeated contacts with juvenile justice authorities often show little concern over threats from probation officers, however. In such instances, caregivers, probation officers, and other concerned adults will need to combine resources to increase their leverage over the youths.

Other extended family and community members also might be asked to facilitate treatment goals, and the roles that they serve can vary greatly. Examples range from calling the caregiver if they notice the youths out at night, to agreeing to provide a job for the youths, to providing social support for the caregivers. The inclusion of external members often is critical to achieving and sustaining clinical progress in the natural environment.

Finally, the role of other treatment providers should be noted. A precondition for the establishment of an MST program is that the team has primary clinical decision-making authority for the families served—with the exception of officials that have legal mandate over the youths. Moreover, MST therapists provide comprehensive services to minimize the potential of working at cross purposes with case managers from other agencies involved with the family. When outside consultation is sought (e.g., legal, medical, psychiatric), the role of the service provider is limited to the specific need for which consultation was requested. Great care is taken in such instances to establish a collaborative relationship between the service provider and the MST therapist and family and to ensure that recommendations are consistent with MST philosophy and treatment goals.

Therapeutic Roles and the Engagement Process in the Case of Mike

Several probable roles in the treatment can be identified based on the information provided. Both Ms. D. and Mr. D., as the parents, will be involved intensively in all aspects of treatment. Mike's sister will play an additional role, as will the school officials. Other resources likely will be drawn upon, including peers of Mike and of his parents, the probation officer, and other members of the system identified during the course of treatment.

Although development of a therapeutic alliance between Mike and the therapist is valuable, the primary individuals that the therapist will target for engagement are Ms. D. and Mr. D. Therapists and caregivers influence each other's behaviors in the treatment through the reciprocal nature of their interactions (Cunningham & Henggeler, 1999). Therapist behaviors with caregivers therefore influence whether or not the family remains involved in services. Nearly half of all clients who are referred for usual mental health services do not attend their first session and of those who do, a large percentage do not return after their initial appointment (Garfield, 1994). The multiproblem families that are usually referred to MST programs by juvenile authorities are especially difficult to engage. Hence, therapists devote their greatest resources and skills to those family members who have the power to decide whether the family will collaborate with treatment or not. Those members are usually the caregivers.

During initial meetings with Ms. D. and Mr. D. the therapist will listen to their concerns, provide hope for change, and normalize their feelings of frustration regarding Mike's situation. Key members of the caregivers' indigenous support systems (e.g., Ms. D.'s sister) will be involved in engagement as they might assist in interventions, provide encouragement to the caregivers, and help Mr. and Ms. D. sustain treatment gains once treatment is completed. When Mike is involved in the sessions, the therapist will play a directive role in facilitating conversation and interactions between Mike and his family members. Attempts will be made to reframe his negative statements (e.g., "I hate being at home" to "Right now there are a lot of difficulties to face at home. Sometimes I would prefer not to deal with them because it is hard to think about sadness and disappointments.") and to reinterpret his behaviors for his parents. When negative interactions occur between Mike and his parents, the therapist is careful not to align with Mike, but rather to help the family problem solve the challenging interaction.

Rapport building with external system members is also critical to treatment success. Prior to meeting with the school officials and Ms. D. and Mr. D. together, the MST therapist will meet the school personnel alone. This will allow for further assessment and provide the opportunity for school personnel to air any complaints they might have, without antagonizing the parents directly. The MST therapist will empathize with teachers and school authorities who are frustrated with Mike, while simultaneously empowering them to feel that positive change is possible if a team approach is used. These interactions will also be used to obtain information to design effective interventions. Similarly, although Mike and his family might view the probation officer as "the enemy," the MST therapist will work hard to establish positive rapport with the officer to ensure that he or she does not undermine the therapeutic plan (e.g., making idle threats regarding consequences). Developing a positive relationship with the juvenile officer is often essential to achieving favorable clinical outcomes. For example, the probation officer might interpret a temporary setback (e.g., shoplifting arrest) as evidence of clinical failure, and consequently advocate for incarceration. Such outcomes can be averted when therapists have strong working relations with juvenile justice staff.

Treatment Implications and Outcome
Specific Techniques and Strategies
The MST model incorporates evidence-based intervention techniques derived primarily from the behavioral, cognitive-behavioral, and pragmatic family

therapy models. These techniques, however, are delivered within a social–ecological conceptual framework, a program philosophy that views caregivers as critical to achieving long-term outcomes, an organizational commitment to overcoming barriers to service delivery, and an ongoing quality assurance system. The following are examples of strategies that might be used with this particular case.

Increasing parental monitoring.   The first step in achieving this goal is to engage Ms. D. and Mr. D. in a cooperative agreement to help their son. Once this first step is accomplished, the MST therapist will work with Ms. D. and Mr. D. to develop a list of rules for Mike to follow regarding his activities. They will initially be asked to "brainstorm" their ideas, and the therapist will help pare the list down to a manageable and reasonable number and framework. A relatively short list increases the likelihood of success. Ms. D. and Mr. D. will be encouraged to develop concrete consequences for rule violations that they are confident can be enforced.

Table 8.1 provides examples of rules and consequences that might be developed initially to increase parental monitoring while simultaneously addressing other overarching goals. The therapist will help the parents establish the set of rules in a positive manner. Mike might object to the rules and feel that they treat him too immaturely. Ms. D. and Mr. D., however, will remind him that he has had the opportunity to be responsible without the rules, but has chosen to behave otherwise. They will let him know that the rules are in place because they love him and want him to succeed and meet his personal goals in life (e.g., graduating high school). The following are examples of concrete rules that might be developed.

RULE 1.   Ms. D. and Mr. D. have given Mike a curfew of midnight on weekends. Both caregivers and Mike will synchronize their watches with an alarm before Mike leaves for the evening, so there will be no confusion over the time that he is to be home. Because Mike alternates households on the weekends, the parent with whom he is staying will wait for him to come home. If the alarm sounds at midnight and Mike is not home, the parent will keep track of the minutes that Mike is late. If Mike arrives 5 minutes late, the next evening he will have to be home 10 minutes before midnight. Once he is home, a phone call is made to the other caregiver to notify him or her that Mike is home safely, and whether or not he is on time. By making the phone call, Mike will see that his parents are working together to change his behavior and the chances for splitting behavior (i.e., giving one caregiver some information and the other different information) are decreased. Furthermore, communicating about Mike's behavior will allow both parents to

TABLE 8.1

Example of Concrete Rules and Consequences Developed to Increase Parental Monitoring, While Simultaneously Addressing Problems Related to School

Mike's rules (to be posted someplace visible at both Mom and Dad's homes)	
Rule	Consequence
In the house by midnight on weekends. Weeknight curfew dependent on activity. Curfew will be determined at the time that permission is granted to be out.	Sanction: For every minute late, the next weekend night Mike will be home double the amount of time early. If late by more than 1 hr, the therapist will be notified. If late by 2 hr, the authorities will be notified. If late on a school night, Mike loses the privilege of going out the next time he requests it on a school night. Reward: If Mike is on time three weekends in a row, he will earn an extra 30 min out on the evening of his choice, the following weekend.
Attend school daily	Sanction: Mother (or therapist or father) will attend school with Mike the next day. He will work off the money lost by missing work, by completing household chores. Reward: Each week that Mike attends school daily, as verified by school officials, he will earn money for entry into a school activity (e.g., football game).
Attend tutoring twice a week	Sanction: Mike will be picked up after school the following day and taken to his mother's office. He will sit in her office and be required to study until she is able to leave for the day. Reward: Every week that Mike attends both of his tutoring sessions, he will be able to go out on Friday night. If he skips tutoring, Mike will spend his Friday night studying.

either praise his success or, if necessary, know what consequences to enforce the next evening.

Rule 2. In light of the risk that Mike will be charged with truancy if he misses anymore school, Ms. D. and Mr. D. decided to place special emphasis on his school attendance. Depending on how Mike gets to school in the mornings (e.g., bus, walking, friends), his method of transportation might need to be changed. Because of Ms. D.'s early work schedule, her sister (i.e., Mike's aunt) agreed to take Mike to school. However, Mike can still choose to skip school once he is dropped. Both Ms. D. and Mr. D., therefore, will meet Mike's teachers, guidance counselor, and attendance officer. Ms. D. and Mr. D. will learn which classes Mike is skipping and seek the assistance of school personnel who would be most helpful. For example, if Mike has been leaving school before his third period history class, Mike's history teacher might agree to notify the attendance office as soon as she is sure that Mike is not attending her class. The attendance office will then contact Ms. D. to notify her of Mike's truancy. Ms. D. will contact Mr. D. and the therapist, and the therapist will meet one or both of the parents as soon as possible and attempt to track Mike down. If located, the parent will immediately bring him back to school. Arrangements will be made for one of the parents, with help from the therapist and other indigenous supports, to shadow Mike for the next couple of days (i.e., sit with him in school), and he will also be given significant additional chores to complete at the house (e.g., cleaning bathrooms, washing floors) as penalty.

RULE 3.   Mikes' academic performance is below his level of capability. Ms. D. and Mr. D., therefore, will have him attend tutoring that is offered at the school twice a week. This intervention aims to improve his grades and provide increased monitoring. Mike's attendance will be verified by one of his parents, and the therapist will randomly stop by the tutoring sessions to monitor Mike's efforts. If Mike fails to attend a tutoring session, he will be picked up from school the next day and taken to his mother's office where he will study under her supervision. If she has a meeting scheduled, he will be supervised by his aunt.

Although each of the preceding rules has negative consequences for noncompliance, Ms. D. and Mr. D. will also work with the therapist to reward Mike's responsible behavior. For example, if Mike does not violate his curfew and is home without incident on Friday and Saturday for three consecutive weekends, he might be allowed to stay out until 12:30 A.M. on the fourth weekend or receive some other desired reward.

In addition to setting concrete rules around specific behaviors, the therapist will help Ms. D. and Mr. D. increase Mike's participation in prosocial recreational or extracurricular activities of his own choice. Mike likely will be more motivated to participate if he selects his own activities. Moreover, participating on a school sports team or in a club will increase Mike's contact with positive peers and provide an environment that includes adult supervision. The parents also might encourage Mike to spend his free time responsibly by gaining an age-appropriate part-time job (e.g., mowing the neighbors' lawns).

It is important to note that the therapist will also assist Ms. D. and Mr. D. in developing a plan to monitor Mike's friendships. The parents will become familiar with their son's peers, and meet his peers' parents. If Mike is going to a friend's home, one of the parents will call the friend's parents ahead of time to verify that the boys will be there. Similarly, if Mike is spending the night at a friend's home, he will be expected to call his mother or father to check in. The therapist will ask the parents to encourage Mike to have his friends over to their house so that he can be monitored more closely.

By increasing parental monitoring, Ms. D. and Mr. D. are not only improving Mike's school attendance, academic performance, and peer relationships, they are enhancing the positive affect between themselves and Mike. Toward this end, part of the therapist's role is to buffer the frustrations that caregivers experience during the process of altering problem behavior toward more responsible conduct. The therapist will reframe caregiver frustrations while simultaneously providing social support. For example, the therapist might say, "I know it gets you angry when Mike violates his curfew. You are really worried and concerned for his safety when he is late. But please remember that you are doing an exceptional job of helping him become more responsible. He should be expected to try and test his limits. That is why you have a consequence already laid out for him, and I have full faith that you are going to follow-through. I know that this is difficult, but you are doing an excellent job of letting him know that you love him and care about his safety." When concrete rules and consequences are in place, along with a social-support system, power struggles between the youths and caregivers should eventually be reduced.

Smoking marijuana.   As shown in Figure 8.5, parental monitoring and truancy have been identified as key determinants of Mike's substance use. The strategies suggested previously for addressing these factors, therefore, will also address his marijuana use. To further facilitate reductions in substance use, the therapist will also implement a substance use-specific contingency management system (Cunningham et al., 2003) based on emerging MST research with substance-abusing juvenile offenders (e.g., Randall, Henggeler, Cunningham, Rowland, & Swenson, 2001). This particular contingency management approach is derived from the highly successful behavioral clinical and research programs developed by Donohue and Azrin (2001) with adolescent substance abusers and Budney and Higgins (1998) with adult substance abusers. Briefly, substance use is monitored frequently via urine drug screens and other biological indices, and consequences are provided contingently. Clean screens earn the participant points that can be redeemed for valued awards, whereas dirty screens result in subtracted points and corresponding loss of privileges. Each point, for example, is equal to a dollar, and points can be exchanged for prosocial activities (e.g., entry fee to a school event) or items (e.g., a new basketball).

In the current case, the therapist would first help Mike and his parents develop a list of rewards that outweigh the benefit of smoking marijuana. These could be earned with clean drug screens. Mike then would identify his most valued privileges, and these would be maintained or lost based on the results of the drug screens. Initially, the therapist would assist the parents in implementing the system, with the eventual goal of transferring the system to parental oversight.

In addition to establishing a behavioral system to decrease Mike's marijuana use, the therapist will teach Mike to develop drug avoidance strategies. Based on a functional analysis of his substance-use patterns, the therapist will help Mike identify the frequency of his smoking, the amount of time spent using marijuana, the triggers or range of situations and activities that influence his drug use, and the resulting positive and negative consequences. Such information will form the basis of his drug avoidance strategies. For example, Mike might indicate that he often smokes marijuana when he is with his friend Sam. Sam gets the marijuana from his step-brother Joe, who visits every other weekend. Mike therefore knows that there is a great likelihood that he and Sam will smoke marijuana if he goes to Sam's house the week after Joe's visit. Knowing the consequences of a dirty urine drug screen, Mike is coached to use strategies for avoiding this high-risk situation. Ideal strategies are those that are low cost to Mike (e.g., require minimal risk of peer rejection), but are likely to be successful. For example, Mike might tell Sam that his probation officer is having him tested for drugs every day and has threatened to lock him up the next time he fails a drug test. On the other hand, when a youth's drug cravings and triggers for use are internal (e.g., anxiety), alternative coping mechanisms (e.g., exercise) might be required. For example, Mike might substitute playing a fast-paced game of basketball with positive peers for smoking marijuana as a method of decreasing anxious thoughts.

Finally, as Mr. D. has a history of substance abuse and Mike identifies closely with him, an intervention involving Mr. D. could be highly beneficial to Mike's success. The therapist would meet Mr. D. and discuss the impact that his substance use had on his behaviors in the family. Mr. D. would be asked to identify techniques that he has used to maintain his abstinence. The therapist then would facilitate a conversation between Mike and his father in which Mr. D. would reinforce Mike's drug refusal and encourage him to abstain from further substance use.

Low parent–child affect.   Several aspects of MST facilitate positive communication and affect between family members. The level of positive affect between caregivers and youths is increased by interventions that (a) reframe negative feelings (e.g., anger is really concern or hurt), (b) encourage caregivers to provide praise and notice when their child is succeeding, (c) depend on caregivers to advocate for their child (e.g., holding a school meeting), and (d) help caregivers engage in constructive problem-solving conversations. In addition, interventions that increase the amount of positive time spent together that is noncontingent on youth behavior can provide a forum for "enjoying each other" and learning more about each other's interests.

Examining Figure 8.5, several drivers for low parent–child affect have not yet been addressed by other interventions. Ms. D. identified that Mike's difficult temperament dates back to his infancy. The therapist might work with Ms. D. to "let go" of the past and, instead, to focus on Mike's current strengths. The therapist, for example, might learn that Ms. D. felt incompetent in her ability to parent and soothe Mike during his infancy, which generalized to her overall self-perception of her parenting ability. As a result, she became emotionally detached from her son. The therapist could assist Ms. D. by providing affirmation of her strong parenting efforts currently. Furthermore, contributing to the detachment, Ms. D. labeled Mike as being "just like his father." In contrast, the therapist could encourage Ms. D. to identify traits in Mike that are more similar to her own qualities (e.g., he is very sensitive), or are his own independent strengths. Through such interventions and spending more enjoyable time together, Ms. D. and Mike can likely improve their emotional relationship.

Aggression toward sister.   Ideally, successful interventions developed to target other overarching goals will indirectly influence and decrease Mike's aggression toward his sister. For example, as Ms. D. begins to attend to Mike's successes and praise him more often, the discrepancy between the level of praise awarded to him and his sister will not be as great (see Figure 8.5). In addition, as Ms. D. and Mr. D. learn to communicate more cooperatively around parenting issues, the level of conflict regarding Mike's sister's refusal to visit her father might decrease. Mike has a long-standing history of using aggression toward his sister during conflictual interactions, however, and thus, additional interventions might be indicated.

Drawing again on the functional analysis, the MST therapist would work with Mike to identify antecedents, behaviors, and consequences regarding his aggression. For example, Mike might indicate that his sister calls him "a loser" and teases him about privileges that she has, which are not available to him (e.g., she can drive because she is 16 and he is underage). He acknowledges that and then pushes her out of his room and makes verbal threats. The consequence is that she tells their mother, who in turn yells at Mike and makes idle threats. An appropriate intervention, therefore, would include increased monitoring of both Mike and his sister's comments toward one another, and deliver predetermined concrete consequences for both of them when aggressive interactions occur. In addition, the therapist might work with Mike on issues of anger management, using a cognitive-behavioral approach to identify and alter cognitive distortions that hinder his ability to choose nonaggressive solutions to interpersonal challenges (Henggeler et al., 1998).

Mechanisms of Change

When conceptualizing client characteristics from an MST perspective, emphasis is placed on the youth's family as the client, rather than the individual youth. Parents, in particular, are the primary agents of change. The primary mechanisms of change involve altering the family system to increase monitoring and contingencies for behavior, while also focusing on the strengths and needs of the youth along with other members of his or her social ecology. These strengths are considered in goal setting and treatment planning. Continuous assessment of client functioning and dangerousness is required throughout the various phases of treatment. Furthermore, assessment of therapist–client rapport, with a focus on caregiver engagement, is critical for successful intervention implementation. Therapeutic practices draw on the techniques of behavioral, cognitive-behavioral, and pragmatic family therapies, with an emphasis on developing caregiver competencies.

Medical and Nutritional Issues

There are no specific medical or nutritional issues that appear to be of concern in this case, or that would require attention from the MST team.

Potential Pitfalls

Youths with serious behavioral problems and their families present many potential barriers to successful interventions. A critical component of MST programs, however, is the explicit assumption that the therapist and team are responsible for delineating and developing strategies to overcome any barriers to behavior change that emerge. Indeed, considerable resources (e.g., low caseloads, considerable supervisory and consultant support) are available to address barriers to change. Moreover, the therapist should anticipate many of these barriers and address them proactively. For example, the therapist anticipated that Ms. D. and Mr. D. might have considerable difficulty developing a cooperative parenting relationship. The therapist therefore predicted for both parents that such cooperation would be challenging and provided support around their emotional vulnerabilities. The therapist was prepared to engage in communication training with both parents and knew to establish ground rules for interactions. There is, however, a risk that Ms. D. and Mr. D. would not agree to work together or that once they interacted, their maladaptive means of communicating would resurface. Because a member of the MST team is available 24 hours a day, a therapist was available to assist and support the parents during emotionally charged and challenging situations. If parental cooperation was not feasible, alternative strategies focusing on the mother (as Mike spent the most time with her) would be implemented. Specifically, the MST therapist would bring the "lack of divorced parents cooperation" problem to supervision, and the MST team would reconceptualize the fit assessment (see Figure 8.3) and develop an alternative strategy to meet the overarching goal (e.g., the therapist meets each of the parents individually). Similarly, Mike is expected to resist his new rules and structure, use marijuana again, and resist participating in after-school activities. Likewise, the parents are expected to be lax in their follow-through with positive and negative consequences for Mike's behavior change. More seriously, Mike might engage in more illegal behavior and come in further contact with criminal justice authorities. Although these barriers appear to target different treatment issues, the method for overcoming them remains the same. That is, the MST therapist returns to the analytical process and reassesses the fit, "tweaking" the interventions as necessary and obtaining advice and support from the supervisor and MST consultant to eventually design and implement effective change strategies.

Termination and Relapse Prevention

Although not discussed extensively in the case description provided, MST interventions almost always encourage caregivers to increase their level of indigenous support. Support can come from extended family members, friends, coworkers, or neighbors. During the termination phase of treatment, the MST therapist weans the family from relying on the therapist for external support. Rather, one of the markers for termination is that the caregivers can implement successful interventions to increase youth responsible behavior on their own with indigenous support. Drawing on the skills and competencies developed during treatment, the caregivers can develop solutions to curb youth misbehavior and seek validation and reinforcement from their naturally occurring support systems. Depending on the severity and potential chronicity of the case, a referral might be made to less intensive services for aftercare.

Termination begins after the therapist has determined that the overarching goals have been obtained or that treatment has reached a point of diminishing returns for time invested. If successful, the caregivers should have the skills needed to maintain their progress. The therapist begins to reduce the number of sessions held with family members, while maintaining availability for times of crisis. The therapist predicts that Mike might show a lapse in his progress, but emphasizes that the parents now have strong plans for turning things back around. Both Ms. D. and Mr. D. have ample evidence that they are capable of handling new or recurring problems, as they, not the therapist, were responsible for implementing interventions to change Mike's behavior. Termination from treatment is viewed as a celebration of family achievements and might be marked by providing the family with a certificate of successful completion, having a termination party, or another symbolic sign of the family's accomplishments.

Summary

MST is differentiated from many other psychotherapeutic interventions by the conceptualization and method of overcoming barriers to successful advances in treatment. When treatment gains are limited, the MST therapist and team are responsible for determining the factors contributing to the lack of progress. The therapeutic team revisits the analytical process and devises alternative strategies for overcoming barriers. The time for termination is usually determined by attainment of overarching goals and the caregivers' ability to successfully monitor and maintain responsible behavior for themselves and their child.

ACKNOWLEDGMENTS

This manuscript was supported by grants DA17487, DA015844, and DA10079 from the National Institute on Drug Abuse; MH65414 and MH60663 from the National Institute of Mental Health; AA122202 from the National Institute on Alcoholism and Alcohol Abuse; H79TI14150 from the Center for Substance Abuse Treatment; and the Annie E. Casey Foundation. The views represented in this chapter are those of the author alone and do not necessarily reflect the opinions of the Annie E. Casey Foundation.

REFERENCES

Ackerman, M. J., & Kane, A. W. (1990). *How to examine psychological experts in divorce and other civil actions.* Eau Claire, WI: Professional Education Systems.

American Psychiatric Association. (2000). *Diagnostic and statistical manual of mental disorders* (4th ed.). Washington, DC: American Psychiatric Press.

Aos, S., Phipps, P., Barnoski, R., & Lieb, R. (2001). *The comparative costs and benefits of programs to reduce crime* (Document 01-05-1201). Olympia, WA: Washington State Institute for Public Policy.

Azar, S. T., Robinson, D. R., Hekimian, E., & Twentyman, C. T. (1984). Unrealistic expectations and problem-solving ability in maltreating and comparison mothers. *Journal of Consulting and Clinical Psychology, 52,* 687–691.

Borduin, C. M., Henggeler, S. W., Blaske, D. M., & Stein, R. J. (1990). Multisystemic treatment of adolescent sexual offenders. *International Journal of Offender Therapy and Comparative Criminology, 34,* 105–113.

Borduin, C. M., Mann, B. J., Cone, L. T., Henggeler, S. W., Fucci, B. R., Blaske, D. M., & Williams R.A. (1995). Multisystemic treatment of serious juvenile offenders: Long-term prevention of criminality and violence. *Journal of Consulting and Clinical Psychology, 63,* 569–578.

Bronfenbrenner, U. (1979). *The ecology of human development: Experiments by design and nature.* Cambridge, MA: Harvard University Press.

Brown, T. L., Henggeler, S. W., Schoenwald, S. K., Brondino, M. J., & Pickrel, S. G. (1999). Multisystemic treatment of substance abusing and dependent juvenile delinquents: Effects on school attendance at posttreatment and 6-month follow-up. *Children's Services: Social Policy, Research, and Practice, 2,* 81–93.

Budney, A. J., & Higgins, S. T. (1998). *A community reinforcement plus vouchers approach: Treating cocaine addiction.* Rockville, MD: U. S. Department of Health and Human Services, National Institutes of Health, National Institute on Drug Abuse.

Center for Substance Abuse Prevention (CSAP). (2001). *Exemplary substance abuse prevention programs award ceremony.* Washington, DC: CSAP, Substance Abuse and Mental Health Services Administration.

Cunningham, P. B., Donohue, B., Randall, J., Swenson, C. C., Rowland, M. D., Henggeler, S. W., & Schoenwald, S. K. (2003). *Integrating contingency management into multisystemic therapy.* Charleston, SC: Family Services Research Center.

Cunningham, P. B., & Henggeler, S. W. (1999). Engaging multiproblem families in treatment: Lessons learned throughout the development of multisystemic therapy. *Family Process, 38,* 265–286.

Curtis, N. M., Ronan, K. R., & Borduin, C. M. (2004). Multisystemic treatment: A meta-analysis of outcome studies. *Journal of Family Psychology, 18,* 411–419.

Doherty, W. J., & Needle, R. H. (1991). Psychological adjustment and substance use among adolescents before and after parental divorce. *Child Development, 62,* 328–337.

Donohue, B., & Azrin, N. H. (2001). Family behavior therapy. In E. F. Wagner, & H. B. Waldron (Eds.), *Innovations in adolescent substance abuse interventions* (pp. 205–227). New York: Pergamon Press.

Ducibella, J. S. (1995). Considerations of the impact of how children are informed of their parent's divorce decision: A review of the literature. *Journal of Divorce and Remarriage, 24*, 121–141.

Elliott, D. S. (1994). *Youth violence: An overview.* Boulder, CO: University of Colorado, Center for the Study and Prevention of Violence, Institute for Behavioral Sciences.

Garfield, S. L. (1994). Research on client variables in psychotherapy. In A. E. Bergin, & S. L. Garfield (Eds.), *Handbook of psychotherapy and behavior change* (pp. 190–228). New York: Wiley.

Haley, J. (1976). *Problem solving therapy.* San Francisco: Jossey-Bass.

Henggeler, S. W. (1998). Delinquency. In S. B. Friedman, M. Fisher, S. K. Schonberg, & E. M. Alderman (Eds.), *Comprehensive adolescent health care* (pp. 862–867). St. Louis: Quality Medical Publishing.

Henggeler, S. W., & Borduin, C. M. (1990). *Family therapy and beyond.* Pacific Grove, CA: Brooks/Cole.

Henggeler, S. W., Borduin, C. M., Melton, G. B., Mann, B. J., Smith, L., Hall, J. A., Cone, L., & Fucci, B.R (1991). Effects of multisystemic therapy on drug use and abuse in serious juvenile offenders: A progress report from two outcome studies. *Family Dynamics of Addiction Quarterly, 1*, 40–51.

Henggeler, S. W., Clingempeel, W. G., Brondino, M. J., & Pickrel, S. G. (2002). Four-year follow-up of multisystemic therapy with substance-abusing and substance-dependent juvenile offenders. *Journal of the American Academy of Child and Adolescent Psychiatry, 41*, 868–874.

Henggeler, S. W., Melton, G. B., Brondino, M. J., Scherer, D. G., & Hanley, J. H. (1997). Multisystemic therapy with violent and chronic juvenile offenders and their families: The role of treatment fidelity in successful dissemination. *Journal of Consulting and Clinical Psychology, 65*, 821–833.

Henggeler, S. W., Melton, G. B., & Smith, L. A. (1992). Family preservation using multisystemic therapy: An effective alternative to incarcerating serious juvenile offenders. *Journal of Consulting and Clinical Psychology, 60*, 953–961.

Henggeler, S. W., Pickrel, S. G., & Brondino, M. J. (1999). Multisystemic treatment of substance abusing and dependent delinquents: Outcomes, treatment fidelity, and transportability. *Mental Health Services Research, 1*, 171–184.

Henggeler, S. W., Rodick, J. D., Borduin, C. M., Hanson, C. L., Watson, S. M., & Urey, J. R. (1986). Multisystemic treatment of juvenile offenders: Effects on adolescent behavior and family interactions. *Developmental Psychology, 22*, 132–141.

Henggeler, S. W., & Schoenwald, S. K. (1998). *The MST supervisor manual: Promoting quality assurance at the clinical level.* Charleston, SC: MST Services.

Henggeler, S. W., & Schoenwald, S. K. (1999). The role of quality assurance in achieving outcomes in MST programs. *Journal of Juvenile Justice and Detention Services, 14*, 1–17.

Henggeler, S. W., Schoenwald, S. K., Borduin, C. M., Rowland, M. D., & Cunningham, P. B. (1998). *Multisystemic treatment of antisocial behavior in children and adolescents.* New York: Guilford Press.

Henggeler, S. W., Schoenwald, S. K., Rowland, M. D., & Cunningham, P. B. (2002). *Serious emotional disturbance in children and adolescents: Multisystemic therapy.* New York: Guilford Press.

Howell, J. C. (2003). *Preventing and reducing juvenile delinquency: A comprehensive framework.* Thousand Oaks, CA: Sage.

Huey, S. J., Henggeler, S. W., Brodino, M. J., & Pickrel, S. G. (2000). Mechanisms of change in multisystemic therapy: Reducing delinquent behavior through therapist adherence and improved family and peer functioning. *Journal of Consulting and Clinical Psychology, 68,* 451–467.

Kazdin, A. E. (1994). *Behavior modification in applied settings.* Pacific Grove, CA: Brooks/Cole.

Kazdin, A. E. (2003). Problem-solving skills training and parent management training for conduct disorder. In A. E. Kazdin, & J. R. Weisz (Eds.), *Evidence-based psychotherapies for children and adolescents* (pp. 241–262). New York: Guilford Press.

McBride, D. C., VanderWaal, C. J., Terry, Y. M., & VanBuren, H. (1999). *Breaking the cycle of drug use among juvenile offenders.* Washington, DC: National Institute of Justice, NCJ 179273.

McCabe, K. M. (1997). Sex differences in the long term effects of divorce on children: Depression and heterosexual relationship difficulties in the young adult years. *Journal of Divorce and Remarriage, 27,* 123–135.

Minuchin, S. (1974). *Families & family therapy.* Cambridge, MA: Harvard University Press.

Moffitt, T. E. (1993). Adolescence-limited and life-course-persistent antisocial behavior. A developmental taxonomy. *Psychological Review, 100,* 674–701.

National Institute on Drug Abuse. (1999). *Principles of drug addiction treatment: A research-based guide.* NIH Publication No. 99–4180. Rockville, MD: Author.

Ogden, T., & Halliday-Boykins, C. A. (2004). Multisystemic treatment of antisocial adolescents in Norway: Replication of clinical outcomes outside the US. *Child and Adolescent Mental Health, 9,* 77–83.

President's New Freedom Commission on Mental Health. (2003). *Achieving the promise: Transforming mental health care in America.* Rockville, MD: President's New Freedom Commission on Mental Health.

Randall, J., Henggeler, S. W., Cunningham, P. B., Rowland, M. D., & Swenson, C. C. (2001). Adapting multisystemic therapy to treat adolescent substance abuse more effectively. *Cognitive and Behavioral Practice, 8,* 359–366.

Roizblatt, A., Rivera, S., Fuchs, T., Toso, P., Ossandon, E., & Guelfand, M. (1997). Children of divorce: Academic outcome. *Journal of Divorce and Remarriage, 26,* 51–56.

Schaeffer, C. M., & Borduin, C. M. (2005). Long-term follow up to a randomized clinical trial of Multisystemic Therapy with life course persistent offenders. *Journal of Consulting and Clinical Psychology, 73,* 445–453.

Schoenwald, S. K. (1998). *Multisystemic therapy consultation guidelines.* Charleston, SC: MST Institute.

Schoenwald, S. K., & Henggler, S. W. (2003). Current strategies for moving evidence-based interventions into clinical practice: Introductory comments. *Cognitive and Behavioral Practice, 10,* 275–277.

Schoenwald, S. K., Henggeler, S. W., Brondino, M. J., & Rowland, M. D. (2000). Multisystemic therapy: Monitoring treatment fidelity. *Family Process, 39,* 83–103.

Schoenwald, S. K., Letourneau, E. J., & Halliday-Boykins, C. A., (2005). Predicting therapist adherence to a transported family-based treatment for youth. *Journal of Clinical Child and Adolescent Psychology, 34,* 658–670.

Schoenwald, S. K., Ward, D. M., Henggeler, S. W., Pickrel, S. G., & Patel, H. (1996). Multisystemic therapy treatment of substance abusing or dependent adolescent offenders: Costs of reducing incarceration, inpatient and residential placement. *Journal of Child and Family Studies, 5,* 431–444.

Shaw, D. (1991). The effects of divorce on children's adjustment. *Behavior Modification, 15,* 456–485.

Silitsky, D. (1996). Correlates of psychosocial adjustment in adolescents from divorces families. *Journal of Divorce and Remarriage, 26,* 151–169.

Stanton, M. D., & Shadish, W. R. (1997). Outcome, attrition, & family-couples treatment for drug abuse: A meta-analysis and review of the controlled comparative studies. *Psychological Bulletin, 122,* 177–191.

Strother, K. B., Swenson, M. E., & Schoenwald, S. K. (1998). *Multisystemic therapy organizational manual.* Charleston, SC: MST Institute.

U.S. Department of Health and Human Services. (1999). *Mental health: A report of the Surgeon General.* Rockville, MD: U.S. Department of Health and Human Services, National Institutes of Health, National Institute of Mental Health.

U.S. Public Health Service. (2001). *Youth violence: A report of the Surgeon General.* Washington, DC: U.S. Public Health Service.

CHAPTER 9

The Continuum of Residential Treatment Care for Conduct-Disordered Youth

Robert D. Lyman and Christopher T. Barry

TREATMENT MODELS

Residential placement for children and adolescents with conduct problems is a frequently considered and often implemented treatment option. This treatment alternative is appealing to both parents and civil authorities because it removes the troublesome youths from the family and community, and presumably reduces the probability of further episodes of acting-out behavior (at least during the period of placement). Historically, such placements have been implemented within either the juvenile correctional system or public or private mental health facilities. In recent years, however, these systems have increasingly begun to resemble each other: detention centers and other correctional facilities typically implement individual treatment plans and milieu therapy programs, while residential treatment facilities and inpatient psychiatric programs serve increasing numbers of delinquent youths and have developed enhanced mechanisms for behavior control and security. Therefore, in this chapter, no firm distinction will be made between correctional facilities and treatment programs, and models and data from both realms will be discussed.

Despite the appeal of residential treatment for youths with conduct problems, there are a number of practical and theoretical drawbacks to such treatment. Barker (1993) reported that the data supporting the effectiveness of residential treatment compared to less invasive, nonresidential interventions are less than conclusive. In fact, extended residential treatment can produce institutionalized and excessively externally governed behavior in children and adolescents. Barker also noted that youths in residential treatment may learn additional dysfunctional behaviors from other youngsters in treatment with them. Disengagement from the family and difficulty re-entering the family system after discharge from residential treatment are two other potential problems. Finally, the expense of residential treatment (for both private individuals and governmental units) and its limited availability in many cases are other variables to be considered.

In addition to these practical drawbacks to residential treatment, Barker (1993) mentions several "theoretical" objections to the implementation of such treatment. These include the context-dependent nature of children's conduct problems and their remediation, and the increasing emphasis on treating childhood behavior problems within the context of the family system (Everett & Volgy, 1993). He also discusses societal disenchantment with "institutional" solutions to human problems in a variety of areas (mental health, housing, poverty, corrections) and a consequent turn to more family- or community-based approaches to such problems. Such approaches de-emphasize the role of residential treatment, particularly if it is long term and institutional in nature. In-home interventions (Kinney, Madsen, Fleming, & Haapala, 1977), day-treatment approaches (Ghuman & Sardes, 1998), and the provision of comprehensive "wrap-around" services (VanDenBerg, 1993) are more consistent with this noninstitutional bias.

Despite these objections, Barker (1993) notes several indications for its use, including the presence of family dysfunction as a significant causal and/or maintaining variable in child conduct problems, safety considerations (both the child's and others'), and the need for specific treatment procedures that cannot be implemented in the home environment.

Common presenting issues for children and adolescents diagnosed with conduct problems who are admitted to residential treatment include poor impulse control, erratic or disorganized behavior, threats of harm to themselves or others, contact with law enforcement and juvenile authorities, social skills deficits, depression, anxiety, and noncompliance with parental control efforts (Frensch & Cameron, 2002; Lyman & Campbell, 1996; Quinn & Epstein, 1998; Whittaker, Archer, & Hicks, 1998). The family histories of many of the children referred for residential treatment are suggestive of significant turmoil. For instance, Quinn and Epstein (1998) observed that only a small percentage of children referred for such treatment live with both biological parents, and the majority have a history of placement outside the family home. Significant family histories of substance abuse, alcoholism, mental illness, violence, and criminal activity have also been noted for many of these children (Frensch & Cameron, 2002; Husey & Guo, 2002; Moore & O'Conner, 1991; Quinn & Epstein, 1998; Timbers, 1990). Finally, the families of children referred for out-of-home treatment have been noted to be characterized by less cohesion and fewer support networks (Frensch & Cameron, 2002; Jenson & Whittaker, 1989). Husey and Guo (2002) contend that, given the disordered family backgrounds of these children, "increased periods of more stable functioning for such youth may be a more realistic goal than seeking a 'once and for all cure'" (p. 408). It has also been concluded that a focus on reintegration back into the community is more productive than orienting interventions toward long duration of residential treatment (Landsman, Groza, Tyler, & Malone, 2001).

Wilson and Lyman (1982) cite four principles that should guide the decision-making process concerning treatment environment. First, treatment should be provided in the setting that is least disruptive of the child's natural environment, but still allow for effective intervention. This principle has had increasingly significant implications for residential treatment in terms of services provided, the cost of those services, and the types of children referred and treated (Frensch & Cameron, 2002). This decision requires consideration of the full range of residential and nonresidential treatment options and analysis of each option's potential for both treatment effectiveness and disruptiveness. Such an analysis is not always straightforward. It may be difficult, for example, to determine if a year in residential treatment is more disruptive to a child's life or offers more potential for effective remediation than 3 years in day treatment while living at home. In conducting such an analysis, it is important that the entire continuum of treatment alternatives be considered. This continuum is briefly delineated below, roughly in order of increasing disruptiveness to the child's life.

Outpatient Treatment

Such treatment can range from play therapy (O'Connor, 1991) to psychotherapy (Russ & Freedheim, 2001), to behavior therapy (Powers, 2001), and to family therapy (Sayger, 2001). Outpatient treatment may continue for years or terminate after only a few sessions. Evidence as to its effectiveness varies widely, with behavioral and cognitive-behavioral approaches generally better able to document effectiveness than other approaches (Kazdin, Bass, Ayers, & Rodgers, 1990; Weisz & Weiss, 1993). Generally, there is relatively little disruption to a child's life with outpatient treatment. Treatment usually requires no more than 2 or 3 hours per week, and school attendance and community activities are minimally affected.

Historically, many children with severe conduct problems have been viewed as not suitable for outpatient, in-home, or in-school treatment. However, outcome data on children treated in selected programs suggest that they can be treated effectively without removal from their homes. At times practitioners may enter the home environment to treat the child and/or family. Examples of such in-home interactions with demonstrated efficiency for conduct-disordered youths include the Homebuilders model (Haapala, 1996) and multisystemic therapy (Henggeler, Schoenwald, Borduin, Rowland, & Cunningham, 1998, see chapter 8 of this book). A variant of in-home treatment is "in-school" treatment, in which group or individual interventions are implemented in the school environment. An example of such an intervention, which has been shown to be effective for conduct problems, is Lochman's Coping Power program (Lochman, Lampron, Gemmer, & Harris, 1987, see chapter of this book).

Day Treatment, Partial Hospitalization, and Special Education Programs

Providing mental health services for extended periods of time during the day offers the advantage of expanded treatment contact without the disadvantages of removing the child from his or her home (Gabel, 1989). Frequently, such programs offer some form of milieu therapy in addition to academic programming and behavioral management. In addition, a variety of therapeutic approaches, ranging from group and individual psychotherapy to pharmacological treatment, can be incorporated into the treatment day.

Shelter and Respite Care

Residential care provided for short periods of time (12 hours to 3 weeks) is generally termed respite care if its purpose is to aid and support parents or other caretakers and shelter care if the purpose is to protect and help the child (Marc & McDonald, 1988). These two purposes frequently overlap. Such care is often provided in response to emergencies such as abuse, abandonment, or parental substance abuse, or in response to parent requests for relief from caretaking strain or reports of inability to control a child. Frequently, shelter or respite care is offered as adjunctive treatment by a residential treatment facility, child welfare agency, or juvenile court. Programs may offer formal therapeutic programming, including group and individual counseling and some form of milieu therapy; however, many provide only temporary housing and supervision (Seng, 1989; Weinman, 1984).

Foster and Group Home Care

One of the most common forms of out-of-home treatment for conduct-problem youths is placement in foster or group homes. These categories of care are differentiated by the number of children placed in a home (generally 1–3 for foster care; 3–12 for group care). They are similar in that the children reside with surrogate parents in a home-like environment. Usually, there is relatively little in the way of formal treatment interventions, although the foster or group home parents may have received specialized training and adjunctive counseling may be provided by child welfare workers or others. Foster and group homes are often operated on a contract basis by child welfare agencies. Group homes are generally more institutional than foster homes, as they may have behavior-management programs in place and may maintain formal case files. The duration of placement in such programs may range from weeks to years, with some children growing to adulthood in such settings. The Achievement Place or Teaching Family model (TFM) (Blase, Fixsen, Freeborn, & Jaeger, 1989) is a variation on the group home format that has been shown to be efficacious with conduct-disordered youths.

Residential Treatment Centers

Residential treatment centers are characterized by a stronger "agency" identification than group and foster homes and by correspondingly less similarity with children's natural environments (Lyman & Campbell, 1996). Programs are often more isolated from the community than group homes and may rely on in-house educational and recreational programming rather than utilizing community resources. There is usually a well-developed, formal treatment program and staff in addition to, or other than, houseparents to implement it. Usually, treatment responsibility resides with licensed mental health professionals rather than parent surrogates. Although residential treatment programs may serve 100 or more children at one site, usually functional units of no more than 15 or 20 children are housed together.

Because residential settings, by nature, involve close contact among youths with histories of emotional and behavioral problems, specific, safe, and well thought-out intervention procedures are required. Direct-care staff in these facilities should be intensively trained in those procedures and mechanisms for reporting the outbreak of disruptive behaviors and the necessary use of more intensive intervention strategies (e.g., restraint, seclusion) should be in place. Similar to the idea that the setting itself should be the least restrictive setting possible for the child, the prevailing principle for the use of behavior-management principles within a residential facility is that the least intrusive behavior control intervention should be used initially, with more intrusive interventions only used later as necessary (Jones & Downing, 1991).

Inpatient Hospitalization

Hospital inpatient units are usually much less similar to children's natural environments than group homes or residential treatment centers. Therefore, inpatient hospitalization tends to be more disruptive to the "flow" of a child's life (Dalton, Bolding, Woods, & Daruna, 1987). Nursing staff are typically used rather than houseparents or child care workers, and there tends to be more formality and regimentation to daily activities. Such normal childhood activities as snacking and playing outside are often unavailable. Schooling may be suspended during hospitalization or may be offered on the hospital ward. Parent contacts are often restricted. Often, pharmacological treatments or other biological interventions are considered to be the primary therapeutic modalities, with relatively little attention given to the impact of the hospital milieu. Twenty or more years ago, inpatient psychiatric hospitalization sometimes lasted for extended periods (up to a year or more). However, in today's managed care environment, most inpatient psychiatric hospitalizations have a duration of less than 1 month. Inpatient hospitalization is more often a crisis-stabilization intervention than a form of residential treatment.

Institutional Treatment

Institutional care is defined by the absence of normalizing environmental experiences and a de-emphasis on re-entry into the child's natural environment upon discharge (Lyman & Campbell, 1996). Such programs are frequently both physically and attitudinally isolated from the community and offer few opportunities for residents to leave the facility. Daily routines are often regimented and impersonal. Frequently, the average duration of treatment is years. Residents are afforded little personal freedom in such matters as dress, daily activities, and room decor. Personal possessions may be minimal and parent contact infrequent. Schooling is almost always provided at the institution. Placement in such facilities is usually extremely disruptive to a child's life and development. Previously, a number of conduct-problem youths were treated in state psychiatric hospitals with institutional characteristics; however, in recent years these programs have reduced services to this diagnostic group, leaving state (or other) juvenile correctional facilities as the primary institutional facilities serving conduct-disordered youngsters. These programs frequently provide minimal therapeutic services and residents' primary staff contact is with paraprofessionals whose orientation is correctional rather than therapeutic.

As stated earlier, a guiding principle in making treatment decisions or recommendations across this continuum is that treatment should be provided in the least disruptive environment possible. Thus, outpatient interventions should generally be tried (or at least considered) prior to residential modalities. The appropriate exceptions to this principle are cases requiring immediate placement because of danger to the child or others, or instances in which there is clear need for medical treatment or diagnosis requiring an inpatient setting. However, recent research suggesting that even severe conduct problems can be managed without out-of-home placement (Weisz, Walter, Weiss, Fernandez, & Mikow, 1990) indicates that even in these circumstances caution in considering residential options is advisable.

A second guiding principle elucidated by Wilson and Lyman (1983) is that treatment should be provided in the setting that allows for maximum treatment effectiveness. For example, problems stemming from dysfunctional communication between parents and child probably cannot be effectively treated in an environment that does not involve parents in the treatment process. Similarly, school-performance or behavior problems cannot be addressed in a treatment environment that does not have an educational component. Of critical importance is the need to maximize treatment generalization from the therapeutic environment back to the child's natural environment. It does little good to have a child demonstrate substantial progress within a residential treatment environment if that progress is not sustained after discharge. One way of maximizing the probability that treatment effects will generalize back to the home environment is by minimizing dissimilarities between the treatment environment and the home environment (Conway & Bucher, 1976). Obviously, more home-like (or more school-like) treatment programs offer substantial advantages in this regard and should be considered over more institutional or inpatient options because of the greater probability of effective generalization of treatment effects.

The third guiding principle cited by Wilson and Lyman (1983) is that treatment should be implemented in the most cost-effective way possible. Clearly, one component in an analysis of cost-effectiveness is treatment effectiveness. A treatment option cannot be viewed as cost-effective (even if it is very inexpensive) unless it produces the desired therapeutic outcome. Most evaluations of residential and inpatient treatment for conduct-disordered youths demonstrate that most (but not all) children show significant improvement while the child is in treatment, with this conclusion typically based on behavioral or psychometric assessments made at the time of admission compared to similar assessments conducted at the time of discharge. Research has generally indicated that behavioral and cognitive-behavioral approaches are more effective than intrapsychic or dynamic interventions. Long-term follow-up data are less positive than short-term results (Lyman & Campbell, 1996). More detailed treatment outcome results will be discussed later in this chapter.

The second element of cost-effectiveness appraisal is a consideration of direct cost, treatment duration, and the social cost of treatment failure. Five years of weekly outpatient therapy at $100 per hour may prove more costly than 9 months of residential treatment at $250 a day if these factors are adequately considered. Cost and treatment effectiveness need to be considered in comparing the different modalities of residential treatment to each other and in comparing residential treatment to alternative treatment options. For example, some wilderness treatment programs treat conduct-disordered youths for less that $100 per day with outcome results comparable to those of $300 per day traditional residential programs. In this case, is there any real justification for recommending the more expensive program? Similarly, day treatment programs may deliver comparable treatment outcomes at one-third the cost of residential programs, suggesting that real consideration should be given to their utilization rather than out-of-home placement. However, considerations of child safety or protection of the community may supercede issues of cost-effectiveness and lead to a residential placement recommendation. In recent years, the spread of managed care philosophies in both private and public sectors combined with demands for greater fiscal accountability by taxpayers has made issues of cost-effectiveness increasingly important in the area of youth treatment. Residential treatment and other "deep-end" interventions have been objects of close scrutiny, with a number of public entities choosing privatization as the method to achieve both accountability and cost control (Ogles, Trout, Gillespie, & Penkert, 1998).

The fourth guiding principle expressed by Wilson and Lyman (1983) is that a child's clinical condition, diagnosis, and behavior should be matched to the philosophy, structure, and capabilities of the treatment environment. Some youths require placement in programs with more resources, such as nighttime nursing staff and locked wards, while other children need only home-like conditions with houseparent supervision. Placement of children in a program with inadequate resources can lead to dangerously uncontrolled behavior, staff burnout, and a lack of improvement in the child. On the other hand, placement of children in programs with more structure and resources than necessary may result in loss of treatment effectiveness because of minimal generalization to the home environment and inappropriate utilization of limited or expensive treatment resources.

Another important aspect of matching a child's treatment needs to a program's capabilities concerns the underlying treatment philosophy of a program and the primary therapeutic interventions that stem from this philosophy. Youths with limited verbal abilities and short attention spans are unlikely to derive much benefit from a program utilizing traditional verbal psychotherapy as its primary treatment approach. Similarly, children with depression and anxiety as primary symptoms are unlikely to show improvement if enrolled in a program that uses a points and levels system to manage disruptive behavior as its main treatment intervention. Staff in medically oriented inpatient programs may be unfamiliar with educational remediation approaches and may de-emphasize the role of learning disabilities in a child's adjustment problems. The above-described "mismatches" represent poor choices of treatment options because of incompatibility between program philosophy and child needs.

Six theoretical models have had the greatest influence on treatment within the context of residential care. They are briefly described in the text that follows.

The Psychoanalytic Model

Best represented by Bettelheim (1950, 1974, also see chapter of this text), the psychoanalytic model of residential treatment emphasized the removal of children from "psychogenic" family environments and the provision of psychoanalytic therapy within the safety of residential care. Redl (1966) expanded the psychoanalytic model to include treatment interventions by child care workers (life space interviews), but the mainstream of psychoanalytic thought de-emphasized the importance of the residential milieu, believing that by far the most important components of residential treatment were the efforts of the psychiatrist, psychologist, and social worker (the child guidance team; Whittaker, 1979).

Psychoanalytically based residential treatment was the dominant model from the 1930s until the 1960s and continues to be influential today (Stamm, 1989). However, as noted earlier, these programs have failed to provide much empirical support for their effectiveness and are largely inappropriate for the majority of conduct-disordered youths.

The Behavioral (Cognitive-Behavioral) Model

Behaviorally based residential treatment emerged during the 1960s as part of the more general development of treatment approaches for psychological and behavioral disorders based on laboratory-derived learning principles

(Lazarus, 1960; Ross, 1964; Wolpe, 1958). In addition, the failure of psychoanalytic residential programs to document discernable treatment effects and the lack of applicability of psychoanalytic techniques to many clinical populations encouraged the application of behavioral principles within the context of residential treatment. A number of comprehensive models of behavioral residential treatment were developed that de-emphasized the role of individual psychotherapy and instead focused on the systematic manipulation of positive and negative consequences to shape behavior. As a result of this change in philosophy, the role of residential staff came to be regarded as more important, and such staff came to be viewed as the primary agents for implementing highly structured programs to regulate and remediate children's behavior within the residential environment. The previously mentioned Achievement Place program (Blase et al., 1989) provided substantial early data indicating the effectiveness of behaviorally based residential treatment for conduct-disordered youths. A number of research studies have found that residential treatment programs employing behavioral and/or cognitive-behavioral approaches produce improved behavioral functioning *within the residential treatment setting* (Day, Pal, & Goldberg, 1994; Friman, Toner, Soper, Sinclair, & Shanahan, 1996; Larzelere et al., 2001), although the benefits of these approaches have not been well tested in direct comparison to other theoretical approaches to residential treatment.

The Psychoeducational Model

The psychoeducational model is a variant of the cognitive-behavioral model. It is best represented by the Project Re-Ed program founded by Nick Hobbs in Tennessee (Hobbs, 1966; Lewis & Lewis, 1989). The psychoeducational model stresses the teaching of more appropriate behaviors and coping skills to children and adolescents rather than focusing primarily on reinforcing such behaviors as they occur, as does the behavioral model. A fundamental part of the psychoeducational model is an emphasis on continued community involvement for the child in residential care and continued contact between the child and family. As a result of these emphases, psychoeducational model programs appear to be particularly effective in promoting generalization of treatment effects to the home environment. Like behavioral programs (and unlike psychoanalytical programs), psychoeducational programs also appear to have applicability to a wide variety of client types and clinical conditions, particularly externalizing disorders. They also (like behavioral programs) emphasize the importance of online staff's efforts and the effect of the therapeutic milieu rather than individual or group psychotherapy.

The Medical Inpatient Model

Since the formation of the first children's psychiatric units in general hospitals, such as the one begun in Johns Hopkins Hospital in 1930 (Freedman, Kaplan, & Sadock, 1972), there has been a tremendous increase in the number of such units. Although they initially had a strong psychoanalytic orientation, in recent years most of these programs have adopted an eclectic, almost atheoretical orientation that emphasizes medical diagnosis and treatment (Perry, 1989). Although many psychiatric inpatient units serve conduct-disordered youths (particularly those with substance abuse problems) because of availability, parental desperation, and the realities of insurance coverage, they actually appear to be most effective in treating youths whose mental health problems are specifically linked to organic causes or are responsive to biological intervention. Given the very limited duration of most inpatient stays, long-term interventions are not feasible. As pointed out earlier, inpatient programs usually do not offer good environments for dealing with school or family problems because of the lack of emphasis on (and expertise in) educational programming and the limited contact between treatment staff and the child's family. Staff in medical inpatient programs are usually more familiar with medical diagnostic and treatment procedures and tend to emphasize organic etiological factors over psychosocial and psychoeducational ones. Two roles of increasing importance for medical inpatient programs are the periodic hospitalization of chronically mentally ill children and youths for the purpose of providing parental respite and crisis stabilization, and the housing of children briefly while complex medical diagnostic tests are performed. Both of these functions appear to be less applicable to conduct-problem youths than to other clinical populations. Another role mentioned earlier that is a specialization for some medical inpatient units is the provision of time-limited (1 month, usually) treatment for adolescent substance abuse. Such treatment is usually more expensive when delivered in a hospital setting rather than a "nonmedical" residential setting and there appears to be little justification for this added expense, except for the fact that some insurance carriers will pay for the service only when it is provided in a hospital.

The Peer Culture Model

The peer culture model stresses the importance of interpersonal factors, particularly with regard to peers, in therapeutic functioning. Raush, Dittman, and Taylor (1959) and Polsky (1961) were among the first to formally recognize that peer influences often have more impact on child behavior than formal treatment interventions. Following this recognition, several authors (Flackett & Flackett, 1970; Vorrath & Brendtro, 1974) developed treatment approaches designed to mobilize peer support for adaptive rather than mal-adaptive behaviors in residential treatment. Most peer culture programs use group discussions as well as group control of privileges or rewards for this purpose. Frequently, these procedures are collectively termed the "thera-peutic community." The effectiveness of this treatment approach appears to derive from both the confrontation and feedback in group discussion and the reinforcement of adaptive behaviors with positive consequences. Par-ticipation in peer culture model programming requires moderate verbal and cognitive capabilities, and staff must be significantly involved to ensure the therapeutic nature of group processes and consequence decisions. However, much of the effectiveness of these programs can be attributed to interactions between residents.

As mentioned earlier, the peer culture model has become the model of choice for inpatient adolescent substance abuse programs, as well as for a number of other short term, inpatient, adolescent treatment programs serving more diverse populations. This appears logical because such a high percentage of adolescent substance abuse programs appear to be related to peer influence. The same logic applies to a variety of other adolescent-conduct problems that are maintained by peer attention; however, internal-izing disorders appear less appropriate for intervention via the peer culture model.

The Wilderness Therapy Model

Contact with nature and involvement in "natural" activities have long been assumed to have therapeutic value. In the 1920s camps with an overtly therapeutic focus were established for underprivileged urban youngsters (McNeil, 1962), and by the 1930s programs specifically for youths with mental health problems were in existence (Young, 1939). Since that time, there have been two directions in wilderness program development. On the one hand, a wide range of camping programs have developed that utilize traditional child mental health interventions such as group and individual therapy, levels systems, etc., to treat children in a camp or wilderness set-ting. Many of these programs are time limited (usually summer), whereas others operate year round. Some are adjuncts of more traditional residen-tial programs, while others are free-standing. They may range in theoretical orientation from behavioral to psychodynamic and may serve clients whose diagnoses range from autism and mental retardation to conduct disorder. A number of published studies suggest that such programs are as effective as traditional residential programs at much lower cost (e.g., Plouffe, 1981; Rickard & Dinoff, 1974). Additional advantages to such programs are that placement tends to be less stigmatizing than for traditional residential treatment programs and that time-limited summer programming allows uninterrupted enrollment in school.

Wilderness therapy programs are the second direction followed by outdoor treatment programming. These are primarily derived from the Outward Bound model originated by Kurt Hahn (Richards, 1981). Such programs attempt to offer transcendent, real-life, challenging experiences in the natural environment that will call forth adaptive and prosocial values and behaviors in children and adolescents. Wilderness therapy programs are primarily group oriented and offer challenges to comfort and safety that, when successfully managed, facilitate the growth of a new repertoire of coping skills and enhanced feelings of self-esteem for the participants. In addition, new patterns of relating to others are developed. The specific challenges offered can range from hiking, canoeing, and mountain climbing to sailing open waters in a small boat or living off the land for extended periods of time. A number of research studies have demonstrated the effectiveness of such interventions (Burton, 1981; Gibson, 1981). One problem that has recently emerged with wilderness therapy programs is the issue of forced enrollment and aggressively demanded performance of physical challenges. Several instances have been reported in the national media in which youths who were forced by parents to enroll in wilderness therapy programs were injured or killed when supervisors in these programs demanded more physical effort or participation than the youngsters were capable of giving. These events represent a distortion of the wilderness therapy model and suggest that monitoring of safety must take precedence over implementation of challenge activities, and that supervisors should be selected more for therapeutic sensitivity and training than prowess in wilderness activities. The unfortunate events also illustrate the difficulty governmental monitoring and certification agencies have in determining which programs are treatment programs and how to adequately monitor the safety and appropriateness of their interventions.

The Boot Camp Model

A "treatment" model specific to the remediation of conduct problems in adolescents and young adults that has emerged fairly recently and proved remarkably popular is the "boot camp" or "shock incarceration" model (Simon, 2002). These programs were first introduced in Georgia and Oklahoma in the early 1980s (Osler, 1991) and can now be found in over 30 states (MacKenzie, 1993). The Juvenile Justice and Delinquency Prevention Act of 1993 stipulated the conversion of 10 closed military bases into boot camps for juvenile offenders (Simon, 2002), ensuring their continued popularity.

AQ1

Boot camps are evidently based on the philosophy that the harsh regimentation and discipline of military-style basic training will remediate conduct problems in youngsters within 90–120 days. Programs typically include military-style marching, physical training, strenuous manual work with little or no skills training, and harsh verbal correction and immediate physical punishment (usually push-ups or laps) for misbehavior, backtalk, or failure to follow commands. Staff almost always have a military or law enforcement background, dress in military-style uniforms, and act like drill instructors with residents. Some programs incorporate elements of substance abuse treatment and may have some form of therapeutic counseling. Quite often, first offenders are sent to boot camps by juvenile court judges as an alternative to incarceration in traditional juvenile institutions. Outcome data on boot camps suggest that recidivism rates are only marginally better than those of other juvenile correctional institutions and that cost savings over such institutions are negligible (MacKenzie, 1994).

PROGRAM ATTRIBUTES

There are significant theoretical and philosophical differences across the residential programs previously described, but they all must address a number of practical issues that, to a large extent, determine the nature and effectiveness of any program, regardless of theoretical orientation. A brief discussion of these program attributes is presented below.

Physical Facilities

Although a program's theoretical orientation may, to some extent, shape its physical facilities, such practical considerations as funds available, location, intended population, zoning laws, and community acceptance are more likely to determine the nature of these facilities. Attention to physical facilities in the residential treatment literature varies widely, ranging from Bettelheim's detailed discussion of the importance of the appearance of bathrooms in helping children work through their psychosexual conflicts (Bettelheim & Sanders, 1979), to the failure of most authors to mention the topic at all. Group and foster homes are usually located in "regular" family homes with only modest modifications for safety purposes. Residential treatment centers typically are less "homey" facilities. There is usually an administration and/or education building, housing units that bear little resemblance to family homes, and specific facilities (gyms, pools, etc.) for recreation. In addition, these facilities often include elements that are necessary for client containment and/or safety (childproof or unbreakable windows, for example) or which are required by specific treatment interventions (e.g., locked seclusion rooms). Institutional (mental health or correctional) and inpatient programs are often quite sterile and impersonal. Housing units feature nursing stations or correctional "control" stations, and bedroom and bathroom fixtures are often designed with durability or safety as higher considerations than comfort or aesthetics (beds bolted to the floor, one-piece stainless-steel fixtures). Very often access to the outside is restricted in these programs and high fences surround play areas. Dining facilities also tend to be impersonal, and typically residents have no access to food between scheduled meal times. Residential programs also vary in the amount of personal space and privacy afforded to residents, with more home-like programs allowing more of both than institutional programs. All of these characteristics of the residential environment would appear to be important elements of the child's milieu and, therefore, factors in program effectiveness. However, there have been few empirical investigations reported in the research literature to guide the development of physical facilities for residential treatment. A critical treatment concern that has already been mentioned is enhancement of treatment generalization. This principle would suggest the preferability of more home-like, community-based residential treatment facilities; however, no empirical research exists to support this logical conclusion.

Staffing

Although staff are considered important elements in almost every treatment model, there are significant differences of opinion as to the relative importance of different staff members. The psychoanalytic idea of the therapist as the central figure, with other staff members considered secondary and part of the "other 23 h" (Trieschman, Whittaker, & Brendtro, 1969), has largely given way to a recognition that all members of the milieu are important and that those who spend more time with the child (direct care staff such as child care workers, nurses, houseparents, and teachers) are more likely to have an impact on the child's adjustment and progress than those who see the child no more than 5 h a week. A paradox in this area is that more training, higher salaries, and greater input into the treatment plan are almost universally given to those who spend the least time with the residents. Programs vary widely in how much attention is given to the selection, training, and supervision of direct care staff and how involved such individuals are in treatment planning. The unfortunate reality, however, is that, in most cases, the profession of child care worker is not a life-long career and, as a result, direct care staff tend to be young and relatively inexperienced. Houseparents also tend to turn over fairly frequently (probably because of the stress of the position) and therefore are often fairly inexperienced. Programs vary in whether direct care staff are nurses, child care workers, or houseparents. Financial and treatment advantages (and disadvantages) can be cited for each staffing model, but again there is little empirical evidence for the advantages of one staffing philosophy over another. Some treatment models do seem to dictate certain staffing patterns. One would expect a medical inpatient program to be staffed by nurses who could administer pharmacological treatments, whereas an institutional correctional facility would be unlikely to employ houseparents. However, these expectations may merely represent "fossilized" thinking and may deserve further critical appraisal.

One study isolated the variable of resident-to-staff ratio in assessing residential treatment outcome. Specifically, residential treatment outcomes for children treated with a lower resident-to-staff ratio were compared with those for less severely disturbed children treated with a higher resident-to-staff ratio. These outcomes were then also compared to outcomes from inpatient care with more severely disturbed children (Friman, Toner, Soper, Sinclair, & Shanahan, 1996). Findings indicated that a lower resident-to-staff ratio can result in behavioral improvements to a level comparable to that of less disturbed children, leading the authors to conclude that more heavily staffed residential programs can serve as an alternative to more costly inpatient programs for severely disturbed children.

Characteristics of Children Served

Most residential programs serving conduct-problem youths have stated eligibility criteria, usually expressed most clearly in terms of exclusion criteria. Common reasons for not considering children for programs include low IQ, fire-setting, self-injurious or suicidal history, co-morbid psychotic disorder, and medical problems. Unfortunately, these criteria are often based more on liability concerns or staff uneasiness than on an empirical assessment of the program's capabilities.

It is shortsighted to focus on the child's behavior as the primary criterion for program admission or exclusion. As previously mentioned, other variables such as the range of alternative, nonresidential services available, family resources and capabilities, and the community's tolerance for acting-out behavior must be considered. Residential treatment is indicated by a gap between a child's needs and the resources available in his or her natural environment, rather than by a certain diagnosis or pattern of behavior.

The Role of Psychotherapy

In the past, verbal psychotherapy was often seen as the primary agent of change in residential treatment, with the rest of the residential program merely providing adjunctive care. Today, however, residential programs for which formal psychotherapy is considered the primary treatment modality are in the minority, and such a treatment model is increasingly considered invalid. "A truly therapeutic milieu cannot be organized around the concept of individual psychotherapy as the central mode of treatment" (Whittaker, 1979, p. 56).

So, what exactly is the role of psychotherapy in residential treatment? Reviews of the effectiveness of child mental health treatment (Kazdin et al., 1990; Weisz & Weiss, 1993) have yielded mixed results, which suggest that verbal psychotherapy should not be the treatment of choice for most children and adolescents. Additionally, psychotherapy within the context of residential treatment is subject to constraints and expectations that differ considerably from those associated with outpatient psychotherapy. Psychotherapy may be requested by residential staff for a child when he or she is behaving badly and may be viewed by both children and staff as merely an extension of the program's behavior-management system. There are also significant issues regarding confidentiality and client advocacy that must be addressed when a child is seen in psychotherapy within a residential program (Monahan, 1989).

The Role of the Group

Regardless of the explicit model on which a residential treatment program is based, group factors and influences will be critical in determining treatment outcome. Peer influences are extremely powerful within the residential group (Polsky, 1961; Polsky & Claster, 1968), and unfortunately these influences are often in the direction of encouraging and reinforcing maladaptive behaviors (Buehler, Patterson, & Furniss, 1966). As previously mentioned, the peer culture model attempts to use peer influences to promote positive behaviors (Brendtro & Wasmund, 1989; Vorrath & Brendto, 1974), and some behaviorally oriented programs have attended to these influences through techniques that include the use of peer managers and peer monitoring (Blase et al., 1989; Phillips, Phillips, Fixsen, & Wolf, 1972). Other techniques that have been employed to make the group a therapeutic agent include the use of group problem-solving sessions (Rickard & Lattal, 1969) and the use of group contingencies and reinforcement (Swain, Allard, & Holborn, 1982).

Adaptive Skills Training

The learning of adaptive behaviors is an important component of many residential treatment programs. Project Re-Ed (Hobbs, 1966; Lewis & Lewis,

1989), for example, "stresses the teaching of competence across the total spectrum of the child's development as the fundamental purpose of the helping environment" (Whittaker, 1979, p. 71). Behavioral programs, including the TFM (Blase et al., 1989) also include the learning of specific adaptive behaviors as goals for children in treatment and include direct instruction as well as reinforcement for target-behavior demonstration. Specific intervention techniques that have been used to teach adaptive skills include social skills training (Shure, 1992), modeling interventions (Marion, 1994), and contingency management procedures applied to academic performance (DuPaul & Eckert, 1997). Specific social skills training programs developed for outpatient use such as Lochman's Coping Power program (Lochman et al., 1987) can also be adapted for use within a residential treatment context.

Behavior Management and Control
Issues of behavior management and control are critical for all residential programs, even those whose primary client population is not conduct-problem youth. Approaches to these issues vary widely, from the permissive tolerance of inappropriate behavior seen at some psychodynamically oriented programs (Bettelheim, 1974) to the highly structured behavior-management systems in place at more behaviorally oriented programs (Blase et al., 1989). A number of specific behavior-management techniques have demonstrated efficacy within residential treatment environments, such as the use of points and levels systems (Johnson, 1995), overcorrection techniques (Matson, Manikam, & Ladatto, 1990), behavioral contracting (Allen, Howard, Sweeney, & McLaughlin, 1993), self-instructional training (Ollendick, Hagopian, & Huntzinger, 1991), and time-out procedures (Roberts & Powers, 1990).

The limitations of highly structured behavior-management systems should also be recognized. The ultimate purpose of residential treatment is to improve a child's functioning in his or her natural environment, not to control it within the residential treatment environment. Behavior-management techniques are only truly effective when they bring about behavior change that generalizes and is maintained past discharge from treatment.

Assessing Effectiveness of Residential Treatment and Its Alternatives
A comprehensive analysis of the effectiveness of residential treatment for conduct-disordered youths cannot focus just on residential treatment but must also include alternative treatment modalities. It is impossible to determine if residential treatment is the best treatment option if one does not know how effective that treatment is in comparison to day treatment or

in-home treatment. Therefore, this review, although not including outpatient treatment (see Kazdin et al., 1990, and Weisz & Weiss, 1993 for reviews of the effectiveness of outpatient therapy), will begin with a brief review of effectiveness data on day treatment and community-based services for conduct-disordered youths before proceeding to a selective review of residential treatment outcome data.

Alternatives to residential treatment.   Prentice-Dunn, Wilson, and Lyman (1981) investigated the treatment outcome of externalizing disordered children placed in behaviorally oriented day and residential treatment programs at the same facility. They found that both groups demonstrated equivalent, moderate improvement on behavioral ratings and academic measures and that greater parental involvement was a predictor of improvement in both settings. The two groups were found to be equivalent in severity of disorder at admission, with placement in day treatment rather than residential treatment occurring as a function of family residence within commuting distance to the center rather than as a result of child diagnostic or behavior-management variables.

Velasquez and Lyle (1985) compared the efficacy of a day treatment program emphasizing counseling and school advocacy to residential treatment through the use of a quasiexperimental post-test comparison design. Subjects were adjudicated youths and status offenders. Both interventions were found to produce significant reductions in status offenses, and no significant differences were found between the groups in postdischarge school attendance, social workers' assessments of adjustment, or maintenance of a family living situation.

An interesting study that did not specifically target conduct-disordered youths but offers meaningful data on the questions of comparative cost and treatment effectiveness of day and residential treatment was conducted by Grizenko and Papineau (1992). They compared the outcome and cost of treating 23 children with mixed mental health diagnoses in residential treatment with the outcome and cost of treating 23 similar children in the same unit after it had been converted to a day treatment program. They found no differences between the groups in age, diagnosis, severity of psychopathology, and family functioning. Treatment outcomes for the two groups were also not significantly different, although there was a trend for more improvement in the day treatment group. Average length of treatment was 6.1 months for the day treatment program versus 19.6 months in the residential program, and the average cost per child for day treatment ($9213) was less than one-sixth the per-child cost for residential treatment ($61,412).

Carlson, Barr, and Young (1994) examined factors associated with treatment outcomes of male juvenile offenders treated in either day or residential treatment and found no significant difference in outcome between the two groups. Overall, 76% of parents felt that their children had shown behavioral improvement, although objective data indicated that only 35% of the youngsters demonstrated a significant reduction in antisocial behavior.

Lyman, Prentice-Dunn, and Wilson (1995) compared children in residential treatment with children in day treatment at the same facility and found that children in residential treatment were rated by staff as making significantly greater behavioral improvement than the children in day treatment. However, parents did not rate the two groups as differing significantly in behavioral improvement, and there were no differences in academic progress or in the number of disruptive incidents between the two groups.

The preceding findings suggest that day treatment programs can provide safe, cost- and treatment-effective intervention to youths with conduct problems equivalent in severity to those of youngsters commonly served in residential treatment. The issue is likely to be whether such programs are available.

In-home or community-based treatments usually involve intervention teams that implement some combination of group and individual therapy, milieu therapy, parent training, psychopharmacological treatments, behavior management, and crisis intervention. Treatment is usually delivered at least partially in the home or neighborhood.

Winsberg, Bialer, Kupietz, Botti, and Balka (1980) compared outcomes for 49 conduct-disordered children who received either 6 months of inpatient care or community-based treatment following brief inpatient crisis care. They found that the children who received community-based treatment showed significantly greater improvement than the group that received extended hospital care. Long-term follow-up (1.5–3 years) found that almost half of the inpatient group was later placed in residential treatment versus less than 30% of the community-based treatment group.

The Homebuilders model (Haapala, 1996) of community-based treatment has been evaluated in a number of studies. This model targets children at high risk for removal from their homes and consists of intensive, in-home crisis intervention conducted by therapists who are on call 24 hours per day and provide case management, behavior modification, crisis intervention, parent training, and family therapy services. Teams frequently provide more than 10 hours per week of services to an individual family.

Kinney et al. (1977) found that during the initial period of service delivery, 90% of Homebuilders child clients were able to be maintained in their homes rather than being removed, and a 16-month follow-up showed that 97% of the clients who avoided out-of-home placements initially were still residing at home. Haapala and Kinney (1988) conducted another evaluation of the effectiveness of the Homebuilders model and found that only 13% of status-offending youths received out-of-home placement during 12 months following Homebuilders intervention. This figure was in contrast to 34% of these same youths who experienced out-of-home placement prior to Homebuilders intervention. Bath, Richey, and Haapala (1992) found similar results regarding out-of-home placements and also found that child age (0–2, over 9), gender (male), parent mental health problems, low child IQ, low family income, child delinquency, and child physical violence were predictors of out-of-home placement.

Other models of community-based services for conduct-disordered youths that have reported encouraging results include Henggler's multisystemic therapy model (Henggeler et al., 1998, see chapter 8 in this text) and the wrap-around model (VanDenBerg, 1993). This model, rather than basing treatment on one service modality, emphasizes the development of a continuum of treatment services that can be applied individually to a case as needed. The wrap-around model therefore moves beyond the discussion of residential versus nonresidential treatment to a consideration of matching service needs to resources for an individual child.

The Willie M. Program in North Carolina is one of the more ambitious attempts to provide wrap-around services for conduct-disordered youths. An array of services, including residential care, vocational training, structured recreation, and psychotherapy, were provided to disturbed youths who were assaultive or violent. Weisz et al. (1990) evaluated the program and found that lower arrest rates after termination from the program were nonsignificantly associated with longer term involvement in the Willie M. program.

Residential Treatment

One of the earlier scientifically sound studies assessing outcome of residential treatment for conduct-problem youngsters was done at Cumberland House, the original Project Re-Ed facility in Nashville, TN, by Weinstein (1969, 1974). He found that after an average of 8 months of residential treatment, approximately 90% of treated participants were rated as moderately or much improved, while control participants failed to demonstrate significant change. This progress was maintained after discharge as indicated by the fact that 92% of the residentially treated children were rated as severely disturbed at admission, but only 44% and 51% were so rated at 6-month and 18-month follow-ups. A more recent evaluation of the Re-Ed program (Lewis, 1988) found that family variables were better predictors of residential treatment progress than child variables.

Jesness (1971, 1975) conducted several studies evaluating residential treatment for delinquent youths. He found that placement in prescriptive, individualized treatment programs rather than the standard training-school milieu resulted in some differences in the number of behavior problems during treatment but had little effect on recidivism after discharge.

The TFM (Blase et al., 1989), originated at the Achievement Place group home, has been the subject of several outcome evaluations. The program is a behavioral one, with a comprehensive points and levels system in which appropriate behaviors earn privileges and inappropriate behaviors lose privileges. Braukmann, Kirigin, and Wolf (1976) found a much lower rate of legal offenses for Achievement Place residents than other group-home residents while they were in treatment, but no difference in the number of offenses committed in the year following discharge, although Achievement Place youths were institutionalized at less than half the rate (14%) of comparison youths (31%). Kirigin, Braukmann, Atwater, and Wolf (1982) compared 13 TFM group homes with 9 comparison group-homes. They found nonsignificant trends for boys (57% vs. 73%) and girls (27% vs. 47%) in TFM homes to have lower rates of offense following discharge than youngsters in the comparison homes. Similarly, Weinrott, Jones, and Howard (1982) compared the effectiveness of 26 TFM homes with that of 25 other group homes. They found improvements in behavioral adjustment for the youths treated in both sets of group homes, but no significant advantage for the TFM homes.

Cavior and Schmidt (1978) compared a residential program of individualized treatment interventions, including behavior modification, group and individual therapy, and reality therapy, to a traditional juvenile correctional program and failed to find any differences in postdischarge parole performance and recidivism. It is discouraging to note that the recidivism rate during the 3-year follow-up period was approximately 58% for each group.

Spence and Marzillier (1981) found a significant in-program and follow-up advantage in target-behavior demonstration for delinquent youths who were exposed to social skills training in residential treatment versus those who did not receive such training. However, no significant difference was found between the groups on such variables as self-report of delinquency and legal convictions at discharge or follow-up.

Barton, Alexander, Waldron, Turner, and Warburton (1985) evaluated the results of a behavioral family therapy program with youths in a state training school and their families. They found that at a 15-month follow-up, 60% of the family therapy subjects had been charged with subsequent offenses versus 93% of the youths exposed to the standard treatment protocol. It is difficult, however, to view a 60% recidivism rate as an indication of program effectiveness.

Glick and Goldstein (1987) implemented an aggression control training program within a residential facility for delinquent youths and found that the treatment group performed better than controls on measures of acting-out, impulsivity, and social skills. They also found that the treatment group was rated as significantly improved in four of six areas of postdischarge community functioning.

Day et al. (1994) found significant and sustained improvement on behavioral ratings following a behaviorally oriented residential program for children aged 6–12 with conduct problems. Improved academic outcomes have also been found for youths following residential treatment compared to youths who received another form of treatment (Thompson et al., 1996).

In a recent residential treatment outcome study, Larzelere et al. (2001) found that a cognitive-behavioral residential treatment program produced improvements in residents' behavior ratings in various domains from admission to discharge. Many of these improvements were still apparent 10 months after discharge, and notably, there was more placement stability for these children who, prior to residential treatment, had a history of unstable living situations. The children who received residential treatment demonstrated a prolonged reduction in property offenses, aggression, and run-away attempts. There was little or no reduction, however, in the referral problems of substance use, truancy, fire setting, and lying. The residential program evaluated comprised individual, group, and family therapies, as well as special education. The program was psychoeducational in nature and also included an extensive contingency management system, behaviorally oriented social skills training, and opportunities for residents to practice acquired skills in the milieu. Emphasis was placed on generalizing skills to the postdischarge environment.

Brendtro and Wasmund (1989) reviewed functioning of positive peer-culture treatment programs in residential settings and concluded that such programs "can have a positive impact on individual youths in areas of self-esteem, personal responsibility, academic achievement, and prosocial values" (p. 94). Unfortunately, the studies they review provide little follow-up data, relying mostly on in-program psychometric change as evidence of improvement. A similar review of wilderness therapy programs (Bacon & Kimball, 1989) documents therapeutic changes in conduct-disordered youths following enrollment in such programs, including significant reduction in recidivism rates (Kelly, 1974; Kelly & Baer, 1968; Wilman & Chunn, 1973).

Garrett (1985) conducted a meta-analytic investigation of juvenile offenders treated in institutional or community residential (i.e., group home) programs. She found that behavioral treatment approaches were generally more effective than other approaches and that contingency management, family treatment, and cognitive-behavioral interventions were the most effective specific treatments. Overall, effect sizes were only marginally significant.

Whitehead and Lab (1989) also conducted a meta-analysis of juvenile correctional treatment. They included 50 outcome studies published from 1975 to 1984 in their analysis, excluding a number of others for reasons such as lack of objective data, failure to include a control group, and lack of clear specification of the treatment method. In this analysis, Whitehead and Lab included seven studies of what they classified as institutional/residential programs. Of these seven studies, four yielded negative phi coefficients, indicating an adverse effect of the treatment on the participants. Of the remaining three studies, only one (Adams & Vetter, 1982) had a statistically significant positive treatment effect. The authors concluded that their analysis provided "little encouragement" regarding the efficacy of residential/institutional treatment for conduct-disordered youths.

Bates, English, and Kouidou-Giles (1997) found the effects for structured residential treatment to be weak and not clearly better than those for unstructured therapeutic group homes or inpatient treatment. However, a problem with this review, as with most others in this area, is determining a clear definition of the treatment that was to be implemented and assessing whether or not it was enacted as prescribed.

Other broad-based meta-analytic studies of child mental health treatment outcome that have been done have largely ignored residential and inpatient treatment for conduct disorders as a specific variable. Casey and Berman (1985) reviewed 64 outcome studies of child treatment. Their sample included only 8% inpatients, but they did compute an effect size for the inpatient treatment group (0.42) that was significantly lower than the effect size found for outpatients (1.11). Weisz, Weiss, Alicke, and Klotz (1987) conducted another meta-analytic treatment outcome study, but they specifically excluded residential and inpatient interventions. Kazdin et al. (1990) conducted a meta-analysis of 105 child and adolescent treatment studies that included 3% inpatients and 1% incarcerated adolescents; however, although they reported an overall effect size of 0.88 compared to no treatment, they did not specifically analyze for an inpatient/residential treatment effect. Durlak, Fuhrman, and Lampman (1991) conducted a meta-analysis of 64 preadolescent treatment studies in which 19% of the subjects were in residential treatment; however, again, they did not specifically analyze for a residential treatment effect. Weisz, Weiss, Morton, Granger, and Han (1992), and Hazelrigg, Cooper, and Bourduin (1987) similarly conducted meta-analyses of child treatment studies that included participants in residential or inpatient treatment but did not analyze for a residential treatment effect.

A review of the literature evaluating residential and inpatient treatment for conduct disorder suggests that earlier studies generally cited positive effects of such treatment but that these results were less than convincing because of experimental design flaws, such as the failure to utilize comparable control groups, and the use of poorly defined, subjective outcome measures. More recent, better designed research indicates that residential treatment for conduct problems only inconsistently produces positive treatment outcomes from admissions to discharge, and that generalization of treatment to the postdischarge environment is questionable, with longer follow-up intervals producing less compelling results. Behavioral and cognitive-behavioral approaches have been shown to be more effective than other models of intervention, and several child and family characteristics are associated with positive treatment outcomes. These include higher IQ, more parental involvement in treatment, and the absence of psychotic or psychopathic behaviors. It is apparent that more research in this area is needed, with more detailed analysis of the effect of specific components of residential treatment on specific outcome measures, particularly in the child's postdischarge environment.

Investigating and understanding residential treatment outcomes has been a difficult undertaking, in part because of the numerous forms such treatment takes. Frensch and Cameron (2002) contend that, because of this difficulty, there has been a virtual lack of progress over time in evaluating such programs. Furthermore, studies that have shown positive treatment effects have been largely unable to isolate specific treatment strategies within the residential milieu that serve as the primary mechanisms of improvement. Regrettably, research has also indicated that behavioral improvements made in residential treatment tend to dissipate over time (Frensch & Cameron, 2002; Lyman & Campbell, 1996).

THE CASE OF "MIKE"
Conceptualization, Assessment, and Treatment Planning
Referral for residential treatment may be appropriate for Mike because of his worsening behavioral problems, previous unsuccessful attempts at outpatient treatment, and the presence of family discord. An alternative to such a referral would be home- or community-based treatments such as Homebuilders (Haapala, 1996) or multisystemic therapy (Henggeler et al., 1998); however,

for the purposes of this chapter, we will proceed with a discussion of residential treatment as applied to Mike's case.

Given Mike's IQ score (in the average range), cognitive-behavioral treatment approaches are appropriate, especially considering that the current trend in residential treatment is toward these behavioral and cognitive-behavioral interventions, and residential approaches incorporating behavioral emphases would likely result in improved performance for Mike while in treatment (Frensch & Cameron, 2002). However, there is no clear indication from the literature that such specific treatment strategies would automatically result in maintenance of emotional and behavioral gains after discharge from the residential setting. Instead, the involvement of the family support system during treatment and the stability of the postdischarge environment are the best predictors of a positive outcome for Mike after residential treatment (Frensch & Cameron, 2002). Therefore, an additional consideration for residential treatment is that the facility be in close proximity to Mike's family to allow exploration and treatment of underlying family issues.

Other Information

The initial intake, conducted in the form of interview and observation, would include an evaluation of Mike's mental status, discussion of the referral concerns and/or precipitating events, information regarding his treatment history, and gathering of other relevant background information to ensure that residential treatment would be appropriate (Hendren, 1991). Informed consent for the treatment would be obtained from Mike's parents and treatment procedures (i.e., residential milieu, classroom structure and objectives, psychotherapy, medications, other treatment modalities, and crisis-intervention procedures such as restraint and seclusion) would be discussed in detail with Mike and his family at the time of admission. Any necessary releases of information (e.g., Mike's previous school, probation officer, prior therapists) would also be obtained at this time.

Ideally, Mike would also be informed of his rights in the residential setting. In some treatment centers, these are posted in visible areas, and a copy is given to children in age-appropriate language. The rights communicated to Mike would include guarantees of "protection, sustenance, freedom from undue invasion of privacy, access to family and friends, respect for one's cultural and religious values, confidentiality, and treatment and other services that foster developmental progress" (Lyman & Campbell, 1996, p. 70).

Visits to the facility prior to admission, if feasible, might allow for a smoother transition to residential treatment for Mike and his family. Otherwise, admission procedures would include a tour of the facility, including recreational areas, living quarters, and classrooms. Mike would also meet his direct-care staff and other residents during this time. During, or shortly after admission, Mike would meet his individual therapist to begin establishing rapport. Many residential settings would also allow for Mike to bring important, yet safe, "transitional objects" from home to further ease his adjustment to the facility (Lyman & Campbell, 1996).

Therapeutic Goals

An important aspect of residential treatment based on cognitive-behavioral models is the development of a detailed, individualized treatment plan at admission. Treatment plans are most often geared toward goals or desired outcomes in presenting areas of concern. Mike's parents and, if deemed necessary by the court, his probation officer should be actively involved in the process of devising his treatment plan. A primary treatment emphasis for Mike would be decreasing his conduct-problem behaviors. Behavioral modification efforts will likely be effective in promoting positive behaviors for Mike within the treatment setting. However, much therapeutic effort should be geared toward cognitive and behavioral strategies that will help Mike to generalize improved behavioral choices to his natural environment. An additional treatment goal would target the factors in Mike's social context that promote substance use and to determine Mike's motivation to decrease substance use, as well as his social skills at resisting peer pressure. Such a concern could be addressed in individual, family, and group therapy sessions. Integrating the family into treatment and focusing on interventions to aid in family communication and reduce conflict would also be an important aspect of Mike's treatment.

Finally, treatment plans in residential settings often focus on recognizing and promoting a youngster's areas of strength or competency. For Mike, these strengths may become increasingly apparent as he is observed by staff in the residential setting and through discussions with him about his areas of interest and self-perceived competence. Even at admission, the treatment plan will most likely include some consideration of aftercare planning so that throughout Mike's placement, staff can implement strategies that will provide the best opportunity of success and maintenance of therapeutic gains postdischarge. Provisions for trial visits to Mike's home environment would also begin to be discussed at admission. The treatment plan would be reviewed with Mike as it is being developed, seeking his feedback, and it would be updated regularly during his placement.

Mike's treatment team would most likely consist of professionals from disciplines such as psychology, psychiatry, social work, and special education. In addition, consultation would likely be available from nutrition, pediatrics, neurology, speech and language, etc., as needed (Lyman & Campbell, 1996). Mike's previous assessment information, frequent assessment of his mood and mental status, as well as continued behavioral observations of him in treatment and while interacting with others, would inform the treatment team in terms of differential diagnosis and the need for specific intervention strategies.

Treatment Implications and Outcomes
Therapuetic Techniques and Strategies
The weekly schedule for Mike would include times for individual therapy, school, some form of expressive therapy, recreation, psychoeducational activities, and group therapy (Lyman & Campbell, 1996). For example, group therapy from a cognitive-behavioral model could focus specifically on increasing recognition of the connection between behaviors and consequences, social skills and communication, and improving emotional coping skills. However, group therapy can also provide an opportunity for residents to process their feelings regarding each other, the milieu, or other issues and to get feedback from same-aged peers regarding social, emotional, and behavioral issues. The classroom would likely involve self-paced lessons based on Mike's grade and achievement level. In many cases, direct-care staff would be available in the classroom to assist teachers in behavioral management. Mike's treatment goals can and should be targeted in each of his scheduled activities. His individual therapy work would likely include support regarding family and adjustment issues, as well as work on developing more constructive approaches to dealing with his anger.

Residential treatment often includes a trial of some form of psychotropic medication. The residential setting is often ideal for implementing this form of treatment, given the accessibility of the prescribing psychiatrist and the opportunity for close observation of the benefits and side effects of a given medication regimen. However, Mike's history does not clearly indicate areas for which medication might be helpful. Most likely, continued assessment and observation of Mike's attentional capabilities and affective state, including any signs of depression or mood swings, would occur before any determination would be made about need for medication.

As noted previously, Mike's parents would be included throughout treatment by their involvement in treatment planning and revision, planned visits to the treatment center, off-campus visits, parent support groups, if available, and education concerning Mike's emotional and behavioral issues, as well as any medication that might be recommended. In short, family interventions would be geared toward improving the family's support network, reducing conflict, improving communication, and psychological education, especially pertaining to child development (see Lyman & Campbell, 1996). Even though Mike's parents are divorced, his frequent contact with his non-custodial parent (i.e., father) would indicate the need for both parents to be engaged in all familial components of treatment. Mike's sense of continued connectedness to his family and community would be a crucial component of treatment.

There is also increasingly a move toward promoting a resident's active participation in treatment in the form of "challenges" (e.g., ropes courses, raising animals, etc.) that promote teamwork, seeking appropriate assistance from adults, and self-esteem based on actual accomplishments (Beker, 2001). The availability of such activities for Mike would greatly depend on the location of the residential treatment center and the available community resources. Presumably, such activities would also serve to decrease boredom, a particular issue for residents in Mike's general age group.

The therapeutic milieu itself is the most important component of Mike's residential treatment (Lyman & Campbell, 1996; Woolston, 1991). The daily and weekly schedule would likely be quite structured so that the general routine is predictable and to allow adequate time for transition between activities. At the same time, aspects of the schedule and programming need to be flexible enough to provide for unique opportunities (e.g., field trips, presentations) or special occasions (e.g., birthdays). That is, although the residential setting would be designed to provide a relatively high degree of structure, it should also be designed to provide children and adolescents with a set of experiences that could be considered as typical as possible for their age. On a day-to-day basis this is hopefully accomplished by the milieu functioning as a home would, with residents being allowed to decorate their rooms but also being responsible for basic chores such as keeping their rooms clean and putting away laundry to decrease their dependence on staff (Lyman & Campbell, 1996). Time would be allowed for meals, snacks, rest, recreation, hygiene, school, and treatment activities. For Mike's age group, schedules could be presented to each resident individually at the beginning of the week, given that they will likely understand the routine and concept of time.

Upon entry to the milieu, Mike would likely be given limited freedom or privilege options, and a great deal of external control would be provided by direct-care staff. Nevertheless, the number of explicitly stated rules should be few, clear, and enforceable (Lyman & Campbell, 1996). For adolescents in particular, it will be especially important for firm limits to be established regarding aggression and sexual acting-out. The rationale for such an approach at the beginning is to provide control for children and adolescents who presumably lack self-control and/or come from environments in which there was little consistency or clarity of behavioral expectations. Such clear expectations also help promote a sense of physical and psychological security (Lyman & Campbell, 1996). It will be important that the milieu be set up so that Mike can gradually earn more freedom and privileges as he makes further progress in the residential setting and his behavior warrants them. Furthermore, despite the clear expectations and methods of maintaining safety and control, the tone of the setting should be positive and nurturing, rather than punitive or repressive (Lyman & Campbell, 1996).

Positive reinforcement as a behavioral technique should be a central aspect of Mike's residential experience and likely would be effective in promoting behavioral gains (Murray & Sefchik, 1992). Provisions for positive reinforcement could include immediate rewards or could be comprised of more elaborate systems such as a token economy or a system of "levels," which involves increasingly attractive privileges as behavior is more appropriate and adaptive (Moss, 1994). The reinforcement schedule for Mike should be initially short term and focused on personal improvement so that the link between his behavior and positive consequences in the milieu becomes clear. With time, it would be expected that social reinforcers such as praise from staff or special activities with staff or peers would become more meaningful as Mike becomes more comfortable with his surroundings (Lyman & Campbell, 1996).

Redirection for inappropriate behavior should progress from the least intrusive possible method to the most intrusive method necessary. For example, selectively ignoring inappropriate attention-seeking behaviors might be effective if the behaviors are relatively minor and do not endanger anyone. Altercations involving Mike and his peers may require verbal redirection, problem solving, separation of the involved parties, or timeout. Timeout or other forms of seclusion should only be used when less intrusive methods have failed or cannot maintain the safety of the milieu. A debriefing of the incident should follow once consequences (e.g., timeout) are complete and/or the situation appears to have stabilized. Staff consistency in implementation of consequences and their ability to de-escalate conflicts, rather than to become engaged in them, will help Mike and his peers learn the consequences of their behaviors and also serve to model effective problem-solving skills.

As would have been described during Mike's intake interview, provisions for crisis management would also be in place for more severe episodes in which the safety of those on the residential unit might be compromised. The most common of such strategies involve physical restraint, seclusion, and ideally less often, chemical restraint. Seclusion could involve any procedure from isolating an individual in an area away from the group to placing an individual in a specified, locked room (Lyman & Campbell, 1996). Again, this procedure should be implemented only after less intrusive methods have failed and is utilized solely to prevent injury or help the individual gain self-control, not as a punishment (Lyman & Campbell, 1996). Behaviorally, there is little evidence supporting a therapeutic benefit to seclusion (Goren, Singh, & Best, 1993). In addition, seclusion carries a risk of injury to residents and staff, and Mike and his family should have been thoroughly advised of the use of crisis management and potential risks at intake (Blair, 1991).

Intensive staff training in the use of physical restraint (i.e., procedures involving some form of physical holding) is crucial for the safe implementation of this procedure. Such training may also involve staff trainees practicing restraint holds on each other. This strategy would likely increase safety in the use of restraint and allow staff to understand what it is like to be restrained. Should Mike, for example, require physical restraint, it has been suggested that staff send calming messages to him while implementing the restraint, remove any articles of clothing or objects from pockets that could pose a potential for self-injury (e.g., shoes/shoe laces), and intervene if there is any attempt by Mike at self-harm (Wherry, 1986). In addition, Wherry suggests that seclusion be implemented by staff more familiar with Mike, that they be aware of their feelings during all phases of the procedure, be aware of Mike's feelings, get other staff assistance only if needed, plan for removal of other residents from the situation, and debrief with Mike once the incident is over (see Lyman & Campbell, 1996).

Although there is no reported history of suicidality for Mike, provisions for suicide assessment and prevention would be provided for all residents. First and foremost, the physical environment should be safe in terms of areas of resident access and materials to which they may have access. The degree of suicide precaution for Mike individually would be determined at intake but also would be continually re-evaluated depending on his apparent mood and behavior on the unit. Staff communication during a crisis with suicidal residents should be supportive and oriented toward helping the individual cope with the precipitating issue(s) (Lyman & Campbell, 1996).

Initial individual and group therapy sessions should focus first on issues surrounding confidentiality, the importance of maintaining the confidentiality of other group members, and circumstances under which information given during therapy sessions would have to be shared with other staff and/or individuals outside the treatment center. Of course, it will also be important for therapists to establish rapport with Mike and to gauge his initial impressions of, and adjustment to, the residential setting. Any concerns regarding implementation of behavioral management and crisis-intervention strategies raised by Mike should be taken seriously and, depending on the potential risk of harm indicated, should be communicated to the treatment team and staff. As therapists and staff get to know Mike, they can shape their interventions and interactions with him toward his specific strengths and interests (e.g., sports). Interactions between staff and residents will be enhanced through staff communication at shift change regarding Mike's performance so far that day, his strengths, and areas of concern.

Mechanisms of Change

Overall, the available literature suggests that a cognitive-behavioral treatment within the residential milieu would likely result in behavioral and emotional improvements for Mike while in treatment. Nevertheless, it will be critical for treatment to also focus on the environment (especially the family) to which Mike will return and to plan for less restrictive follow-up interventions after discharge.

REFERENCES

Adams, R., & Vetter, H. J. (1982). Social structure and psychodrama outcome: A ten-year follow-up. *Journal of Offender Counseling, Services, and Rehabilitation, 6,* 111–119.

Allen, L. J., Howard, V. F., Sweeney, W. J., & McLaughlin, T. F. (1993). Use of contingency contracting to increase on-task behavior with primary students. *Psychological Reports, 72,* 905–906.

Bacon, S. B., & Kimball, R. (1989). The wilderness challenge model. In R. D. Lyman, S. Prentice-Dunn, & S. Gabel (Eds.), *Residential and inpatient treatment of children and adolescents.* New York: Plenum Press.

Barker, P. (1993). The future of residential treatment for children. In C. E. Schaefer, & A. J. Swanson (Eds.), *Children in residential care: Critical issues in treatment* (pp. 1–16). Northvale, NJ: Jason Aronson.

Barton, C., Alexander, J. F., Waldron, H., Turner, C. W., & Warburton, J. (1985). Generalizing treatment effects of functional family therapy: Three replications. *American Journal of Family Therapy, 13,* 16–26.

Bates, B. C., English, D. J., & Kouidou-Giles, S. (1997). Residential treatment and its alternatives: A review of the literature. *Child and Youth Care Forum, 26,* 7–51.

Bath, H. L., Richey, C. A., & Haapala, D. A. (1992). Child age and outcome correlates in intensive family preservation services. *Children and Youth Services Review, 14,* 389–406.

Beker, J. (2001). Back to the future: Effective residential group care and treatment for children and youth and the Fritz Redl legacy. *Child and Youth Care Forum, 30,* 443–455.

Bettelheim, B. (1950). *Love is not enough.* New York: Free Press.

Bettelheim, B. (1974). *A home for the heart.* New York: Knopf.

Bettelheim, B., & Sanders, J. (1979). Milieu therapy: The Orthogenic School model. In J. D. Noshipitz (Ed.), *Basic handbook of child psychiatry* (Vol. 3, pp. 216–230). New York: Basic Books.

Blair, D. T. (1991). Assaultive behavior: Does it begin in the front office? *Journal of Psychosocial Nursing, 5,* 21–26.

Blase, K. A., Fixsen, D. L., Freeborn, K., & Jaeger, D. (1989). The behavioral model. In R. D. Lyman, S. Prentice-Dunn, & S. Gabel (Eds.), *Residential and inpatient treatment of children and adolescents* (pp. 43–59). New York: Plenum Press.

Braukmann, C. J., Kirigin, K. A., & Wolf, M. W. (1976, August). *Achievement place: The researchers perspective.* Paper presented at the annual meeting of the American Psychological Association, Washington, DC.

Brendtro, L. K., & Wasmund, W. (1989). The peer culture model. In R. D. Lyman, S. Prentice-Dunn, & S. Gabel (Eds.), *Residential and inpatient treatment of children and adolescents* (pp. 81–96). New York: Plenum Press.

Buehler, R. E., Patterson, G. R., & Furniss, J. M. (1966). The reinforcement of behavior in institutional settings. *Behavioral Research and Therapy, 4,* 157–167.

Burton, L. M. (1981). A critical analysis and review of the research on Outward Bound and related programs (Doctorial dissertation, Rutgers University, 1981). *Dissertation Abstracts International, 42,* 1581B.

Carlson, B. E., Barr, W. B., & Young, K. J. (1994). Factors associated with treatment outcomes of male adolescents. In G. Northrup (Ed.), *Applied research in residential treatment* (pp. 39–58). New York: Haworth.

Casey, R. J., & Berman, J. S. (1985). The outcome of psychotherapy with children. *Psychological Bulletin, 98,* 388–400.

Cavior, H. E., & Schmidt, A. A. (1978). Test of the effectiveness of a differential treatment strategy at the Robert F. Kennedy Center. *Criminal Justice and Behavior, 5,* 131–139.

Conway, J. B., & Bucher, B. D. (1976). Transfer and maintenance of behavior change in children: A review and suggestions. In J. Mash, L. A. Hamenlynck, & L. C. Handy (Eds.), *Behavior modification and families* (pp. 119–159). New York: Brunner/Mazel.

Dalton, R., Bolding, D. D., Woods, J., & Daruna, J. H. (1987). Short-term psychiatric hospitialization of children. *Hospital and Community Psychiatry, 38,* 973–976.

Day, D. M., Pal, A., & Goldberg, K. (1994). Assessing the post-residential functioning of latency-aged conduct disordered children. *Residential Treatment for Children and Youth, 11,* 45–61.

DuPaul, G. J., & Eckert, T. L. (1997). The effects of school-based interventions for attention-deficit/hyperactivity disorder: A meta-analysis. *School Psychology Review, 26,* 5–27.

Durlak, J. A., Fuhrman, T., & Lampman, C. (1991). Effectiveness of cognitive-behavior therapy for maladapting children: A meta-analysis. *Psychological Bulletin, 110,* 202–214.

Everett, C. A., & Volgy, S. S. (1993). Treating the child in systemic family therapy. In T. K. Kratochwil, & R. J. Morris (Eds.), *Handbook of psychotherapy with children and adolescents* (pp. 247–257). Boston: Allyn & Bacon.

Flackett, J. M., & Flackett, G. (1970). Criswell House: An alternative to institutional treatment for juvenile offenders. *Federal Probation, 34*, 30–37.

Freedman, A. M., Kaplan, H. I., & Sadock, B. J. (1972). Child psychiatry: Introduction. In A. M. Freedman, H. I. Kaplan, & B. J. Sadock (Eds.), *Modern synopsis of comprehensive textbook of psychiatry* (pp. 574–583). Baltimore: Williams & Wilkins.

Frensch, K. M., & Cameron, G. (2002). Treatment of choice or last resort? A review of residential mental health placements for children and youth. *Child and Youth Care Forum, 31*, 307–339.

Friman, P. C., Toner, C., Soper, S., Sinclair, J., & Shanahan, D. (1996). Maintaining placement for troubled and disruptive adolescents in voluntary residential care: The role of reduced youth-to-staff ratio. *Journal of Child and Family Studies, 5*, 337–347.

Gabel, S. (1989). Outpatient treatment as an alternative to residential treatment or inpatient hospitalization. In R. D. Lyman, S. Prentice-Dunn, & S. Gabel (Eds.), *Residential and inpatient treatment of children and adolescents* (pp. 147–161). New York: Plenum Press.

Garrett, C. J. (1985). Effects of residential treatment on adjudicated delinquents: A meta-analysis. *Journal of Research in Crime and Delinquency, 22*, 287–308.

Ghuman, H. S., & Sardes, M. D. (1998). *Handbook of child and adolescent outpatient, day treatment, and community psychiatry.* New York: Brunner/Mazel.

Gibson, P. (1981). The effects of and the correlates of success in a wilderness therapy program for problem youths (Doctoral dissertation, Columbia University, 1981). *Dissertation Abstracts International, 42*, 140A.

Glick, B., & Goldstein, A. P. (1987). Aggression replacement training. *Journal of Counseling and Development, 65*, 356–362.

Goren, S., Singh, N. N., & Best, A. M. (1993). The aggression-coercion cycle: Use of seclusion and restraint in a child psychiatric hospital. *Journal of Child and Family Studies, 2*, 61–73.

Grizenko, N., & Papineau, D. (1992). A comparison of the cost-effectiveness of day treatment and residential treatment for children with severe behavior problems. *Canadian Journal of Psychiatry, 37*, 393–400.

Haapala, D. A. (1996). The Homebuilders model: An evolving service approach for families. In M. C. Roberts (Ed.), *Model programs in child and family mental health* (pp. 295–315). Mahwah, NJ: Erlbaum.

Haapala, D. A., & Kinney, J. M. (1988). Avoiding out-of-home placement of high-risk status offenders through the use of intensive home-base family preservation services. *Criminal Justice and Behavior, 15*, 334–348.

Hazelrigg, M. D., Cooper, H. M., & Bourduin, C. M. (1987). Evaluating the effectiveness of family therapies: An integrative review and analysis. *Psychological Bulletin, 101*, 428–442.

Hendren, R. L. (1991). Determining the need for inpatient treatment. In R. L. Hendren, & I. N. Berlin (Eds.), *Psychiatric inpatient care of children and adolescents: A multicultural approach* (pp. 37–65). New York: Wiley.

Henggeler, S. W., Schoenwald, S. K., Borduin, C. M., Rowland, W. M., & Cunningham, P. B. (1998). *Multisystemic treatment of antisocial behavior in children and adolescents*. New York: Guilford Press.

Hobbs, N. (1966). Helping disturbed children: Psychological and ecological strategies. *American Psychologist, 21*, 1105–1151.

Husey, D. L., & Guo, S. (2002). Profile characteristics and behavioral change trajectories of young residential children. *Journal of Child and Family Studies, 11*, 401–410.

Jenson, J. M., & Whittaker, J. K. (1989). Partners in care: Involving parents in children's residential treatment. In R. D. Lyman, S. Prentice-Dunn, & S. Gabel (Eds.), *Residential and inpatient treatment of children and adolescents* (pp. 207–227). New York: Plenum Press.

Jesness, C. F. (1971). The Preston Typology Study: An experiment with differential treatment in an institution. *Journal of Research in Crime and Delinquency, 8*, 38–52.

Jesness, C. F. (1975). Comparative effectiveness of behavior modification and transactional analysis programs for delinquents. *Journal of Consulting and Clinical Psychology, 43*, 758–779.

Johnson, C. R. (1995). Unit structure and behavioral programming. In R. T. Ammerman, & M. Hersen (Eds.), *Handbook of child behavior therapy in the psychiatric setting* (pp. 133–149). New York: Wiley.

Jones, R. N., & Downing, R. H. (1991). Assessment of the use of timeout in an inpatient child psychiatry treatment unit. *Behavioral Residential Treatment, 6*, 219–230.

Kazdin, A. E., Bass, D., Ayers, W. A., & Rodgers, A. (1990). Empirical and clinical focus of child and adolescent psychotherapy research. *Journal of Consulting and Clinical Psychology, 58*, 729–740.

Kelly, F. (1974). Outward bound and delinquency: A ten-year experience. Paper presented at the Conference on Experimental Education. Estes Park, CO.

Kelly, F., & Baer, D. (1968). *Outward bound schools as an alternative to institutionalization for adolescent delinquent boys*. Boston: Fardel.

Kinney, J. M., Madsen, B., Fleming, T., & Haapala, D. A. (1977). Homebuilders: Keeping families together. *Journal of Consulting and Clinical Psychology, 45*, 667–673.

Kirigin, K. A., Braukmann, C. J., Atwater, J. D., & Wolf, M. M. (1982). An evaluation of teaching-family (Achievement Place) group houses for juvenile offenders. *Journal of Applied Behavior Analysis, 15*, 1–16.

Landsman, M. J., Groza, V., Tyler, M., & Malone, K. (2001). Outcomes of family-centered residential treatment. *Child Welfare, 80*, 351–379.

Larzelere, R. E., Dinges, K., Schmidt, M. D., Spellman, D. F., Criste, T. R., & Connell, P. (2001). Outcomes of residential treatment: A study of the adolescent clients of girls and boys town. *Child and Youth Care Forum, 30*, 175–185.

Lazarus, A. (1960). The elimination of children's phobias by deconditioning. In H. J. Eysenck (Ed.), *Behavior therapy and the neuroses* (pp. 114–122). New York: Pergamon Press.

Lewis, W. W. (1982). Ecological factors in successful residential treatment. *Behavioral Disorders, 7,* 49–56.

Lewis, W. W. (1988). The role of ecological variables in residential treatment. *Behavioral Disorders, 13,* 98–107.

Lewis, W. W., & Lewis, B. L. (1989). The psychoeducational model: Cumberland House after 25 years. In R. D. Lyman, S. Prentice-Dunn, & S. Gabel (Eds.), *Residential and inpatient treatment of children and adolescents* (pp. 97–113). New York: Plenum Press.

Lochman, J. E., Lampron, L. B., Gemmer, T. C., & Harris, S. R. (1987). Anger-coping interventions for aggressive children: Guide to implementation in school settings. In P. A. Keller, & S. Heyman (Eds.), *Innovation in clinical practice: A source book* (Vol. 6, pp. 339–356). Sarasota, FL: Professional Resource Exchange.

Lyman, R. D., & Campbell, N. R. (1996). *Treating children and adolescents in residential and inpatient settings.* Thousand Oaks, CA: Sage.

Lyman, R. D., Prentice-Dunn, S., & Wilson, D. R. (1995). Behavioral day treatment as an alternative to residential or inpatient treatment. *Continuum, 2,* 71–83.

MacKenzie, D. L. (1993). Boot Camp Prisons in 1993. *National Institute of Justice Journal, 227*(November), 21–24.

MacKenzie, D. L. (1994). Boot camps: A national assessment. *Overcrowded Times,* 5,1.

Marc, D. L., & MacDonald, L. (1988). Respite care: Who uses it? *Mental Retardation, 26*(2), 93–96.

Marion, M. (1994). Encouraging the development of responsible anger management in young children. *Early Child Development and Care, 97,* 155–163.

Matson, J. L., Manikam, R., & Ladatto, J. (1990). A long-term follow-up of a recreate the scene, DRO, overcorrection, and lemon juice therapy program for severe aggressive biting. *Scandinavian Journal of Behavior Therapy, 19,* 33–38.

McNeil, E. (1962). Forty years of childhood: The University of Michigan Fresh Air Camp, 1921–1961. *Michigan Quarterly Review, 1,* 112–118.

Moore, L. M., & O'Connor, T. W. (1991). A psychiatric residential centre for children and adolescents: A pilot study of its patient characteristics and improvement while resident. *Child: Care, Health, and Development, 17,* 235–242.

Moss, G. R. (1994). A biobehavioral perspective on the hospital treatment of adolescents. In P. W. Corrigan, & R. P. Liberman (Eds.), *Behavior therapy in psychiatric hospitals* (pp. 109–127). New York: Springer Publishing Co.

Murray, L., & Sefchik, G. (1992). Regulating behavior management practice in residential treatment facilities. *Children and Youth Services Review, 14,* 519–539.

O'Connor, K. J. (1991). *The play therapy primer: An integration of theories and techniques.* New York: Wiley.

Ogles, B. M., Trout, S. C., Gillespie, D. K., & Penkert, K. S. (1998). Managed care as a platform for cross-system integration. *Journal of Behavioral Health Services & Research, 25*, 252–268.

Ollendick, T. H., Hagopian, L. P., & Huntzinger, R. M. (1991). Cognitive-behavior therapy with nighttime fearful children. *Journal of Behavior Therapy and Experimental Psychiatry, 22*, 113–121.

Osler, M. W. (1991, March). Shock incarceration: Hard realities and real possibilities. *Federal Probation*, pp. 34–42.

Perry, R. (1989). The medical inpatient model. In R. D. Lyman, S. Prentice-Dunn, & S. Gabel (Eds.), *Residential and inpatient treatment of children and adolescents* (pp. 61–79). New York: Plenum Press.

Phillips, E. L., Phillips, E. A., Fixsen, D. L., & Wolf, M. M. (1972). *The teaching family handbook*. Lawrence: University of Kansas Printing Service.

Plouffe, M. M. (1981). A longitudinal analysis of the personality and behavioral effects of participation in the Connecticut Wilderness School: A program for delinquent and pre-delinquent youth (Doctoral dissertation, University of Connecticut, 1981). *Dissertation Abstracts International, 41*(12-B), 4683.

Polsky, H. W. (1961). *Cottage six: The social system of delinquent boys in residential treatment*. New York: Sage.

Polsky, H. W., & Claster, D. S. (1968). *The dynamics of residential treatment: A social system analysis*. Chapel Hill: University of North Carolina Press.

Powers, S. W. (2001). Behavior therapy with children. In C. E. Walker, & M. C. Roberts (Eds.), *Handbook of Clinical Child Psychology* (3rd ed., pp. 825–839). New York: Wiley.

Prentice-Dunn, S., Wilson, D. R., & Lyman, R. D. (1981). Client factors related to outcome in a residential and day treatment program for children. *Journal of Clinical Child Psychology, 10*, 188–191.

Quinn, K., & Epstein, M. H. (1998). Characteristics of children, youth, and families served by interagency systems of care. In M. H. Epstein, K. Kutash, & A. Duchnowski (Eds.), *Outcomes of children and youth with emotional and behavioral disorders and their families* (pp. 81–114). Austin, TX: Pro-Ed.

Raush, H. L., Dittman, A. T., & Taylor, J. J. (1959). The interpersonal behavior of children in residential treatment. *Journal of Abnormal and Social Psychology, 58*, 9–26.

Redl, F. (1966). *When we deal with children*. New York: Free Press.

Richards, A. (1981). *Kurt Hahn: The midwife of educational ideas*. Unpublished doctoral dissertation, University of Colorado, Boulder.

Rickard, H. C., & Dinoff, M. (Eds.). (1974). *Behavior modification in children: Case studies and illustrations from a summer camp*. Oxford, UK: University of Alabama Press.

Rickard, H. C., & Lattal, K. A. (1969). Group problem-solving in therapeutic summer camp: An illustration. *Adolescence, 4*, 320–332.

Roberts, M. W., & Powers, S. W. (1990). Adjusting chair timeout enforcement procedures for oppositional children. *Behavior Therapy, 21*, 257–271.

Ross, A. O. (1964). Learning theory and therapy with children. *Psychotherapy: Theory, Research and Practice, 1*, 102–108.

Russ, S. W., & Freedheim, D. K. (2001). Psychotherapy with children. In C. E. Walker, & M. C. Roberts (Eds.), *Handbook of Clinical Child Psychology* (3rd ed., pp. 840–859). New York: Wiley.

Sayger, T. V. (2001). Family psychology and therapy. In C. E. Walker & M. C. Roberts (Eds.), *Handbook of clinical child psychology* (3rd ed., pp. 860–880). New York: Wiley.

Seng, M. J. (1989). Child sexual abuse and adolescent prostitution: A comparative analysis. *Adolescence, 24*(95), 665–675.

Shure, M. B. (1992). *I can problem solve (ICPS): An interpersonal cognitive problem solving program*. Champaign, IL: Research Press.

Silver, S. E., Duchnowski, A. J., Kutash, K., Friedman, R. M., Eisen, M., Prange, M. E., Brandenburg, N. A., & Greenbaum, P. E. (1992). A comparison of children with serious emotional disturbance served in residential and school settings. *Journal of Child and Family Studies, 1*, 43–59.

Spence, S. H., & Marzillier, J. S. (1981). Social skills training with adolescent male offenders: Short-term, long-term, and generalized effects. *Behavior Research and Therapy, 19*, 349–368.

Stamm, I. (1989). A psychoanalytic model. In R. D. Lyman, S. Prentice-Dunn, & S. Gabel (Eds.), *Residential and inpatient treatment of children and adolescents* (pp. 25–42). New York: Plenum Press.

Swain, J. J., Allard, G. B., & Holborn, S. W. (1982). The good toothbrushing game: A school-based dental hygiene program for increasing the toothbrushing effectiveness of children. *Journal of Applied Behavior Analysis, 15*, 171–176.

Thompson, R. W., Smith, G. L., Osgood, D. W., Dowd, T. P., Friman, P. C., & Daly, D. L. (1996). Residential care: A study of short- and long-term educational effects. *Child and Youth Services Review, 18*, 221–242.

Timbers, G. (1990). Describing the children served in treatment homes. In P. Meadowcroft, & B. A. Trout (Eds.), *Troubled youth in treatment homes: A handbook of therapeutic foster care* (pp. 21–32). Washington, DC: C.W.L.A.

Trieschman, A. E., Whittaker, J. K., & Brendtro, L. K. (1969). *The other 23 hours*. Chicago: Aldine.

VanDenBerg, J. E. (1993). Integration of individualized mental health services into the system of care for children and adolescents. *Administration and Policy in Mental Health, 20*, 247–257.

Velasquez, J. S., & Lyle, C. G. (1985). Day versus residential treatment for juvenile offenders: The impact of program evaluation. *Child Welfare, 64*, 145–156.

Vorrath, H. H., & Brendtro, L. K. (1974). *Positive peer culture*. Chicago: Aldine.

Weinman, K. (1984). Encouraging youth in shelter care. *Individual Psychology: Journal of Adlerian Theory, Research and Practice, 40*, 212–216.

Weinrott, M. R., Jones, R. R., & Howard, J. R. (1982). Cost-effectiveness of teaching family programs for delinquents: Results of a national evaluation. *Evaluation Review, 6*, 173–201.

Weinstein, L. (1969). Project Re-Ed schools for emotionally disturbed children: Effectiveness as viewed by referring agencies, parents, and teachers. *Exceptional Children, 35,* 703–711.

Weinstein, L. (1974). *Evaluation of a program for re-educating disturbed children: A follow-up comparison with untreated children* (Final Report to the Bureau for the Education of the Handicapped, Project Nos. 6-2974, 552023). Washington, DC: U.S. Department of Health, Education & Welfare.

Weisz, J. R., & Walter, B. R., Weiss, B., Fernandez, G. A., & Mikow, V. A. (1990). Arrests among emotionally disturbed violent and assaultive individuals following minimal versus lengthy intervention through North Carolina's Willie M. Program. *Journal of Consulting and Clinical Psychology, 58,* 720–728.

Weisz, J. R., & Weiss, B. (1993). *Effects of psychotherapy with children and adolescents.* Thousand Oaks, CA: Sage.

Weisz, J. R., Weiss, B., Alicke, M. D., & Klotz, M. L. (1987). Effectiveness of psychotherapy with children and adolescents: A meta-analysis for clinicians. *Journal of Consulting and Clinical Psychology, 55,* 542–549.

Weisz, J. R., Weiss, B., Morton, T., Granger, D., & Han. S. (1992). *Meta-analysis of psychotherapy outcome research with children and adolescents.* Unpublished manuscript, University of California, Los Angeles.

Wherry, J. N. (1986). The therapeutic use of seclusion with children and adolescents. *Residential Treatment for Children & Youth, 4,* 51–61.

Whitehead, J. T., & Lab, S. P. (1989). A meta-analysis of juvenile correctional treatment. *Journal of Research in Crime and Delinquency, 26,* 276–295.

Whittaker, J. K. (1979). *Caring for troubled children.* San Francisco: Jossey-Bass.

Whittaker, D., Archer, L., & Hicks, L. (1998). *Working in children's homes: Challenges and complexities.* New York: John Wiley and Sons.

Wilman, H. C., & Chunn, F. Y. (1973). Homeward bound: An alternative to the institutionalization of adjudicated juvenile offenders. *Federal Probation, 37,* 52–57.

Wilson, D. R., & Lyman, R. D. (1982). Time-out in the treatment of childhood behavior problems: Implementation and research issues. *Child and Family Behavior Therapy, 4,* 5–20.

Winsberg, B. G., Bialer, I., Kupietz, S., Botti, E., & Balka, E. B. (1980). Home vs. hospital care of children with behavior disorders: A controlled investigation. *Archives of General Psychiatry, 37,* 412–418.

Wolpe, J. (1958). *Psychotherapy by reciprocal inhibition.* Stanford, CA: Stanford University Press.

Woolston, J. L. (1991). Psychiatric inpatient services for children. In M. Lewis (Ed.), *Child and adolescent psychiatry: A comprehensive textbook* (pp. 890–894). Baltimore: Williams & Wilkins.

Young, R. A. (1939). A summer camp as an integral part of a psychiatric clinic. *Mental Hygiene, 23,* 241–256.

CHAPTER 10

Psychopharmacologic Considerations in the Treatment of Conduct Disorder

Douglas Mossman and Christina G. Weston

THE TREATMENT MODEL

Although most child therapists practice eclectically, they usually describe their treatments as following a particular model—psychodynamic, cognitive-behavioral, family therapy, etc.—that informs how they conceptualize children's emotional and behavioral problems. In deciding whether pharmacological therapy might help Michael, a child psychiatrist ideally would apply several conceptual models simultaneously. But this does not mean that, if asked, the psychiatrist would *explicitly* endorse all, or even one, of these models as having guided his pharmacological treatment plan. During their training, physicians focus on learning about what works, and they receive little or no instruction about theories of what works. Because of this, models of treatment often operate implicitly, without the practitioner being aware of their influence. Yet, if the following four treatment models were presented to our child psychiatric colleagues, most would endorse the models as capturing, in abstract terms, the kinds of factors that underlie their concrete recommendations about specific medications.

The Biopsychosocial Model
The biopsychosocial model is a viewpoint on the nature of illness most closely associated with George Engel (Engel, 1977, 1980). Engel maintained that

any comprehensive, scientific account of medical disorders must recognize that such conditions emerge within individuals who are part of a system. The system has increasingly complex subpersonal elements (atoms, molecules, cells, and organ systems) and suprapersonal contexts (family, community, culture, and society) that can be regarded as having a hierarchical organization. At each point in the hierarchy, lower levels are necessary but not sufficient to describe or explain the phenomena that we observe.

As a practical matter, psychiatrists know that for some mental disorders —for example, schizophrenia and manic-depressive illness—psychotropic medication is the mainstay of successful treatment, without which psychological and social interventions may be futile. Yet the biopsychosocial model reminds psychiatrists that psychotropic drugs usually are only partial solutions to the problems that ail their patients, which means that in most cases, medications should constitute just one aspect of a patient's treatment plan. Ideally, medication is a biological intervention that complements other treatment interventions that address the patient's emotions and behavior, and the family, educational, and social contexts in which the patient lives.

In Michael's case, a child psychiatrist should remember that whatever physical impact drugs might have on the youth's nervous system, a prescription for medication also conveys nonbiological messages. For example, a prescription for Michael suggests that the interpersonal conflicts that led to the consultation reflect something that is "wrong" with Michael as an individual, rather than a dysfunction in the mother–son dyad or a child's reaction to his parents' separation and divorce. Michael's presentation for evaluation followed his having broken the law, yet a prescription for medication will redefine his delinquency as a manifestation of an individual's improperly functioning nervous system. Finally, because Michael is a minor, the decision whether to accept the medication will be his mother's, not his; prescribing medication thus reinforces Michael's membership in a category that is legally and socially subordinate.

The Medical Model
The medical model of illness gives psychiatrists a second set of principles that shape prescribing decisions. The term "medical model" often is used pejoratively, implying a compassionless approach to medicine that mistakenly reduces human illness to biological processes, and that mistakenly reduces the physician's task to diagnosing diseases and providing drugs or surgery to "cure" them. In fact, the medical model, as applied to addictions or other behavioral problems, embodies a compassionate view of the sufferer: his problems are regarded as disorders analogous to physical conditions, rather

than moral defects. This implies that a patient's problems require and should be addressed by therapy, not moral condemnation and punishment. Thus, a psychiatrist applying the medical model to Michael's misbehavior (e.g., his shoplifting and fighting) will regard this as a matter that can be treated rather than something that, for example, should simply be discouraged with stern admonitions.

The medical model also tells psychiatrists that diagnoses matter. In modern clinical medicine, diagnoses and treatment rest on understanding the pathology that underlies observed signs and symptoms. In most medical specialties, physicians employ a remarkable array of tests—including chemical evaluations of body fluids, imaging tissues with X-ray, and ultrasound technologies, biopsies, and genetic analyses—to make diagnoses and to evaluate the progress of treatment. Thoughtful child psychiatrists are painfully aware of the imperfections in current schemes for diagnosing mental disorders and the near-absence of psychiatric diagnostic technologies. Nonetheless, most of us believe that current psychiatric diagnoses have some practical utility: accurate psychiatric diagnoses (however imperfect they currently are) provide some information about the expected course of an ailment and what treatments might be expected to alleviate that ailment (Robins & Guze, 1970). Thus, one of the chief tasks of a psychiatrist evaluating Michael's need for psychotropic will be to discern whether Michael has any diagnosable disorder for which medication typically is effective.

By itself, conduct disorder is not a condition for which psychiatrists can offer a medication that delivers much improvement. That is why a psychiatrist seeing Michael will likely wonder, "Is there anything else going on?" Many children with conduct problems have comorbid disorders that may contribute to some of their delinquent acts (Loeber, Burke, Lahey, Winters, & Zera, 2000); for example, if delinquent acts are but one manifestation of a broader problem with impulsiveness and inattentiveness, this suggests that the conduct problems are features of attention deficit/hyperactivity disorder, and that taking medication for ADHD might help the child reduce his misbehavior. Such a finding is all the more significant in view of the data suggesting that many children with conduct disorder have ADHD (Loeber et al., 2000), that those children whose conduct disorder is complicated by ADHD have poorer outcomes (Satterfield & Schell, 1997), and that boys who have ADHD are more likely to develop conduct disorder at an earlier age than those who do not have ADHD (Loeber, Green, Keenan, & Lahey, 1995). Also, having conduct disorder increases the risk of developing other disorders in the future. In one study, 35% of children with conduct disorder were later found to have ADHD (Offord et al., 1992). In a longitudinal study of the prevalence of psychiatric disorders, conduct disorder occurred in 9% of the children by age 16, and was comorbid most often with depressive disorders, substance use disorders, and ADHD (Costello, Mustillo, Erkanli, Keeler, & Angold, 2003). Some children who are depressed "just don't care" about consequences and do "whatever they want;" for these children, antidepressant therapy may alleviate conduct problems along with dysphoric mood.

The Psychopharmacological Model

A third model implicitly invoked by child psychiatrists relates to the ways in which psychotropic medications work. Although physicians do not understand as much about how psychotropic drugs work as we understand, for example, about the reasons that antibiotics are effective, we do know much more than we did 40 years ago—a time when many still-used medications were prescribed mainly because doctors knew *that* they worked, if not *why* they worked.

Most currently prescribed psychotropic drugs exert their effects by influencing or altering the ways *neurotransmitters* interact with the brain's nerve cells, or neurons. Neurotransmitters are substances (usually molecules) that convey signals between neurons. These substances typically are synthesized in neurons and stored in *terminals* before being released into *synapses*, or regions between nerves. There, the neurotransmitters interact with other neurons typically by binding to *receptors* on those other neurons. This binding action sets in motion one or more of a series of events. Examples include transmission of electrical signals along the cell surface and altering synthesis of proteins, RNA, and compounds within the cells to which the neurotransmitter binds (Wilcox, Gonzales, & Miller, 1998).

Most current psychotropic drugs act by altering the actions of one or more of just a few neurotransmitters: dopamine, serotonin, norepinephrine, acetylcholine, and γ-aminobutyric acid. For example, antipsychotic drugs (used in the treatment of many psychiatric disorders, including schizophrenia) block the action of dopamine at receptors, while stimulants (e.g., amphetamine, used to treat attentional problems and hyperactivity) enhance release of dopamine into the synapse. The psychopharmacological model tells psychiatrists that psychotropic medications reduce or eliminate symptoms of mental disorders by virtue of their effects on neuronal transmission. However, medications do not "cure,"—that is, solve the underlying problem that has caused those disorders.

The psychopharmacological model also tells psychiatrists that certain drugs are likely to have beneficial effects on specific types of symptoms irrespective of a patient's diagnosis. For example, antipsychotic drugs will attenuate or stop many patients' psychotic symptoms (e.g., hallucinations and delusions), whether those symptoms occur during an episode of schizophrenia, mania, or depression. A few studies suggest that atypical antipsychotics and divalproex sodium, which have antiaggressive actions in mania and schizophrenia, also alleviate aggression in children with conduct disorder (McDougle, Stigler, & Posey, 2003; Steiner, Petersen, Saxena, Ford, & Matthews, 2003).

Whether children with conduct disorders have specific neurotransmitter abnormalities is a matter that is not yet clearly understood. Some studies point to abnormalities in the activity of norepinephrine and dopamine (Lahey, McBurnett, Loeber, & Hart, 1995; Rogeness, 1994). Other studies point to relationships among aggression, serotonin, and whether the onset of conduct disorder occurs in childhood or adolescence (Unis et al., 1997). These studies point to possible biological underpinnings that may contribute to aggression in conduct disorder, and may suggest potential avenues for psychopharmacologic treatments. For example, three recent double-blind studies have found that risperidone, an antipsychotic drug that interacts with dopamine and serotonin receptors, can reduce aggression behavior in children with conduct disorder (Aman, De Smedt, Derivan, Lyons, & Findling, 2002; Findling et al., 2000; Snyder et al., 2002). It should be noted, however, that research has not yet demonstrated whether pharmacologically lowered scores on measures of aggression are associated with reduced frequency of rule violations, incarceration, or other undesirable social outcomes associated with having conduct disorder.

The psychopharmacological model also reminds psychiatrists that nicotine and marijuana are psychotropic drugs. Nicotine probably has little impact on Michael's mood, but if he is addicted to the substance, this may help explain why he repeatedly has smoked cigarettes in the school bathroom. Marijuana is usually not addictive, but Michael's frequent use may play a significant role in his mood problems, irritability, and volatility. Also, continued use of marijuana may subvert any therapeutic interventions, including pharmacological treatments.

The Developmental Model

A final set of considerations informing child psychopharmacology relate to the patient's age, emotional and physical growth, social maturity, and all the other features of what mental health clinicians call "childhood development." Some of Michael's presenting problems—curfew violations and truancy—represent his failure to adhere to age-appropriate expectations for American youths in the 21st century, but would not be problems if he were a few years older. At

13 years of age, Michael's needs for parental care and nurture are susceptible to disruption by divorce, and his reactions to this event will be very different than would be the case if he were in early latency or late adolescence.

Level of development affects not only how a child reacts to events, but also how clinical syndromes display themselves. Preadolescent children, typically, will not describe themselves as "depressed," although they may feel tired, have crying spells, look sad, and think about suicide. The information requested from and obtained during a psychiatric interview with Michael should reflect what things Michael is developmentally capable of describing as well as how psychiatric symptoms manifest themselves in young teenage boys.

Psychiatrists now know that many major mental illnesses, including manic-depression, have a median age of onset during adolescence, and that most psychiatric problems that come to clinical attention during adulthood have antecedents earlier in the patient's life. Oftentimes, the adolescent emotional and behavioral problems that augur the onset of severe mental illnesses in adults become clear only in retrospect. This is particularly true in the case of conduct disorder and oppositional defiant disorder (ODD). A recent study by Kim-Cohen and colleagues found that among adults with serious mental disorders, 25–60% turn out to have met criteria for conduct disorder or ODD during childhood or adolescence (Kim-Cohen et al., 2003).

CLINICIANS' PROFESSIONAL SKILLS AND ATTRIBUTES

Making a recommendation about pharmacological treatment involves a diverse set of child psychiatric skills and attitudes, which require that the psychiatrist do much more than merely know what medications might be helpful and what kinds of symptoms or conditions medication might address. First, the psychiatrist must recognize that any pharmacological interventions will take place in a larger treatment context. In situations like Michael's, where the psychiatrist serves as a potential coprovider of treatment and as a consultant to the primary therapist, the psychiatrist can expect to work with the child, his family, one or more other clinicians, and agencies that also are providing services. A child psychiatrist needs to understand the purpose and potential therapeutic impact of the other services Michael is receiving.

The child psychiatrist also should be able to gather information from other caregivers and other parties, for example teachers, to integrate that information with the psychiatrist's own direct clinical observations, and to construct a comprehensive overview of Michael's situation and problems. Patients with conduct disorder often minimize their own problems and the extent of their difficulties, which is one of several reasons why practice parameters on the assessment and treatment of conduct disorder promulgated by the American Academy of Child and Adolescent Psychiatry (1997) emphasize the need for multidimensional assessment.

Second, the psychiatrist needs a set of interpersonal therapeutic skills that foster a treatment alliance, or that engage the cooperation and faith of the child and his parents. Although the psychiatrist may be focusing his efforts on providing drug therapy, he still needs to employ the interview skills that a good therapist uses. The psychiatrist needs to convey quickly to the parents and the child that he is interested in understanding how they feel and what they experience. This is especially true for children like Michael, who understandably feels reluctant about coming for psychotherapy, let alone the prospect of having to take medication. The doctor must let the child know that what he experiences is important and that his perspective on his difficulties really matters.

Simultaneously, the psychiatrist must impart a similar message to the child's parent or guardian. One of the most difficult tensions in child psychiatric work—one exemplified in the vignette about the initial consultation with Michael—is that parents and children often are at loggerheads when they arrive at the doctor's office. The child psychiatrist must nonetheless both understand views of the problem and convey respect for both perspectives, even though these perspectives seem mutually incompatible. Of course, in a consultant's position, the child psychiatrist's role and time with the family will be limited, and efforts to foster a therapeutic alliance may have been aided by the family's prior contact with the primary therapist.

A third set of skills come into play if the psychiatrist's evaluation indicates that a medication might indeed be helpful. The psychiatrist needs to respond empathically to the child's feelings about getting a prescription. A prescription may signify to a child that he is abnormal or that all his family's problems are his fault. Some children (along with some parents) expect that medication will solve all problems, although this is true only occasionally. Many children experience gratitude at receiving a prescription, because the doctor has recognized and is offering relief from the dysphoria that the child has long suffered. Whatever their initial reactions, parents and children must also understand that, however thoughtfully medication is prescribed, there is no guarantee that it will work or be free of noxious side effects. An explanation of expected benefits, possible adverse effects, and alternatives (including no drug treatment at all) is part of the informed consent process involved in proper psychiatric practice (Gutheil & Appelbaum, 2000).

Taking medication effectively requires that the child patient and his parents become, in effect, collaborators in an experiment to see whether the medication is helpful. The child psychiatrist can make this point explicitly, adding that part of the experiment is to gather data about whether the drug is really helping. The process of taking psychotropic medication may include obtaining information about treatment responses not just from the child, but also from the parents, teachers, and others in the child's environment who can see how the child is doing.

THE CASE OF "MIKE"

Conceptualization, Assessment, and Treatment Planning
Additional Information and Assessment Tools

Information in the case vignette is typical of—and in some ways more complete than—what a psychiatrist usually receives before evaluating a child's need for medication. We have a rich description of mother–son interactions, the father's attitudes, and even intelligence testing, which eliminates several diagnostic possibilities (e.g., learning disabilities). Still missing, however, are many kinds of information that a psychiatrist seeks when considering medication.

Typically, the decision to prescribe medication hinges on whether a patient has symptoms that indicate the presence of disorders that a medication might address. The vignette contains hints about some possible disorders: Michael seems moody and may be depressed; there also are suggestions that he may have ADHD. The psychiatrist would begin the process of getting more information during the clinical interview, asking questions about a variety of possible symptoms and their course, hoping to rule in or rule out various conditions that might coexist with Michael's conduct problems.

For example, the vignette gives some hints that Michael may be depressed. Children of Michael's age are articulate about certain features of depression and unaware of other features, in part because of their still-limited ability to talk about feelings. Michael may supply information about whether he often feels "down," "tired," or "sad," about his sleep patterns, his concentration, and whether he had thought about death or suicide. Other indicia of childhood depression—for example, diminished interest in things, abrupt deterioration in school performance—might be discussed with Michael's parents, who might also report on any outwardly visible changes in mood. Parents are often the best source of information about ADHD problems, for example, they are the ones most likely to recall whether, early in elementary school, Michael's teachers reported that he could not pay attention or sit still.

A few children who receive diagnoses of conduct disorder later develop psychotic disorders or major affective illnesses. In Michael's case, such problems seem very unlikely, but psychiatrists routinely ask about hallucinations or delusions and occasionally patients' answers surprise us. If psychotic symptoms are present, they exert a strong influence on both diagnosis and the types of recommended pharmacological treatment. If a family psychiatric history (usually obtained from a parent) reveals that Michael's first-degree relatives have experienced major mental illnesses, this raises the likelihood that Michael may be developing such problems. For example, persons who develop bipolar disorder often do not display any mental symptoms at age 13, but a prominent family history of manic-depressive illness would raise the possibility that Michael's moodiness may be a prelude to a major affective disorder.

Psychiatrists typically inquire about whether trauma or abuse has occurred because such experiences often are associated with post-traumatic stress disorder. Psychiatrists also ask about past suicide attempts, current suicidal thinking, and thoughts about hurting other people. Such phenomena occur often during depressive and psychotic illnesses, and may indicate the need for immediate intervention—for example, hospitalization—rather than simply providing a prescription.

Psychiatrists also ask children about their use of drugs and alcohol. Having a diagnosis of conduct disorder is associated with higher rates of substance abuse (Whitmore et al., 1997). Literature also suggests that persistent hyperactivity symptoms are associated with subsequent conduct problems and substance abuse (Mannuzza et al.,1991; Mannuzza, Klein, Bessler, Malloy, & LaPadula, 1993), and that delinquent behavior antecedes or coincides with a child's initial experimentation with substances (Huizinga, Loeber, & Thornberry, 1993).

As the preceding paragraphs suggest, accurate diagnosis may take considerable time and is sometimes difficult. For example, child psychiatrists frequently need to distinguish boys who are merely rambunctious from those who suffer from ADHD. Some helpful clues include the child's degree of impairment in many settings and accounts of problems that date back to preschool. Learning that a child was expelled from several daycare centers and that his parents could not work because his babysitters could not tolerate his hyperactivity and aggressiveness suggest an unusual and probably pathological level of impulsiveness. Complimenting such accounts may be recollections from early school years, when the child struggled academically because he could not function appropriately in classrooms and had trouble keeping friends because he said mean things and struck other children. Such information may give the psychiatrist the sense of a chronic impairment that ADHD would explain. Even if, at Michael's age, such behaviors have waned, their presence early on raises the chance that he has a condition that medication might alleviate.

Although most clinical data are gathered by interviewing, psychiatrists can have parents or teachers complete questionnaires to flesh out diagnostic information. Useful examples include the Mini International Neuropsychiatric Interview, a short, structured interview that screens for several psychiatric conditions, including eating disorders, panic disorder, obsessive–compulsive disorder, and social anxiety disorder (Sheehan et al., 1998). The Child Behavior Checklist (Achenbach & Rescorla, 2000) is a convenient tool for systematic gathering observations and perspectives of parents and teachers, and covers a broad base of symptoms and diagnoses. If initial investigation discloses substantial problems with attention, hyperactivity, or impulsiveness, an ADHD symptom questionnaire (e.g., the Conners' Ratings Scales–Revised, Conners, 1997; reviewed by Collett, Ohan, & Myers, 2003) completed by parents and teachers can document both the extent of ADHD and, later on, response to treatment.

Finally, psychiatrists will obtain information about a child's physical health, including allergies, currently treated problems, past medical problems, date of the last physical examination, and the examination's results. In some cases, psychiatrists will recommend obtaining laboratory studies— for example, blood tests—to rule out medical causes of what appear to be psychological symptoms. Many times psychiatrists will get "baseline lab tests" before starting medications when administering a drug requires laboratory monitoring of side effects.

Therapeutic Goals

The therapeutic goals for Michael's pharmacological treatment depend on his psychiatric diagnosis and the role medication (if any is prescribed) could potentially play in his overall treatment. If a psychiatric evaluation showed that Michael had conduct disorder uncomplicated by any other significant psychiatric condition, then the primary therapeutic goal would be to reduce aggressive actions and other violations of society's rules, and help him avoid further legal involvement or incarceration. Secondary goals would include helping Michael to improve his academic functioning, to develop relationships with peers who are not engaged in lawbreaking activities, and to reduce his abuse of marijuana and other substances. Medication might help achieve these goals by affecting his impulsiveness or proneness to do the first thing that comes to his mind.

If psychiatric evaluation showed that Michael had other disorders that were more amenable to pharmacological medication treatment, for example ADHD, then reducing impulsiveness with medication and improving his academic abilities (to attend school, to be organized about and do his homework) might well become primary goals that might lead to more socially approved behavior in contexts away from school. If Michael were depressed, then improving his mood and decreasing his neurovegetative symptoms would become primary goals, successful achievement of which might lead to better interpersonal and academic functioning.

Immediate and long-term results.   Assuming that evaluation disclosed reasons to think medication might help Michael, the hoped-for results of treatment would hinge on what condition was diagnosed and the anticipated benefits of medication for that condition. But to focus on how medication would address conduct disorder problems, desired changes would include improving his frustration tolerance and decreasing the frequency and severity of anger outbursts. One would also like Michael to substitute verbal expression of anger (e.g., yelling) for physical expression of anger (e.g., fighting), which might lead to improved relationships with peers, family, and teachers. The psychiatrist would hope that, over the longer term, development of improved social skills would permit gradual reduction and discontinuation of medication.

If Michael indeed suffers from ADHD, immediate goals would include improving his attention span and decreasing his impulsiveness, which would help him make better behavioral choices. ADHD is often a chronic condition that might lead Michael to need medication for an extended period, perhaps through high school and beyond.

If Michael received medication to treat depression, expected results would include improvements in mood over a period of 1–6 months, along with a concomitant increase in capacity to tolerate stressors without becoming irritable and aggressive.

Length of Treatment and Session Frequency

The time-line for pharmacotherapy depends on the problem for which Michael receives treatment. In most cases where a careful assessment leads to initiation of a medication trial, Michael should return within (at most) 2 weeks to assess side effects, and then at least monthly to assess treatment response. With some medications, for example stimulants for ADHD, one may know about their positive results within as little as a week, although dosage adjustments may continue for some time thereafter. For other medications—antidepressants are an example—it takes a month or more for changes in neurotransmission to produce symptomatic improvement. As part of the process of prescribing medication, psychiatrists should explain to children and their parents (who may hope for immediate results) how long they should expect to wait before noticing any benefits or side effects. In the case of antidepressants, child patients need especially close monitoring over the first 2 weeks because of risks for agitation, mania, and thoughts about suicide.

Once an appropriate medication dose is found (and assuming it has been beneficial), patients may need to be seen every 2 or 3 months for reassessment appointments, during which the doctor would determine whether the drug was still helpful and not causing side effects. The data about how long children should take antidepressants are limited, but for adults, the consensus is that treatment should continue for 6–12 months *after remission of symptoms* before attempting to lower and discontinue medication (American Psychiatric Association, 2000; Gruenberg & Goldstein, 2003). As previously noted, pharmacotherapy with a drug for ADHD might continue for years if treatment has proved beneficial.

Case Conceptualization

In his book *Listening to Prozac*, psychiatrist Peter Kramer (1993) described his experiences with giving antidepressants to adult patients who then experienced not only improvement in mood, but also changes in what we typically think of as enduring features of personality: perceptions of self-worth, interpersonal confidence, sensitivity to rejection, and willingness to take risks. Though Kramer has an uncommon ability to describe his clinical observations, the types of observations he reports are far from unusual. By the time they have completed their residency training, most psychiatrists have treated several patients in whom longstanding, seemingly "psychological" problems—maladaptive personality traits, behavioral disturbances, mood difficulties, or faulty cognitions—resolved quickly once those patients took an adequate dose of the right medication. When considering whether to recommend pharmacological treatment, a psychiatrist is implicitly asking, "To what extent are the patient's problems a reflection of a biological state that medication might alter?"

In Michael's case, getting the information discussed in the previous sections may provide the answer to this question. That information will complement information the psychiatrist knows about the co-occurrence of various disorders with conduct problems. Although estimates vary, recent studies suggest that in teens with conduct disorder, approximately 80% have comorbid substance problems, 50% also have ADHD, and 20–30% suffer from co-occurring affective disorders (Bukstein, Glancy, & Kaminer, 1992; Loeber et al., 2000; Milan, Halikas, Meller, & Morse, 1991).

The Therapeutic Relationship

As previously noted, even a medication consultation requires the psychiatrist to establish a type of therapeutic relationship with Mike and his parents. The quality of that relationship could influence treatment compliance and, by extension, treatment response. Below we address special issues the child psychiatrist might consider in the psychopharmacological relationship.

Special Cautions, Potential Resistance

Although a list of all possible cautions would require discussion going far beyond the scope of this chapter, earlier sections have included examples of potential side effects that medications can cause. When prescribing a medication, it is helpful for psychiatrist to emphasize common or especially serious adverse effects to parents and to supplement this oral discussion with written information that parents can take home. Psychiatrists can also urge patients and their parents to call if they develop concerns or have urgent questions about medication that develop between appointments. Such efforts may help address and overcome resistance to taking medications that might understandably arise from experiencing unexpected medication side effects. These efforts may also open chances for dialog with patients who are anxious about taking medication and may therefore over-interpret normal bodily sensations as side effects.

Another special caution (also mentioned previously) is that parents must supervise the child's taking of medication, including where and how medication is stored. This can help avert many potential problems, including serious ones that might arise if, for example, an impulsive child reasoned, "Things aren't going well, I'll take two or three times my usual dose."

Many children and parents are reluctant to have what seem like behavioral problems addressed through medication. Of course, very resistant families will not even come for a many medication evaluation. However, if other forms of therapy have been tried unsuccessfully, parents may be more interested in and receptive to hearing about scientific evidence supporting the potential helpfulness of medication for their child, and the potential consequences of leaving a problem untreated. With ADHD, for example, good evidence suggests that stimulant medications are very helpful and lower the risk that children will later develop substance use problems and have worsening of conduct problems. With conduct disorder alone, evidence is much less solid, which is why psychiatrists may often decide not to recommend medication.

Areas to Avoid

In Michael's case, the psychiatrist should avoid doing some things himself despite knowing that those things should be done. In a collaborative treatment, the psychiatrist's role usually is not that of being the child's or the family's primary therapist. Although the psychiatrist may know about many or all of the issues that the primary therapist is aware of, the psychiatrist should avoid addressing family dynamics and individual problems that do not relate directly to taking medication. The delineation of and restrictions on the psychiatrist's role can be accomplished by having the psychiatrist, other treating mental health professionals, and patient(s) agree in advance on how various treatment issues will be handled and who will handle those issues. This is not to say that psychiatrists should ignore what they perceive as emergencies, but only those complex issues that are being addressed in Michael's nondrug therapy should remain the province of his other therapists (Ellison & Harney, 2000; Sederer, Ellison, & Keyes, 1998).

If Michael or his family bring a therapy issue to the psychiatrist's attention, the psychiatrist should listen carefully, clearly convey concern, and acknowledge the issue's importance. The psychiatrist may then wish to ask about how the patient and primary therapist are addressing the issue, thereby providing a response that has two functions. First, such a response provides additional opportunity for discussion and for the psychiatrist to gain more information about it. Second, asking about how the issue is being addressed in treatment supports the psychiatrist's colleague while reinforcing the importance of dealing with the issue in its proper treatment setting.

Patient's Strengths

Despite his difficulties, Michael has normal intellectual capacities. Being a 13-year-old of normal intelligence means that he has a substantial ability—well above the ability of most children his age whom child psychiatrists treat—to understand the role of medication in his care, what its expected benefits might be, why he should take medication only as prescribed, and what the side effects of the medication might be. He could also communicate about these matters fairly well with the doctor and his mother, which will help the psychiatrist determine whether the medicine was effective.

Another strength is that Michael's mother recognizes that her son's difficulties are matters that merit intervention by mental health professionals. Many parents of children with conduct problems do not bring them for treatment. Were Michael's mother to initiate psychotherapy and also investigate pharmacological treatment, this would suggest that Michael had his mother's support for looking at his problems and making changes. Such support would help his chances in benefitting from nonmedication therapy, and might increase Michael's benefit from medication by improving the likelihood that he would take it properly.

Boundaries

As with all therapeutic relationships, medication consultation relationships should have established boundaries. In pharmacotherapy, "boundaries" and "limit-setting" have meanings that are more concrete than is the usual case in psychotherapy. Michael and his mother must understand and agree that medication should be taken as the psychiatrist prescribes it, and that they should discuss matters with the doctor before making any changes in medication. If side effects develop, they need to stop the medication and promptly tell the psychiatrist about the problem.

When stimulants are prescribed, parents (and when appropriate, child patients) should understand that they are controlled substances. They should know that doctor will keep track of how many stimulant prescriptions are written to make sure that no extra pills are available for misuse or potentially illegal use.

Further "limits" would include telling Michael that he should not use alcohol, marijuana, or other "recreational" drugs. Substance use might make his medication ineffective or interact with his medication in ways that could cause serious health problems. Indeed, Michael probably should be told by all his caregivers, "If you continue to use drugs, you will make it very difficult for us to help you with your problems." The psychiatrist might consider arranging for periodic or random drug screens as a way of checking on Michael's self-reports about drug use.

Involvement of Others

Children simply cannot receive or benefit from medication without some involvement of the important adults in their lives. Michael's other caregivers must support his taking medication and provide other interventions, because medication alone probably will not address all his problems. Because he is a minor, Michael cannot receive medication without the consent of one custodial parent and a parent's financial support in paying for the medication. Both of Michael's parents should participate in (and hopefully agree about) any trial of medication; they should help to make sure Michael takes medication, and help to monitor for improvements and side effects. Michael's primary care physician (typically a family practitioner or pediatrician) should know about the medication that is being prescribed; they may also be able to alert the psychiatrists about drug interactions or other medical issues that must be considered in prescribing decisions.

In addition to taking his medication, Michael and his parents will need to monitor symptoms and reactions to the drug outside of the office contact. Occasionally, psychiatrists have patients or parents keep more or less formal logs that chart changes in mood or behavior.

Treatment Implications and Outcomes
Special Techniques and Strategies
In the role of a psychopharmacological consultant, the child psychiatrist specifically directs his attention toward learning whether a medication might help, and then providing that medication. For most psychiatric conditions—and certainly in Michael's case—psychiatrists would not regard medication as a complete solution or sufficient psychiatric treatment. Because of this, the psychiatrist would expect to collaborate with one or more other mental health professionals helping to provide other features of Michael's care. This means that Michael's mental health professionals will need to agree on their particular roles and how they will divide responsibilities for his care, and will need to take time (often unremunerated time) to speak with each other during treatment. To do this well, the psychiatrist must find a way to cordially resolve turf battles effectively with his mental health colleagues.

Other special techniques have been mentioned earlier, and involve ways to obtain information relevant for treatment from sources beyond Michael and his mother. Particularly where medication for ADHD is prescribed, the psychiatrist may wish to distribute questionnaires for teachers as well as parents, which may then be reviewed to monitor response to medication.

Mechanisms of Change
As we noted earlier, psychiatrists prescribe medication in the belief that by altering neuronal transmission, individuals will experience improvement in behavior or relief from the symptoms they are experiencing. Thus, if medication helped Michael, it would presumably reflect a connection between altering

his brain functioning manifested outwardly in new patterns of behavior, improved mood, or changes in his attitude and outlook. Put another way, one would expect changes in neuronal transmission to bring about changes in Michael's patterns of thinking and acting, which would then lead to fewer of the rule-violating social interactions that are the basis for diagnosing conduct disorder.

In providing stimulant medications to treat ADHD, for example, the psychiatrist hopes that by altering dopamine transmission, the drug will improve an otherwise distractible patient's ability to focus attention on matters that require attention and to maintain attention without being distracted. As a behavioral matter, altered dopamine functioning would "translate" into Michael's being less impulsive and more capable of considering a broad range of social issues before he makes his judgments. Were Michael to receive treatment for depression, one might expect that his feeling better would coincide with reduced irritability and better sleep. These improvements might, in turn, help Michael to avoid getting into conflicts with his mother and fights with other kids, to feel more motivated to do schoolwork, and to achieve more academic success.

Medical and Nutritional Issues

With regard to medical issues, the first question that might be posed is, "Is medication warranted?" and then, "What effect might medication have?" The answer to the first question is very simple: we do not know. The case vignettes provide some hints that Michael might have problems that medication would help. The strongest hints concern problems with attention and depression. If psychiatric diagnosis revealed the presence of ADHD, depression, or any other disorder amenable to medication, we might expect that taking medication would help some of Michael's problems to abate fairly quickly. The impulsiveness and inattention associated with ADHD could well improve within a week or two of starting a medication once an adequate dose was reached. If Michael were depressed, if he and his parents decided to accept medication as a treatment for his depression, and if he tolerated medication well, Michael might look and feel somewhat better within as little as 2 weeks after starting treatment, although it would require 1–2 months to know whether antidepressant medication would really work well.

Potential Pitfalls

Distinguishing those children who are likely to benefit from medications from children who have problems that medicines cannot address may be complicated, and often requires considerable time and attention from a psychiatrist. Psychiatrists who provide psychopharmacological consultation in cases such as Michael's may experience (or at least perceive) pressure from the referring clinician or parents to "do something" to "fix" a very troublesome situation. This can lead psychiatrists to prescribe medications even when clinical evidence provides far-less-than-solid justification for doing so. Also, external demands or contextual features of the consultation—for example, limitations on time allotted for the consultation or on the psychiatrist's potential reimbursement—may impede careful evaluation.

Because a prescription conveys a message that the problem is "biological," children or adults may assume or act as though child patients have *no* responsibility to control behavior or develop better self-control. Examples of such thinking include a child's saying, "I forgot to take my pill today, so that's why I misbehaved." Although having a disorder or not taking medication may explain some aspects of a child's problems, this does not necessarily mean that *all* misbehavior and law-breaking is not the child's fault. Here, misplaced hopes that medication will quickly and inexpensively make everything better may be augmented by resistance to therapeutic soul-searching and the hard work of making changes in behavior, thinking patterns, and patterns of interaction within the family.

A further potential pitfall in medication therapy is noncompliance. Some children and teens experience side effect or dislike how medications make them feel, and respond by not taking them. While psychiatrists should encourage teenage patients to be somewhat independent and responsible for their mental health treatment, parents still need to monitor what their kids are doing to help assure that children take their medications. This can add to difficulties caused by pre-existing anger or power struggles between child and parent.

For children who take stimulants, psychiatrists must remain alert for possible misuse of medications. Short-acting methylphenidate sometimes has a "street value," and children are known to crush and snort the drug. Michael's possibly having substance use problems already would heighten the psychiatrist's concerns here.

All medications have potential side effects about which patients and parents should be cautioned, and for which psychiatrists should provide careful monitoring. Close follow-up (to include the psychiatrist's telephone availability and frequent in-person visits) is especially when patients are initiating treatment with any psychotropic drug. In October 2004, the FDA notified that prescribing information for antidepressants carry a "black box" warning concerning their potential to induce suicidal ideation in children (Harris,

2004). Though this risk—and others, such as the possibility of inducing mania—should induce caution in prescribing, it does not mean that Michael should not receive a trial of antidepressants, especially if evaluation shows that he has persistent mood problems that nonpharmacological therapies cannot resolve. Depression itself is associated with a greatly increased risk of suicide (Shaffer et al., 1996), and a recent review suggests that increased prescribing of antidepressants by physicians may have lowered the suicide rate among teens (Gould, Greenberg, Velting, & Shaffer, 2003). Studies also demonstrate that fluoxetine alleviates depression in children (Emslie et al., 1997; March et al., 2004), and many clinicians' experience convinces them that other antidepressant drugs work, too.

Termination, Relapse Prevention

Many problems treated with psychotropic medications arise from conditions that, without treatment, would last for years or would be characterized by remissions and relapses. Answering questions about when Michael's psychopharmacologic treatment might stop and how relapses might be prevented depends heavily on his diagnoses and the success that medication had in addressing problematic aspects of his clinical presentation.

If, for example, psychiatric evaluation disclosed that Michael had ADHD problems as a young child and that these had continued to affect his functioning during adolescence, he might anticipate having continuing problems with inattention and impulsiveness that lasted well into early adulthood. Michael and his parents would need to know that pharmacological benefits from his problem might continue for years without any clear point at which medication would be stopped. This would mean that his contact with a child psychiatrist might continue throughout his teenage years.

If Michael turned out to have depression, to take antidepressant medication, and to benefit from it, he might expect to continue taking medication for up to a year—months after his symptoms had remitted. At his point, most child psychiatrists would discuss trying to taper and stop the medication rather than have Michael continue his exposure to a drug, the long-term consequences of which are still ambiguous. His parents would need to understand that Michael would still remain at risk for recurrence of depressive symptoms and would therefore need to remain under the psychiatrist's supervision during tapering and the initial months after discontinuation. If Michael weathered this process well, his regular contact with the psychiatrist might end, with the understanding that restarting medication might be necessary several months or years in the future.

REFERENCES

Achenbach, T. M., & Rescorla, L. A. (2000). *Manual for the ASEBA school-age forms and profiles.* Burlington, VT: University of Vermont, Research Center for Children, Youth, and Families.

Aman, M. G., De Smedt, G., Derivan, A., Lyons, B., & Findling, R. L. (2002). Double-blind, placebo-controlled study of risperidone for the treatment of disruptive behaviors in children with subaverage intelligence. *American Journal of Psychiatry, 159*, 1337–1346.

American Academy of Child and Adolescent Psychiatry. (1997). Practice parameters for the psychiatric assessment of infants and toddlers. *Journal of the American Academy of Child and Adolescent Psychiatry, 36.*

American Psychiatric Association. (2000). Practice guideline for the treatment of patients with major depressive disorder (revision). *American Journal of Psychiatry, 157*(4 Suppl), 1–45.

Bukstein, O. G., Glancy, L. J., & Kaminer, Y. (1992). Patterns of affective comorbidity in a clinical population of dually diagnosed adolescent substance abusers. *Journal of the American Academy of Child and Adolescent Psychiatry, 31*, 1041–1045.

Collett, B. R., Ohan, J. L., & Myers, K. M. (2003). Ten-year review of rating scales. V: Scales assessing attention-deficit/hyperactivity disorder. *Journal of the American Academy of Child and Adolescent Psychiatry, 42*, 1015–1037.

Conners, C. (1997). *Conners' rating scales-revised technical manual.* North Tonawanda, NY: Multi-Health Systems.

Costello, E. J., Mustillo, S., Erkanli, A., Keeler, G., & Angold, A. (2003). Prevalence and development of psychiatric disorders in childhood and adolescence. *Archives of General Psychiatry, 60*, 837–844.

Ellison, J. M., & Harney, P. A. (2000). Treatment-resistant depression and the collaborative treatment relationship. *Journal of Psychotherapy Practice and Research, 9*, 7–17.

Emslie, G. J., Rush, A. J., Weinberg, W. A., Kowatch, R. A., Hughes, C. W., Carmody, T., & Rintelmann, J. (1997). A double-blind, randomized, placebo-controlled trial of fluoxetine in children and adolescents with depression. *Archives of General Psychiatry, 54*, 1031–1037.

Engel, G. L. (1977). The need for a new medical model. *Science, 196*, 129–136.

Engel, G. L. (1980). The clinical application of the biopsychosocial model. *American Journal of Psychiatry, 137*, 535–544.

Findling, R. L., McNamara, N. K., Branicky, L. A., Schluchter, M. D., Lemon, E., & Blumer, J. L. (2000). A double-blind pilot study of risperidone in the treatment of conduct disorder. *Journal of the American Academy of Child and Adolescent Psychiatry, 39*, 509–516.

Gould, M. S., Greenberg, T., Velting, D. M., & Shaffer, D. (2003). Youth suicide risk and preventive interventions: A review of the past 10 years. *Journal of the American Academy of Child and Adolescent Psychiatry, 42*, 386–405.

Gruenberg, A. M., & Goldstein, R. D. (2003). Mood disorders: Depression. In A. Tasman, J. Kay, & J. A. Lieberman (Eds.), *Psychiatry* (2nd ed., pp. 1207–1236). Hoboken, NJ: Wiley.

Gutheil, T. G., & Appelbaum, P. S. (2000). *Clinical handbook of psychiatry and the law* (3rd ed.). Philadelphia: Lippincott Williams & Wilkins.

Harris, G. (2004, October 16). *F.D.A. toughens warning on antidepressant drugs.* The New York Times, p. A9.

Huizinga, D., Loeber, R., & Thornberry, T. P. (1993). Longitudinal study of delinquency, drug use, sexual activity, and pregnancy among children and youth in three cities. *Public Health Reports, 108*(Suppl 1), 90–96.

Kim-Cohen, J., Caspi, A., Moffitt, T. E., Harrington, H., Milne, B. J., & Poulton, R. (2003). Juvenile diagnoses in adults with mental disorder: Developmental follow-back of a prospective-longitudinal cohort. *Archives of General Psychiatry, 60*, 709–717.

Kramer, P. (1993). *Listening to Prozac.* New York: Penguin Books.

Lahey, B., McBurnett, K., Loeber, R., & Hart, E. (1995). Psychobiology. In P. Scholevar (Ed.), *Conduct disorders in children and adolescents* (pp. 27–44). Washington, DC: American Psychiatric Press.

Loeber, R., Burke, J. D., Lahey, B. B., Winters, A., & Zera, M. (2000). Oppositional defiant and conduct disorder: A review of the past 10 years, part I. *Journal of the American Academy of Child and Adolescent Psychiatry, 39*, 1468–1484.

Loeber, R., Green S. M., Keenan, K., & Lahey, B. B. (1995). Which boys will fare worse? Early predictors of the onset of conduct disorder in a 6-year longitudinal study. *Journal of the American Academy of Child and Adolescent Psychiatry, 34*, 499–509.

Mannuzza, S., Klein, R. G., Bessler, A., Malloy, P., & LaPadula, M. (1993). Adult outcome of hyperactive boys. Educational achievement, occupational rank, and psychiatric status. *Archives of General Psychiatry, 50*, 565–576.

Mannuzza, S., Klein, R. G., Bonagura, N., Malloy, P., Giampino, T. L., & Addalli, K. A. (1991). Hyperactive boys almost grown up. V. Replication of psychiatric status. *Archives of General Psychiatry, 48*, 77–83.

March, J., Silva, S., Petrycki, S., Curry, J., Wells, K., Fairbank, J., et al. (2004). Fluoxetine, cognitive-behavioral therapy, and their combination for adolescents with depression: Treatment for adolescents with depression study (TADS) randomized controlled trial. *Journal of the American Medical Association, 292*, 807–820.

McDougle, C. J., Stigler, K. A., & Posey, D. J. (2003). Treatment of aggression in children and adolescents with autism and conduct disorder. *Journal of Clinical Psychiatry, 64*(suppl 4), 16–25.

Milan, R., Halikas, J. A., Meller, J. E., & Morse, C. (1991). Psychopathology among substance abusing juvenile offenders. *Journal of the American Academy of Child and Adolescent Psychiatry, 30*, 569–574.

Offord, D. R., Boyle, M. H., Racine, Y. A., Fleming, J. E., Cadman, D. T., Blum, H. M., et al. (1992). Outcome, prognosis, and risk in a longitudinal follow-up study. *Journal of the American Academy of Child and Adolescent Psychiatry, 31*, 916–922.

Robins, E., & Guze, S. B. (1970). Establishment of diagnostic validity in psychiatric illness: Its application to schizophrenia. *American Journal of Psychiatry, 126*, 983–987.

Rogeness, G. (1994). Biological findings in conduct disorder. *Child and Adolescent Psychiatry Clinics of North America, 3*, 271–284.

Satterfield, J. H., & Schell, A. (1997). A prospective study of hyperactive boys with conduct problems and normal boys: Adolescent and adult criminality. *Journal of the American Academy of Child and Adolescent Psychiatry, 36*, 1726–1735.

Sederer, L. I., Ellison, J., & Keyes, C. (1998). Guidelines for prescribing psychiatrists in consultative, collaborative, and supervisory relationships. *Psychiatric Services, 49*, 1197–1202.

Shaffer, D., Gould, M. S., Fisher, P., Trautman, P., Moreau, D., Kleinman, M., & Flory, M. (1996). Psychiatric diagnosis in child and adolescent suicide. *Archives of General Psychiatry, 53*, 339–348.

Sheehan, D. V., Lecrubier, Y., Sheehan, K. H., Amorim, P., Janavs, J., Weiller, E., et al. (1998). The Mini-International Neuropsychiatric Interview (M.I.N.I.): The development and validation of a structured diagnostic psychiatric interview for DSM-IV and ICD-10. *Journal of Clinical Psychiatry, 59*(Suppl 20), 22–33.

Snyder, R., Turgay, A., Aman, M., Binder, C., Fisman, S., & Carroll, A. (2002). Effects of risperidone on conduct and disruptive behavior disorders in children with subaverage IQs. *Journal of the American Academy of Child and Adolescent Psychiatry, 41*, 1026–1036.

Steiner, H., Petersen, M. L., Saxena, K., Ford, S., & Matthews, Z. (2003). Divalproex sodium for the treatment of conduct disorder: A randomized controlled clinical trial. *Journal of Clinical Psychiatry, 64*, 1183–1191.

Unis, A. S., Cook, E. H., Vincent, J. G., Gjerde, D. K., Perry, B. D., Mason, C., & Mitchell, J. (1997). Platelet serotonin measures in adolescents with conduct disorder. *Biological Psychiatry, 42*, 553–559.

Whitmore, E. A., Mikulich, S. K., Thompson, L. L., Riggs, P. D., Aarons, G. A., & Crowley, T. J. (1997). Influences on adolescent substance dependence: Conduct disorder, depression, attention deficit hyperactivity disorder, and gender. *Drug and Alcohol Dependence, 47*, 87–97.

Wilcox, R. E., Gonzales, R. A., & Miller, J. D. (1998). Introduction to neurotransmitters, receptors, signal transmission, and second messengers. In A. F. Schatzberg, & C. B. Nemeroff (Eds.), *The American Psychiatric Press textbook of psychopharmacology* (2nd ed.). Washington, DC: American Psychiatric Press.

CHAPTER 11

Comparative Treatments of Conduct Disorder

Summary and Conclusions

K. J. Hart, W. Michael Nelson III, and A. J. Finch, Jr.

When the topic of conduct disorder arises, many of us face questions that, although phrased in very different ways, inquire about the distinction between this diagnostic category and "just plain bad kids." Even within the Juvenile Justice system, some judges, magistrates, probation officers, and treatment professionals question the utility and meaning of identifying "bad" behavior as indicative of a disease or disorder. Whether we believe that youths who exhibit the behaviors characteristic of conduct disorder are bad or "disordered," most clinicians (and citizens) would agree that these youths pose significant challenges to their families, their peer groups, their schools and teachers, their neighborhoods, and society at large. For this reason, regardless of one's view of the nature of the problem, we are in need of effective interventions for these youths. However, it is our beliefs about the causal factors of conduct disorder that guide our intervention attempts. Thus, theories are related to practice in a circular and mutually reinforcing manner. Theories offer a preconceived way of examining clinical data and clearly bias our observations. Nevertheless, they impose order on the "chaos" of clinical data by organizing our awareness and helping us make sense of what we need to do to effectively intervene in these youths' lives.

Across the chapters of this book, we have analyzed the case of "Mike" from eight different theoretical perspectives, ranging from person-centered analytic treatment to the community-based interventions of Multisystemic Therapy (MST). Needless to say, the interventions differ greatly in both conceptualization of Mike's difficulties and the description of the optimal intervention(s) needed to change his deviant behavior. Despite these differences, there are similarities among several of the interventions that are worth highlighting. For example, authors of nearly all the chapters specifically address the need to establish a "therapeutic relationship" with the youth and/ or his parents as a fundamentally important component of the treatment. Additionally, several of the approaches recognize the role that parent and/or family dynamics play in Mike's behavior (e.g., family therapy, MST, behavior therapy, and the Coping Power Program/cognitive-behavioral therapy). Several other approaches acknowledge the role that peer group and community factors play in Mike's behavior (e.g., behavioral therapy and Coping Power/ cognitive-behavioral therapy), although the Multisystemic approach attempts to affect these influences most directly. The identification of these factors by the other approaches indicates that our field has begun to recognize that we need to broaden our "clinical view" and create interventions that affect a wider number of forces that are related to externalizing behavior. This recognition poses a challenge to mental health professionals to not only change our intervention scope, but also to rethink our use of diagnoses, which are focused on "the person."

Striking differences exist across the chapters. The most apparent difference, perhaps, is the amount of research available to support the effectiveness of the intervention described. Both MST and the Coping Power Program have considerable empirical support. Behavioral interventions are also based on well-researched (i.e., "validated") methods, and some pharmacotherapy practices are based on controlled drug trials that measure symptom change following the introduction of medication. In contrast, self psychology and the family therapy approaches have relatively few empirical studies to support the use of these methods in the treatment of conduct disorder. This absence may be due, at least in part, to the degree of importance given to empirical outcome studies by proponents of these approaches. Instead, the support for these intervention approaches is more often gained from case studies and clinical description. This preference for clinical "data" is based, in part, on the nature of the primary outcomes of these approaches (i.e., ego development in self psychology or family interaction patterns in family therapy), which are much more difficult to measure than overt behavior change.

In a similar vein, Lyman and Barry's comprehensive review of the variety of residential treatment approaches (chapter 9) provides us with information that should give us pause. They repeatedly remind us that residential treatment generally has not been shown to produce lasting change in youth's behavior and adjustment. They feel that this failure arises because the youth's behavior is not treated in the contexts in which it naturally occurs. Residential treatment programs remain common, particularly for youths with conduct disorder and other highly disruptive behaviors, despite a fair amount of data suggesting that these programs are often no more effective than nonresidential programs. This information points to a need to educate the professionals who come into contact with these youths, including family and juvenile court personnel, to consider using community-based interventions. This finding also poses a challenge to mental health professionals to continue developing interventions that affect "community" factors that influence behavior. We will touch on this point again at the conclusion of this chapter.

As a way to allow the reader to compare various features of the intervention approaches, we have provided a brief summary of the treatment models and the other elements of treatment provided in response to each question posed of the chapter authors, and then offer an overall integration of the information provided in this volume. Much of this information is also summarized in table form in Appendix A to assist the reader in a quick comparison of the methods proposed by each chapter author.

TREATMENT MODEL

The self psychology approach views Mike's behavior as arising from trauma or denial of needed relationship experiences. Mike is "stalled" in the development of self as a result of ineffective parental relationships; the therapeutic relationship allows for interpersonal experiences that reinvigorate that development, and, when successful, produce a self that is resilient. The resilient self can manage life's frustrations and disappointments without emotional or behavioral disruption. As a result, the self psychology approach has as its focus on the relationship that is formed between the therapist and Mike. It is through the development of an empathic, therapeutic relationship that Mike will experience elements that he lacked in his relationship with his parents. The therapist's ability to create an atmosphere of empathic understanding of Mike's subjective world, to successfully interpret Mike's behavior, and process the transferences that develop in their relationship allows for a "cure" of the root of Mike's deviant behavior. Whereas the therapeutic relationship is the means to an end with the other approaches, the relationship formed in self psychology treatment is the desired "end." In this approach, Mike's behavior outside the therapy is of less concern or interest, except as "fodder" for interpretation by the therapist. The empathic atmosphere of the therapeutic relationship and the developing transferences will allow Mike to feel fully "understood," and will allow for Mike's development of self to progress on its own. When development takes place on a track that leads to wholeness and cohesion, the need to act out or experience emotions that interfere with functioning no longer exists.

Pharmacotherapy for disorders also assumes that the "cause" for deviant or maladaptive behavior arises from factors that reside "within" the individual. In this case, those causes are assumed to be biological features, most likely related to the effect that neurotransmitters (or the lack thereof) have on signal transmission within the brain. Medications are provided to alter the biological condition that produces the undesired behavior, but does not provide a permanent change or cure for the condition the medications are designed to treat. Mossman and Weston remind us that there is no known biological condition that has been identified for conduct disorder, but that Mike may have a comorbid condition (such as ADHD or depression) that might respond to medication and, by extension, improve other areas of this functioning, as well.

The identified youth also is the focus of residential treatment programs. Despite data suggesting that the effectiveness of residential treatment are limited, residential treatment for conduct disorder remains common, and is appealing in many situations. By its very nature, the residential treatment approach assumes that the youth is the primary individual in need of intervention, and there appear to be a number of advantages with residential treatment. By placing the youth in a regulated setting, there can be a high level of control of the environment, and reinforcement contingencies can be managed consistently and with maximal structure. Theoretically, that will provide the most rapid change in a youth's behavior. Other types of intervention (individual and group therapy, for example) can be delivered more frequently than is typical in a nonresidential setting. In addition, it can provide a degree of public safety when it removes a youth who is dangerous to the public from the community. Residential treatment also carries a punitive feature, because it removes that youth from his natural setting, which is assumed to be preferred over placement. In addition, the removal of the "problem" is negatively reinforcing to the individuals involved in the placement process. The punitive feature of residential placement is especially appealing to those who work in the court systems. Unfortunately, as is acknowledged in the chapter, residential treatment has a number of disadvantages that appear to outweigh these advantages for many youths. Outcome data suggest that any change in behavior that occurs during the course of residential treatment typically does not persist when the youth returns to home and community. Most residential treatment programs acknowledge the importance of involving parents in treatment so as to maintain treatment gains, but their attempts to do so appear to have been met with limited success.

The behavioral approach assumes that Mike's deviant behavior is a product of learning. Just as the behavior developed through modeling and environmental contingencies, so will behavior change take place. Behavior therapy for Mike involves using learning principles, especially positive and negative reinforcement and punishment, to produce more adaptive behavior patterns. Behavior therapy for conduct disorder acknowledges that all behavior, including deviant behavior, takes place in a broad social context, so various levels of this context (parents, family, and community) need to be considered and addressed. The mechanisms for making changes beyond the family do not appear to be well developed at this point, and show us areas where behavioral interventions can continue to develop.

Family therapy approaches shift the focus of attention from the individual to a broader system. In general, family therapy holds that examination of family interaction patterns is the best way to understand the behavior of any individual within that family. In contrast to the behavioral approach, family therapists do not see a linear, cause-effect relationship between the behaviors of family members (i.e., the parent's behavior does not cause the child to react in a particular way). Instead, the focus is on the complex patterns of reactions among family members. Structural family therapy examines family transactional patterns, with particular emphasis on the organization (or structure) of the family. Structural family therapists attempt to understand how family subsystems are defined, and the nature of the boundaries among those subsystems. When there are problems with the boundaries among those subsystems (either being too rigid or too flexible), problem behavior in family members can arise. The Bowenian approach to family therapy attempts to understand family interaction patterns across generations, with particular attention to how families have managed anxiety across generations. A primary task for families is to allow members to individuate and differentiate from other family members. The goal of the Bowenian approach is to promote insight into these family patterns, so that members can understand how early family experiences influence current family functioning.

The Coping Power Program is based on cognitive-behavioral and social learning principles. The premise of this approach is that thoughts influence behavior, and that effective interventions aim to alter both an individual's general behavior patterns and the thoughts (cognitions) that accompany that behavior. This model acknowledges that both child factors (such as poor self-regulation, poor social problem-solving skills, and poor ability to resist peer pressure) and contextual factors (such as poor parental involvement and poor disciplinary practices) account for the development of Mike's problem behavior. Intervention ideally addresses both of these factors. The Coping Power Program involves manual-based interventions for both Mike and his parents. Broader social risk factors, such as the level of neighborhood crime, are also acknowledged to play a role, but are not directly targeted in this intervention. The child component to this intervention focuses on anger management and social problem solving. In both of these features of the intervention, Mike is taught to understand (and then replace) the cognitive distortions that limit his ability to regulate his emotional arousal or manage social information. Mike's mother (and, ideally, his father) is instructed to use more effective discipline practices and to increase monitoring of Mike's behavior.

The cognitive-developmental model sees behavior as multidetermined—a result of learning, genetics, and cognitive schema—and it attempts to marry many features of cognitive-behavioral therapy with important ideas about the parental relationship drawn from attachment theory. In addition to recognizing the role that cognitions (about self, about the effectiveness of behavior patterns, and about the motives of others) play in our behavior, this approach recognizes that features of the child-parent attachment are important in producing—and maintaining—the youth's deviant behavior. This approach uses many of the components seen in other cognitive-behavioral approaches, but it pays special attention to the repair of the parent–child relationship.

The intervention that takes the broadest approach to the treatment of conduct disorder is MST, which has been designed specifically to treat CD and antisocial behavior of teens. MST is based on the premise that behavior is seen as multidetermined and bidirectional in nature. Antisocial behavior arises out of some combination of many factors, and effective intervention requires change on multiple levels. That is, Mike is involved in many systems (family, school, peers, neighborhood) that have reciprocal influence on behavior. MST targets all of these systems, from family peers, school, and neighborhood. Caregivers and parents are key in MST, and they often appear to be the "target" of therapy. As in the Coping Power Program, Mike's parents are assisted in developing more effective discipline practices and better monitoring and supervision of Mike's behavior. MST takes advantage of the youth's "social ecology" by providing treatment in the home with parents, at school with teachers, or on the practice field with coaches, rather than in an office. This is seen as providing a direct way to obtain information about Mike and his family, and to promote behavior change. In this way, MST breaks many of the traditional therapy "boundaries" by involving many individuals and by occurring in the natural environment.

To summarize, the treatment approaches presented in this volume vary in emphasis on Mike versus the systems in which he lives. They all aim to alter Mike's behavior, but they vary with regard to how directly they attempt to achieve that behavior change. Some approaches (self psychology, Bowenian family therapy) assume that insight and understanding will ultimately result in more adaptive behavior. In contrast, other approaches target behavior change more directly, through the use of medication, altered family interaction, altered environmental contingencies, and learning new skills.

THERAPIST SKILLS AND ATTRIBUTES

It goes without saying that applying each treatment approach requires specialized training and supervised experience in the special techniques and strategies of that approach. In addition to the specific background, however, the approaches described in this volume vary in some of the features that the practitioner brings to the treatment, primarily with regard to the degree to which the therapist must engage in introspection or self-review. The self psychology approach seems to require the greatest amount of reflection. Not only must the therapist reflect on the behavior and feelings of the patient, but he or she must also reflect on and analyze his or her own feelings and behavior in session, in order to understand countertransference issues and other elements that play a role in analytic therapy. For these reasons, many analytic therapists engage in ongoing supervision and/or analysis to assist their own role as a therapist. Likewise, Bowenian family therapists often engage in a guided review or analysis of their families of origin. This degree of personal review was not evident in the other approaches presented.

Although it takes a very different approach, MST also requires ongoing supervision to assist the therapist in problem solving the needs of individual clients. In contrast to most of the other approaches in this volume, MST is implemented by practitioners at a Masters' level, and amount of training has not been found to be directly related to treatment outcome in the studies on MST efficacy. Likewise, the cognitive-behavioral Coping Power Program, which follows a treatment manual, is often provided by individuals who do not provide treatment independently. Nonetheless, in both of these approaches, the ability to flexibly apply the treatment program was seen as a valuable attribute to bring to the treatment. That is, one must adhere to the treatment model, but be flexible in its application so as to take advantage of naturally occurring "teachable moments" when they occur. Insofar as these interventions are typically offered outside of a traditional office setting, these therapists must also be comfortable working in a variety of environments, including schools or low-income neighborhoods. It was also described that the MST therapist should be energetic and positive in his or her view of the child and family. Communicating a positive view and the potential for change may, in fact, be an essential element in therapy from many different perspectives.

Some features of the optimal attributes of physicians offering medications to children and adolescents also deserve special mention. Although this intervention may be seen by some practitioners as an "adjunct" to other therapies, the need to establish a therapeutic alliance in this consulting relationship was emphasized. A working, therapeutic relationship between the physician and the parent and child is necessary to assure optimal communication regarding medication response and side effects, but also likely influences compliance with the recommended medication.

Many of the approaches described similar personal attributes that are felt to play an important role in treatment. Qualities such as being flexible, tolerant, and being able to convey empathy to both Mike and his parents were seen as being important in implementing most of the approaches. In addition, several of the approaches describe the need to work with many members of a child's world, such as school personnel, parents, other caregivers, and other mental health professionals. When assuming a role that requires one to "wear many hats," several of our authors acknowledged the need to be aware of ethical obligations (particularly, confidentiality issues) that can arise in these situations. Regardless of the approach, and even for the approaches (such as Coping Power and MST) that follow prescribed protocols, all chapter authors saw the need to attend to the relationship the therapist forms with Mike and/or significant others in his world. Traditionally, the analytic approaches have emphasized the therapeutic relationship more than the behavioral or cognitive-behavioral approaches. The former uses the relationship between therapists and client as being the most critical factor. In the latter, relationship is considered a necessary, but not sufficient, condition for successful treatment. In other words, the more behaviorally oriented the therapist, the more the assumption that their clients are helped primarily by the specific change techniques employed rather than by their relationship with the therapist. Although not specifically addressed, it is likely that nearly every one agrees that techniques alone do not make for a successful intervention. Personal qualities, like the ability to join with clients and form a therapeutic relationship, demonstrate respect for people, offer hope to individuals, and demonstrate a compassionate understanding of other people's sufferings are important in any therapeutic endeavor, regardless of one's theoretical orientation.

THE CASE OF "MIKE": SPECIFIC TOPICS
Further Information and Assessment Tools

Most of the approaches required information in addition to, or instead of, the information provided in the case presentation and psychological evaluation. Without exception, each approach required information that was specific to its conceptualization of Mike's difficulties and treatment approach. Both the behavioral and MST approaches described a need to gather specific information about the features of Mike's environment that contribute to, or allow, and/or reinforce his deviant behavior, typically through questionnaires or checklists. In both of these approaches, in particular, assessment was seen as an ongoing process. In addition, some approaches (pharmacotherapy, cognitive developmental, and behavioral) felt the need to rule out comorbid ADHD, depression, or learning disability. It is likely that all the approaches would consider this, at least to some degree, even though it was not specifically mentioned.

Because of the nature of these treatments, both self psychology and family therapy approaches required much more information about specific features of Mike's functioning. Specifically, the self psychology approach felt that detailed information about Mike's "self" could be gathered through personal histories and projective testing, and the family therapies required much more information about family functioning and relational patterns. Both of the family therapy models presented in this volume are "systems oriented" in that Mike's behavior is viewed as a larger part of the family system in which all members function interactively. In a sense, they attempt to look past individual personalities to the patterns of influence that shape family members' behavior. In both the self psychology and family therapy approaches, additional testing could be completed (projective measures for self psychology and family mapping for family therapy, for example), but ongoing "assessment" is also a component of both these therapy approaches, through observations made during sessions. The Coping Power Program, which emphasizes the role of social cognitive processing, also sees the benefit of additional information about Mike's ability to problem solve when in social situations, and his ability to assume the (cognitive) perspective of others. The cognitive-developmental approach also attempts to identify Mike's attributions about his behavior, his beliefs about the role his behavior plays in helping him reach desired goals, and his views about his relationship with his parents. Notably, both the MST and the Coping Power approaches expressed the desire to have information about Mike's strengths—a feature that is typically absent in many problem-focused psychological evaluations.

THERAPEUTIC GOALS

In nearly all of the approaches presented in this volume, the primary aim is to decrease Mike's deviant behavior. The path to that change, of course, varied significantly from approach to approach. The behavioral approach, perhaps, attacks this change in behavior most directly, by altering the reinforcement contingencies in Mike's environment. Thus, many behavioral approaches say little about systems and treat individuals as separate but interactive entities who mutually influence each other, primarily as stimuli and reinforcers. Many of the other approaches are less direct in attempting to facilitate the desired behavior change. In family therapy, change occurs when the dysfunctional family relationships are changed, and in Coping Power and cognitive-developmental approach, behavior change occurs when Mike learns more effective ways to problem solve social situations and can better regulate his emotional behavior. In pharmacotherapy, aggressive behavior and rule violations may decrease with medication.

In contrast, the aim of self psychology is to restart the development of the self, which has been arrested by ineffective parenting. Mike's ego has been fractured by failed or ineffective parental relationships, and this fracture is repaired by establishing a therapeutic relationship that provides him with mirroring and the idealizing transferences necessary to develop the mature narcissism that will allow him to be resilient to the stresses and challenges of life. Theoretically, this will not require that he engages in deviant behavior, but behavior change is not a stated goal of this treatment.

LENGTH OF THERAPY

Although effective treatments are being developed for conduct disorder, it remains a difficult problem to treat, and many of the approaches in this volume describe fairly lengthy treatment. For example, behavior therapy would likely occur over the course of a year, and many residential treatment programs for conduct disorder are 12 months in duration; cognitive developmental typically requires at least 6 months of weekly sessions. The structured approach offered by Coping Power involves sessions that occur over the course of 15–18 months for Mike and 3–4 months for his parents. In contrast, Family Therapy is typically offered as a brief treatment of

12 sessions over the course of 3–4 months. MST treatment is also relatively short, typically 3–5 months, although it should be noted that the services offered during this period are very intense, often with daily contact in the early phases of treatment. Length of self psychology treatment is difficult to predict, but this is generally a much longer treatment, and very intense, with sessions ideally occurring four to five times per week. Because the changes to neuronal functioning that occur as a result of medication do not endure after the medication is stopped, pharmacotherapy will last as long as there seems to be a continuing need for the medicine, potentially for several years. There may not be frequent contact with the psychiatrist over the course of this intervention, however. If the medication is well tolerated, brief contact may occur only once every 3–4 months.

CASE CONCEPTUALIZATION

Many of the approaches in this volume recognize Mike's behavior as determined by multiple factors. The behavioral, cognitive-behavioral (Coping Power), cognitive-developmental, and MST approaches see Mike's behavior as strongly influenced by the environments in which he lives, at home, school, and in his neighborhood. These three approaches also view Mike's behavior as a result of reciprocal influences from those environments—Mike's behavior is influenced by contingencies around him, but his behavior, in turn, influences his environment and the contingencies that it provides. The behavioral and cognitive-developmental approaches, for example, recognize the role that temperament plays in fueling a stressed system, resulting in the poor parenting that contributes to the development of conduct disorder. In addition, the cognitive-behavioral and cognitive-developmental approaches view Mike's understanding of his environment (i.e., his cognitions, attributions, and beliefs) as another important influence on his behavior, and a potential source for behavior change. To some extent, these approaches shift the focus of treatment from Mike exclusively, and work with his environment (parents, teachers, and others) to help produce a change in his behavior. Even more explicitly, Family Therapy shifts focus from Mike as the problem to the family relationships as the problem. Exactly how this is conceptualized varies by Family Therapy approach: for a structural family therapist, Mike's behavior arises out of disturbances in the family subsystems (i.e., its "structure"), whereas Bowenian therapists see behavior disturbance as a result of poorly balanced needs for emotional autonomy and closeness, along with triangulated family relationships.

In contrast to these approaches, both self psychology and pharmaco-therapy view the cause of Mike's maladjustment as something within Mike. In pharmacotherapy, the source is a disturbance in neuron functioning within Mike's brain. Although it is important to note that there is no specific medication to treat conduct disorder, Mike's clinical presentation raises the possibility of a comorbid disorder such as ADHD or depression that might respond to medication. Improvements in those conditions, in turn, could decrease Mike's irritability, aggressiveness, and/or impulsivity. In a different way, the self psychology view is that Mike experiences a Narcissistic Behavior Disorder and a failure to develop adequate self-soothing functions as a result of a failure in narcissistic development. Mike's arrested development is likely related to the physical (due to the divorce) and psychological (due to father's style of engaging with Mike) loss of his father.

THERAPEUTIC RELATIONSHIP

The self psychology approach and residential treatment are designed to work with Mike, with no direct attention given to others in his life. The focus of treatment in self psychology is what transpires in session; in fact, some might argue that the therapeutic relationship is the treatment. In self psychology treatment, there is no need to involve others in the process. Residential treat-ment, by its very nature, would remove Mike from his family and other fea-tures of his natural environment, and the focus also would be on Mike and his behavior. Most research on the efficacy of residential treatment demon-strates limited generalization of behavior change when a youth returns home, so there are attempts in many facilities to engage parents and other caregivers in treatment in an attempt to improve treatment generalization.

One might view the therapeutic relationship necessary for successful pharmacotherapy as unnecessary, but there is a need to engage both Mike and his parents in a therapeutic relationship, even if the physician is "just" prescribing medication. As the authors articulate, accurate assessment of Mike's difficulties and treatment compliance will rest on the quality of the alliance built between the physician and Mike and his parents.

Many of the approaches in this volume recognize the need to involve various members of Mike's environment in the treatment. Most obviously, family therapy involves all members of the nuclear family, including divorced parents. Indeed, Bowenian therapy focuses on the parents, with occasional sessions for other members of the nuclear family. Behavioral, Coping Power, and MST explicitly involve others in the treatment. In behavioral and Coping Power, parents are the most active others involved in the treatment, but teachers are also often drawn into the intervention. In MST, the net is cast even wider to involve other caregivers, coaches, ministers, or any others who are actively involved in Mike's life.

The role played by the therapist also varies widely across the approaches. A Bowenian family therapist assumes the role of teacher who helps family members identify family relationship patterns. Both the behavioral approach and MST describe the role of the therapist as collaborator. Coping Power involves a great deal of skill instruction, which places the role of the therapist as a teacher or coach in skill development. In self psychology, the therapist is a "mirror" to reflect Mike's behavior and emotional experiences in therapy. As previously mentioned, all approaches acknowledge the need to build a positive therapeutic alliance in order to assist Mike and his parents on the difficult road to change. Qualities such as warmth, responsiveness, and reliability are likely important factors in the therapeutic relationships built across all the approaches.

THERAPEUTIC TECHNIQUES AND STRATEGIES

Specific strategies used by the approaches in this volume may seem to vary widely, but a closer examination yields some similarities. For example, MST "borrows" techniques used by other approaches to construct a package of interventions to address the challenges posed by a particular youth and his family. In constructing the "package," MST employs those techniques that have been supported in the research literature. Most commonly, they employ techniques from behavior, cognitive behavioral, and pragmatic family therapy, although there is emphasis placed on delivering these techniques within a social ecological conceptual framework.

With regard to Mike's case in particular, several approaches (MST, behavioral, and Coping Power) focused on the need to increase parental monitoring and develop effective rules or behavioral expectations for Mike as a critical part of successful treatment. For both MST and behavior therapy, the construction of rules and expectations would be based on an in-depth analysis of the current expectations and contingencies for Mike's behavior. Needless to say, most of the "work" for this portion of the intervention would be done with Mike's parents, rather than with Mike. In the Coping Power approach, general principles for behavior management are provided in the parent portion of the program. The cognitive-developmental approach takes a slightly different stance with regard to parents, with emphasis placed on building a stronger parent–child relationship to repair suspected difficulties in attachment.

Several of the other approaches focus on features of the therapeutic relationship as particular techniques in the treatment. Specifically, Mossman and Weston feel that building a therapeutic alliance is a critical feature to successful pharmacotherapy, as it increases communication and treatment compliance. In structural family therapy, the therapist must "join" with the family and, at least initially, adopt family patterns of interaction. This strategy appears to increase the therapist's ability to later change those patterns of interaction through boundary restructuring and increased (direct) communication among family members. Needless to say, self psychology is based in the therapeutic relationship, and the therapist makes interpretations of Mike's actions and associations in order to help "restart" Mike's ego development. Bowenian family therapy differs from the other approaches in its strategy of analyzing and theorizing with family members to help them appreciate how family emotional processes and transgenerational influences affect current family functioning.

MECHANISMS OF CHANGE

Several of the approaches in this volume conceptualize Mike's behavior as a product of many features, events, and characteristics. Obviously, those interventions that viewed Mike's behavior as a result of multiple factors attempt to change more than one feature, and see the sources of change as arising from features that are not within Mike. In particular, the Coping Power Program, behavior therapy, cognitive-developmental therapy, and MST view the role of parents as critical elements to produce change in Mike's deviant behavior. Indeed, one might argue that these approaches view the changes in parents' behavior as the primary mechanism of change in Mike's behavior. This is most explicit in MST, which views the parents as the primary "client." Similarly, much of the work of the behavior therapist will be with the parents, as opposed to Mike. Coping Power provides interventions for both Mike and his parents, but much of the content of the parent sessions aims to change parent behavior in areas that are similar to those targeted by behavior therapy and MST, especially adequate parent supervision and contingencies for behavior.

Family therapy also views the mechanism for change as "outside" of Mike, but with a different perspective than the other interventions. Here the source of change comes from changes in interaction, rather than specific behaviors. In structural family therapy the source of change is how family members experience one another, and in Bowenian therapy, change occurs as family members reflect on family behavior across generations.

Although our authors acknowledge that there is limited research on the features of residential treatment that result in changes in behavior, there is an assumption that external factors (such as a more structured environment) play an important role. There is also recognition that, unless the family is involved, any changes in Mike's behavior are not likely to generalize to the community. There is also recognition that peers likely play an important (but often unrecognized) role in Mike's behavior (and behavior change), thus citing another "external" mechanism of change.

In contrast to the other interventions, self psychology and psychopharmacology view change as a function of factors within Mike. Medication changes neuronal transmission in relevant brain regions and this is assumed to be the primary reason for changes in behavior, mood, or social interaction. In self psychology, change occurs through therapeutic transferences, especially idealizing, mirroring, and twinship transferences. These events ultimately result in changes in Mike that allow him to remobilize his self-object needs. This remobilization allows Mike to resume self-development in a manner that will not require deviant behavior, and/or to develop compensatory skills that will not require that he engage in deviant behavior.

It is important to acknowledge that several other approaches also strive to produce changes within Mike, in addition to making changes to external forces. Specifically, the Coping Power and cognitive-developmental interventions attempt to teach Mike specific skills in order to increase his ability to manage problems more effectively (for example, through improved social problem-solving skills) and regulate his emotional reactions more effectively (through anger management training and affect regulation skills).

MEDICAL AND NUTRITIONAL ISSUES

Virtually none of the approaches see medical or nutritional issues as critical features of Mike's behavior or adjustment. Generally, these features do not seem to be given much attention by treatment providers. Several of the authors note that Mike may benefit from medication to treat a comorbid disorder, such as depression or ADHD. The consultation that might result in this intervention could require medical tests, in addition to monitoring for adverse reactions to or potential side effects from the medication. In the family therapy chapter, however, DeRoma emphasizes the possible role that poor nutrition or less than optimal eating habits may have on Mike's overall adjustment. She suggests that poor nutrition could account for features of Mike's behavior, such as his irritability and poor learning. Possible use of illicit substances could also be seen as a medical issue: not only can substances change behavioral and emotional reactions, but they can also create health problems. At minimum, DeRoma advises that therapists working with adolescents should inquire about, and consider, the role that health and nutrition issues might play in behavior and adjustment.

POTENTIAL PITFALLS

Just as several of the authors saw relationship building as an important feature of the therapeutic relationship, the theme of therapeutic relationships resurfaced as authors considered potential obstacles to treatment. Likewise, several of the authors acknowledged that many of the factors that initiate, contribute to, or maintain Mike's deviant behavior remain outside the traditional therapy relationship and can, in fact, undermine the strategies being implemented to create behavior change. This issue was perhaps most directly stated with reference to problems that arise in residential treatment. Regardless of the theoretical orientation of the programs, residential treatment typically involves bringing together youths with similar difficulties, in this case deviant or antisocial behavior. Peer influence is well acknowledged to be a strong factor in conduct disorder. When Mike lives in the community, he has access to nondeviant peers, but this access is greatly diminished when he enters a residential program. In fact, the greatest pitfall of residential treatment relates to Mike's potential exposure to "deviant" peers who may reinforce antisocial attitudes and behavior, rather than support positive behavior change.

In family therapy, the primary difficulties seem to center around the participation of all family members, and the attention the therapist must pay to family behavior, not just what family members say. Failing to take that necessary time to join the family can also interfere with family treatment, as premature attempts to intervene in the family will be unsuccessful. Time is also at issue in medication consultation, and this is likely a feature that is not well appreciated by insurance companies and other mental health professionals. Specifically, failure of the psychiatrist to adequately evaluate Mike or to communicate adequately about a medication recommendation can undermine the utility of that intervention. Medication also can communicate to Mike (and his family) that he is not responsible for his behavior, which could undermine other attempts to intervene to decrease Mike's deviant behavior.

When using a behavioral approach, failure to adequately engage enough people in Mike's environment to affect the contingencies for his behavior can impede or prevent successful behavior change. For example, improvements in Mike's behavior may threaten his father, who has been the "successful" disciplinarian in the past, and this could lead him to undermine Ms. D.'s parenting. If his father has been actively involved in the behavioral program, he may feel less need to "act out" against the improvements in behavior. In cognitive-developmental intervention, Mike's likely resistance to treatment was seen as a potential pitfall, as was Ms. D.'s frustration at her inability to help Mike up to this point. In addition, Mr. D.'s apparent lack of investment in treatment could undermine any attempts at intervention.

Conducting interventions in natural environments, such as schools, bring a number of advantages in treatment, but the setting can also pose challenges that can impede treatment response. The Coping Power Program, which is often run in school settings, has experienced interruptions to treatment attendance due to school assemblies, school holidays, field trips, standardized testing, and other school activities. Coordination with, and support of, school personnel is critical to prevent these types of features from interfering with program delivery. A primary role of the MST team is to identify "barriers" to treatment, many of which are the types of difficulties described above. A common impediment to treatment response is attendance at sessions, which is a primary reason why MST is delivered in the home or as close to home as possible. The team also attempts to identify barriers such as recognizing efforts by family members that are undermining treatment, and devise strategies to change or decrease the impact of that barrier.

TERMINATION AND RELAPSE PREVENTION

The Coping Power approach is a time-limited intervention, and issues related to termination are included in the treatment program. Particularly in the parent groups, information is provided in notebooks to allow parents to refer to the strategies they have been taught. This approach also uses skills building and generalization exercises to prevent relapse. As progress is made in response to interventions, families are "weaned" from the involvement of the MST. Termination occurs when caregivers can demonstrate that they can implement successful interventions without the assistance of the MST team. As is the case with Coping Power, the caregivers have been given the skills necessary to manage Mike, and other supports have been established in the community to decrease the likelihood that Mike will revert to previous behavior patterns. Family therapy also typically ends when treatment goals have been met; in Mike's case, this will likely occur when family members demonstrate that they can articulate more explicit family rules, and a greater understanding of the problems in the family. Return to treatment is encouraged if family members experience difficulties. Termination in self psychology is also based on treatment progress, although in this case it follows Mike's "lead" and his demonstration of his ability to manage loss. Termination is seen as a critical phase of treatment, and it progresses slowly. Although sessions may cease, the treatment is not typically felt to have "ended" and the door remains open to future sessions without the stigma that future sessions communicate a "relapse." Termination of behavior therapy and cognitive-developmental treatment is also based on treatment response, but attention to "consensus" is also recommended. That is, there should be agreement by family members that they are ready to end treatment. Most commonly, session frequency decreases gradually, and therapists are advised to consider scheduling "booster sessions" following cessation of regular sessions in order to monitor behavior change and the family's use of newly acquired skills in order to prevent relapse. Warning that some relapse is likely, and providing a plan to manage any such relapse also seem to be effective strategies.

As previously mentioned, studies on the efficacy of residential treatment have suggested that relapse is common once a youth returns to the community. As discharge from the facility approaches, focus of treatment should shift from Mike to his "natural" environment, especially his family. Additionally, support services in the community (such as individual or family therapy) should be in place before discharge to help maintain progress made in treatment.

CONCLUSIONS

Remarkable gains have been made in the treatment of children and adolescents over the past 2 decades. There are over 550 different types of psychotherapies for children and "new" treatments continue to emerge (Kazdin, 2004). Such a proliferation of intervention approaches has both advantages and disadvantages. Particularly for clinicians working with children and adolescents, there are a variety of special challenges in identifying what problems warrant treatment, how to assess functioning, intervening when the child or adolescent may not see any need for treatment, deciding on the focus or range of therapy, and keeping the child and/or family involved in therapy. The initial task of identifying problems that require, and will benefit from, treatment is not as easy as it may seem. Whereas very extreme and pervasive departures from "typical" development are easily identified as needing special intervention (e.g., autism, childhood psychosis), many of the symptoms of CD (such as threatening or intimidating others, bullying, fighting, stealing, destroying others' property, deceitfulness, theft, curfew violations, skipping school) are often present and even relatively common, at least to some degree, at different points in child and adolescent development (e.g., DiClemente, Hansen, & Ponton, 1996). Thus, one of the challenges in dealing with CD is deciding whether the qualitative or quantitative characteristics of the disorder are maladaptive or within the typical range given the child's developmental level. The problem is even further complicated by making judgments that are influenced by the family's socioeconomic status, neighborhood, ethnicity, race, and/or culture. As a result, multimethod assessment has been advocated as the "best strategy" for assessing any disorder of childhood. The multimethod assessment approach emphasizes the importance of obtaining information from different informants from a variety of settings, and employing a variety of procedures (e.g., clinical interviews, direct observations, parent/teacher questionnaires, psychological tests of individuals and/or families, and, if possible, interviews of peers). It should be noted, however, that in the context of obtaining data from multiple sources in the assessment phase, research suggests that reports from parents, teachers, and the children themselves do not correlate very well. In generally, there is no "gold standard" that could be recommended for all clinicians to employ in assessing CD. The clinical assessment actually consists of many strategies and procedures with the purpose of better understanding the child's thoughts, feelings, and behaviors that occur within the family, community, and school settings. Clinical interviews can be conducted with parents and children either separately or jointly. Comprehensive assessment also requires consideration to evaluating the child's difficulties and weaknesses but also his or her strengths.

Although the pros and cons of structured versus semistructured or even nonstructured interviews are beyond the scope of this text, most clinicians do not use formal structured interviews when gathering clinical information. Formal, standardized rating scales [e.g., Revised Behavior Problem Checklist (Quay & Peterson, 1983, 1984), Child Behavior Checklist (Achenbach, 1991), Children's Inventory of Anger (Nelson & Finch, 2000)] are strongly recommended not only because they assess several domains of the child's functioning, but also because they also provide normative data, which allows the clinician to better understand some of the developmental nuances related to the acting-out difficulties the child is presenting.

The clinician needs to carefully assess the family's motivation for seeking treatment, as children rarely refer themselves. In fact, acting-out youngsters often minimize or deny experiencing stress, symptoms, or problems. Problems may also arise when parents do not feel their child needs assistance, but others (such as the school or court) feel they do. This situation may be more common in CD; one study found that only 31% of parents of children with CD in a community sample thought that assistance was needed (Boyle,

1991). Some other parents believe that problems with their children will simply resolve themselves with time, which also decreases the likelihood that they will seek treatment (Pavuluri, Luk, & McGee, 1996).

In assessing the child, the importance of early (childhood) versus late (adolescent)-onset psychopathology is important. From a family perspective, conduct-disordered children may arise in families where the severely acting-out children have close relationships with their parents but have difficulty interacting effectively in the broader community. Their lying, cheating, stealing, and fighting clearly creates problems for others but the crisis does not occur until the child gets into trouble outside the home, most typically with school or legal authorities. Such families may be inappropriately protective of such children and the parents themselves may exhibit antisocial behaviors (e.g., lying, gambling, cheating, having affairs, cheating on income taxes, bragging about shady business deals, fixing tickets, pilfering at work). They may teach their children that such behavior is "smart" rather than wrong. Such children may grow up never having had to face the world's consequences until they get into trouble outside the home when they are caught shoplifting or cheating. The parents may simply be seeking treatment to help protect the child by wanting a letter to legal authorities that the child really "could not help it." On the other hand, other families may be disengaged to the point that there is limited interaction; the children simply spend time in their rooms, spend more time with their peers, break curfew, and skip school. The parents may act like they want to parent their child but are oftentimes tired of being parents and/or frightened of it. These uninterested or disengaged parents may simply view the behavior as typical or they may rationalize their children's behavior as just going through "growing pains."

Clearly, the etiology involved in CD is multidetermined. Among others, specific causal factors have been genetic problems; birth disorders; prenatal and postnatal problems; learning disabilities; hyperactivity; related emotional disorders; models for aggression; rejection by normal peers and/or by teachers; breakdown of family management skills, including monitoring, supervision, problem solving, consistent discipline, and warmth; incompetent parenting; severe physical illness; poverty; alcoholism/drug abuse in the family; child abuse; lack of interest or experience in parenting; high emotional or physical neglect by overly committed parents; marital conflict or divorce; affiliation with deviant peers; deficient problem-solving ability; and poor cognitive processing or other cognitive deficiencies. Even as we gain greater understanding of the etiology of CD, the challenges children and adolescents with CD pose to our neighborhoods, schools, and society at large compel us to continue our efforts to intervene in the lives of these youths.

Perhaps the greatest challenge the therapist faces is to change the hopelessness that the parents experience, and the inertia that stems from their despair. Parents of children and adolescents with CD can become paralyzed into an emotional stupor, and their helplessness can feed their ineffective interactions with their youngsters. The emotional resources required of parents can affect their willingness to continue parenting under extremely difficult situations and can lead to exhaustion as they try to cope with what they perceive as an impossible situation. They can come to believe that nothing can be done, and in some cases it appears that these parents feel they have been abused themselves, a situation that Price (1996) has labeled "parent abuse." Some children and adolescents emotionally blackmail their parents with provocation through vulgarity and personal attacks, severe disrespect; self-destructive acts such as quitting school, running away, using drugs, indiscriminant sex, threats of suicide, threats of impending physical assault; and even reporting their parents to child protective services for "child abuse" that has not really occurred. An important role for the therapist in these situations, in particular, is to communicate a sense of hope and to empower them to mobilize and deal with the severe behavior problems exhibited by their out-of-control children.

Parent management training seems to be one of the most empirically supported procedures in interventions for CD. It teaches parents to alter their child's behavior in the home using contingency management techniques and improving parent/child interactions to enhance other parenting skills (e.g., improving parent/child communication, monitoring, and increased supervision). There have been a number of excellent treatment manuals and materials developed that have facilitated parent management training (e.g., Barkley, 1997; McMahon & Forehand, 2003). Although these have not been developed specifically for CD, they should be helpful for many of these parents.

Change in the child's or adolescent's problem behavior is also of paramount importance for these families, as they are under pressure from schools, courts, and other forces to improve the youth's behavior. Behavior modification and cognitive behavior interventions are also well supported by empirical studies and many programs are available in treatment manual form (e.g., Coping Power Program by Lochman & Wells, 2003; "Keeping Your Cool" by Nelson & Finch, 1996). These skills training approaches focus on the cognitive deficiencies, distortions, and emotional regulation problems that can underlie problem behavior. Generally, these types of programs teach children various anger management skills, such as problem solving, self-talk, assertion training, and relaxation to modify maladaptive thoughts, feelings, and behaviors in problem social situations.

Without a doubt, the most extensive family community-based program for conduct-disorder adolescents who are at risk for out-of-home placement is multisystemic treatment (Henggeler & Lee, 2003). In this approach, the youth with CD is viewed as functioning within interconnected social systems of family, school, neighborhood, as well as court and juvenile services. The severe acting-out is viewed as being maintained by the transactions within or between any of these systems, and intervention seeks to empower caregivers to improve the family functioning. As such, treatment is carried out with all family members, school personnel, peers, juvenile justice staff, and other individuals in the youngster's life. Although some of the behavioral, cognitive behavioral, and multisystemic intervention approaches have been given empirical support, the effectiveness of such interventions has not yet differentiated between those youth who show life course persistent disruptive behavior and those who show adolescent-limited patterns of conduct disorder.

The approaches described in this volume certainly provide the practitioner with a variety of theoretical orientations and tools to consider using when helping children and families with conduct disorder. The approaches vary in the amount of empirical support they have received, but we doubt that any of the authors feel that the approaches they have described are the "final word" on effective interventions for these youths and their families. The trend among the interventions however appears to be toward broadening our focus, sometimes seeking to change or muster support from the community. Considering the impact of conduct disorder, which affects not just the child and his family but often the greater community in very direct ways, this level of intervention may represent the next challenge for clinical psychology. That is, we may need to develop interventions or programs that help us create the "village" that provides the support, nurturance, and structure that all children need and deserve in order to become productive, happy adults.

REFERENCES

Achenbach, T. M. (1991). *Manual for the Child Behavior Checklist/4–18 and 1991 Profile*. Burlington: University of Vermont, Department of Psychiatry.

Barkley, R. A. (1997). *Defiant children: A clinician's manual for assessment and parent training* (2nd ed.). New York: Guilford Press.

Boyle, M. H. (1991). Children's mental health issues: Prevention and treatment. In L. C. Johnson, & D. Barnhorst (Eds.), *Children, families, and public policy in the 90s* (pp. 73–104). Toronto: Thompson Educational.

DiClemente, R. J., Hansen, W. B., & Ponton, L. E. (Eds.) (1996). *Handbook of adolescent health risk behavior*. New York: Plenum Press.

Henggeler, S. W., & Lee, T. (2003). *Multisystemic treatment of serious clinical problems.* In A. F. Kazdin, & J. R. Weisz (Eds.), *Evidence-based psychotherapies for children and adolescents* (pp. 301–322). New York: Guilford Press.

Kazdin, W. E. (2004). Psychotherapy with children. In M. J. Lambert (Ed.), *Bergin and Garfield's handbook of psychotherapy and behavior change* (5th ed.). New York: Wiley.

Lochman, J. E., & Wells, K. C. (2003). Effectiveness study of Coping Power and classroom intervention with aggressive children: Outcomes at a one-year follow-up. *Behavior Therapy, 34,* 493–515.

McMahon, R. J., & Forehand, R. L. (2003). *Helping the non-compliant child: Family-based treatment for oppositional behavior* (2nd ed.). New York: Guilford Press.

Nelson, W. M. III, & Finch, A. J., Jr. (1996). *"Keeping your cool": The anger management workbook (Parts 1 and 2).* Ardmore, PA: Workbook Publishing.

Nelson, W. M. III, & Finch, A. J., Jr. (2000). *Children's Inventory of Anger (ChIA).* Los Angeles, CA: Western Psychological Services.

Pavuluri, M. S., Luk, S. L., & McGee, R. (1996). Help seeking behavior problems by parents of preschool children: A community survey. *Journal of the American Academy of Child and Adolescent Psychiatry, 35,* 215–222.

Price, J. A. (1996) *Power and compassion: Working with difficult adolescents and abused parents.* New York: Guilford.

Quay, H. C., & Peterson, D. R. (1983). *Interim manual for the Revised Behavior Problem Checklist.* Unpublished manuscript, University of Miami.

Quay, H. C., & Peterson, D. R. (1984). *Appendix I to the interim manual for the Revised Behavior Problem Checklist.* Unpublished manuscript, University of Miami.

Appendix

CONCEPTUALIZATION, ASSESSMENT, AND TREATMENT PLANNING

A. Further Information

1. Assessment Tools

Self psychology	Requires an intrapsychic evaluation to determine the state of Mike's self. Projective testing provides helpful information, as does careful observation of Mike's response to the therapy.
Family therapy	Further assessment of family relational patterns is needed; some gathered through interview and observation of family interaction in session. Formal techniques such as family mapping or self-report measures related to family relationships can be helpful.
Residential treatment	Medical information to provide for 24-h care; inform Mike and his family of all aspects of the program, including rules; and obtain consent for all features of treatment.
MST	Assessment is an ongoing process, requiring identification of the mechanisms that "drive" problem behavior. Assessment to identify strengths and needs by interviews and observation of family members and other caregivers such as teachers, coaches, and others who interact with Mike and his family.

Cognitive-behavioral coping power	History of social relationships and information about how Mike processes social information, and his abilities related to perspective taking. Problem-solving measures can be helpful. Information about school and neighborhood factors (such as amount of criminal activity). More information about Mike's strengths would also be desirable.
Medication	Rule out possible ADHD and depression through further clinical interview and information from parents related to specific symptoms. Gather information about the extent of Mike's substance use, general medical health, and family medical and psychiatric history.
Behavioral	A functional analysis to determine the current contingencies for Mike's maladaptive behavior, done through behavior checklists, behavior logs, and/or direct observation. Further evaluation to rule out ADHD and/or LD.
Cognitive developmental	Using diagnostic interviews, such as the K-SADS, can help clarify diagnosis of CD and identify other possible diagnoses such as ADHD and/or substance abuse. Assessment should also identify Mike's attributions about his behavior, beliefs about his behavior, and his views regarding his relationships with his parents.

2. Therapeutic Goals

Self psychology	Restart the development of self so that patient can develop a resilient self through mature narcissism. Repair fractured ego development through the therapeutic relationship, with particular focus on failure in relationships with parents.
Family therapy	Repair dysfunctional family relationships and behavior patterns that maintain Mike's behavior, and to reframe the focus of the problem from Mike to the family. Structural therapy: rearrange family structure through boundary modification (e.g., strengthen parent boundaries). Bowenian: decrease emotional fusion.
Residential treatment	Would depend on theoretical orientation of program, but most aim to decrease the behavior that brought the youth into treatment. Using the feature of increased contact with other youth in program, many also work to increase social skills such as peer resistance and problem-solving skills.

MST	Establish hierarchy of overarching goals to decrease primary behavior problems, e.g., increase parents' monitoring of Mike's behavior to decrease substance use and truancy; intermediate goals are steps to achieve the overarching goals.
Cognitive-behavioral coping power	To have Mike reduce his conduct problems and substance use to normative levels and to increase prosocial activities and interests.
Medication	If diagnosis other than Conduct Disorder is identified, medications to treat that diagnosis might focus on decreasing aggressive actions and rule violations, and improve academic functioning.
Behavioral	Primary goal is to reduce the conflict between Mike and his mother, and to reduce Mike's conduct problem. Improving Mike's prosocial behavior may be an important step in that process.
Cognitive developmental	Reduce the frequency of Mike's shoplifting and theft from home, improve class attendance, reduce his feelings of anger and frustration, reduce the frequency and severity of conflict with his sister, reduce severity and frequency of oppositional behavior with mother and teachers, and reduce or eliminate cannabis use.

3. Length of Treatment

Self psychology	Difficult to determine, as aim is for psychic growth, not behavior change. Psychic growth is difficult to predict. Twice weekly sessions, at least; four to five times per week if improvement is not seen.
Family therapy	Both approaches would likely be relatively brief, 12 sessions.
	Weekly sessions in Structural.
	Twice monthly in Bowenian.
Residential treatment	Ranges from 5 to 7 days for inpatient hospitalization to 12 months for other residential programs. If part of court involvement, length might be dictated by the Court, rather than by achievement of treatment goals.
MST	Typical treatment is between 3 and 5 months. Session frequency varies, but is often daily during the initial weeks of intervention. Twenty-four-hour assistance by phone is available throughout treatment.
Cognitive-behavioral coping power	Manualized treatment offered across 20–33 weekly sessions over the course of 15–18 months for Mike and 10–16 weekly sessions for his parent(s).

Medication	After initial assessment, return in 2 weeks and then monthly for several months. Could extend to every 3 months for medications that are used long term and do not pose significant side effect risks.
Behavioral	To implement both parent training and a program to improve Mike's prosocial behavior will likely require 40 weeks of hourly sessions.
Cognitive developmental	Generally, sessions are held weekly and treatment typically lasts 6 months.

4. Case Conceptualization

Self psychology	Mike experiences as Narcissistic Behavior Disorder as a result of failure in narcissistic development related to the physical and psychological loss of his father, and a failure to develop self-soothing functions.
Family therapy	In both approaches, the focus shifts from Mike as the "problem" to family relationships as the problem. Structural: Mike's behavior arises from disturbed executive (parental) subsystem functioning and diffusion of child–parent boundaries. Bowenian: needs for emotional autonomy and closeness are not well balanced, and family relationships are triangulated.
Residential treatment	Varies by program orientation.
MST	Behavior is multidetermined and bidirectional in nature. Mike is nested within multiple systems that have reciprocal influences on behavior. Mike presents many strengths that can serve to promote positive behavior change.
Cognitive-behavioral coping power	Mike's behavior is the product of the interplay among multiple aspects of his social network. Cognitions influence behavior, with recognition that child level factors (such as anger arousal and social information processing) and contextual factors (level of parental involvement and skill; level of neighborhood violence) also play important roles.
Medication	Although conduct disorder alone does not warrant medication, it is frequently comorbid with other conditions that might respond to medication. For Mike, a psychostimulant to treat possible ADHD and/or an antidepressant to treat mood problems could lead to less impulsivity and irritability.

Behavioral	Mike's difficult temperament, the disruption posed by his parent's divorce, and Ms D's decreased availability to provide supervision combined with developmental affiliation with peers led to undesirable peers and conduct problems.
Cognitive developmental	Mike's parents may have responded in a less than optimally consistent, reliable, and supportive manner to Mike's difficult, frustrating temperament; the attachment may be insecure, avoidant, or disorganized, which can create tacit, maladaptive beliefs about relationships with others.

B. The Therapeutic Relationship

1. Roles in a Therapeutic Relationship

Self psychology	Therapist provides a safe, secure, and empathic environment. Therapist serves as a transference object onto which Mike can project his need for understanding and admiration; accepting of Mike's world view.
Family therapy	Structural: all relevant family members participate, including divorced parents; therapist "joins" system to help effect change.
	Bowenian: focus on parents, with occasional session for members of a nuclear family; therapist as teacher.
Residential treatment	In most programs, relationships with direct care staff (nurses, child care workers, houseparents) will be most influential. To maximize program effectiveness, involvement of parents and treatment after-care plan is also critical to generalize any behavior change.
MST	A collaborative approach to treatment with therapist as "coach"; guide and educator to help all those in system to develop the skills and resources necessary to function adaptively; frequent involvement of others in Mike's social environment. Caregivers key to behavior change, and must be engaged; that is the primary therapeutic relationship.
Cognitive-behavioral coping power	Recognition that the therapeutic alliance has an effect on compliance and investment in treatment. Confidentiality and limit-setting are also important. Also need to consider therapeutic relationships in four sets: clinician–school personnel; clinician–group; clinician–child (Mike); clinician–parent/caregivers.

Medication	Although often seen as a "consultant" to other treatment, the psychiatrist will need to form a therapeutic relationship with Mike and his parents, both to gather relevant information and to keep open communication in order to monitor symptom response, compliance, and side effects.
Behavioral	Therapist must form relationships with Mike, his mother, and perhaps with others in his life, such as his teacher and probation officer. Empathy, positive regard, and genuineness are helpful features to bring to all those relationships.
Cognitive developmental	Emphasis is placed on therapeutic warmth, responsiveness, reliability or consistency, nurturance, and predictability as a foundation for the therapeutic process.

C. Treatment Implications and Outcome
1. Therapeutic Techniques and Strategies

Self psychology	Interpretation of Mike's actions and associations in a manner that Mike can understand.
Family therapy	Structural: therapist "joins" the family, initially by adopting family patterns of interaction, later playing a directive role in restructuring boundaries and facilitating communication among family members.
	Bowenian: analyzes and theorizes with family members to help them appreciate how family emotional processes and transgeneration influences affect current family functioning.
Residential treatment	Varies by orientation, but most include program-wide behavior management systems (e.g., levels system) and individualized behavioral goals.
MST	Uses evidence-based intervention techniques from behavior, cognitive-behavioral, and pragmatic family therapy, delivered in a social–ecological conceptual framework. Primary focus will be to increase parent monitoring and rule development with specific consequences.
Cognitive-behavioral coping power	Anger management to decrease emotional outbursts; problem-solving skills to improve Mike's ability to evaluate situations more accurately and behave less impulsively. Parent training to help develop and support use of effective disciplinary techniques.

Medication	Psychiatrist likely to be in collaborative role with other professionals, and agreement about roles will be important. Forming a therapeutic alliance and communicating about the role medication plays in Mike's overall treatment is important, especially given what that might say to Mike about his need to assume responsibility for his behavior.
Behavioral	Performing a functional analysis to understand the contingencies for Mike's behavior, then changing those contingencies to negatively reinforce and/or punish negative behavior and positively reinforce adaptive and prosocial behaviors.
Cognitive developmental	Work to strengthen the parent–child relationship by reflecting on times when the relationship was happy (or, at least, better). Also work to help parents be effective as parents, and to help Mike learn how to regulate his emotional reactions.

2. Mechanisms of Change

Self psychology	Through the therapeutic transferences (especially, idealizing, mirroring, and twinship transferences), self-object needs are remobilized. This allows development to proceed and/or compensatory skills to develop.
Family therapy	Structural: change occurs because family members experience each other differently.
	Bowenian: family develops curiosity about sources of family behavior across generations and enthusiasm for separateness.
Residential treatment	Few studies have clearly identified which of many facets of residential treatment are most critical. Peer influence is likely important, and can be used to program's advantage. Involvement of family to maintain behavior change is also critical for long-term outcome.
MST	Family, especially parent, is seen as client. Focus on increasing the strength of parents, and identifying youth strengths to assist in goal setting. Meeting needs in the larger system (social ecology) also supports positive change.
Cognitive-behavioral coping power	By altering both child and parent factors through this empirically supported program, significant changes in behavior can be seen.
Medication	Medication changes neuronal transmission in key brain regions, and this is assumed to be the primary reason for changes in behavior, mood, or social interactions.

Behavioral	Intervening in the coercive cycle by altering events that provoke negative behavior and the contingencies for that behavior. Forming a collaborative partnership with Mike and his family will facilitate their participation in this program.
Cognitive developmental	Supporting the development of affect regulation skills; changing maladaptive beliefs about the appropriateness and value of aggressive and oppositional behavior; changing tacit maladaptive beliefs or schema about relationships with others; improving social problem-solving skills; and improving the quality of parent–child relationships.

3. Medical and Nutrition Issues

Self psychology	None specifically mentioned.
Family therapy	Information about family member's health status might help in understanding how dysfunctional family patterns developed. Poor nutrition of adolescents has been associated with decreased energy and learning problems, and should be explored.
Residential treatment	None specifically mentioned.
MST	None specifically mentioned.
Cognitive-behavioral coping power	Suggest referral to physician for evaluation of irritability and subclinical–attentional problems to determine if intervention for those features might be helpful. Otherwise, these are not the focus of treatment.
Medication	Appropriate work-up and follow-up for possible medical side effects of medication.
Behavioral	Other than referral for medication, if indicated, for ADHD, there are no specific medical or nutritional issues for Mike.
Cognitive developmental	Medications to treat comorbid conditions such as ADHD or depression should be considered, if those conditions are identified.

4. Potential Pitfalls

Self psychology	Through the necessary process of therapy, Mike will experience his feelings more intensely, leading to increased acting-out. Parents may withdraw him from treatment prematurely, and/or his escalating behavior may result in criminal charges; may also have difficulty in understanding or acknowledging the boundaries of the relationship.

Family therapy	Need to insist that all family members participate, and to focus on family behavior, not what is said. Must also spend time "joining" the family and to be able to implement the specific family therapy strategies correctly.
Residential treatment	If influence of peers is not managed, exposure to other behavior-disordered youth can further reinforce negative behavior. Positive changes occurring in residential treatment may not generalize to community.
MST	MST team established with an eye to identify and overcome barriers to change. For example, focus on parents' communication with each other to increase adherence to consequences for rules.
Cognitive-behavioral coping power	Implementing the program at school can produce interrupted attendance due to assemblies, field trips, etc. Organizing the groups at times when school activities are least likely to interfere is helpful. Accommodating parent schedules also helps parents' attendance—scheduling in evening or providing babysitting.
Medication	It can require considerable time and evaluation by psychiatrist to determine if medication is appropriate and what meds to consider. Not all systems provide for this level of contact. Meds can also communicate to Mike that he is not responsible for his behavior; side effects can pose a problem with compliance.
Behavioral	Failure to adequately engage enough people in Mike's environment to affect the contingencies for his behavior and failing to adequately manage the frustration or emotion that working with challenging youth can bring.
Cognitive developmental	Teens with CD often resist treatment, and parents often expect immediate solution or behavior change, although they have difficulty implementing changes in the home. Ms. D.'s frustration, Mr. D.'s lack of investment in treatment, and Mike's peer group may also impede treatment progress.

5. Termination and Relapse Prevention

Self psychology	A critical phase of treatment, to begin when Mike demonstrates how far he has come in managing loss. Termination process progresses slowly and the door remains open to future session. Must take Mike's lead; future treatment is not described as a "relapse."

Family therapy	When goals of treatment achieved, termination can be considered. In particular, when family shows more explicit rules and greater understanding of problems. Should be encouraged to return if any family members experience difficulties.
Residential treatment	Best for treatment to end when pre-established goals have been met. As termination approaches, focus should shift to the "natural" environment (especially, family). Adequate after-care plan (i.e., established services in the community) to help maintain progress made in treatment.
MST	Family is "weaned" from MST team as progress is achieved. Termination occurs when caregivers can implement successful interventions.
Cognitive-behavioral coping power	This is a time-limited program, and termination is built into the sessions through review and closure activities. Participants receive notebooks with handouts and worksheets to which they can refer in the future. There are also skill-building and generalization exercises to help prevent relapse.
Medication	Will depend on the comorbid diagnosis, but Mike and his parents will need to understand that symptoms could return or increase if successful medication regime is discontinued.
Behavioral	Termination should be based on family consensus, and with information from sources other than just Mike. Tapering sessions and booster sessions are typically helpful. Informing Ms. D. of "signs" to look for as indications of relapse will help the family return to treatment before all previous gains have been lost.
Cognitive developmental	Termination issues are likely if a therapeutic relationship has been established, and should be addressed early. Often helpful to taper session frequency and use booster sessions, and to coordinate family and community resources to serve as supports for changes made in treatment.

Index

Springer Series on Comparative Treatments for Psychological Disorders

Arthur Freeman, EdD, ABPP, Series Editor